The Associated Board
of the Royal Schools of Music

A Social and Cultural History

The Associated Board
of the Royal Schools of Music

A Social and Cultural History

David C. H. Wright

THE BOYDELL PRESS

First published 2013
The Boydell Press, Woodbridge

This special edition:
The Associated Board of the Royal Schools of Music
in association with Boydell & Brewer Ltd.
Distributed by ABRSM

ISBN 978 1 84849 579 1

The Boydell Press is an imprint of Boydell & Brewer Ltd
PO Box 9, Woodbridge, Suffolk IP12 3DF, UK
and of Boydell & Brewer Inc.
668 Mount Hope Ave, Rochester, NY 14620-2731, USA
website: www.boydellandbrewer.com

A catalogue record for this book is available
from the British Library

The publisher has no responsibility for the continued existence
or accuracy of URLs for external or third-party internet websites
referred to in this book, and does not guarantee that any content
on such websites is, or will remain, accurate or appropriate

Papers used by Boydell & Brewer Ltd are natural, recyclable
products made from wood grown in sustainable forests

MIX
Paper from
responsible sources
FSC® C013604

Designed and typeset in Adobe Warnock Pro by
David Roberts, Pershore, Worcestershire

Printed and bound in Great Britain by
CPI Group (UK) Ltd, Croydon, CR0 4YY

Contents

List of Illustrations   vi

List of Tables   vii

Preface   ix

List of Abbreviations   xii

Miscellaneous Conventions   xiii

Introduction: The Context for a History   *1*

I THE BACKGROUND

1 Music Exams and Victorian Society   *19*

2 Competing for Candidates: TCL, ABRSM and the Society of Arts   *42*

II THE BOARD ESTABLISHED, 1889–1920

3 The ABRSM Idea and the First Exams, 1889–91   *63*

4 The Early History, 1892–1920   *76*

5 The ABRSM and the 'British World'   *92*

III THE INSTITUTIONAL CULTURE, 1920–83

6 The Inter-War Years   *105*

7 The Board in Wartime   *129*

8 The Post-War Board   *135*

9 Too Much Success: the 1960s and 1970s   *144*

IV THE BOARD REVIVED, 1983–2009

10 The Reconstitution, 1983–5   *171*

11 Reconnecting with its Market: the Smith Years, 1983–92   *181*

12 Redefining its Role: the Morris Years, 1993–2009   *209*

Appendix 1   Speech and Drama Examinations   *257*

Appendix 2   ABRSM Personalia, 1889–2010   *259*

Select Bibliography   *261*

Index   *267*

Illustrations

1 George Watson, the ABRSM's first Secretary, with Frederic Cliffe, one of the Board's intrepid early overseas examiners
(Reproduced by kind permission of the RCM Centre for Performance History) *64*

2 Extract from the ABRSM's first examination paper, 1890
(Reproduced by kind permission of the ABRSM) *70*

3 Bedford Square, where the ABRSM had its headquarters from 1907 to 2000
(Reproduced by kind permission of the ABRSM) *85*

4 Title page of the ABRSM's 1911 piano exam music as published by Augener
(Reproduced by kind permission of the ABRSM) *88*

5 Sir Hugh Allen, who reshaped the Board between the wars; portrait (pencil on paper) by John Singer Sargent (1856–1925)
(© Courtesy of the Warden and Scholars of New College, Oxford/
The Bridgeman Art Library) *106*

6 Title page of the ABRSM's famous 'Craxton/Tovey' Beethoven edition, 1931
(Reproduced by kind permission of the ABRSM) *118*

7 Ronald Smith, Chief Executive, 1983–1992, and a key figure in changing the ABRSM
(Reproduced by kind permission of the ABRSM) *182*

8 Richard Morris, Chief Executive, 1993–2009, who set the ABRSM in new directions
(Reproduced by kind permission of the ABRSM) *208*

9 24 Portland Place, the ABRSM's headquarters from 2000 *220*

10 Cover of the ABRSM's new Barry Cooper Beethoven edition, 2007
(Reproduced by kind permission of the ABRSM) *252*

Tables

2.1 Music exams offered by the Society of Arts in 1896   *53*

2.2 Local Exam provision offered by TCL and the ABRSM in 1891   *56*

2.3 Diploma provision offered by the most reputable exam boards in 1890   *58*

4.1 Levels in ABRSM Practical Examinations, 1890–1933   *77*

4.2 Levels in ABRSM Written Examinations, 1890–1933   *78*

4.3 Assessment criteria for Piano and Violin from 1896 Local Centre Exam syllabus   *79*

4.4 Music prescribed for Piano Local Centre Examinations in 1901   *80*

4.5 Entries to ABRSM Local Centre and School Exams, 1912/13–1920/21   *87*

7.1 UK music exam entries and ABRSM income, 1938–45   *133*

8.1 Sources of RCM income, 1953–60   *138*

9.1 Composer representation in selected ABRSM Piano syllabuses, 1933–83   *147*

9.2 ABRSM UK examination trends in selected instruments and theory, 1950–85   *149*

9.3 Proportion of Theory to Practical grade exams in the UK and overseas   *154*

9.4 Grade 5 as a Proportion of all Theory grade exams in the UK   *155*

9.5 Take-up of Theory exams by grade in 2009   *156*

11.1 Ratio of Overseas to UK candidates in 1983 and 2009   *206*

12.1 Major new ABRSM initiatives (excluding publishing), 1993–2009   *222*

12.2 Complaints and appeals against examiners in the summer exam periods, 1993–6   *231*

For my wife, Penny

Preface

T HE Associated Board of the Royal Schools of Music, better known by its acronym as the ABRSM, has influenced the musical lives and tastes of millions of people since it conducted its first exams in 1890. This history explores how and why the ABRSM became such an important influence for British musical life, and looks at some of the consequences that have followed from that influence. It examines how much latitude the ABRSM has had to impose its musical view of things, and the extent to which its exams respond to the market by taking account of the circumstances and musical preferences of its customers. These enquiries shape much of what follows.

The book is an institutional history of the ABRSM, placing it in its social, cultural and economic context, and showing how it has negotiated – or, at times, has been unresponsive to – the changing social, educational and cultural landscape. It does not seek to provide a comprehensive historical account of ABRSM events, even though the discussion is structured chronologically. Also, though an organization like the ABRSM offers considerable scope for anecdotal character portraits, this temptation is almost entirely resisted. Nor does this book study in any detail the changing fashions in individual instrumental/vocal teaching and repertoire revealed by the ABRSM syllabuses. Although points about this aspect are made in a general way there remains considerable scope for future, more specifically centred, instrumental/vocal studies looking at the syllabuses themselves. Thus it is to be hoped that this general sweep across the ABRSM's institutional history may prompt other, differently focused, histories.

Some aspects of the Board's history have been deliberately constricted or excluded. For example, the focus is very much on the ABRSM's work in the UK, and so discussion of its overseas examinations has been confined to the way this activity fed in to the British World concept (Chapter 5) and about its significance for today's ABRSM, with particular reference to the Far East and China (Chapters 11 and 12). There is also very little discussion of the Speech exams, which were always very much an ancillary activity. (A brief outline of these exams is given in Appendix 1.)

The historical account opens with two chapters which set out the rise and significance of the music exam phenomenon. Readers who do not wish to spend time on the Victorian social context may want to skip Chapter 1 and proceed to Chapter 2 (a discussion of the exams of the Society of Arts and the circumstances surrounding the founding and first exams of Trinity College of Music, the Royal Academy and the Royal College) or even move directly to Chapter 3 (setting up the ABRSM and its first exams).

It is important to make clear that this is an independent scholarly study and was not commissioned by the ABRSM. The book's independence was common ground between the Board and myself from the first exploratory meeting held to discuss my idea to write a history, back in May 2006. The understanding was that the ABRSM would support the idea of a serious history being written about it, and co-operate by providing access to its archives and giving me the facility to talk to staff. I undertook to respect confidentiality with respect to any 'live' commercial, strategic or institutional information. This has proved a very happy basis for my work, and everyone at the ABRSM has been scrupulous, as well as steadfast, in respecting this history's independence. I wish to express my considerable gratitude to Richard Morris, the ABRSM's former Chief Executive, for supporting the idea of this history and to Leslie East, Executive Director: Syllabus and Publishing, who has been my official point of institutional contact. Both have been enormously encouraging and very open in answering any questions I have raised. I am also very grateful to Guy Perricone, Chief Executive from 2010, for his similarly strong support for the project. Other ABRSM Directors have also been very encouraging and helpful, giving me information and patiently answering my questions, particularly Tim Arnold, Richard Crozier, Tim Leates, Penny Milsom and Nigel Scaife. I am grateful to Lynne Butler and Robert Sargant, who took trouble to further my understanding of things relating to their areas of work. There are many other ABRSM staff who befriended this historian leading a sometimes peripatetic existence in their midst. Mainly based in the Chief Examiner's department and UK Operations while I used the archives, I greatly benefited from the help and kindness shown at various times by, particularly, Mary Bullard, Jacqui Larkin, Heather Leeson, Louise Leigh, Celia Pudwell, Donald Scott and Ruth Turner, and from the cheerfulness of all – it was very enjoyable to work there. Former members of the ABRSM who kindly agreed to be interviewed were Jenny Jones, Philip Mundey and Ronald Smith. I am also very grateful to Sir David Willcocks, Sir John Manduell, Sir David Lumsden and Sir Douglas Morpeth for agreeing to be interviewed.

I have incurred many other debts in the course of researching and writing this book. I gratefully acknowledge the support of the British Academy for its award of a Small Research Grant. For kind permission to quote and to reproduce illustrations from archive and library holdings, I am grateful to the following institutions: the ABRSM; the Royal College of Music, London; the Royal Academy of Music, London; Trinity College London Archive; the William Alwyn Foundation Archive. I am grateful to the following individuals for permission to quote from their private materials or unpublished sources: the Dunhill family in respect of Thomas Dunhill's diaries; Hermione Lockyer to quote from the diaries of her late father, Thornton Lofthouse; Gill Agnew for permission to quote from the diary of her late father, Richard O. Latham; Mrs Lovedy Cornish for permission to quote from the correspondence of her late cousin Henry Moule. I am most grateful to the libraries and librarians of the British Library, the RCM Library and its Centre for Performance History, the Royal College of Organists' Archive, the Royal Society of Arts, Margaret Jones (of the William Alwyn Archive) and the staff of the Anderson Room at Cambridge University Library. I should also like to express my gratitude to that wonderful resource 'MeasuringWorth' (www.measuringworth.com) for its economic calculators and supporting explanations.

I owe a particular debt to that doyen of music's social historians, Cyril Ehrlich, who did so much to develop and shape my thinking in these areas. He used to say that he hoped that his *Music Profession*, which he wrote as a survey of this hitherto unexplored field, would encourage others to make their own detailed investigations of some of its aspects. This history is one such offshoot, and I hope that he would not have been too vexed by its shortcomings. Very sadly, two people who contributed to this book did not live to see it published. One was the social historian of sport and leisure the Revd John Lowerson, who gave me much practical support, encouragement and invaluable early feedback. His friendship continues to be missed by many. The other is Clara Taylor, until 2010 the ABRSM's Chief Examiner. Clara's enthusiasm for the nuggets the research occasionally produced was a great antidote to archival longueurs, and I hope she would have forgiven my inserting so many footnotes.

I am grateful to Bruce Philips for his support of the idea of turning my early researches on the ABRSM into a book. For encouragement, help, information and hospitality in the process of writing I should like to thank William and Gill Agnew, Chris Andry (for information on his grandfather Hilary Macklin), Paul Banks (who also drew my attention to the Frederic Cliffe materials in the RCM's Centre for Performance History), Ian Bartlett, Christina Bashford (for sharing with me her researches on the College of Violinists), Frank Bongiorno, Paul Collen, Kieran Crichton, Ian Curror, Andrew Dilley, Hildur Eriksson, née Sandquist (for her reminiscences of ABRSM examiners in Canada in the 1930s), Ruth Finnegan, Oliver Gledhill, David Harpham, Wendy Hiscocks (for information on Arthur Benjamin), Anne Holmes MBE (for her generous loan of material relating to Cao Qun, Wuhun and the Grimsby International Singing Competition), Joseph Horovitz, Peter Horton, Leanne Langley, Vanessa Latarche, Andrew McCrea, Simon McVeigh, Maureen Smith, Barry Sterndale Bennett. I also thank those involved in the publication process at Boydell, Michael Middeke and, in particular, Megan Milan and David Roberts. Marija Đurić Speare gave invaluable help at the proofreading stage. I wish to thank those who have read some of the text and given me responses at different stages, especially Arnold Whittall, Trevor Herbert, Christina Bashford and members of the 'Music in Britain' seminar at the Institute of Historical Research. I owe particular gratitude to Penny Milsom, whose many perceptive comments on the text as it progressed have been to its very considerable benefit. Needless to say, such errors and inconsistencies that remain are entirely my own responsibility.

Finally, it gives me immense pleasure to acknowledge the debt due to my wife, Penny, incurred over many years, for her encouragement and unwavering support. I owe her more than I can express, and the book's dedication to her is but a small acknowledgement of that.

Abbreviations

ABMB	Associated Board Minute Book
ABRSM	Associated Board of the Royal Schools of Music
ABRSMA	Associated Board of the Royal Schools of Music Archives
DES	Department of Education and Science (1964–92)
DfEE	Department for Education and Employment (1995–2001)
GME(s)	Grade Music Exam(s)
HLR(s)	Honorary Local Representative(s)
ISM	Incorporated Society of Musicians
LCE	Local Centre Exams
LEA	Local Education Authority
LSE	Local School Exams
MMA	Music Masters and Mistresses Association
MT	*The Musical Times*
NTSM	National Training School for Music
ODNB	*Oxford Dictionary of National Biography: From the Earliest Times to the Year 2000*, ed. H. C. G. Matthew and Brian Harrison, 60 vols. (Oxford University Press, 2004)
RAM	Royal Academy of Music, London
RAMA	Royal Academy of Music, London, Archives
RCM	Royal College of Music, London
RCMA	Royal College of Music, London, Library Archives
RCMp	Royal College of Music, London, Centre for Performance History
RMCM	Royal Manchester College of Music
RNCM	Royal Northern College of Music, Manchester
RPI	Retail Price Index
RSAMD	Royal Scottish Academy of Music and Drama, Glasgow (from 2011 called the Royal Conservatoire of Scotland)
RSMs	Royal Schools of Music
TCL	Trinity College London (the examination branch of TCM)
TCLA	Trinity College London Archives
TCM	Trinity College of Music (the conservatoire, from 2005 called Trinity Laban)

Miscellaneous Conventions

⫽ RPI Conversions

Conversions of historical amounts into 2009 RPI equivalents are from Lawrence H. Officer, *Five Ways to Compute the Relative Value of a UK Pound Amount, 1830 to Present* (www.measuringworth.com/ukcompare). The values presented are as given on the access date; the tables themselves continue to be revised in the light of new information.

⫽ Keys

Minor keys are indicated by lower-case letters (e.g. Valse in a), and major keys by capitals (Study in G).

⫽ Pre-decimal currency

One pound (£1) had 20 shillings (20s).
One shilling (1s) had 12 pence (12p).
One guinea (the traditional unit for charging professional fees) was £1 1s.
Half a guinea was 10s 6d.

Introduction
The Context for a History

⁄⁄ The Associated Board

THE Associated Board of the Royal Schools of Music (ABRSM) is the extramural examining body set up by the Royal Academy of Music and the Royal College of Music in 1889. The Royal Manchester College of Music (now the Royal Northern College of Music) and the Royal Scottish Academy of Music and Drama (now the Royal Conservatoire of Scotland) joined the Board as subsidiary partners in 1947, becoming full partners in a major restructuring of the ABRSM that took place in 1985. (To avoid the tedious repetition of its acronym, I shall refer to the ABRSM variously in the text as 'the Associated Board' or just 'the Board'.)

What is the Associated Board, and what does it represent? Despite its ubiquitous presence in music education, relatively few know much about this institution and the basis on which it determines standards, writes syllabuses and runs its exams. In fact the Board is one of the significant legacies of Victorian Britain, generated as part of that society's concern to expand the technological and professional workforce needed to run the Empire. And, as with some other Victorian inceptions, the Board's system of exams – designed to provide for the objective assessment of progress in learning an instrument or voice, and applied on an industrial scale – was a symbiosis of educational purpose and entrepreneurial enterprise. Moreover the system has proved itself remarkably adaptable in meeting the changes in educational and musical environments during the course of its history. Some 120 years of the ABRSM has stamped in the public mind the idea of the eight music grades as a sort of *gradus ad Parnassum* that transforms the neophyte from Grade 1 beginnings to the pre-professional stage of Grade 8.

Early on, the ABRSM enjoyed little institutional weight or substance of its own. Tightly controlled by its two owner RSMs, the Associated Board was constructed as the neutral ground on which these two uneasy partners could meet to conduct business together – an administrative space defined by the mutual perception of common interests. Over time this began to change as the scope and scale of the Board's operations extended well beyond the capacity of the Schools to exercise detailed oversight, and so the ABRSM began to establish and develop a distinctive identity in its own right. The story of the modern ABRSM since its reconstitution in 1985 is about its emergence from under the coat-tails of the Royal Schools into an institution that projects a clear sense of its own identity. Mention the ABRSM to parents and pupils, and the reaction is likely to be 'music exams'; it is most improbable that any specific connection will be made to the RSMs themselves. In the course of its 120 years few institutions can be said to have had a greater effect on people's musical lives across the world. This account of the ABRSM seeks to explain how and why it is that the Board has become such a significant force.

⁄⁄⁄ Why a history?

I NTERESTINGLY, one or two people reacted with some scepticism when I said that I was researching a history of the ABRSM, surprised at the thought that anything to do with music exams offered much scope for any sort of history. Speculation as to the likely outcome ranged from expectations of ineluctable boredom (along the lines of '... and the highlight that year was a change to the scales in the clarinet syllabus') to dark mutterings of the need to expose colonialism and profit making. (Possibly influencing these individuals' reactions were their own experiences, and possibly a vestigial memory of the 'good news–bad news story' of music grades: the good news is that you have passed, the bad news is that now you must study for the next grade. Arguably, though, that was a better outcome than the 'bad news–bad news' version: you have failed the exam and you will take it again until you pass.) But as a social historian of music, the answer to the 'What sort of history?' question was clear to me from the outset, although the question of how to balance it all into a satisfactory whole within the restriction of space has remained very much a live issue in the process of writing.

Music examinations are something of an emotive subject for obvious reasons. Many do remember them as uncomfortable or frightening, regardless of the result. Even the idea of being 'examined' in music can seem unnatural – the antithesis of the sort of spontaneous pleasure that playing an instrument or singing is supposed to give. It is perhaps too easy to imagine that those candidates who go on to become professional performers take their grade exam experiences happily in their stride, treating them as the merest formalities of a successful musical progress, soon forgotten as they develop into mature artists. There is also much anecdotal evidence that some with modest grades – but achieved against the odds – continue to carry their success as a badge of honour well into their adult life.[1] But regardless of the degree of musical success or the level of attainment that people reach, many agree that their grade exam experiences are formative in terms of personal development, offering maturing experiences that help focus personal discipline and prompt ways of coping with nerves or stress.

Significant though music exams are to the individual concerned, they have much wider significance to the historian. They provide valuable evidence of change and continuity about the technical and cultural processes of musical formation. Essentially, these exams are an encapsulation of musical attitudes. Their syllabuses are a rich source of information about didactic materials and changing fashions in teaching instruments and singing. If we follow the Board's syllabuses over a period of time, we can observe the formation of a repertoire of teaching pieces that travelled the world. Some of the pieces in this repertoire are indeed exemplary in the canonic sense, holding firmly on to their place by reappearing time and again in the lists; others, however, often composed in idioms that tell

---

[1] Indicative of the value of early achievement as meaningful to the individual is the example kindly given to me by Professor Ruth Finnegan of someone she encountered who despite having later achieved a university degree in music and compositions to their name still mentions their ABRSM Grade 5 in their CV (Private communication, 27 November 2007).

us much about contemporary tastes and musical values, are transient. So, taken as a whole, we see that there are many ways in which music exams determine the cultural expectations of those learning to play or sing. And as well as this, grade exams have come to constitute the vocabulary of individual musical progress and a means to label standards of attainment. Thus, in a variety of ways, grade exams, as in 'doing the grades', have fashioned many people's understanding of what constitutes 'normal' practice in music teaching.

One reason why the ABRSM has been such a rewarding subject to study is because examination processes tell us so much about the wider social and historical context. And an integral part of its history has been the question of what it is about the British milieu that has enabled the ABRSM to exercise such an enormous influence on music education from its inception in 1889. Explaining this requires some contextual discussion of music in its wider social, economic, educational and cultural environment over the period of the Board's history. Bringing these sorts of considerations into play generates very different insights about music and its circumstances than those we get from conventional musical histories, with their traditional emphasis on composers and works, and changes in compositional idioms between epochs.

Study of examination syllabuses tell us not only about the music that was set and the related technical requirements, but also conveys something of the attitudes and expectations – the implied relationships – between the exam board, teacher and candidate. For example, we learn much about how an exam board relates to its market from the way it words its examination rubrics; its descriptions of the examination process; the assistance or contact it offers to teachers; and the feedback it gives its candidates. These details help us build a larger picture: were exam boards all vying for the same candidate market, for example, or did they seek to differentiate themselves in musical or social terms? If they were after the same sorts of candidates, then how did that competition express itself? The entry fee charged by different exam boards is a simple but useful piece of information, because it gives us an immediate point of comparison. For example, does the willingness to pay 2 guineas to be examined by the Associated Board (President, the Prince of Wales) in 1890, rather than the one guinea for the rival exams offered by Trinity College London, mean the expectation of a better sort of exam, or is it about something else entirely, such as a statement of social class?[2]

Does a class difference between the early ABRSM and other examining bodies help to explain the surprisingly large and rapidly growing number of candidates entered for the Board's very expensive exams? And why were so many teachers prepared to apply to become 'registered teachers' of the Board in its early days at the cost of one guinea? If such a class difference was at work, certain decisions, such as which exams to use – the Royal Schools' or Trinity's – and which colleges to study at, were perhaps more socially grounded than we might have imagined. Or should we interpret entry to the early Associated Board exams as an expression

[2] Leisure activities as the expression of class culture is a rewarding theme explored by H. Cunningham, 'Leisure and Culture', in *The Cambridge History of Britain*, vol. 2: *People and Their Environment*, ed. F. M. L. Thompson (Cambridge: Cambridge University Press, 1990), 279–339.

of deeper musical seriousness because it bought the opportunity to be examined by one of the several national figures who were the Board's examiners? The fact that the Associated Board could boast examiners such as Charles Stanford, Hubert Parry and the organist Walter Parratt (all later knighted) was in itself eloquent expression of the potency of its musical status.

My original interest in the Associated Board came from my work on the founding and the early development of the Royal College of Music.[3] There was really no British precedent for the RCM, which from its beginnings offered what we should still today recognize as a 'modern curriculum' with delineated elements of study and courses of specified length. The College had originated as an educational corrective to the perceived institutional and musical inadequacies of the RAM. The fundraising process to establish the RCM had generated mutual antagonism between the two institutions, and there was considerable jealousy of the RCM's royal and aristocratic backers. The idea of an 'Associated Board' was a way to circumvent the otherwise unseemly spectacle of the two chartered national music institutions being publicly at each other's throats. (However, institutional rivalry had not dissuaded several of the country's most distinguished instrumentalists from being simultaneously on the staff of both RSMs.)

Sir George Grove, the RCM's Director, and Alexander Mackenzie, the RAM's newly arrived Principal, realized that an Associated Board offered mutual financial benefit. For the single most pressing issue facing both the RAM and RCM was a debilitating lack of money, an ongoing problem without any immediate prospect of solution. It is the amount of one-to-one vocal or instrumental teaching that makes conservatoire education such a notoriously expensive form of training – then as now. Moreover, in those days, students received not only individual first study lessons, but also individual second study and harmony lessons. Financially the RAM was dependant on fees from paying students plus the few scholarships its Subscribers could fund. The RCM had the funding for fifty scholarship places (some with maintenance) but needed to attract a hefty number of additional paying students to balance its books, and this problem was further exacerbated in 1893 by its move into the new, much larger, building on Prince Consort Road. Undoubtedly, therefore, the strongest inducement to establish the ABRSM was financial, with the anticipated profits from the exam fees providing a vital income stream that would alleviate the pressures on both Schools.

However, the concept of an Associated Board of the two RSMs was also attractive because Grove would have seen it as offering a ready and financially self-supporting way of fulfilling the responsibility laid upon the RCM at its foundation by its royal charter, namely to work:

> to the advancement of the Art of Music by means of a central teaching and examining body ... rewarding with academical degrees and certificates of proficiency ... persons, whether educated at the College or not [and working to the] promotion and supervision of such musical instruction in schools and elsewhere as may be thought most conducive to the cultivation

[3] David Wright, 'The South Kensington Music Schools and the Development of the British Conservatoire in the Late Nineteenth Century', *Journal of the Royal Musical Association* 130/2 (2005), 236–82.

and dissemination of the Art of Music in the United Kingdom ... [and] throughout our dominions.

The RCM's charter, requiring it to undertake a wider responsibility for the promotion and supervision of musical instruction, was to be the legitimizing instrument of the ABRSM. (Grove also felt that this charter laid upon the Board a responsibility to drive all unchartered institutions out of the music exam market.)[4] But clearly a scheme of music exams properly run through an Associated Board by the two RSMs would be effective in boosting the status of music training and thereby the individual and joint national standing of the RAM and the RCM.

It is difficult now to be certain how many of the benefits brought about by the creation of the Associated Board were foreseen by Grove and Mackenzie, and how many were serendipitous. Looking back, it is clear that in its early days the ABRSM did indeed play a significant part in raising the profiles of the Royal Schools. First, as the ABRSM exams (and their imposing certificates) spread across the country, they helped to establish the musical authority of the College and Academy in the public mind. Secondly, music exams helped to professionalize the activity of music teaching itself; this development encouraged more middle-class families to see music teaching as a respectable career for their children (particularly daughters), and so made them more inclined to invest in the fees to buy a conservatoire training. Thirdly, the Board's exams were a practical means of assisting former Academy and College students to make their way in setting up teaching practices and competing for pupils. The thinking behind this was that conservatoire training made for better-quality teachers, and that this would be demonstrated by the abundance of ABRSM examination successes achieved by pupils of RSM-trained teachers. Fourthly, the ABRSM syllabus (by prescribing appropriate technical exercises and pieces) would expand the potential pool of better prepared and more accomplished students for the Royal Schools. Grove and Mackenzie might also have had another practical benefit in mind: ABRSM examining would be a powerful form of financial patronage that would give the RAM and the RCM some useful extra leverage over their professorial workforce. Teaching fees at the College and the Academy were low (the ubiquitous title of 'professor' helped dignify the situation), and so the chance of additional income and status from ABRSM examining (initially examining was almost exclusively confined to those on RSM staffs) offered the compensation of an additional professional benefit. Some RSM staff made a substantial proportion of their living as examiners, especially from overseas tours. Others, however, never really took to the work of examining, constantly declaring themselves unavailable for examining tours and doing the bare minimum required to keep themselves on the panel of examiners, much to the Board's chagrin. Even at their most motivated, the panel of examiners remained a slightly restive workforce, always believing the Board could afford better rates of pay and expenses. Later, of course, the institutional hold would evaporate completely when the success of the ABRSM meant that the

---

[4] In his speech to the Associated Board's third Annual Dinner, Grove declared that 'in a short time I trust that we shall find the whole of the examinations in our hands, conducted in a way which nobody but this Board can conduct them'. *Proceedings of the Third Annual Dinner* (14 July 1892), 15 (ABRSMA).

demand for more examiners far outstripped the Royal Schools' ability to provide them, and so recruitment had to be opened out much more widely across the profession.

Very soon after its first British exams, in the mid-1890s, the Board was invited to conduct examinations in South Africa; it then began to offer its exams in Australasia and Canada, and subsequently across the Empire. This Empire-wide presence means that the Board has sometimes been represented as something of an imperial adventurer, seeking to make a profit out of the sentimental associations bound up in Dominion markets. As is discussed in Chapter 5, some recent histories of the British Empire have argued that there was a much more reciprocal relationship between Britain and its Dominions than post-colonialist theories have allowed. The history of the ABRSM's early Australian operation is certainly remarkable more for what it reveals about a sense of obligation within the Board's psyche to develop the standards of music teaching in Australia, than for any achievement of profit; indeed, for more than half their years of operation, the Australian exams ran at a significant loss. A loss was not surprising, given the difficulties imposed by the country's vast spaces, attenuated lines of communication and the difficulty of ensuring the availability of exam music. But periods of financial deficit were characteristic, too, of the Board's position in other colonies; and for many years the Board's UK income underwrote, or cross-subsidized, its colonial examining. Despite these losses, the Board continued to hold to its commitment of providing colonial scholarships and exhibitions for study at the Royal Schools. Although some scholars, such as the Australian Arthur Benjamin, stayed on to make their career in London, many other colonial students returned to develop the musical life at home. Interestingly, too, the Board lost some of its examiners, such as Edgar Bainton (Director of the Sydney Conservatorium), to the Empire, because their examining tours gave them a taste for the contrasting life-styles they experienced in the Dominions.

Because music grades have become so much part of the warp and weft of British classical music, few really stop to consider the system's wider significance. For one thing, the grade process is a conditioning factor in the musical taste, habits and attitudes of candidates and their teachers, and, by extension, it also affects the many parents and siblings who are inescapably caught up by it. In other words, the huge market for grade exams that has taken hold since the late nineteenth century means that the syllabuses put out by examination boards have shaped the way that very many teachers teach, and have defined musical standards and musical taste for millions of people. For most classically trained musicians the grade system has had a determining effect on at least some of the pieces, scales and technical exercises that they have learned, prescribing at exactly what stage in their development they were taught them. Secondly, the economic significance of the grade exam system on music teaching is a significant but relatively understated aspect (the matter of exam fees excepted). The pressure on passing music exams has done much to reinforce the idea that good music teaching is a skilled service with verifiable outcomes that can be linked to financial value. For good or ill, effective grade exam results are a way of defining success in this music teaching market, which makes the system a stimulus to competition. For this reason, one significant effect of grade exams has been to encourage more explicit comparisons between teachers.

But this can also represent one of the abuses of the grade system, because in reality, proper comparisons of successful teaching rest upon very much more than exam statistics. Nevertheless, teachers with a strong record of examination results can sometimes command a corresponding premium in the fees they charge. In this context, one of the generally beneficial consequences of the grade system has been to increase the standing of music teaching as a professional activity, something that was one of the original objectives of the ABRSM. The economic significance of the grade system extends to other forms of supply. The music retail trade has been a major beneficiary because grades make a real impact through sales of examination music and stimulating the demand for musical instruments and a range of assorted accoutrements. Additionally, the local music shop is often a networking centre for the teachers in an area, and sometimes it is also a centre at which grade exams are held. It is significant that although the ABRSM has developed a strong online presence for its publications, it has also been careful to maintain its support for local retailing in the UK.

Power relationships

I SUSPECT that one of the negative reactions to my idea of a history about the ABRSM sprang from reservations people hold about a grade system that can appear something of a summary judgement, *de haut en bas*. But researching the ABRSM's history has made me more conscious of just how much more complex and encompassing this whole process of musical assessment is when seen in relation to the social and musical interaction that is involved. Each individual grade exam is the cumulative point of an integrated and consensual educational process. If we break this process down, we see that the requirements made for each grade are far from arbitrary; rather, they reflect the common teaching experience and a shared musical culture. In fact these exams represent more of a broad consensus among users than the surrounding mythology of examination board diktat might sometimes indicate. Of course, as far as the individual candidate is concerned, their music exam is likely to be the culmination of much preparation and possible anxiety, and he or she is possibly the last person to appreciate that the brief event which has caused them such apprehension is such a fascinating nexus of the professional, social, economic and institutional spheres.

The occasion of the music exam is the obvious key moment. In practice, there is all the folklore that surrounds this event. Formally, the examiner is the Board's representative, the agent charged with maintaining and implementing its standards. But in the immediacy of the exam centre itself, examiners are sometimes seen and treated as the exam board itself in anthropomorphic guise, a construction that can invest their every mundane act with immense, external significance, whether it be the selection or rejection of biscuits, a nice smile or an expressed fondness for cats. In this situation, the examiner dominates all, a position that some have been very ready to exploit. But, if we stand back from this human situation and analyse the power relationships involved in these exams, we see that the candidate is not necessarily in the weakest or most critical position. There are two others – the teacher and the examiner – who as well as the candidate constitute the dramatis personae of the grade exam, and each of these two has an important professional and economic stake also invested in the process. Put another way, this triangle of candidate, teacher and examiner represents a complex interaction or negotiation of mutual interests. It is because the whole process surrounding the exam involves the *interaction* of these interests that it is less obviously hierarchical and one-sided than traditional perceptions of examination power play might have us believe.

One way of explaining how this interaction works in practice is to ask the question: 'Who is the subject of scrutiny in this examination process – the candidate, the teacher or the examiner?' That question will continue to resonate in various guises during the course of this book. But it should be emphasized that in its early days, much of the Board's initial focus was on testing the teacher. One of the justifications given for setting up the Board was that success in its exams would function as an objective measure of a teacher's effectiveness – these exams were never solely about the pupil *per se*. The idea was that by drawing attention to the results of good music teaching and exposing the bad, the ABRSM exams would be the means of ridding the market of inferior teachers. That outcome would fulfil the responsibility laid on the ABRSM by the RCM's charter. Early in its history the Board's confident expectation was that the adverse publicity generated by poor results would be the means by which inadequate teachers would see their supply of pupils gradually wither away. And, as mentioned earlier, in today's climate exam success is certainly considered a key indicator of any teacher's quality.

Just as the candidate is not the only one under scrutiny in the exam process itself, so the exam board itself is perhaps rather less dominant than it might seem. Because there are several grade music exam boards, there is potential for negotiation in the relationship between teacher and exam board. The continuing loyalty of teachers to an exam board often depends upon that board prescribing music that is rewarding for pupils to study and for teachers to teach. This makes the selection of exam music a crucial commercial, as well as educational, decision. The music that is prescribed must appeal to a wide range of tastes, while at the same time being worth while to study from both the technical and interpretative perspectives. A busy teacher will often find him- or herself teaching several pupils at the same grade, and it doesn't take much imagination to realize the effect this can have if they feel antipathetic to the pieces they are required to teach. Therefore the basic expectation of teachers is that their exam board will continue to provide good syllabus content at every stage. If a board gets this wrong, it can mean significant drops in numbers of exam entries with the ultimate danger that an ill-judged syllabus could prompt teachers to migrate to another exam board – perhaps permanently.

Exam syllabuses are designed to influence the process of cultural and technical formation, but critics of the grade system feel that the necessarily detailed and prescriptive scheme of step-by-step music grades produces a treadmill that enforces conformity on teachers and pupils alike. Against this is the argument that the variety of musical circumstances and the sheer disparity of teaching standards to be encountered make it more educationally responsible to provide a complete scheme of musical development that some can dip into as required and others follow much more systematically. In educational terms this means that the syllabus has to be robust enough to work under different sorts of situations. At one end of the teaching spectrum is the musically confident, self-sufficient teacher who typically uses grade exams as an occasional tool to give their pupils and their parents external verification of progress. But against that are teachers less well placed in terms of their own individual musical and teaching skills, and who, from necessity, become dependent upon an exam board's syllabus as their (sometimes only) source of teaching materials, taking their pupils relentlessly through the successive grades, with little or no intermission for any independent exploration of repertory. In this situation the exam syllabus becomes by default the dominant musical influence over teacher and pupils.

As we shall see, different markets use grades in different ways, and there is much less uniformity in practice than is often supposed. The major challenge for the Associated Board in recent years has been to meet the needs of new teaching developments, such as group instruction, or non-classical musical idioms that people like to learn, such as jazz. Another initiative has been that the Board has involved itself with the professional development of teachers, designing courses and mentoring events, something that represents a radical departure from the ABRSM's historical past. (In its early years the Board had studiously avoided involvement in anything other than the formal process of assessment and awards, believing that to do so would be to compromise its objectivity and independence.) One view of the Board's recent entry into the field of professional development sees it as a ploy designed to reinforce dependency on the ABRSM 'brand'. Another would be to see the Board stepping into something of a void. Although much government emphasis is currently being placed on the need for professionals to continue to upgrade their skills during their working lives, at present there is very little professional development provision for independent instrumental music teachers, many of whom feel increasingly isolated as their years of formal education recede. As will become apparent in the course of this book, the once unquestioned high cultural status of classical music has been reduced as society has changed. One simple illustration is the change in UK newspaper coverage: where once discussion or reviews of classical music dominated, now it is usually relegated to being a minority interest. The once large mainstream or 'middlebrow' audience for classical music has been diminished by the appeal of other musical idioms, and digital technology has made individuals musically much more self-sufficient. In this situation the traditional, independent music teacher is ever more vulnerable, and it is in the Board's own longer-term interest to do all it can to foster the quality of teaching available to those taking its exams.

The examiner

FOR all that the examiner appears to be the dominant figure in this three-way interaction of candidate, teacher and examiner, it is in fact the examiner's role that is the most scrutinized and externally accountable. The basic expectation made of examiners is that their marking should show a demonstrable level of fairness, appropriateness and consistency, and that their marks and comments should signify the Board's criteria and standards. An exam board has everything to lose if its examiners do not perform their roles well, or are deficient in any way that suggests a lack of professionalism or quality of judgement. Even in the early days when examiners were thought to operate in a more autocratic, less accountable manner, the files show that the ABRSM was certainly aware of the damage that was incurred when an examiner behaved inappropriately. Although it would uphold an examiner's verdict where possible, if it judged him (and until 1956 it was always a male examiner) to be at fault it was also ready to discipline or dismiss the offender depending on circumstances. Until 1930 the candidate received no feedback in the form of examiner's comments – only a bald statement of marks (awarded under the assessment criteria set out for each instrument), and even this they had to pay for separately.

When full examiners' reports of marks and comments began to be issued during the 1920s, it proved something of a mixed blessing. Though intended to help the candidate, they also drew attention to any unfortunate deficiencies in the examiner's arithmetic, grammar and handwriting. Sorting out examiners' reports threatened to swamp the administration, and in 1931 it was declared that these reports would be passed on to candidates 'without discussion or revision' – effectively a public declaration that the onus was on the examiner – though for obvious reasons the Board continued to check the examiner's addition before the result was released. Today's quality-assurance climate requires a much more transparent process, making the examiner much more accountable to the candidate and to the Board. For its part, the ABRSM has had to become much more open in its relationship with both teacher and candidate, and this has involved the instigation of an appeals process to safeguard teachers' and candidates' interests. In its early history the Associated Board traded very much on the aura that its aloofness generated, whereas today's observer is more likely to be struck by the extent to which it is seeking to demythologize itself by publishing explanatory material, seeking feedback and hosting teachers' forums on its website.

The Board's overriding objective in selecting and training its examiners is to have the confidence that not only will they be able to deliver consistent standards on their own, individual, account, but also that the marks they award will be felt by teachers to relate to the verdicts delivered by the Board's other examiners across the years. This raises two points. One is that there has to be a strong sense of collective responsibility about being an examiner, a willingness to adopt wholeheartedly the received standards of the marking body as a whole. The other is that there is something transcendental about the belief that assessment values can be transmitted unchanged down the years, and while historically this is unverifiable, it is an idea that many are happy to believe because it gives the system a desirable sense of consistency and security of judgement. Over the years, the ABRSM has tried several methods to standardize the way its examiners mark. Early on in its history, very few pieces were set for each grade and this gave the marking a certain focus at a time when there was no training of examiners, as such – everyone was just expected to 'know' instinctively the standards to apply at each grade. Then, as more alternative pieces were added to the syllabus and the number of examiners increased as the uptake of the exams continued to grow, the need to standardize examiners' marking became a much more pressing issue. The method eventually adopted was for the Secretary to calculate the marking average of the panel as a whole at each grade and to issue warnings (that marking was too high or too low) to those examiners who deviated unacceptably from this average. The 1960s and 1970s saw the appointment of moderators who visited examiners at work and who could advise them as necessary. Later came formal examiners' meetings and seminars, and the institution of mock exams as part of the training process.

From the Board's first exams there seems to have been general public acceptance about the broad consistency of marking standards. The national profile of many of the early examiners was undoubtedly one reason why its grades became so quickly established and certainly helped to generate trust in the exams, whether the examining was necessarily consistent or not. But the Board's long delay in doing anything positive to develop their examiners' skills was indicative of its institutional conservatism both socially and professionally. It stubbornly held to its belief that examiners would simply absorb the collective standard through a sort of osmosis. Indeed, the idea of calling examiners together for a training meeting appeared to have been considered an affront to their professional dignity – and, worse, they would have needed paying. But clearly such attitudes could not hold, and the shake-up of society in the wake of the Second World War, and especially from the 1960s (when British society became progressively more questioning of establishment authority), brought about considerable change in the Board as it did in so many other aspects of British life.

Out of date and out of touch

AT various times in its history the Board has been criticized as a reactionary or conservative musical force. Often this has been for musical reasons, such as its very conventional and unadventurous choice of repertoire. But in the matter of women examiners (discussed in Chapter 8) the Board chose to be reactionary in an important social respect too. Its continual refusal to appoint women examiners was particularly striking because it flew in the face of the attitudes of that part of the profession – the staffs of the RSMs – from which it mainly drew its examiners. Women had been allowed to mark music theory papers and, from the 1920s, to join the panel of elocution examiners, but not to examine music grades. The issue had been simmering for a while, but matters were brought to a head in 1945 when RAM and RCM male staff submitted a petition for women to become examiners. A placatory decision in principle had been taken by the Governing Body to accept women examiners, but despite periodic reminders given by one of its members, Percy Buck, the heads of the Academy and the College, Sir Stanley Marchant and Sir George Dyson, refused to appoint any. They maintained their obduracy despite a post-war crisis in which the Board found itself swamped by a significant increase in the number of candidates and an acute shortage of male examiners. Such was the pressure that in 1947 the Board was actually considering implementing measures designed to *reduce* entries by making the exams a less attractive proposition! And all this in the year that the Royal Manchester College and the Royal Scottish Academy became junior partners of the Board, which made their staffs eligible for selection as examiners. It was only in 1956 that the first women practical examiners were nominated. It is difficult not to conclude that, in their prejudice against women examiners, Dyson and Marchant were more prepared to damage the Board than to concede the gender issue. The injustice had considerable economic significance, because the Board was effectively disenfranchising women from a significant element of professional musical activity. It was an inauspicious beginning to the post-war era that also marked a quiescent period in its history in which the Board simply left things to run along their established lines without any fresh thinking.

Quite apart from its gender, the constitution of the post-war examining panel was very restricted in other ways too. There was an overwhelming predominance of keyboard players, some singers and a very thin sprinkling of other instrumentalists. This imbalance reflected the pattern of conservatoire employment. Though obviously the conservatoires employed distinguished orchestral players, it was simply not viable for working orchestral musicians to become Board examiners. Membership of the examining panel was based on availability for a minimum of three one-week periods each year. But the extraordinary hours orchestral players were required to work to maintain their position and income made it most unlikely that they would be able to offer anything like this. So throughout much of its history the average Board examiner was a keyboard player. He would be either a pianist or organist on the Royal Schools' staff, a cathedral organist, or a public school director of music – who was usually a keyboard player in any case. But that sort of examiner profile was not as inappropriate then as it would be today, because the market for the Board's exams in the 1940s and 1950s was still primarily the drawing-room instrument constituency of pianists, singers, violinists and cellists (plus organists) who had been the candidates in the 1890s – so what was there to interest an orchestral player in examining a shoal of keyboard players? The change in the make-up of ABRSM candidates really began only in the 1960s. Or, put another way, in the world of the 1940s and 1950s, the keyboard weighting of the examining panel was a close reflection of the nature of the candidate base. While this keyboard dominance caused periodic disgruntlement among the teachers of other instruments, the Board gave little shrift to any complaints, pointing out that its examiners were interested primarily in the musical quality of the playing when reaching their assessment, and only secondarily in how it was achieved. On this basis, the undoubted musical quality of the examiners concerned sustained the position without compromise to the integrity of the exams themselves. Periodically there have been calls for specialist examiners to examine their own instrument or voice, and the issue of specialist or generalist assessment continues to rumble. One change between the post-war and today's examining panel is that the presence of RSM staff is much diminished and now there is a more open process intended to draw examiners from a much wider professional constituency. However, the piano-based aural tests continue to discourage orchestral players with weak keyboard skills.

The ultimate sanction for a teacher dissatisfied with the syllabus or the examining standards of one examining board is to switch to another. Thus no examination board can afford to lose touch with its own core market; this inserts a useful competitive element between them. History shows that competition in the music exam market does not always work as might be expected, because all the indications are that teachers tend to react strongly against any perceived dilution of standards. The danger of opportunist competition lies less in the lowering of standards than in the restriction of the breadth of musical demands that an exam makes, or in the slide into more conservative forms of musical taste, something in which both teachers and exam board can become complicit. The ABRSM of the 1940s and 1950s fell heavily into the trap of conservatism. There was a deadening effect that resulted from the predominance of elderly and traditionalist members of its Governing Body (no matter how personally illustrious) who were very happy to see the continuation of the status quo. And because the Governing Body then heavily controlled the Board's operations, there was really no impetus to revitalize its syllabuses. Eventually the Board woke up to the uncomfortable amount of external criticism that it was facing. Increasingly teachers and educationalists characterized it as distant, narrow-minded and largely indifferent – when not actually oblivious – to the needs of its users. As earlier indicated, the ABRSM's exam base continued to lie primarily with the piano, violin, cello and voice, as well as in music theory – significantly those were the only exam subjects that each drew more than a thousand candidates in 1960. Not until 1969 did the ABRSM make a serious investment in published wind and brass syllabuses, a realignment that brought about a considerable transformation of its situation. In 1970, candidates in the flute, clarinet, oboe and trumpet either comfortably, or substantially, exceeded the thousand threshold and, significantly, Grade 8 was attracting a much stronger range of orchestral instrument entries; this was all very different from the 1960 situation.

The extensive realignment of the candidate base that happened in the 1960s and 1970s shows just how outmoded the Board had become, content simply to operate on the basis of traditional assumptions, regardless of the ways that music education had been developing. The successive generations of its Governing Body had been dominated by organists (virtually all the heads of the Royal Schools had been organists), and over time their musical values had shaped the ABRSM's mindset. By tradition the organist was the general practitioner of the musical world and, whether based at the diocesan cathedral or a large town parish church, he was likely to find – or make – himself the focal point of much local music-making, directing the local choral society or orchestra, and often being the principal grammar school music teacher. This pattern was now long established in British musical life, and had become deeply embedded in the ABRSM's thinking. This explains why it took so long for the Board to widen its instrumental base to take in the orchestral world. But another factor was the traditional self-sufficiency of the brass band world in the training of its instrumentalists, and this had played a crucial role in keeping those instruments outside the grade system. Change began in the post-war period with the appearance of a new educational force in music – Local Authority instrumental services. It was the increase of school-based instrumental teaching that generated a substantial demand for orchestral instrument exams.

⁄⁄⁄ Changing things around

T HE event that paved the way for the transformation of the ABRSM into its modernized counterpart was the 1985 reconstitution of the Board. This had a fundamental effect. First, it brought the Manchester and Scottish Royal Schools into full partnership of the ABRSM, on an equal basis with the original London partners. Secondly, it precipitated a new way of collective thinking. With the charitable donations now to be shared between four equal partners, it was clear that the Board needed to increase its income if it were to continue to contribute to the RSMs in any meaningful way. In April 1983, after having had two organist Secretaries, William Cole and Philip Cranmer, the Board broke decisively with the past by appointing Ronald Smith to be the Board's executive head with the new title 'Chief Executive and Director of Examinations'. Smith came to the Board after a period as county music adviser for Avon, giving him a base among school and instrumental teachers. His experience of the practicalities of instrumental musical education began the revivification of the Board as a modern institution.

Under Smith, the Board began to shed its paternal image. He instigated a raft of changes to the exams, supported by more developed quality-assurance processes, a more sophisticated examinations administration and new marketing and overseas initiatives. All this began to make the Board a much more complex organization. A further break with the past came in 1993 with the appointment of Richard Morris as Smith's successor. Morris was the first non-professional musician to be the ABRSM's executive (rather than administrative) head, and he held the post until his retirement at the end of 2009. Morris's time saw the Board pursuing a future much more on its own terms, stepping out of some of the shadows of its past, not least by bringing the Board into the political debate about music education. He undertook a vigorous development of the Board's overseas markets, particularly in the Far East, a strategy epitomized by securing an examining presence in China. Morris also initiated new strategic directions in what the Board now offers, enhancing its profile within music education. One fresh approach has been to offer more extended forms of assistance to instrumental music teachers through formal, award-bearing professional development courses. Another development has been to instigate a strong ABRSM web presence that including the informality of teachers' forums and podcast discussions.

As will become evident, for much of its time the Board was essentially happy to continue to do what it had always done, catering for its traditional middle-class instrumental base without really thinking about whether it had the potential to benefit music education rather more broadly across society. The post-war explosion of instrumental music teaching in schools transformed things, but the Board was no more than a passive beneficiary of this change. The expansion of instrumental learning brought about by Local Education Authority (LEA) music services generated a significant increase in woodwind and brass grade exams, but even then it did not seem to strike the Board that this development represented both a need and the opportunity for an expansion of its work. That can be the only explanation for the Board's failure to publish dedicated syllabuses for the brass and woodwind families, which, as we have seen, did not happen until the late 1960s – until then teachers were obliged to write to the Board for the requirements for their individual instrument. As mentioned, once they were fully integrated within the grade system, it very quickly became as routine for woodwind and brass players to take grade exams as it was for keyboard and string players and singers. Looking back, the 1960s, 70s and most of the 80s were something of a golden era for young British musicians as the instrumental lesson provision made freely available to schools through the music services of LEAs enormously broadened children's access to learning instruments. For a while the LEA music services provided not only lessons and instruments to children, regardless of parental income, but also – importantly – opportunities for talented players to progress to play at county and national level, a system which fed some very fine instrumentalists into the conservatoires. The breakdown of this system in the late 1980s, with the dismantling of its financial base by the 1988 Education Reform Act, had a strongly adverse effect on British music education, because, once again, it made a child's opportunity to learn an instrument largely dependent upon parental finance.

A new environment

T HE 1988 Education Reform Act changed British music provision. The Act provided for the local management of schools, giving individual schools the opportunity to control their own budgets. The devolving of financial responsibility from local government to schools meant that instead of instrumental music provision being made freely available to schools through their LEA, music became a resource to be competed for within a school's overall budget. LEA music centres were reformed, many replaced by financially self-supporting music services providers, usually operating on a fee basis. In consequence, unless music was seen as a priority by a school, it tended not to fare very well in the new climate, and so instrumental lessons, always a cost-intensive resource, became a frequent casualty. Increasingly instrumental training was again to depend upon parental willingness and capacity to pay. This development held huge implications for the ABRSM. The shrinking of the candidate base at the lower grades now threatened the pyramid structure that had been so vital in sustaining the traditional educational and economic model of the eight-grade system. (The reference is to the very broad base of early grade learners which then tapers off significantly towards the higher grades.)

Hard on the heels of the damage to instrumental learning that the 1988 Act had caused by reducing opportunities and increasing costs to parents, came a more insidious type of harm done to classical music's social image. The 1997 Labour government brought a much more consciously populist approach to the arts and their funding. Particularly detrimental to classical music's social and cultural image was politicians' targeting of it as an elitist and middle-class activity. The irony is that until the effect of the 1988 Act took hold, entry to the conservatoires had been characterized by musicians drawn from right across the social spectrum, their talent fostered by LEA music provision. Increases in the direct costs of learning an instrument inevitably changed that social balance, because it made access to music tuition more economically exclusive, but observing the effect of this change then encouraged politicians to draw a connection between classical music training and social advantage. Classical music has become something of a punch bag in the contentious polarization between elitist values and populist culture, one reason why the ABRSM has recently involved itself more in the political debate about music education. Another response by the Board has been to develop new exams (such as 'Music Medals') that are outside the traditional eight-step grade system and which take account of some of the new circumstances affecting early-stage instrumental learning.

The purpose of this Introduction has been to give a context for the history that follows. I hope it will have indicated that the history of the ABRSM is more interesting than might have been expected, not least because it is about so much more than just the act of examining. In relating it, I hope to convert some of those who were originally sceptical about whether such a history was worth while. The ABRSM is an institution that has touched our musical culture in so many respects, generally for the good, though also sometimes less admirably. Core to the ABRSM is the relationship of candidate, teacher and examiner, and this account shows how the Board has handled this interaction at different phases of its history, according to the social and cultural context and the conventions of the day. Other themes also play their part in illustrating how the Board has adapted – or failed to adapt – to changing circumstances. The ABRSM's combination of the educational and commercial polarizes attitudes. Crucial to the public image of the ABRSM brand is the Board's ability to demonstrate that it keeps its educational and commercial aspects in an acceptable balance. The two main arguments for the Board's commercial success are, first, that its profits go to music education in the form of charitable donations, and, second, that an entrepreneurial approach is key to the Board maintaining its relevance in the fast-changing environment of music education – only current economic success can fund the research and development of new products necessary to avoid the ossification of reliance on past formulas. It will already be clear that responsibility in music examining is as much about meeting the needs and expectations of users across an evolving musical canvas as it is about the technicalities of music. Accordingly this history seeks to place the work of the Associated Board within those changing cultural, social and educational circumstances.

I The Background

1 Music Exams and Victorian Society

﹉ The context

THE system of grade and diploma music exams that is now so familiar to us is a product of the attitudes and social circumstances of Victorian society. To explain the origin of these exams and why they proliferated so rapidly into something of an industry requires a broad social history perspective. These exams are part of a fascinating context that sees music teaching mutate from an occupation that many considered evidence of low social standing, into the middle-class respectability of a 'profession'. And because graded exams established standardized assessments of musical attainment, they were significant in changing music education from something of an *ad hoc* pursuit into a more systematic and educationally significant process. Because grade exams also enabled musical progress to be measured and defined as clearly and unambiguously as achievements in school-based subjects, they secured more general acceptance of music as a discipline within the conventions of the wider education system.

At first it may not seem obvious that larger historical and social processes should have played much of a part in shaping our music exam culture. But this chapter argues that contemporary social and economic factors were just as formative in making late nineteenth-century Britain such an opportune time to invent the musical exam system as was the astonishing transformation and efflorescence of its musical life. Music exams and a vital musical culture were each legacies of the Victorian and Edwardian periods. But for a long time we have been conditioned against taking a positive view of the musical life of this period. One reason has been the reluctance of the musicological mindset to present British musical life within its wider, energizing, context. In truth, very few music historians have said much that is complimentary about British music at this time, because traditional music histories take the view that the measure of the health of a nation's musical life lies in its compositional achievement. But to anyone wanting an account of the musical life of a society in the round, as it were, this approach is clearly problematic, because self-evidently composition constitutes only one aspect of musical life. Discussion of other activities that are essential to a flourishing musical culture, such as performance and music teaching, are conspicuously absent from conventional musical histories. In recent years this emphasis on composition has been challenged by accounts that have looked at musical life in a more comprehensive way, and from a range of other perspectives: social, economic, concert life and its repertoires, amateur music traditions, etc.[1] It is because the

---

[1] See, *inter alia*, R. Nettel, *Music in the Five Towns, 1840–1914* (London: Oxford University Press, 1944); E. D. Mackerness, *A Social History of English Music* (London: Routledge & Kegan Paul, 1964); Cyril Ehrlich, *The Music Profession in Britain since the Eighteenth Century: A Social History* (Oxford: Clarendon Press, 1985); Ruth Finnegan, *The Hidden Musicians: Music-Making in an English Town* (Cambridge: Cambridge University Press, 1989; 2nd edn, Middletown, CT: Wesleyan University Press, 2007); Dave Russell, *Popular Music in England, 1840–1914*, 2nd edn (Manchester: Manchester University Press, 1997); Ronald Pearsall, *Edwardian Popular Music*

music exam phenomenon makes no sense unless it is considered within its social as well as musical context that this chapter looks at the wider reasons behind the provision and take-up of music exams in late nineteenth-century Britain. Likewise, subsequent chapters assess the ways that this examination culture has continued to exercise a significant, but often unrecognized influence, on our musical lives today.

This chapter outlines what it was about the patterns of Victorian musical life that made it such a propitious environment for the music exam culture to take root. Much of this has to do with the way that a substantial amount of British musical life was concentrated in the spheres of amateur music-making, such as the choral society, the brass band, competitive music festivals of all kinds, and, of course, music in the home. Despite the celebrated epithet *Das Land ohne Musik*, the proliferation and abundance of musical activity in Victorian Britain made it the land with – rather than without – music; something that will be returned to. But because this view flies so strongly in the face of established opinion it is advisable to unpick here some of the negative myths and labels of convenience that have become too readily attached to this period. Appreciating some of the evidence that points to the vigour of amateur musical activity helps us understand just why the exam culture became so readily accepted and so enthusiastically taken up that it became a formative aspect of our national musical mindset. Even the necessarily brief outline given below emphasizes just how complex are the interlocking social and economic strands at work here, a complexity augmented by

(Rutherford, NJ: Fairleigh Dickinson University Press, 1975); Cyril Ehrlich, *The Piano: A History*, rev. edn (Oxford: Clarendon Press, 1990); Lewis Foreman, *Music in England, 1885–1920, as Recounted in Hazell's Annual* (London: Thames Publishing, 1994); Michael Musgrave, *The Musical Life of the Crystal Palace* (Cambridge: Cambridge University Press, 1995); Andrew Blake, *The Land without Music: Music, Culture and Society in Twentieth-Century Britain* (Manchester: Manchester University Press, 1997); Gareth Williams, *Valleys of Song: Music and Society in Wales, 1840–1914* (Cardiff: University of Wales Press, 1998); Christina Bashford and Leanne Langley (eds.), *Music and British Culture, 1785–1914: Essays in Honour of Cyril Ehrlich* (Oxford: Oxford University Press, 2000); Paula Gillett, *Musical Women in England, 1870–1914* (Basingstoke: Macmillan, 2000); Trevor Herbert (ed.), *The British Brass Band: A Musical and Social History* (Oxford: Oxford University Press, 2000); Derek Scott, *The Singing Bourgeois*, 2nd edn (Aldershot: Ashgate, 2001); Jeffrey Richards, *Imperialism and Music: Britain, 1876–1953* (Manchester: Manchester University Press, 2001); John Lowerson, *Amateur Operatics: A Social and Cultural History* (Manchester: Manchester University Press, 2005); Margaret Handford, *Sounds Unlikely: Music in Birmingham*, rev. edn (Studley: Brewin Books, 2006); Rachel Cowgill and Peter Holman (eds.), *Music in the British Provinces, 1690–1914* (Aldershot: Ashgate, 2007); Christina Bashford, *The Pursuit of High Culture: John Ella and Chamber Music in Victorian London* (Woodbridge: Boydell Press, 2007); Jenny Doctor, David Wright and Nicholas Kenyon (eds.), *The Proms: A New History* (London: Thames & Hudson, 2007); David Wright, 'Music and Musical Performance: Histories in Disjunction?', in *The Cambridge History of Musical Performance*, ed. Colin Lawson and Robin Stowell (Cambridge: Cambridge University Press, 2012), 169–206. From a more sociological perspective, see Peter J. Martin, *Sounds and Society: Themes in the Sociology of Music* (Manchester: Manchester University Press, 1995).

the ambiguous attitudes to music held by some elements of Victorian society. Part of the Victorian paradox was that, while collective amateur music-making was generally considered a wholesome enterprise, there were aspects of professional musical life that were not: the habitual connections made between dubious morals and professional performing folk – especially if they were foreign – undermined musicians' status and their social standing as a whole. Because exams formalized the musical process and so helped generate an image of music as an improving recreational activity, they played a part in bringing about more serious attitudes to playing and singing and greater respect to those who taught these skills well.

The chapter then looks at the significance this music exam culture was to exert in transforming the standing of music teaching, both in terms of its educational seriousness, and also by helping to increase its social respectability as an occupation. In the early days, music exam boards titled their grade exams 'Local Exams', because that was the label used for the secondary school exams started by Oxford and Cambridge.[2] This had the advantage of associating music exams in the public mind with a type of exam already considered to represent a prestigious measure of scholastic attainment. Furthermore it projected music to be a subject capable of being assessed, both in theory and practice. Success in these exams depended upon pupils being properly taught, and this, in turn, emphasized the value of expert music teaching. Given the low repute in which music teaching was generally held until the latter part of the century, it is not surprising that the collective ambition of many teachers was to change the situation by means of regulated professional structures. Professional respectability meant an enormous amount in Victorian society, not least in terms of social standing, and this explains why the status of a 'profession' was so eagerly pursued by both school and music teachers. In the chartered, self-regulated professions of law, medicine, architecture, etc., the individual practitioner was able to demonstrate certified evidence of their professional proficiency, supported by a sound level of general education. In music this carries us across to the diploma end of the exam culture (discussed in Chapter 2), where we see that the cost of taking the most reputable diplomas came to represent a good investment for those seeking a music teaching career.

'… in no other nation is there, at the present time, greater musical activity …'[3]

DESPITE its manifest vitality, Victorian and Edwardian musical life as a whole has received a bad press at the hands of most music histories because of the perceived failure of British high art composers – Elgar excepted – to match up to the stature of their significant European contemporaries. Few musicologists

[2] In 1858 the University of Cambridge Local Examinations Syndicate was established, with a system of Junior Local Exams for pupils under sixteen, and Senior Local Exams for pupils under eighteen; the University of Oxford Delegacy of Local Examinations, offering a similar scheme, had been established in 1857.

[3] James D. Brown and Stephen S. Stratton, 'Preface', *British Musical Biography: A Dictionary of Musical Artists, Authors and Composers* (Birmingham: S. S. Stratton, 1897).

have looked beyond this art music context to see the fecundity and pluralism of the very extensive musical life of the period. Two classic titles typify the narrow polarization and firmly entrenched views of this British musical situation. One is Oscar Schmitz's notorious *Das Land ohne Musik*.[4] The other is Frank Howes's depiction of British compositional progress in his *The English Musical Renaissance*: 'There is a general agreement that English music is better in quality and English musical life healthier than it was in Victorian times.'[5] In fact Schmitz's book is a travelogue about British society in general, in which music plays but a small part. Schmitz, a German author and journalist, records the enthusiasm of the British as musical consumers rather than producers, and remarks upon the tendency of audiences to view the feats of musical virtuosi rather as they would the champions of a particular sport.[6] His damaging verdict that 'the English are the only cultured race without a music of their own (music hall ditties excepted)' is often quoted; usually overlooked, however, is its continuation, 'I say music of their own, for perhaps more foreign music is performed in England than in any other country' (i.e. the British appetite for a wide range of music made them excellent – if, by implication, indiscriminate – consumers).[7] Schmitz's dismissive reference to music hall ditties alerts us to the sorts of moral and artistic values encapsulated within different repertories, and the reference in this context was intentionally pejorative. The issue of music's morality as an art and its suitability as an occupational pastime will resurface across this chapter, but what clearly lies at the heart of the 'Musical Renaissance/land without music' stand-off is the question of national pride. British industrial might, military achievement and the seemingly inexorable spread of the *pax Britannica* until 1914 were all symbols of the country's prowess. However, the uncomfortable truth was that when it came to the writing of high art music, British composers of the period were symphonic and operatic underachievers compared with their European neighbours. In the competitive European environment of these pre-war years, the British capacity to excel in the enjoyment of music from other nations rather than to create its own sublime art had become something of a national embarrassment.

The reality was that virtually no pre-war British compositions, apart from Elgar's, managed to sustain a presence in European concert programmes or opera houses – as opposed to an occasional or one-off hearing. Therefore it may seem paradoxical that those who write enthusiastically about British musical life of the period usually do so from the defensive ideological position of a compositionally centred 'English Musical Renaissance'. Broadly stated, the English musical renaissance constructs British musical history from the 1880s as an account of the musical development generated by the new wave of composers around

---

[4] Oscar A. H. Schmitz, *Das Land ohne Musik: Englische Gesellschaftsprobleme*, trans. H. Herzl as *The Land without Music* (London: Jerrolds, [1926]). The following references are to this translation.

[5] Frank Howes, *The English Musical Renaissance* (London: Secker & Warburg, 1966), 17; the following discussion leaves aside the question of how justifiable it was in the first place to apply the term 'renaissance' to this particular context.

[6] Schmitz, *Das Land ohne Musik*, 83.

[7] Ibid., 26.

Charles Stanford, Hubert Parry and the students (and their successor students) they taught at the Royal College of Music.[8] But as already remarked upon, the musicological tendency to emphasize just the music of the high art tradition gives only a very partial impression of the overall musical environment, and therefore the absence of any other musical and social factors considered within the ambit of this 'renaissance' produces a very distorted interpretation. Howes makes the half-hearted acknowledgement that 'composers do not grow in a vacuum, but only in the right kind of soil',[9] only to avoid undertaking anything as earthy as soil analysis. There was indeed a remarkable upsurge in British musical life from around the 1880s, as is evident in the proliferation of performances of all kinds, both amateur and professional; the establishment of permanent orchestras; the purchase and learning of instruments; the staging of competitive music festivals; and the concert provision – it is not just about composition. It is in the context of these much wider musical circumstances that the revivification of composition in the high art tradition was generated. This chapter argues that what lay at the root of all this transformation were the beginnings of an effective British musical education infrastructure, and that music exams played a significant part in this development. With better opportunities for systematic musical training, and student places with scholarship funding, the breadth of native British musical talent was to become more evident, taken up and realized. There was a further crucial factor behind this sudden manifestation of British musical achievement that Howes does not address. This was the increasing support of society in general for treating music as a more socially reputable and economically viable occupation. It was because of this now more propitious environment for music – educationally, socially and economically – that British musical achievement was to become so coherent and powerful an element within the national profile. Thus the ideology that represents the English musical renaissance in seeming isolation as an autonomous, compositionally driven success story is one that flies in the face of all the historical evidence. The idea of a 'renaissance' in British musical life would therefore be much more useful and appropriate if it were to be understood to represent the richness of the whole and not be confined, as it invariably is, just to the single facet of composition.

---

[8] The tendency has been to concentrate only on the few most celebrated composers, but this significantly underestimates the wider formative influence of Stanford and Parry in training musicians. Stephen Banfield has compiled a list of some seventy Stanford composition students who made something of a name for themselves in different musical and administrative spheres in the UK or the Empire, which he calculates perhaps represents 60–70% of the pupils Stanford may have taught at the RCM; see Stephen Banfield, 'Towards a History of Music in the British Empire: Three Export Studies', in Kate Darian-Smith, Patricia Grimshaw and Stuart Macintyre (eds.), *Britishness Abroad: Transnational Movements and Imperial Cultures* (Melbourne: Melbourne University Press, 2007), 63–89.

[9] Howes, *English Musical Renaissance*, 19.

⁄⁄⁄   Amateur music-making and its market

> The backbone of Music in this country is the Musical Amateur ... that
> large section of individuals who are not 'professing' musicians, but who are
> the cause of all music being made, imported, and encouraged here, who
> patronise it and find the money which pays the orchestras, maintains the
> societies, and, in short, which keeps alive that vast musical machine which
> contributes so largely towards the enjoyment of life.[10]

T HE astonishing increase of musical activity in Britain over the course of the
nineteenth century, as is especially evident through the strength of British
amateur music-making, caused E. D. Mackerness to remark that, 'The social
history of English music in the nineteenth century is largely a history of the
manner in which a vastly increased demand for music of all kinds was met.'[11] Two
contemporary publications support this view. One, the relatively little-known 1897
British Musical Biography, states:

> It is probable that in no other nation is there, at the present time, greater
> musical activity, creative or executive, than is to be witnessed in our own;
> [...]The greater masters [...] have been treated with brevity in order to
> afford space for mention of many worthy, if obscure workers in the cause
> of Art, hitherto passed over by writers of biography. The very large number
> (probably over 40,000) of persons engaged in the musical profession at the
> present time will explain the apparent preponderance of notices devoted to
> living musicians.[12]

Second is George Grove's great four-volume *Dictionary* whose publication, as he
writes in its Preface, was justified, 'owing to the great spread of concerts, musical
publications, private practice and interest in the subject'.[13]

Music accompanied most Victorians throughout the course of their everyday
lives, and increasing economic prosperity enabled music to be taken up with
enormous relish across all society. The vigour of Victorian musical life is as
evident in the brass and wind bands of the urban and rural working classes as
in the domestic music-making and concert hall attendance of the middle
classes, and the craze for choral singing was common to both. Music was also an
essential ingredient or accompaniment to much Victorian entertainment, in the
theatre, music hall, restaurants and cafes. But because recording has now made
it possible for us to use music independently of the presence of those actually
playing it, it is easy to forget that for the Victorians even 'muzak' required live
musicians. So in the days before recording technology, even the most mundane
forms of commodity music were available only through live performance. The
burgeoning of the middle classes prompted aspirations to improve the individual

---

[10] Frederick Crowest, *Phases of Musical England* (London: Remington & Co., 1881),
302–3.

[11] Mackerness, *A Social History of English Music*, 153.

[12] Brown and Stratton, 'Preface', i.

[13] George Grove, Preface to vol. 1 of *A Dictionary of Music and Musicians (AD 1450–1879) by Eminent Writers, English and Foreign* (London: Macmillan, 1879).

family's social status (including a daughter's marriageability) through evidence of cultural attainment. As the effects of affluence, increased leisure time and higher social expectations permeated through society, so they produced new patterns of musical consumption and enjoyment, not only for the bourgeoisie, but also among large sections of the urban working population. In this environment most Victorians saw music as a form of everyday practical activity that their children should be encouraged to learn in order to meet the social expectations of domestic performance and to participate in wider amateur music-making. All this activity demanded a continuous supply of fresh music to play and sing, and clearly the British had sufficient compositional fecundity to keep up with the high level of consumer demand. But the problem (and this is the subtext of the 'Musical Renaissance' representation) was that most British composers of the day – including significant talents such as Sullivan and Edward German – were too adept at writing music with an immediate market appeal, became just too used to the money it brought and so never looked back to the uncertainties of trying to compose symphonic masterpieces in the Austro-German tradition. Understood in these terms, the 'English Musical Renaissance' is a subsequent invention, a musicological construct designed to distinguish those relatively few worthy, or 'high art', British musical works from the abundance of their successful, but commercially tainted, commodified cousins.

The vigorous activity and high levels of consumption of the British amateur music market are evident from the health of ancillary spheres such as the competition festival, instrumental purchase and music retailing. Music competitions – events which crossed the social and musical divides of the brass band, the choral society, and middle-class individuals – became a phenomenon of music-making during the second part of the nineteenth century, and the enormous numbers of participants vividly illustrates the scale of amateur involvement. Enthusiasm for contesting in local and national band festivals was an important stimulus for the very high standards attained by brass bands, and the competitive spirit had become very much part of the brass band ethos.[14] Rivalry was at the heart of the festival movement, something that inevitably made for comparisons with sporting events, though others sought to emphasize the scope of such occasions for individual and collective improvement, as in W. G. McNaught's description, 'The festival is found to provide a novel and instructive entertainment.'[15] Although Mary Wakefield's Westmorland festival in 1885 was far from being the first, it became the archetype of the modern festival, and McNaught estimated that some 50,000 competitors would have been involved in the festivals held during 1907.[16] In the chapter 'The Competitive Movement', part of his general survey of British music,

[14] For an informative account of this world, see Trevor Herbert, 'Nineteenth-Century Bands: Making a Movement', in *The British Brass Band*, ed. Herbert, 10–67; contest rules and the results and repertoire of successful bands in the Open and National Championships, 1853–1997, are given in Appendices 3 and 5; numbers of wind and brass bands were enormous, but difficult to pin down: Dave Russell cites contemporary estimates of between 30,000–40,000 wind bands in 1889! See Russell, *Popular Music in England*, 205.

[15] W. G. McNaught, 'The Competition Festival Movement', *MT* 48 (July 1907), 449–50.

[16] Ibid.

William Johnson Galloway emphasizes just how important the movement was for British musical life, having the power 'to riddle England through and through with music'.[17] Some of the major festivals combined individual competitive classes with involvement in performing the great choral repertory (such as the Brahms and Verdi requiems) that would otherwise be outside the scope of most musical communities; Galloway's description of a favoured festival pattern has the morning given over to contesting and the afternoon being set aside for combined rehearsals in preparation for that evening's concert.[18] The competitive element was a factor that helped the spread of the examination culture: early on, the ABRSM and TCL propagated their work by publishing pass lists and by holding local ceremonies for the distribution of certificates. Local papers would list successful candidates and report on the ceremonies, which were usually dignified by local notables or (as sometimes in the early ABRSM London ceremonies) minor royalty. All this meant that information about the comparative success of different local teachers was readily available, something that generated competition between them, and had obvious implications for their student lists and the fees they were able to charge. All this very much reflected British society's enthusiasm for free trade, something that we also see by the co-existence of a whole raft of music examining bodies in which charlatan and educationally respectable boards intermingled and vied with each other for the candidate market.

The number of pianos produced for the UK market indicates the spread of domestic music-making in this period. These annual estimates suggest that production rose from some 23,000 in 1850 to some 50,000 in 1890, reaching some 75,000 in 1910.[19] This represents an astonishing take-up of piano ownership, but it was possible only because of the 'three year system', or hire purchase, which was widely used by the 1860s.[20] Hire purchase meant that piano ownership was no longer the preserve only of the wealthy, but was now opened up to a much wider section of society. Another illustration of musical growth is the increase in publications of music registered for copyright at Stationers Hall, totals which almost certainly underestimate significantly the number of items actually published. In 1850 registered publications stood at 1,142; in 1880 at 4,432; in 1900 at 7,114 and in 1914 at 11,436 – statistical testimony to the huge market demand for music to be played, sung and enjoyed.[21] One incentive to register a publication

---

[17] William Johnson Galloway, *Musical England* (London: Christophers, 1910), 167–206, the quotation is on 169.

[18] There is a vivid representation of the musical energy of these festivals in Nettel, *Music in the Five Towns*, 36–48; several chapters in Cowgill and Holman, *Music in the British Provinces*, paint a vivid picture of little-known amateur music-making and festival occasions, especially: Sally Drage, 'The Larks of Dean: Amateur Musicians in Northern England'; Rachel Milestone, '"That monstrosity of bricks and mortar": The Town Hall as a Music Venue in Ninteenth-century Stalybridge'; and Catherine Dale, 'The Provincial Musical Festival in Nineteenth-Century England: A Case Study of Bridlington'.

[19] Ehrlich, *The Piano*, app. 2.

[20] Ibid., 98–104.

[21] D. W. Krummel, 'Music Publishing', in *The Athlone History of Music in Britain*, vol. 5: *The Romantic Age, 1800–1914*, ed. Nicholas Temperley (London: Athlone Press, 1981),

was the money to be made from volume sales if the publisher struck lucky. High levels of sales had been made possible by new developments in printing technology. New techniques had lowered the cost of music production, and so, by making sheet music more widely affordable, had stimulated the expansion of the market. One such technique was called stereotyping, a process which had enabled the astutely venturous publisher Novello to generate massive sales of the firm's famous octavo vocal scores. Stereotyping enabled multiple plates to be produced from a single forme of type, so facilitating volume output. Its effect in bringing about the diminution of unit costs is evident from the progressive drop in the price of Handel's *Messiah*. In 1837 an edition of *Messiah* was one guinea, but by 1854 it had dropped to four shillings for an octavo edition, and by the early 1860s it and other oratorios were available at one shilling.[22] The availability of great music in vocal score format at affordable prices had an obvious effect on the very extensive repertoires sung by the great choral societies, as is evident in studies of the Bradford and Huddersfield choral societies.[23] It was also significant in helping the growth of amateur opera societies, fifty-seven of which were affiliated to the National Operatic and Dramatic Association on its formation in 1899, as well as there being others that for various reasons chose not to affiliate.[24]

Sales success did not just depend upon affordable prices – advertising and retailing were critical. Novello owned *The Musical Times*, which became the trade journal of the musical world and assiduously pushed the firm's own publications. With increasing consumer demand, commercial retailing expanded, ensuring the steady supply and distribution of music, even to small communities. Dave Russell presents a striking example drawn from northern British urban centres: Bradford, with a population of nearly 300,000, had forty-six music dealers; Halifax, with a population of approximately 100,000, had eighteen; Batley, with its population of some 30,000, had four; and even Sowerby Bridge, with a population of only 7,500, had two shops that sold music.[25] In the print age, music retail could be good business, as we see from the sales of a perennial Victorian favourite, Stainer's *Crucifixion*. In its first decade to 1898 it sold 88,623 vocal scores (generating Stainer some £785 in royalties) and 362,000 copies of the libretto consisting of text and hymns.[26] Stainer's homely music, with its occasional moments of melodrama, was calculated to offer a rewarding experience to amateur church choirs and to fulfil the taste expectations of Anglican congregations; Novello's astute advertising

---

46–59, table 1.

[22] Miriam Miller, 'The Early Novello Octavo Editions', in *Music and Bibliography: Essays in Honour of Alec Hyatt King*, ed. Oliver Neighbour (London: Clive Bingley, 1980), 160–69; see Russell, *Popular Music in England*, 173.

[23] G. F. Sewell, *A History of the Bradford Festival Choral Society: From its Formation in 1856 to its Jubilee in 1906* (Bradford: G. F, Sewell, 1907); R. A. Edwards, *And the Glory: A History in Commemoration of the 150th Anniversary of the Huddersfield Choral Society* (Leeds: W. S. Maney, n.d.); see also L. C. Venables, *Choral and Orchestral Societies: A Book of Hints on their Organisation, and Business and Musical Management*, 3rd edn (London: J. Curwen & Sons, [1900]).

[24] Lowerson, *Amateur Operatics*, 14.

[25] Russell, *Popular Music in England*, 179.

[26] BL Add. MS 69522, p. 958.

pushed its commercial success. The result was that John Stainer died a multi-millionaire in today's terms, worth some £2.5 million.[27] But the sales of even the most popular choral scores were dwarfed by the sales of sentimental ballads and popular instrumental pieces – the 'easy listening' of their day. Sullivan's 'The Lost Chord' sold some 500,000 copies between 1877 and 1902, and Caroline Lowthian's 'Myosotis [Forget-me-not] Waltz' sold more than 250,000.[28] In 1878 the copyright to W. C. Levey's popular song 'Esmeralda' became available and was bought for £546.[29] An example of the sales potential for popular classical music is Edward German's 'Three Dances' from his incidental music to *Henry VIII*. In 1894 this sold nearly 22,000 in the arrangement for solo piano and some 2,000 in the arrangement for violin and piano.[30] Such a level of sales, designed to satisfy the tastes of the domestic, or drawing-room, musical culture, and marketed to meet the need for multiple instrumental arrangements, shows that there was indeed good and profitable business to be made out of music.[31] Instrumental and harmony tutors were also profitable, and these began selling in good numbers. Again Novello was alert to the possibilities of this new market for musical improvement, and sales of its Primer Series are indicative of the demand, although the firm's sales figures account for only a portion of the numbers of tutors actually sold, because many other publishers were bringing out their own tutors. Taking a yearly average from the Novello publications in the period 1888–92, the sales of Berthold Tours's *Violin* reached some 11,000; W. H. Cumming's *Rudiments* averaged 7,000 (in an especially well-supplied subject); Pauer's *Piano* averaged some 3,300, also against great competition; Stainer's *Organ* nearly 3,700; and Stainer's *Harmony* was averaging nearly 7,300.[32]

But what can be just as revealing as those tutors which sold well are those that failed to find their market, for example, H. Brett's *Cornet*. The very low sales of this tutor indicate the self-sufficiency of the brass band world, which produced its own learning materials, either in-house or taken from specialist brass band publications. The independence of the band world from much for the classical music mainstream (except for the huge crossover of symphonic and operatic repertoire which bands played in wonderfully skilful arrangements) explains the scarcity of brass players (and indeed woodwind players) taking grade music exams until the second half of the twentieth century, when school-based tuition began to be offered independently of the bands themselves.

---

[27] Jeremy Dibble, 'Stainer, Sir John (1840–1901)', *ODNB*; the 'Wealth at Death' figure was converted using the RPI indicator at www.measuringworth.com. For further discussion of Stainer's wealth in relation to other major musical and literary figures of his day, see David Wright, 'Situating Stainer', *MT* 149/3 (Summer 2008), 95–103.

[28] Ehrlich, *The Piano*, 96.

[29] *MT* 20 (January 1879, 33); the sum is equivalent to some £39,000 in RPI terms today.

[30] BL Add. MS 69523, p. 89.

[31] Three informative perspectives on repertoire and taste in the late Victorian and Edwardian music market are: Ehrlich, *The Piano*, esp. chap. 3, 'The British Music Market, 1880–1914'; Richards, *Imperialism and Music*; and Pearsall, *Edwardian Popular Music*.

[32] BL Add. MS 69522, pp. 917–19, 924, 933; Add. MS 69523, p. 808; these are gross figures that include complementary copies.

Of course, music shops were centres for much more than just the purchasing of music and instruments. They became the focus for local musical networks, disseminating by word-of-mouth opinions on local teachers, something that was to be vital in the spread of music exams, as a teacher's successes (or failures) were broadcast around the community. In their study of Victorian leisure-time in rural Sussex (an interesting contrast to the study of the urban north), Lowerson and Myerscough remark on the growth in the demand for private musical tuition throughout the county, with some 131 music teachers listed in *Kelly's Directory* for 1891 (predictably clustered in the seaside towns) supported by thirty-four music dealers and twenty-one piano tuners.[33] But just how many 'professional' musicians were there? Victorian census returns show there had been a big increase in the proportion of musicians to the population as a whole. In 1841 there were nearly 7,000 musicians in a population of some 16 million in England and Wales; the 1851 census showed a 12% increase in this population to 17.9 million, but the number of musicians returned had increased by 60% to over 11,000. The 1891 census shows that the population had expanded to 29 million, with returns by individuals claiming musical employment more than trebling to 38,600. This growth in the number of musicians prompts questions about the sort of musical instruction that was available to them. In earlier days the overwhelming majority would have learned from private teachers or from family members. But, of course, there was also an honourable and well-established tradition of musicians who had learned just by 'picking up' an instrument, a musical form of autodidacticism. The traditional route followed by many church musicians was to be 'articled' to their local cathedral organist, learning on the job as an unpaid assistant and receiving instruction in organ playing, harmony and counterpoint. Until the College of Organists (now the Royal College of Organists) held their first examinations in 1866, there were no diplomas for aspiring organists to take in order to furnish independent evidence of their proficiency. The College's professional-level diplomas (initially Fellowship and later Associateship) were open to any candidate, and tested organists in essential skills such as transposition and score reading as well as in playing. Articled apprenticeship was a route frequently followed by other instrumentalists and singers, too.[34] Apprenticeship was certainly the most usual formal type of education available to talented working-class players or those coming from families of professional or semi-professional musicians, with the cheaper alternative of *ad hoc* private lessons as a fall-back. But children from more affluent backgrounds, such as those with a father in the higher professions, had (if the father permitted musical training) more options, such as to make non-indentured learning arrangements with a celebrated teacher, or to study abroad at one of the European conservatoires. The German conservatoire

[33] John Lowerson and John Myerscough, *Time to Spare in Victorian England* (Hassocks: Harvester Press, 1977), 92.

[34] The census details and a transcript of Articles of Apprenticeship is given in Ehrlich, *The Music Profession in Britain*, 239–40 and Table II; for musical apprenticeship, see also Deborah Rohr, *The Careers of British Musicians, 1750–1850: A Profession of Artisans* (Cambridge: Cambridge University Press, 2001), 68–71.

of Leipzig had the particular cachet of Mendelssohn's name, and many British students studied there.[35]

%% Music and moral anxiety

WHEN we look back on all this musical activity, it does seem astonishing that there should have been very few established music schools in the Victorian period. Apart from the Royal Academy of Music (founded in 1822, and an institution which contemporary opinion held to be neither efficient, nor a reliable source of high-quality orchestral instrumentalists or opera singers) mid-century London had a string of (usually short-lived) private music schools with grand-sounding names, such as the National College of Music (1864–6), the London Vocal Academy and, with rather greater durability, the London Academy of Music (which in 1935 became the London Academy of Music and Dramatic Art).[36] The RAM had been lambasted for its inadequacies in two contemporary sources. One was the important 1865 enquiry mounted by the Society of Arts into the state of musical education in Britain and abroad. This summary of European-wide musical training is rich in the information it contains about contemporary educational practice; but in the process of contrasting how the RAM functioned in comparison with the provision, organization and systematic examinations of the Paris Conservatoire, the Academy was cast in an especially bad light. The other critical publication was a survey carried out by Henry Chorley of the *Athenaeum*.[37] Chorley's case was that the Academy for all its pretension and its Royal title, provided fewer than 25% of the players in the main London orchestras, and that Sir Michael Costa's opera orchestra (generally considered London's finest) had no woodwind player from the RAM.[38] In terms of professional music training, it is significant that (the RAM apart) the conservatoire names that are now so familiar to us are all late nineteenth-century creations: Trinity College London (1874); the Guildhall School of Music (1880); the Royal College of Music (1883); the Birmingham and Midland Institute School of Music (1886), now the Birmingham Conservatoire; the (Glasgow) Athenaeum School of Music (1890), subsequently the RSAMD and now the Royal Conservatoire of Scotland, and the Manchester

---

[35] Details of the establishment, curriculum and student body of the Leipzig Conservatoire are in L. M. Phillips, 'The Leipzig Conservatory, 1843–1881' (PhD diss., Indiana University, 1979); Sir George Grove owned a history of the Leipzig Conservatoire in which he had marked the names of many of its British students. He used this to fundraise for the RCM as evidence of the need for the College's foundation: Dr Emile Kneschke, *Das Conservatorium der Musik in Leipzig ... Festgabe zum 25jährigen Jubiläum zum 2. April 1868* (Leipzig [1872]). RCMA XXII. A.5(1).

[36] These institutions and their provisions are described in the Society for the Encouragement of Arts, Manufacturers, and Commerce, *First Report of the Committee ... on the State of Musical Education at Home and Abroad* (London: Bell & Daldy, 1866), 23–4.

[37] *The Athenaeum*, 10 February 1866.

[38] An admirably pithy summary of both the Society of Arts report and Chorley's analysis is given in Ehrlich, *The Music Profession in Britain*, 79–99.

College of Music (1893), now the Royal Northern College of Music. There was, however, one major exception to the dire state of Victorian professional-level training: that was the Military School of Music at Kneller Hall (1857), which enjoyed a high reputation for its bandsmen and bandmasters. Ehrlich called it 'the most successful of nineteenth-century British music colleges', remarking that it produced 'many of the country's finest wind and percussion players'.[39]

What helps account for this absence of institutions for advanced musical training in the earlier part of the century was the ambivalence of British society towards performers, whether in music or on the stage. This has a long pedigree. Perhaps its most celebrated aristocratic formulation was in a letter by Lord Chesterfield to his son:

> If you love music, hear it; go to operas, concerts and pay fiddlers to play to you; but I insist upon your neither piping nor fiddling yourself. It puts a gentleman in a very frivolous, contemptible light ... Few things would mortify me more, than to see you bearing a part in a concert, with a fiddle under your chin, or a pipe in your mouth.[40]

In truth, it is unlikely that many of the eighteenth-century middle-class intelligentsia would have demurred when Adam Smith referred to the activity of a professional performer as a 'sort of public prostitution', explaining that the 'exorbitant rewards' paid to the most admired players and opera singers not only reflected the rarity and beauty of their talents, but also compensated them for the social 'discredit of employing them in this manner'.[41] Such attitudes made Britain a haven for foreign musicians, and a century later Frederick Crowest, the critic and writer on music, disparaged the dominance of the foreign performer ('... nothing to recommend them but their long hair, their foreign accent, and an untidy appearance'), but recognized that until Britain had a satisfactory system of musical education, 'we must neither envy the foreign element in our places of honour, nor grudge [them] the large sums of money'.[42]

One of the most influential Victorian texts purporting to deal with music's social and moral dimensions was *Music and Morals* by the Rev. H. R. Haweis.[43] First published in 1871, it was republished a number of times, and as late as 1934. The book is really a compendium of Haweis's journalistic writing, a series of assertions, rather than a closely argued philosophical position. It is structured in four sections with its title taken from the first ('Philosophical: Music, Emotion and Morals'). The extensive second section is made up of essentially hagiographic accounts of Handel,

[39] Ibid., 97.

[40] *The Letters of Philip Dormer Stanhope, 4th Earl of Chesterfield*, ed. Bonamy Dobrée (London: Eyre & Spottiswoode, 1932), vol. 4, Letter 1633.

[41] Adam Smith, *The Wealth of Nations* (1776), bk. I, ch. 10, pt. 1, 123–4. The page references are to the 'Modern Library' edition, ed. Edwin Cannan (New York: Random House, 2000).

[42] Crowest, *Phases of Musical England*, 300–301; the Royal College of Music with its modern curriculum was opened two years after publication of Crowest's book.

[43] H. R. Haweis, *Music and Morals* (London: Stathan & Co, 1871); the page numbers for the quotations given below are from the edition published in London by Longmans, Green & Co., 1900.

Gluck, Haydn, Schubert, Chopin, Mozart, Beethoven and Mendelssohn; the third section discusses the evolution of the violin and piano, followed by an account of bells and bell ringing; and the fourth part is made up of a series of miscellaneous articles about music in England, including 'The Musical Amateur' and 'People who Play the Piano'. Haweis's text usefully encapsulates the conflicted Victorian views of music and musicians. He indicates that it is necessary to treat performers with caution, because of the limitations their art imposes on them: 'The [performer's] strict exercise ... admits of very little intellect, imagination or emotion. [...] because it is more mechanical it is therefore less refining and elevating'.[44] He implies that this helps explain why 'it is hardly fair not to recognise in society an under-current of belief to the effect that executive musicians are less distinguished for morality than their neighbours'.[45] And although Haweis recognizes that this perception partly results from the notoriety some famous performers have accrued, he goes on to reinforce the subsidiary status of performers in the musical hierarchy by comparing their character to that of composers: 'if we turn for a moment from the world of Executants to the world of Composers, one fact must strike us – that not only were the great composers as a rule not addicted to the excesses which some would have us believe almost inseparable from a musical temperament, but they appear to have been singularly free from them'.[46] This representation of the inherently ethical nature of the great composers (as set out in the biographical sketches of the book's second part) becomes an argument in support of their music as truly exemplary, morally as well as musically. And, precisely because it is uplifting in moral, as well as musical, terms, this music is worthy of serious study by all. Although this sort of argument would be mocked today, it certainly offered some of Haweis's readership an important reassurance; for segments of society remained uneasy in some respects about the influence of music, especially on the young, despite there being (by Haweis's estimate) some one million people who played the piano: 'Most young ladies play the piano as an accomplishment. A girl's education is as much based on the pianoforte as a boy's is on the Latin grammar.'[47]

Haweis's book certainly did not meet with universal approval, with one commentator scoffing that it 'told us very little that we wanted to know about music, nothing at all about morals, and decidedly less than nothing about the connection between music and morals'.[48] Nevertheless, Haweis's text still illustrates ways in which the situation of music remained complicated because of the ambiguous position musicians held in the social order of things. But to Haweis (an enthusiastic violinist) and others like him, amateur music-making was beneficial both to the individual and to society, not just as an accomplishment in its own right, but because the study of the works of the great composers (i.e. the Austro-German canon) represented an uplifting and worthwhile

---

[44] Haweis, *Music and Morals*, 81.

[45] Ibid.

[46] Ibid., 84.

[47] Ibid., 506.

[48] 'Philomel' in *The Musical Standard*, illustrated series vol. 7 (26 June 1897), 408.

pursuit.[49] But who was to teach all these musical amateurs, and how could they and their families be assured that they were being taught properly? As Crowest indicates, this had become an acute issue for British society:

> As matters are at present, the only course open to the youth or girl, who feels that he, or she, has music in their soul is to go to the local 'professor', or some advertising master; and it need scarcely be pointed out how unsatisfactory and superficial a method such a step too often proves itself.[50]

This situation had come about because for much of the earlier Victorian age, music teaching was not considered a respectable living, and certainly not one that constituted a professional or middle-class occupation. Crowest's anxiety echoed that presented earlier by the Rev. J. M. Capes to the Society of Arts Committee:

> ... music has become a recognized element in British musical life, and its culture is regarded not only as a source of profound and lasting pleasures, but as a powerful instrument for refining and ennobling the mind. Nevertheless, about the last thing that we think of is the ensuring a supply of thoroughly capable musical teachers ...[51]

Because music teaching was entirely unregulated, the public had no independent assurance about the professional quality of individual teachers that diplomas were later intended to provide. Crowest's dismissal of the local 'professor' parallels Capes's concern that:

> The classes of English life which furnish the members of the musical profession are not themselves in a position to supply a good liberal education to their sons and daughters. They cannot afford anything beyond a very unsatisfactory schooling while the embryo musicians are still boys and girls. [...] it is often because an intelligent boy or girl, who shows some fondness for music, can be set up as a 'professor' at a small cost that very many young people are brought up to music, as they might be brought up to any common trade, by way of earning a livelihood.[52]

The exam system was to be significant in changing some of this. Grades and diplomas became the common currency of scholastic and professional attainment, and therefore the single most important factor transforming the status of music teachers and the standing of music teaching. Music's new professional training landscape thus emerged out of the examination culture – albeit in a sometimes confusing jumble of post-nominal letters – as diplomas offered a new respectability that did much to counter ambivalent social attitudes to musicians.

---

[49] Ironically, Haweis's own life was no less morally conflicted than those of the performers he cautioned about, and he had an illegitimate daughter by one of his parishioners: see Bea Howe, *Arbiter of Elegance* (London: Harvill Press, 1967), the biography of Haweis's wife, Mary, the writer and illustrator; also Elizabeth Baigent, 'Haweis, Hugh Reginald (1838–1901)', *ODNB*.

[50] Crowest *Phases of Musical England*, 304.

[51] Society of Arts, *First Report*, Appendix, p. xxvii.

[52] Ibid., 28.

⁄⁄⁄ Music and the social context: the significance of a 'profession'

H o w did grades and diplomas secure acceptance so readily? Part of the answer is that music exams were riding on the back of wider educational change. Two aspects of contemporary educational reform in particular pointed to the way that things would happen in music. One was the drive to make school teaching a recognized profession; the other was the system of externally verified school-based exams. These were developments that reshaped public expectations of education and the quality of teaching, and it was at this time that the Victorian belief in the examination culture was firmly established. All this change was part of the process of the wider reformation of British society, reforms that were perceived as necessary to modernize it, taking it away from the decadence of 'The Old Corruption' – of corrupt patronage and the purchase of posts and promotion – towards the meritocratic ideal of competitive entry and progression on merit as exemplified by the Northcote–Trevelyan reforms in the Civil Service.[53] Those changes replaced Dickens's parody of the Circumlocution Office in *Little Dorrit* with a Whitehall machine capable of running a huge empire, and illustrate the extent of the shift that was modernizing Britain, professionally and socially.

The very tenuous position of music was underlined in Byerley Thomson's 1857 guide to the professions:

> Of all terms indicative of a profession, that of music is, perhaps, the most undefined and vague. ... He may be, for aught we know, an itinerant fiddler, and of the lowest grade of society; or a man of the highest attainments, moving in the most exclusive circles. [...] Undefined indeed, is the status of the musician ... unlike the professions above named [in the earlier chapters], that of music is altogether unprotected. Its portals are open to all who choose to enter.[54]

Thomson's account captures the greater mobility of occupational status and prestige in response to society's changing needs. This mobility had come through the 'advance of education, and the liberality of an improved social condition', with 'new' professions emerging, such as architects, civil engineers, actuaries and other scientific occupations. Thomson distinguishes between the 'privileged' professions – the church, law, medicine, and public civil service, where entry is regulated by law and closed to free competition from without – and the 'unprivileged' professions, which have no restrictions placed on entry to them. The difference between the privileged and the unprivileged professions, says Thomson, is 'less in the light of benefits to themselves [than] as a protection to the public', because some public evidence of competency is required before it can be practised.[55] Thomson's 'protection to the public' is the key phrase here because it identifies the need for the public to be able to take on trust the competency of

---

[53] W. D. Rubinstein, 'The End of Old Corruption in Britain, 1780–1860', *Past and Present* 101/1 (November 1982), 55–86.

[54] H. Byerley Thomson, *The Choice of a Profession: A Concise Account and Comparative Review of the English Professions* (London: Chapman & Hall, 1857), 308.

[55] Thomson, *The Choice of a Profession*, 1–5.

a professional service. This is the precept sometimes referred to as the 'fiduciary principle' and it underpins the development of the Victorian chartered professions. The rise of the chartered professions with their self-regulating responsibilities was to be essential to the modernization of British society.[56]

Today we take it for granted that the services of doctors, architects, accountants and civil engineers, to name only a few, are grounded in an expertise that has been systematically taught, and appropriately and expertly examined under the authority of their regulating professional body. This enables the professional credentials of a qualified practitioner to stand as the assurance of the quality of the service on offer. The legal power for a profession to act to establish and enforce professional discipline derives from its being awarded a royal charter, a form of government regulation given in the sovereign's name. Through a process called 'incorporation', the charter converted a professional association from being a collection of individuals into a single (or corporate) legal entity. As an incorporated body, the institution had the means to set and enforce its practices in such a way that ensured uniform standards of professional competency, admitting new members only after appropriate (usually articled) training and assessment. F. M. L. Thompson summarizes why this system was so attractive to the free trade ethos of Victorian society:

> Short of state-controlled academies and institutions for every profession, the voluntary professional association was the only way which could be devised of fitting professional activities into the workings of a free economy. Rooted at bottom in the economic self-interest of its members, the association was bound to promote the common interest of its profession against the immediate interests of particular members [...] and to persuade members to place a sense of public responsibility and service before their immediate self-interest. The very Victorians who condemned trade unions [...] as unwarrantable interferences with individual liberty, flocked to join professional combinations.[57]

Medicine was a profession that had considerable trouble in establishing a coherent identity for itself, and there are some interesting parallels to be drawn between the struggles of medicine and the struggles of music; those parallels helpfully illustrate some of the issues involved in the professionalizing process. Both professions were notoriously 'fuzzy' to define, because of the sheer range of activities undertaken by and skills (or claimed skills) possessed by those whose work came under each umbrella. Certainly both music teaching and medicine had in common an unenviable reputation for quackery.[58] There had long been

---

[56] See A. M. Carr-Saunders and P. A. Wilson, *The Professions* (Oxford: Clarendon Press, 1933).

[57] F. M. L. Thompson, *Chartered Surveyors: The Growth of a Profession* (London: Routledge & Kegan Paul, 1968), 149; the awarding of a royal charter to the RCM *before* it was established, and on the basis of a mission that predicted a broad range of responsibilities, makes it an interesting anomaly, and explains some of the resentment that its foundation caused.

[58] See Roy Porter, *Quacks: Fakers and Charlatans in Medicine* (Stroud: Tempus Publishing, 1989), esp. chap. 2, 'Medical Entrepreneurship in the Consumer Society',

a distinct social and professional divide between practitioners belonging to the Royal Colleges of Physicians and Surgeons (whose royal charters were granted in 1518 and 1800 respectively) and the plethora of other medical types – a distinction not least reflected in the mode of addressing a surgeon as 'Mr'. The British Medical Association was established in 1856, and the term 'doctor' came to be used for its members. But the BMA was a professional association, not a chartered body, and it was only in 1858, with the passing of the Medical Act and the creation of the General Medical Council, that the medical profession gained by statute the means of self-regulation which obliged medical practitioners to accept compulsory registration, with the checking of an individual's qualifications which this process involved. The inducement for the medical profession to formulate a strong sense of corporate professional identity (the necessary precursor to gaining the ability to regulate its own affairs) is explained by the fact that the granting of a charter conveyed very significant weight and prestige.[59] This is a point that F. M. L. Thompson also emphasizes:

> In the nineteenth century a Charter became established as the status symbol of professional bodies. ... Incorporation by charter was a privilege highly prized by institutions as a mark of their maturity and of their public recognition. This was not so for legal reasons... It was so for social and moral reasons. In part it was because a charter conferred on an institution moral authority over all the members of its profession. [...] the grant of a charter was proof that a society had passed a careful scrutiny of its credentials, its worthiness, its capacity to fulfil its aims, and its generally representative character.[60]

That sort of incentive was never likely to represent much of a prize to music. The idea of musicians bridging across their very different branches of activity in order to unite the music profession under a single chartered body would have been thought by many an extraordinary and incomprehensible concept. For one thing, the division in the basis of the work of different sorts of musicians was just too strong: the marketability of drawing an audience has always been the *sine qua non* of professional performers, and even though most performers teach at sometime or another, many prefer to keep these two spheres of their lives separate. The variety of today's professional music associations illustrates the separation of musical activities. In terms of the nineteenth century's shift to professionalization, it was teachers and organists who, out of the musical community, most craved the professional status of belonging to a chartered body. The major development here was the awarding of a royal charter to the RCM in 1883. (The RAM's royal charter of 1830 was a mark of royal favour that predated the Victorian use of charters as a symbol of professional authority.) Under its charter the RCM was tasked with 'the advancement of the Art of Music', which it was to do through

---

41–92.

[59] The formal qualification of nurses came much later, in 1925, when the General Nursing Council began to regulate the training that led to the status of a State Registered Nurse (SRN).

[60] Thompson, *Chartered Surveyors*, 173–4.

the activities of teaching and examining, awarding degrees and certificates to candidates as appropriate, regardless of whether or not they were educated at the College. The charter also charged the College with the 'promotion and supervision of such musical instruction in schools and elsewhere ... most conducive to the cultivation and dissemination of the Art of Music in the United Kingdom'; it also gave the College a general responsibility to help promote and encourage music in the Empire.[61] This charter effectively made the RCM the chartered institution for music, and this award to a parvenu institution caused considerable resentment among the musical community as well as universities, even though in the end the terms of the charter were less grandiose than had been originally envisaged.[62]

Because the two Royal Schools were then the only musical institutions with royal charters, the ABRSM partnership gave the Board all the appearance of having chartered status. Certainly that was how the Board represented itself. But such an assumption its rivals, particularly TCL, would not concede. Meanwhile, the collective professional weakness of the music teachers' position was further underlined by the threatened national register of teachers. The Parliamentary Bill as proposed in 1891 would automatically have registered all teachers presently in post. The Academy, the College and the ABRSM protested vigorously against the Bill's intention 'to allow so vast a mass of persons to be registered without examination ... [because] It would admit many incompetent persons, and at once place them on an apparent level with some of the most eminent teachers of the profession; while it would exclude many competent teachers under the age of 21, as well as some of the most distinguished musicians of the country, who, although teaching, do not teach in schools'.[63] As Grove put music's position to Sir William Hart Dyke (Chairman of the Select Committee), the Associated Board's exams offered a better solution as far as music teachers were concerned – 'a much surer way of testing teachers is to examine their pupils'. In the event, although the Education Act of 1899 made provision for teachers to register with the Teachers' Registration Council (1902), doing so was voluntary, and the Council was withdrawn in 1907.

The issue, however, was not going to go away, and in 1898 *The Musical Standard* reported that at the 13th Annual Conference of the Incorporated Society of Musicians its Secretary said that the ISM would continue to advocate the registration of teachers of music. Sir John Stainer, speaking as HM Inspector of Music in Schools and Training Colleges, said that 'the State should take music-teaching under its control, and that there shd be one central authority whose certificate would be regarded as proof that its recipient is capable of teaching

---

[61] The charter was reproduced in full in *The Times*, together with the support of a leading article, itself indicative of the status being accorded to the College by the establishment; 'The Royal College', *The Times*, 21 April 1883.

[62] See David Wright, 'Grove's Role in the Founding of the RCM', in *George Grove, Music and Victorian Culture*, ed. Michael Musgrave (Basingstoke: Palgrave Macmillan, 2003), 219–44. Indicative of the controversy in musical circles are the exchanges headed 'The Royal College of Music' in *The Musical World*, 21 January 1882, 41–5; correspondence relating to the protest of universities at the right of the RCM to award degrees is contained in the University of London archives, File RC4.

[63] RCMA, Minute Book: Council, May 1883–February 1894, text inserted opposite p. 171.

music'. Commenting in a leader, *The Musical Standard* remarked that it should not be possible for a musical quack to earn a living, especially in a situation where, as Stainer expressed it, 'music is now recognised as an integral portion of a good education [... and that] the profession of music should do all it can to strengthen its hands, and not to rely on the State to do work which the State has never done'. The remedy was for 'the consolidation of all the examining bodies of repute which now exist [...] then there would be but one examining body, under a royal charter granting certificates for different degrees of proficiency'.[64] A united professional association was a prerequisite to petition for a royal charter, but clearly a united examination front would be an impossibility, given the strength of the antagonism between the Royal Schools and TCL in particular, further compounded by other institutions such as the London College of Music joining the examination merry-go-round. Self-interest meant that the London Royals successfully prevented the Manchester College of Music's first application for a charter in 1893, and then Trinity College's petition in 1917.[65] Had Manchester achieved its charter, the Board's northern market could have been endangered; and had TCL been successful, then as 'Royal Trinity College' not only would its exams have been given a status the existing Royals were desperate to prevent, but it would have made calls (such as *The Musical Standard's*) for a single chartered examination board well nigh irresistible. The Royals were only persuaded not to object to Manchester's second, successful, application for its charter in 1923, on condition 'that a clause was inserted stating that the R.M.C.M. did not propose to hold external examinations or award diplomas to non-students'; in other words, would not damage the ABRSM and the LRAM/ARCM exams market.[66]

School teaching was another of those 'fuzzy' professions in which the range of expertise and differences of status effectively precluded much sense of a coherent professional identity. It is unlikely that teachers in the public schools or the old established grammar schools would have dignified those working in the miscellany of new private secondary and government elementary schools with the title of 'teacher'. In an attempt to improve standards, the College of Preceptors (since 1998 called the College of Teachers) was incorporated by royal charter in 1849. Under the terms of its charter it was to establish a 'competent Board of Examiners to ascertain and give Certificates of the acquirements and fitness for their office of persons engaged or desiring to be engaged in the Education of Youth particularly in the Private Schools of England and Wales'.[67] Accordingly, the College established its own diplomas and in 1850 it also began to run external exams for school boys. This activity by the Preceptors has an obvious parallel with the exams and professional diplomas later offered by the music colleges. The

[64] 'Registrations and Examinations', *The Musical Standard*, illustrated series vol. 8 [full series vol. 53] (8 January 1898), 19–20; the 1899 Education Act provided for the establishment of a register of teachers.

[65] Michael Kennedy, *The History of the Royal Manchester College of Music, 1893–1972* (Manchester: Manchester University Press, 1971), 12; *MT* 58 (April 1917), 168; *MT* 58 (May 1917), 217.

[66] Kennedy, *History of the Royal Manchester College of Music*, 66.

[67] Preamble to the College of Preceptors' royal charter of 1849.

Victorian emphasis on diplomas, rather than degrees, reflects the fact that the total university population in 1871 was just 5,260 (that year's census returned a UK population of 31.8 million).[68] This statistic underlines just how unusual a university education then was, despite considerable reform and expansion of the university sector. Those practical musicians who could afford it would have sought training at one of the music colleges, not a university. One of the attractions of music colleges was that they now had become important networking centres for professional musicians, the places to make useful contacts, a very different musical world from that of university music.

Those who lacked the financial means to study at a music college still depended on *ad hoc* private lessons, or access to those Mechanics' Institutes (which provided adult educational opportunities in a broader range of subjects than their name might suggest) which offered class instruction in music. External music diplomas were a way for such people to secure professional validation for their skills and to even out their lack of formal education. As we have seen, there was a parallel course of action open to school teachers, giving them a leg-up into a more respectable part of the profession; this was to study for one of the diplomas offered by the College of Preceptors. In the later nineteenth century, musicians had one other possible route into professional respectability, frequently chosen by organists, which was to study with a private tutor for one of the several external university music degrees available from Oxford, Cambridge, Durham, London and Dublin. However, because these music degrees did not have the full-time residentiary requirements of a BA degree, and because of their focus on the vocational skills of harmony and counterpoint, they were rather looked down upon by other university graduates. Thus the possessor of one of these external degrees was considered less 'educated' than someone with a BA arts degree who had actually attended university. This explains why someone like John Stainer, already holding the Oxford degrees of BMus and DMus, thought it important to take a BA degree as well, because the BA represented higher educational status and enabled him to proceed to the MA.[69] In order to put music on a par with the other academic disciplines, Stanford drew up a scheme for a complete reform of Cambridge music degrees in the early 1890s, requiring full university residence. This proposal generated fierce controversy among musicians because it would be impossible for a working musician needing to earn a living to fulfil the three-year period of attendance.[70]

---

[68] Michael Sanderson, *Education, Economic Change and Society in England, 1780–1870*, 2nd edn (Cambridge: Cambridge University Press, 1999), 48.

[69] Jeremy Dibble, *John Stainer: A Life in Music* (Woodbridge: Boydell Press, 2007), 102.

[70] Stanford's proposals are set out in Jeremy Dibble, *Charles Villiers Stanford: Man and Musician* (Oxford: Oxford University Press, 2002), 246.

⫽ The school context

T HE system of 'Local Exams' in Music (as grades were originally called) offered by TCL and the ABRSM followed closely the scheme of Local Exams that had been run by the University of Oxford Delegacy of Local Examinations and the University of Cambridge Local Examinations Syndicate from the late 1850s. In a parallel development, the Society of Arts first offered its own programme of examinations in 1856 to those who had left school but were continuing their study at Mechanics' Institutes' classes.[71] As part of its commitment to work for the betterment of individuals and of society generally, the Society of Arts had become involved in the support of the educational programmes (often in technical and scientific subjects) these Institutes offered, and the Society exams (aimed at a working-class constituency) were intended to encourage Institute students to undertake their study on the basis of systematic – rather than occasional – attendance. The Oxbridge Local Examinations were designed for the use of schools, especially for the growing number of private (i.e. fee-charging) schools that catered for the expanding middle-class market outside the public school and endowed grammar school categories.[72] These Oxbridge exams reflected a growing perception that universities had an interest in raising standards in secondary education. This argument, applied to music, was a justification for the ABRSM.

These 'Local Exams' exerted a powerful influence on schools as a means of encouraging both teachers and pupils. They were also innovative because for the first time a syllabus formulated by an independent external authority had the power to shape the educational process. Cambridge's Local Exams in December 1858 followed requests made from various schools, and began with exams sat by 370 candidates in Birmingham, Brighton, Bristol, Cambridge, Grantham, Norwich and London.[73] There were two levels of examination: 'Junior' for under-sixteens and 'Senior' for under-eighteens, a structure later followed by the original ABRSM exams. These school exams were organized on the ground by local representatives, often notables with a strong interest in education,[74] and this administrative model was also adopted by the ABRSM and TCL. Indeed, had these Local Exams not received the wholehearted support and philanthropic commitment of local organizers, it is difficult to see how they would have become established so quickly and securely: the very heavy administrative pressure and concomitant costs of running these schemes would have placed a discouraging burden on the universities themselves. As Andrew Watts points out, the success of this local examination system also depended upon recent technological advances

[71] The basis of the Society of Arts exams are described in Derek Hudson and Kenneth Luckhurst, *The Royal Society of Arts, 1784–1954* (London: John Murray, 1954); a detailed account of the Society's music exams is presented in David Wright, 'The Music Exams of the Society for the Encouragement of Arts, Manufactures and Commerce, 1859–1919', in *Music and Institutions*, ed. Rodmell.

[72] See Andrew Watts, 'Cambridge Local Examinations, 1858–1945', in *Examining the World: A History of the University of Cambridge Local Examinations Syndicate*, ed. Sandra Raban (Cambridge: Cambridge University Press, 2008), 36–70.

[73] Watts, 'Cambridge Local Examinations', 36–7.

[74] Ibid.

that facilitated travel and communications – the railways and the universal postal system.[75]

This system of Local Exams – both in school subjects and later for music grades – offered enormous advantages. It enabled pupils to be tested by specialist examiners in a way that avoided them incurring prohibitive travel costs, and they secured the participation of university and music college teachers, something that greatly enhanced their prestige.[76] As we have seen, and given the very restricted university entrance at the time, this was the closest most of these pupils would come to a university-validated view of their work. London University offered a matriculation exam which some sat as the equivalent of a school leaving exam in order to provide evidence of their general educational attainment, and TCL would also insist upon students for their diplomas first passing the College's own 'matriculation' paper. The perceived value to the universities of these Local Exams is illustrated by the candidate figures: 2,687 candidates had sat local school-based exams in 1870; by 1891, candidate numbers had risen to 11,080.[77] In the 1860s the Cambridge Syndicate (with help from the Colonial Office) discovered that there was a strong overseas market for these exams. In another development Cambridge began to offer comprehensive school inspections (something that the ABRSM would later offer for music) as part of the University extension programme. Clearly, Local Exams with the Oxbridge imprimatur carried both authority and cachet; with this in mind the Royal Schools saw that their own ABRSM system of national music exams had the potential to establish their individual and joint musical authority right across the country.

---

[75] Ibid.

[76] Elizabeth Leedham-Green, 'The University', in *Examining the World*, ed. Raban, 16; theoretically a particularly luckless ABRSM Local Centre Exam candidate might have been faced with both Stanford and Parry as their examiners!

[77] Watts, 'Cambridge Local Examinations', 45.

2 Competing for Candidates:
TCL, ABRSM and the Society of Arts

HISTORICALLY, the most significant of the grade exam boards were the ABRSM and Trinity College London, and for diplomas, the two Royal Schools and Trinity. This chapter begins with a brief outline of these institutions' origins, their characteristics and their antagonisms, and the reasons why they began to offer extramural music exams. But the very first systematic music exams in Britain were being offered to working-class musicians by the Society of Arts, nearly twenty years before Trinity's. The Society's involvement highlights contrasting attitudes about the purpose of music exams between the mid- and the later nineteenth century. One consequence of the music exam industry later in the century was the effect of these exams in professionalizing music education, and thus on the status of music teachers themselves. The pricing and exam structures of each board reveal much about their targeting of the candidate market. The improvement in the professional and social status of music teaching became an incentive for musicians to invest in one of the expensive and challenging music diplomas that the colleges now offered. Diplomas offered a desirable certification of professional ability, and the example of the early ARCM is used as illustration. Some spheres of musical life regarded music exams as antithetical (notably the brass band world, which had its own culture and independent approach to training its instrumentalists), and this explains why grade music exams for so long catered almost exclusively for the drawing-room instrumental culture of the middle classes. Without knowing something of this background, it may otherwise seem incomprehensible why it was not until well after the Second World War that the ABRSM exams catered seriously for the full gamut of orchestral instruments, and began to attract these candidates in appreciable numbers.

⫸ The music college rivals:
the Academy, the College and Trinity

THE escalation of British musical life prompted more concern at Britain's lack of conservatoire provision, something which was central to musical training in continental Europe. Frederick Crowest was only one of a growing chorus spelling out how disadvantageous to the development of a true British musical identity (as much in performance as in composition) was the absence of a national conservatoire, and many argued the case for the government to fund one.[1] The acknowledged model of government-supported conservatoire training was the Paris Conservatoire (founded in 1795), which had played both a distinguished and a determining role in the development of music in France. This extended

---

[1] See also the rationale advanced by Charles Sumner Maine, 'A Conservatoire of Music for England: Report of Prince Christian's Executive Committee since its Foundation by the Prince of Wales', *Macmillan's Magazine* 41, no. 242 (November, 1879), 145–53.

beyond the composers and performers it had directly trained, to the influence it had exerted through the teaching manuals that had been produced under its imprimatur, which set down approved methods of instrumental and vocal training. It was as close to a centralized system of musical education as there could have been, because musicians who had not attended the Conservatoire in person would nevertheless have been likely to have come under its influence by being taught on the basis of an approved Conservatoire method. Contrast the French level of government commitment to music training with that which was on offer in Britain. From 1864 the Treasury contributed annually only £500 grant-in-aid to the RAM, a sum the RCM was also to receive; it was an amount that, astonishingly, was to remain unchanged until 1943. This meant that the RAM, RCM and TCL (TCL had no government support at all) were obliged to operate as financially self-supporting institutions. The refusal of the British government to make a significant contribution to conservatoire funding ensured that the extramural activity of music examining would become a permanent feature of a British music college's income.

The biggest change that conservatoires brought to professional musical training in Britain was gradually to replace the old practice of *ad hoc* occasional private lessons or just 'picking up' an instrument with the provision of systematic and formal 'courses' of musical study. The RCM was the first institution to implement this approach, and Stanford considered that much of the RCM's rapid success happened because scholars and fee-paying students were admitted on the basis that they would complete a three-year course of study – no paying student could enter for less than one year.[2] But three years of study was the period expected of university students, and we have seen from the strong opposition to Stanford's reforms of Cambridge's music degrees that musicians' preference was for non-residential study. So why should RCM students suddenly be prepared to commit to three-year courses? The explanation lies in what the RCM represented to students in terms of their overall experience as well as their individual development. Instruction was offered in all orchestral instruments as well as keyboard and singing, and because some orchestral instrument professors were asked additionally to play as professional 'stiffeners' in the RCM's twice-weekly orchestral class, the College soon became central to the profession, with flourishing orchestral player networks.[3] For aspirant musicians wanting a career in London, the RCM clearly represented a good opportunity to get to know the 'movers and shakers' of that orchestral world and to build up their teaching connections, too.

[2] C. V. Stanford, *Pages from an Unwritten Diary* (London: Arnold, 1914), 216; RCM General Regulations for 1883. One of the issues raised at the Society of Arts Committee hearings was the difficulty the RAM had in retaining students for a long enough period to train them; the students' practice was to leave as soon as they could support themselves in music regardless of fulfilling their potential (Manuel García in evidence, *First Report*, Appendix 6).

[3] The integration of College and profession and the significance of the orchestral class in establishing the RCM within London's music profession is discussed in Wright, 'The South Kensington Music Schools', 266–75; this investment in the orchestral class was considerably reduced in 1895, after Grove's retirement, as an economy measure necessitated by the higher costs of the RCM's impressive new building.

Although there was plentiful employment for musicians, not all of it was very attractive. Ehrlich identified four categories of professional player. At the top were those making a comfortable living and taking their pick of engagements from the opera and concert hall, plus a little teaching; at the next level of affluence were musicians who made their living playing at private social events, such as receptions; then followed the musicians engaged by the forty London theatres, the 'foundation' of London orchestral playing, as Ehrlich describes it; but in the last category were those unable to progress beyond the orchestral sweatshops of the music halls.[4] The key to getting ahead in this professional rat race – then as now – was not just being a good player, but also knowing the orchestral 'fixers' who could supply desirable engagements. As the other conservatoires came to follow the RCM's model, so the best training was consolidated around fewer but more widely recognized institutions. In London it was the Royal Schools, TCL and Guildhall who had the most influential professional networks because they had the pick of London's players on their staff. And the two Royals and TCL had the additional benefit of being on the national map because of their diplomas and schemes of Local Exams which helped make them desirable places to study. Understanding the process of how music colleges established themselves helps to explain how it was that conservatoires – having been previously an irrelevance to British music – became recognized as incubators of national talent and a focus for the profession. In other words, by the end of the nineteenth century, conservatoires had become essential to the national infrastructure of British music, their names symbolic of musical authority.

All this enthusiasm for musical learning in the 1880s and 1890s was a far cry indeed from the environment that the RAM had faced for much of its early existence. Founded in 1822 under the aristocratic figurehead of Lord Burghersh (later Earl of Westmorland), the Academy limped along on a more or less hand-to-mouth existence, training composers, pianists and singers on the basis of income from annual subscribers (including the Queen), miscellaneous charitable donations and the annual parliamentary grant of £500. In 1864, the year of the evidence given to the Society of Arts Committee, there were fifty-nine fee-paying students (38 female, 21 male).[5] The findings of the Society of Arts *Report* emphasized that Britain needed a properly funded national music institution offering free scholarship places. However, the *Report* also concluded that from all the evidence the Committee had received about the extent of the RAM's inadequacy, it was clear that it required fundamental internal reform as well as relocation to more suitable premises. In 1868 the Academy reached a nadir that put its sustainability under serious question. A request to the Chancellor of the Exchequer in May 1867 for an increase in its £500 government grant-in-aid had been refused (it was actually withdrawn for 1868), and so in November a proposal was agreed by the

---

[4] Ehrlich, *The Music Profession in Britain*, 142–3 and 161–3; Ehrlich presents a
    considerable amount of information on orchestral employment around the country in
    chap. 7, 'Players', from which this was drawn.

[5] Society of Arts, *Report*, Appendix, 1. It is worth noting that at this time students could
    enter very much younger than happens today: Sterndale Bennett was only ten when
    he joined in 1826, and George Macfarren was sixteen when he commenced in 1829.

Academy's Board of Directors to close the institution in March 1868.[6] This was revoked in February 1868, but the Academy's continuation with a meagre student body of sixty-six was possible only because its new Principal, Sterndale Bennett, had given up his salary for a while and all its professors forewent a significant proportion of their fees.[7] Meanwhile, the Society of Arts had continued to put pressure on the RAM. But in the face of the Academy's refusal to reorganize itself, the Society – determined to revitalize professional provision – had decided on a self-appointed mission to establish a model musical training school of its own. Accordingly the Society sponsored the founding of the National Training School for Music in South Kensington, on land made available by the Commissioners of the Great Exhibition as part of what came to be called 'Albertopolis', intended as a new cultural and scientific hub for the nation. Despite this threat, the RAM doggedly maintained its independence, and refused offers to merge with the NTSM.[8] Against expectations, its stubbornness paid off, and by 1879 the RAM had achieved a significant recovery. Its student numbers had increased to some 400, generating something over £13,000 in fee income.[9] The downside was that costs had also risen, and the RAM ended the year with a balance of just £87, clearly not enough to enable it to make a serious investment in its premises and future. Shortly after, however, pressure from the Society of Arts ceased because of the embarrassing failure of the NTSM after only six years (1876–82), its demise caused both by the failure of the Society of Arts to persuade the government to take over the long-term funding of the School (its original scholarships were running out), and by Arthur Sullivan's ineptitude as Principal. It was an outcome that must have afforded the RAM very considerable satisfaction.[10]

Relief, though, was to be short lived. Although the NTSM had proved to be a damp squib, plans for its threatened replacement with a 'Royal College of Music' would have caused serious alarm at the RAM. For, this time, no less illustrious a figure than the Prince of Wales (later King Edward VII) was petitioning the Privy Council for a royal charter on behalf of the proposed RCM. The appearance of a second Royal School established with active royal backing, plus a governing council formed of some of the most influential people in public life, and having the redoubtable George Grove as its founding director, all combined to put the RAM's future again in serious doubt. Still the RAM remained defiant, and in a letter that drew attention to its significantly revivified state, it formally refused to surrender its own royal charter, thus ending beyond all doubt any hopes of a single 'national' institution.[11] It also did what it could to spoil Grove's fundraising for the RCM, labelling the new College as merely the plaything of royal and well-connected

---

[6] RAMA, Minutes of the Board of Directors, 1862–79: meetings on 31 May and 20 November 1867. The Treasury's withdrawal of its grant-in-aid is given in a letter dated 14 April 1868.

[7] Ibid: meetings on 15 February and 12 December 1868.

[8] Ibid: meetings on 22 June 1872, 8 February 1873; 20 July and 30 November 1878.

[9] RAMA, Minutes of the Board of Directors, 1879–92: meeting on 15 July 1880.

[10] The NTSM's situation and its failure is analysed in Wright, 'The South Kensington Music Schools', 240–55.

[11] Ibid.

musical amateurs, and claiming that in the eyes of music professionals the RAM fulfilled all that could be required of a national institution. The competing cases are well illustrated in the *Musical World*, which counterpoints one of Grove's RCM fundraising speeches with the case for the RAM by its Principal, Sir George Macfarren. The crackle of institutional antagonism leaps off the page.

The RAM then went on an offensive of its own. Desperately needing the means to create a level of income that would enable it to prepare for the forthcoming competition with the RCM, it established a scheme of music exams. The success of the music exams offered by Trinity College London from the mid-1870s had shown that such exams were an excellent means of simultaneously raising both institutional profile and fee income. Accordingly, the RAM thought that offering its own exams would bring it a competitive advantage that would make it more difficult for the RCM to establish itself. The RAM had first considered offering music exams in 1870, but then shelved the idea on grounds of practicability. In 1880 the idea was resurrected and a scheme of exams put into effect. This was for two different levels of exams: diploma (or 'Metropolitan Exams'), held only at the Academy, and grade (or 'Local Exams'), to be offered on a regional basis. The system of Local Exams was for 'pupils or those who have just left a state of musical pupillage', and was implemented in 1881. The entry fee was to be one guinea. These Local Exams were held at provincial centres across the country (given a minimum entry of twelve candidates), with two examiners, one from the RAM. The second examiner was to be a local representative (also responsible for handling all the practical arrangements) who was to be paid at one guinea an hour, obviously a strong inducement to drum up local business. The Metropolitan Exams, or LRAM, were instituted in 1882. They were aimed at would-be professional musicians ('musical artists and teachers'), and cost 5 guineas for a half-hour exam (the RAM student fees were then some 10 guineas a term). The three examiners were paid 5 guineas each for a seven and half hour examining day, so producing a potential return of 60 guineas on a full day's examining.[12] All seemed to be going well, and by the end of the 1888 financial year receipts for the Local Exams had reached over £1,800, and for the Metropolitan Exams nearly £450.[13] So what induced the RAM to seek the partnership of the RCM – its bitterest rival – in this evidently lucrative operation?

In fact the RAM urgently needed to extricate itself because the way these exams had been run had caused a scandal. The RAM's new Principal, Alexander Mackenzie, explained the situation he had found:

> The slipshod conduct of [the] 'Local Examinations' (held in London and the great provincial centres) brought down a storm of remonstrances and complaints urging an immediate reform of their management.[14]

So instead of enhancing the RAM's reputation, these exams had badly damaged it.

---

[12] Details of these exams and their syllabuses are given in RAM Archives, Minutes of Committee, May 1877–June 1884 and in the RAM Prospectus of July 1881; approval for launching them was given by the Committee of Management, 1 December 1880.

[13] Minutes of the Board of Directors, 1879–92: meeting on 30 March 1889.

[14] Alexander C. Mackenzie, *A Musician's Narrative* (London: Cassell & Co., 1927), 166.

Their administration was inherently corrupt, because at the regional level the way was open for unscrupulous local representatives to poach students from teachers on the grounds that they could give candidates the inside edge necessary to pass. The amounts involved made it worth while for the local examiner to secure desired outcomes if the RAM examiner was open to temptation. Corruption was also endemic within the RAM's own administration, and an audit had exposed a serious level of fraud; the Secretary, John Gill, was dismissed for 'gross and culpable neglect', but no further action was taken against him because the Academy was anxious to avoid the unwelcome publicity that a prosecution would have brought.[15] All the evidence therefore points to the RAM as having every reason to be fearful of the competition it would encounter from the modern-style RCM. So when news reached the RAM that the RCM was about to start its own Local Exams, Mackenzie must have realized that a joint scheme was perhaps the only strategy for dealing with the challenge. It is also indicative of the RAM's perceived vulnerability that George Watson, the College's Registrar and the major administrative force behind the successful establishment of the Associated Board, was loaned to the RAM in 1890 to oversee the reform of its administrative and financial systems.[16]

There were also reasons on the RCM's side why Grove readily accepted the Academy's proposition to form an associated examining board. One was that, given the RAM's weak state, the College was in the position to be the dominant partner (though the proprieties of equality were always carefully observed), and so able to determine the shape of the new examination operation. The way was therefore open for the ABRSM to be established under the legitimacy of the RCM's own charter, with a new scheme of exams organized and run in such a way as to be able to command public confidence. For example, in order to establish a clear distance from the Academy's scheme by removing any taint of corruption, the ABRSM Honorary Local Representatives (HLRs) were unpaid volunteers; moreover, music teachers and professional musicians were excluded from that role. There was a further, perhaps decisive, reason that brought the College into this examination partnership with the Academy. The venture offered a neat solution to the issue of institutional rivalry, and a way of putting to rest press representations of the two Royal institutions as deadly enemies. As the *Musical World*'s coverage had suggested, this had generated an inappropriate public image; far more preferable would be the sporting analogy of two teams in friendly rivalry but united in a single purpose. An Associated Board with a properly formulated and administered scheme of exams was very much in the RCM's own interest.

What also concentrated the minds of Mackenzie and Grove was the success already being achieved in the music exam market by Trinity College. After only around thirteen years Trinity dominated the field. By 1885 TCL was notching up some 5,000 UK candidates a year, examined at some 210 UK centres, bringing in an income of over £6,000.[17] On top of this it had established centres in India,

[15] Minutes of the Board of Directors, 1879–92: meeting on 27 June 1890.

[16] Watson's involvement in the reform of the RAM administration was agreed by the RCM Executive Committee: Minutes of the meeting on 13 March 1890.

[17] Ehrlich, *The Music Profession in Britain*, 117.

South Africa and Australia. Clearly the Royal Schools had quickly to establish their claim to this market. As discussed, conservatoire education was too expensive to be funded only from the fees of paying students and scholarship endowments, and in any case the Schools could not be too ambitious in the fees they charged in case they priced themselves out of the middle-class market. The steadfast refusal of the government to offer serious financial support to music education had put British music colleges in a very different financial position from either the publicly funded conservatoires on continental Europe or the leading American conservatoires which were supported by philanthropic endowments. The importance played by these exams in their early days as both a revenue source and a means of raising awareness of the institutional brand explains why the system of music grades and diplomas became such a particular characteristic of Britain and its Empire.

Today the name of Bonavia Hunt (1847–1914), the clergyman founder of Trinity College London, carries none of the historical weight of his RCM counterpart, Sir George Grove. But in his time, Hunt enjoyed considerable recognition for his determination in establishing Trinity College, for his qualities as a preacher – seemingly Gladstone had offered him a royal chaplaincy – and as a journalist and editor of several popular literary magazines, principally *Cassell's Magazine*, which he edited from 1874 to 1896. While training as a barrister, Hunt had also gained music degrees from Oxford (BMus, 1876) and Trinity College Dublin (DMus, 1887).[18] Initially a choirmaster at South Hackney Parish Church, Hunt set up the Church Choral Society of London, which held weekly rehearsals at Bishopsgate in the East End. The chronology of TCL's subsequent growth can be traced through its appearances in *The Musical Times*. By June 1874 it had become the Church Choral Society and College of Church Music, London, offering 'Examinations for Choral Fellowships (Ch.F.) and Associateships', and exams in harmony and composition. The College was incorporated as Trinity College London in 1875, and that December it was advertising Fellowships and Associateships for males only, and evening classes in Harmony and Counterpoint. In March 1876 it announced its mission as 'the Advancement of Church Music, and the Higher Culture of Church Musicians', offering evening classes in non-musical subjects (Latin, French, Maths, English composition and literature) for the purpose of matriculation, or evidence of general educational attainment, which it made a prerequisite for entering its diplomas. *The Musical Times* for February 1877 lists the results of harmony exams held in London, Manchester and Dublin, at three levels: Licentiates in Music, Associates in Music and Students in Music; as well as in matriculation or Preliminary Arts exams.

The autumn of 1877 saw TCL established in Weymouth Street in the heart of London's West End, offering an extensive programme of evening classes. As well as music paperwork subjects, there was instruction in piano and organ; TCL was also catering for the governess market by providing Higher Exams (diplomas) and a Harmony Class for Women. There was an 'Arts Division' in non-musical subjects (Latin, Greek, French, German, English composition & literature, Maths, Natural

---

[18] For biographical information about Hunt, see Bernarr Rainbow, 'Hunt, Henry George Bonavia', rev. Anne Pimlott Baker, *ODNB*; *The Academic Gazette of Trinity College, London, and Institutions in Union* 1/6 (July 1884), 6–7.

Sciences) and a matriculation class for London University. *The Musical Times* for September 1877 gives the results of Local Exams in Elementary Musical Knowledge held at 'Senior' and 'Junior' levels, which attracted 1,118 candidates, of whom 625 passed. By the next month TCL was advertising a 'complete professional training' of 'three years (twelve terms) duration' for 'Resident' students. The first trial of practical Local Exams in singing and piano was held in December 1878 and the scheme of Local Exams was formalized and advertised across the country in June 1879. Practical diplomas were not instituted until 1892,[19] but from 1879 intending teachers were being offered 'Special Certificates' as validation of their practical skills to complement the theoretical Licentiate and Associate Diplomas.

This chronology suggests a careful but determined process of organic institutional growth, and by 1889, with its local examinations enjoying considerable support, TCL's exam operation was certainly strong enough to hold its own against the threat that the ABRSM would bring. TCL's house journal, *The Academic Gazette of Trinity College, London, and Institutions in Union*, provides detailed information about Trinity's growth, elaborate academic structures and exhaustive regulations. These show, if further proof were needed, that TCL was no fly-by-night operation. By 1888/9 TCL's income from exam fees had reached £8,857. Total candidates examined in the UK and the colonies were given as 8,018, with Local Exams held in Australia, New Zealand, Ceylon and India.[20] By 1890, the year that the ABRSM began its exams, TCL was claiming over 16,000 candidates annually (over a threefold growth in five years) who were sitting exams at more than 160 Local Centres in UK and the colonies.[21] TCL expressed the purpose of its exams as:

> intended to be a means for uniting the whole of the musical profession, and of aiding and co-operating with all qualified teachers of music throughout the Kingdom by supplementing their work with well graduated examination tests, and thereby giving to local teaching the stamp of public, impartial and authoritative approval.[22]

Trinity was seriously dismayed by the threatened appearance of the ABRSM, as *The Academic Gazette* makes clear. Commenting that the ABRSM scheme was a case of 'Imitation is the sincerest flattery', it said that nothing could take away from TCL's pioneering achievement 'to inaugurate a popular educational movement' of local music exams, which to date had examined some 75,000 and which justified 'the far-sighted action taken by Trinity College in this direction seventeen years ago and abundantly prove[d] the national progress in the study of the art of music'.[23] Nothing about this reaction is very surprising. But a rather more idiosyncratic tone is struck in an institutional self-portrait titled 'Parable' (probably written by

---

[19] *The Academic Gazette of Trinity College*, new series 9/1 (June 1892).

[20] *The Academic Gazette of Trinity College* 6/65 (June 1889), 82.

[21] TCL *Calendar for the Academical Year 1890–1*, 102 (TCLA). However, these figures should be treated with some caution as the *Academic Gazette* for July 1890 gives a provisional figure of only half this number.

[22] *Calendar for 1890–1*, 103 (TCLA).

[23] *The Academic Gazette of Trinity College* 6/67 (August 1889), 120–1.

Hunt) that appeared later on in *The Academic Gazette*. In this allegory, Trinity's growth is represented as a strong tree grown from a feeble sapling which achieved its present strength despite many calumnies spread by its opponents. It also survived its opponents stealing cuttings from its wood, 'the subtle flattery of imitation' (i.e. the ABRSM competition). The tree prospered, despite the 'double audacity' of the TCL's founding pioneer in acting 'to raise his tree in the common ground' (a reference to popular music education) because 'it had become a tradition that no such tree could be successfully reared unless planted in one of the royal or parliamentary enclosures' (the College's and Academy's royal charters). In a speech given to a conference of TCL Local Examination Secretaries, Hunt made this 'self-help' basis very clear, saying that Trinity 'had made its way by force of character, by its utility, and not on the strength of any outside (i.e. royal or aristocratic) patronage'.[24] The tone of Hunt's protests may seem naïve to us now, but their palpable sense of injustice gives an insight as to why Trinity was to prove such a determined and doughty opponent to the ABRSM. Trinity's origins are so interesting because they represent a very different sort of institutional beginning and process of growth to those of the two Royals. And in the best Victorian 'self-help' tradition, Trinity was paying its own way on the income it was able to generate for itself, and was proud not to be dependent on a government grant or on the donation of society subscribers flattered by association with a 'royal' institution. Even though Bonavia Hunt was a Church of England clergyman, it may not be too fanciful to see in TCL's determined enterprise to spread popular music education and its fierce independence from the established musical order something of the Nonconformist tone that played such a role in the liberal social conscience of the day.[25] TCL and its graduates also donated the very substantial amount of £5,000 to endow London University's King Edward Chair in music in 1902.

It is clear, from all the vicissitudes that music colleges faced, that the Victorians saw music education as something that could be left to operate freely, supporting itself within the commercial parameters of the free-market context. This should not cause us too much surprise, given the contemporary mindset that saw free trade as an essential condition for a vigorous and productive society. Frank Trentmann captures this attitude in his description of the principle of free trade as 'the closest modern Britain ever came to a national ideology, as important as parliamentary liberty'.[26] Because music exams were a very public expression of music's industry and enterprise, they did much to promote the cause of music education within society as a whole. This free trade environment is very much reflected in the failure of the Society of Arts to persuade the government to assume full financial responsibility for the NTSM, and by the inability of either of the Royal Schools to achieve any immediate increase of its paltry £500 annual grant-in-aid; the government would have seen no reason to intervene in music education when individuals and the market would fund it.

---

[24] *The Academic Gazette of Trinity College* 6/69 (October 1897), 505.

[25] See James Munson, *The Nonconformists: In Search of a Lost Culture* (London: SPCK, 1991).

[26] Frank Trentmann, *Free Trade Nation* (Oxford: Oxford University Press, 2008), 2.

⁂ 'A uniquely British enterprise': the music exam industry and the professionalizing of music education

CYRIL Ehrlich's ground-breaking social history of the music profession in Britain calls the graded musical testing of pupils by dedicated exam bodies 'a uniquely British enterprise'.[27] But apart from Ehrlich's own discussion, which he centres on Trinity's activities, remarkably little attention has been paid to how this market worked. Neither has much consideration been given as to the effects that this market had on the music profession itself. But before discussing the nature and extent of this enterprise, a caveat is needed. To argue the historical position that grade and diploma exams advanced the cause of music education as a professional activity is altogether different from proposing the efficacy of music exams as an educational tool. Because this book is a social and cultural history and not an educational study, it deliberately takes an agnostic stance about the educational benefits – or otherwise – of these exams on the individual.

Music examining constituted an entirely unregulated field, and it was left to chance for the educational wheat to emerge from the examination chaff. This created a situation that offered ample money-making opportunities to charlatan examining bodies whose motivation was primarily financial, more concerned to garner fee income than to improve musical standards. The growth of music-making within the home generated an unprecedented demand for music lessons, as we have seen, and so the availability of meretricious exam certificates and spurious qualifications of attainment posed an obvious problem to the unwary. The method favoured by musical quackery was to produce imposing-looking certificates, on the age-old principle that impressive and elaborate certificates carried the aura of a convincing and reputable authority. These worthless awards inevitably undermined the exams of *bona fide* bodies, and the presence of this charlatan activity also harmed the profession as a whole in the public's eyes. Lack of regulation made legal recourse difficult, while at the same time the tempting income that exam advertising – phoney or otherwise – brought to the musical press ensured maximum confusion. As Percy Scholes acknowledged, 'Like the other musical journals, [*The Musical Times*] admitted the advertisements of bogus institutions to its pages and placed them side by side with those of the genuine institutions.'[28] The music examination business was a lucrative market that at its extremes presented significant opportunities to the canny, unscrupulous operator, and pitfalls to those not in the know. But such market hazards were very much part of the contemporary British free trade nation *par excellence*, with its strong belief that an open unregulated market was essential for the health of civil society. Although the early rush to exploit the income-generating opportunities of the exam market led to all sorts of protestations by contemporary commentators that 'something' be done to regulate the probity of exam bodies, the philosophy of 'laissez-faire' meant that nothing of the kind happened, and the market was left simply to sort itself out.

---

[27] Ehrlich, *The Music Profession in Britain*, 116.

[28] Percy Scholes, 'Professional Diplomas', in *The Mirror of Music, 1844–1944*, 2 vols. (London and Oxford: Novello and Oxford University Press, 1947), 725.

Comparison of the pricing and the categorization of the exams offered by three reputable boards – the Society of Arts, the ABRSM and TCL – gives us a clear indication of the segment of society they were each aimed at. The very first music exams were offered by the Society of Arts as part of their broad programme of exams in the arts and technology. Between 1859 and 1919 the Society offered written music examinations in theory, rudiments, elementary musical composition, harmony and counterpoint; and from 1879 until 1914 it also ran practical instrumental and vocal exams. It might seem surprising that this first system of music exams should have been devised for working-class musicians from the Mechanics' Institutes, and not for the more prosperous middle classes. But the rationale of the Society's exams was to fulfil an essentially philanthropic educational purpose. Its exams were being provided for individuals of the economically hard-pressed working or artisan classes – the social classes least likely to afford systematic music lessons – who wished to improve their circumstances with some official certification of the skills or knowledge they had individually acquired, by whatever means. Thus entrance fees to the Society's exams were kept deliberately low – initially at 2s 6d and never higher than 10s. Table 2.1 sets out a snapshot of the Society's scheme of exams and its entry fees in 1896.

What is immediately striking about the Society's music exams is that grade and diploma levels are mixed together within a single series. These exams were distinctive in several other respects, too. In the ABRSM and TCL exams, musical progress, then as now, was defined by the requirements the syllabus specified for each grade. However, in their original 1879 format, the Society's Practical exams provided no clear identification of the expected musical standard and gave no lists of examination pieces – candidates were free to bring what they wished to perform. Although either a first-class or second-class certificate (later an 'Honours' category was added) could be awarded to the successful candidate, there was no indication as to how these levels were differentiated, and the candidates seem to have been awarded marks on an impressionistic basis for what they did. In 1895 these exams were substantially revised, and from 1896 the syllabus identified four 'standards' or levels of attainment, and listed set pieces for each standard in singing, piano, violin and organ – the most popular exams. Other instrumentalists continued to bring their own pieces, as before. A significant disadvantage that hampered any very wide take-up of the diploma-level Standard 4, was that it carried no entitlement to post-nominal letters, something that put it at very considerable disadvantage against the diplomas on offer from the conservatoires. Neither did the Society publish the names of successful candidates. Thus the Society's Practical exams never attracted candidates in the numbers that entered for the conservatoire exams, and by 1914, examinees had fallen right away to only 244: 205 in piano, 33 in violin and 6 in singing.[29] Compared with the carefully structured levels and precise syllabus stipulations of the modern exam systems offered by the music colleges, the approach taken in the Society's exams seems slightly anarchic, but we need to remember that their primary purpose was much more about encouraging

---

[29] *Journal of the Society of Arts* 63 (2 July 1915), 745.

Table 2.1 Music exams offered by the Society of Arts in 1896

	Examination	Fee	RPI equivalent in 2009*
Paperwork exams (first offered in 1859)	Rudiments of Music (from 1893)	5s	£20.40
	Harmony & Counterpoint (from 1893)	5s	£20.40
Practical exams (first offered in 1879; new format in 1896; candidates could choose between entering for a 'pass' or a 'distinction')	Standard 1 (Easy) [ABRSM equivalent: Grades 4–6]	5s (pass) or 10s (distinction)	£20.40 or £42.90
	Standard 2 (Moderately Difficult) [ABRSM: Grades 5–7]	5s (pass) or 10s (distinction)	£20.40 or £42.90
	Standard 3 (Difficult) [ABRSM: Grade 8/8+]	5s (pass) or 10s (distinction)	£20.40 or £42.90
	Standard 4 (Very Difficult) [Diploma level]	10s	£42.90

* www.measuringworth.com/ukcompare/, accessed 29 September 2010

the individual to pursue an educational path. These exams offered the working-class musician a rare opportunity to gain a certificate attesting their skills.

Tonic Sol-fa was an important gateway to music for many working-class musicians, and initially most of the candidates for the Society's theoretical exams had taken the Tonic Sol-fa class offered by many Mechanics' Institutes.[30] Two notable musicians began in this way: Sir Henry Coward, the famous Sheffield choral conductor, and William McNaught, Stainer's assistant on the School Inspectorate. Coward, the son of a Sheffield cutler, and himself apprenticed to that trade, gained both a first-class certificate in the Elementary Music Composition paper and a second class in Theory of Music in 1871, aged twenty-two – a remarkable achievement for someone who could barely write until he was twenty-one; and later he went on to obtain the Oxford BMus and DMus degrees.[31] In 1876 Coward founded the Sheffield Tonic Sol-fa Association (later the Sheffield Musical Union), and he conducted several other northern choral societies. Greatly admired as a choral trainer in Germany, which his choir visited between 1906 and 1910, Coward won world renown as a choral conductor because of a famous round-the-world concert tour of the Empire that he led in 1911.[32]

[30] See Nettel, *Music in the Five Towns*, 3–11.

[31] F. H. Shera, 'Coward, Sir Henry (1849–1944)', rev. James J. Nott, *ODNB*; see also Mackerness, *A Social History of English Music*, 161–2.

[32] For an account of Coward's achievements, see Richards, *Imperialism and Music*, 450–68.

William McNaught was born in London's Mile End and began his musical life through Tonic Sol-fa; he went on to teach the violin in classes to other East End youths, and conducted a Stepney choir. McNaught was an autodidact of enormous intellectual energy and drive ('devouring the philosophical and scientific writings of Herbert Spenser, Charles Darwin, and others').[33] In 1868 he gained a first-class certificate in the Society's Music (theory) exam, and in 1871 (coincidentally the year of Coward's exam achievements) he won the second prize of £3 in the Elementary Musical Composition Exam. Success in the Society's exams seemed to give McNaught the confidence to give up his job in the coffee trade and enter the RAM (1872–6), an experience as important for its networking as for anything he actually learned, and his career took off. Because of McNaught's Tonic Sol-fa experience, Stainer appointed him one of his Assistant Inspectors of Music; in this role McNaught was estimated to have examined some 20,000 school teachers in the course of their training.[34] It is striking that the Society's exams should have laid the ground for Coward and McNaught's achievements in careers that would have been considered remarkably successful even for those who had enjoyed every educational advantage. These two success stories emphasize the significance of the opportunity that the Society's exams gave to working-class musicians, although it is just as impressive to read of the achievements of a miscellany of others whose entry forms gave their occupations as clerks, storemen, weavers and builders, etc. But the ambiguous nature and uncertain standing of the Society's exams compared with those offered by the conservatoires meant that they had no long-term future. The Society of Arts realized this and approached the ABRSM to take them over:

> In the year 1892 the Society offered to transfer these examinations to the Associated Board of the Royal Academy of Music and the Royal College of Music; *but the Board would not undertake to carry them on at the low fee charged (five shillings), and nothing came of the proposal* [my italics]. Eight years later, in 1900, the question of continuing these examinations was again raised, and some further communications passed between the Associated Board and the Society, but again without result.[35]

In 1914 the Society decided to discontinue its Practical exams (the theory exams continued until 1919), because

> the steady decrease in the number of candidates entering for these Examinations indicates that they are no longer of much practical value, and they have therefore decided not to continue them. They have come to this conclusion with much regret, for they believe that at one time the examinations served a useful purpose, by encouraging youthful students who could not afford to enter for the Examinations of the Royal Academy of Music, at the time when the Society's examinations were started, or in subsequent years for those of the Associated Board of the Academy and the Royal College of Music.[36]

[33] 'W. G. McNaught', *MT* 44 (March 1903), 153–9.

[34] Ibid., 155.

[35] *Journal of the Society of Arts* 63 (2 July 1915), 745.

[36] *Journal of the Society of Arts* 62 (25 September 1914), 919–20.

If we compare the fees that the Society of Arts charged for their series of exams (Table 2.1) with those for the graded exams of the ABRSM and TCL (Table 2.2) and the diplomas offered by the Royal Schools (the ARCM and LRAM), TCL and the College of Organists (Table 2.3), we see the very clear price distinction between the mid-century philanthropic purpose of the Society's exams, and the professionalizing intention and commercial basis of the exams and diplomas offered at the end of the century by the ABRSM, TCL and the Royal Schools. Table 2.2 compares the fees charged by the ABRSM and TCL, and although the difference between the fees charged is sufficiently large to suggest they were each aiming at different social markets, it should also be remembered that the ABRSM Local Centre Exams were assessed by two examiners, as opposed to TCL's single examiner, thereby increasing the Board's costs. The difference in fees may therefore as much reflect the different musical service on offer, with greater objectivity suggested by the presence of two examiners. However, the cachet 'royal' should not be discounted as a means of defining an intended market able to bear the Board's greater fees. Table 2.2 also shows that these exam schemes began by offering many fewer 'grades' than today's standard eight grades. The ABRSM's Local Centre Exams and Local School Exams were intended to correspond to the two levels of the Oxbridge local school exams. (The table gives their approximate modern-day music equivalents.)

⧱ Diplomas

TOWARDS the end of the nineteenth century a consensus had emerged that the market would support two types of exams: the 'formative' process as represented by the grade exams and the 'summative' function of the professional diplomas. Each was intended to fulfil a very different professional purpose.

The grade system offered individual music teachers step-by-step guidance in matters of technical progression and musical formation that could be used to account to parents for their children's development.[37] The music teaching profession itself needed access to a recognized layer of 'summative' or professional-level diplomas, because these qualifications were evidence that the holder had been subjected to a thorough testing by a board of eminent musicians. A diploma's value was clearly related to the reputation of its awarding institution, and accordingly, the best diplomas made very stiff demands on their candidates. In formulating and examining their diplomas, the awarding colleges were operating analogously to a chartered institution. But music's weakness was that instead of there being a single chartered body responsible for setting professional standards, as in the professions regulated by chartered institutes, the sheer variety of available diplomas with very varying reputations had the potential to fracture, rather than to solidify, the

---

[37] This was made explicit in the comments of the Prince of Wales (later Edward VII) to the Board's 1893 AGM, reproduced in the *Fourth Annual Report of the Board* (1893), 31: 'I feel confident that it [the work of the Board] cannot fail both to improve the average standard of teaching, and enable parents to make sure that their children are receiving a careful musical training'; this passage was repeated in the *Seventeenth Annual Report of the Board* (1906), 21.

Table 2.2 Local Exam provision offered by TCL and the ABRSM in 1891

Board	Exams	First offered	Grades available	1891 fees	2009 RPI equivalent*	2010 ABRSM fees
TCL	Local Centre Exams Theory ('Musical Knowledge')	1877	Senior Intermediate Junior	10s 6d 7s 6d 6s 0d	£42.80 £30.60 £24.50	
TCL	Local Centre Exams Practical subjects (1 examiner)	1879	Senior Junior Primary (Piano & Violin only)	£1 1s	£85.70	
ABRSM	Local Centre Exams in practical subjects and Theory of Music (2 examiners)	1890	Senior [approximates to today's Grade 7] Junior (12–16 years) [approximates to today's Grade 6]	£2 2s (this includes the compulsory Preliminary Exam in the Rudiments of Music); each additional subject charged at £1 1s £2 2s	£171.00 £85.70	£61.20 £55.80
ABRSM	Local School Exams 'Preparatory to the Local Centre Examinations' (1 examiner)	1891	Higher [approximates to today's Grade 5] Lower (no age limits) [approximates to today's Grade 4]	10s 6d for one subject; plus 5s 0d for each additional subject NB: each school or teacher entering pupils required to pay a £2 2s Annual Registration fee. In 1892 the Annual Registration fee was reduced to £1 1s, and the exam fees increased to: Higher: 15s 0d Lower: 7s 6d (increases are indicative of the strength of the market)	£42.80 £20.40 £171.00 £85.70 £60.70 £30.60	£47.60 £44.80

* www.measuringworth.com/ukcompare/, accessed 29 September 2010

Sources: TCL, Calendar for the Academical Year 1890–1; ABRSM, syllabuses for the 1890 Local Examinations in Music and the 1890–1 Local School Examinations

public's confidence and provided for much partisan backbiting between teachers whose loyalty was to competing exam boards.

Table 2.3 sets down the diplomas most generally considered reputable. This table includes the specifically vocational diplomas that the College of Organists offered from 1866. These exams had a clear professionalizing purpose because the syllabus prescribed those skills and standards of attainment thought necessary for church organists; in recognition of its work, the College was granted its own royal charter in 1893. Mention should also be made here of the College of Violinists (founded in 1890), which was another reputable specialist examining college that enjoyed the support of many string players on account of its policy of 'expert examination', or 'violinists examined by violinists'.[38] The College examined all stringed instruments, and had the support of some famous players, such as Albert Sammons and Eugene Goossens. Unlike the other boards, the College made very little money, and ran itself on the basis of a 'friendly society' for string players. In addition to the usual raft of grade exams, the College also offered Associate, Licentiate and Fellowship diplomas. But its most interesting and progressive qualification was the Certified Teacher of Violin-playing (CTV), which was designed for those who started teaching early in life and couldn't pursue diplomas on their own account because their financial circumstances meant that they could not afford to reduce their teaching. Teachers seeking the CTV qualification had first to have entered over one hundred pupils for the College's exams, and the award was made on the basis of a teacher's overall results, which the College felt was the real test as to whether someone could teach or not; passing the CTV reflected a success rate that allowed for 'some failures but not an abundance', with honours passes counting to balance some failures.[39]

Anyone seeking to set themselves up in a teaching practice, and who had the necessary financial resources to invest, would likely have aimed for the professional credibility (and post-nominal letters) conferred by one of the conservatoire diplomas; the accumulation of large numbers of 'letters' by music professionals show that, to be on the safe side, many took diplomas from all three institutions. Table 2.3 gives the cost of the Royal Schools' diplomas, whose fees were clearly set at a level that reflected institutional self-image as well as their prestige within the diploma market. The early history of the ARCM indicates why, despite its cost, the diploma was considered a worthwhile investment. The ARCM was conceived as a 'Certificate of Proficiency', attesting 'excellence' in the area examined and competency in other associated musical aspects.[40] The proportion of success for the early ARCM is not always clear, but the failure rate seems to have been high. In its first seven sessions (1886–92), 133 out of 278

[38] Its policy is spelled out in *The Violinists' Gazette* no. 8 (September 1917).

[39] *The Violinists' Gazette* no. 23 (March 1915), 16. I am most grateful to Christina Bashford for so generously sharing with me her research into the College of Violinists, which forms part of a larger project into the violin culture of the late nineteenth and early twentieth centuries.

[40] RCMA, Minute Book: Executive and Finance Committee, vol. 1 (1883–6), meeting on 22 May 1884.

Table 2.3 Diploma provision offered by the most reputable exam boards in 1890

Exam board	Exams	First offered	Fee	2009 RPI equivalent*
College of Organists (Royal College of Organists from 1893)	Fellowship Diploma (FCO)	1866	£1 1s	£85.70
	Associate Diploma (ACO)	1882		
	[From 1871 to 1881 the Associate Diploma was awarded to Fellowship candidates for a 'less high, but satisfactory standard'.]			
TCL	Diplomas in Theory:	c. 1875		
	Associate (AMusTCL)		£2 2s	£171.00
	Licentiate (LMusTCL)		£3 3s	£257.00
	Matriculation (prerequisite for AMus & LMus)		10s 6d	£42.80
	Further Arts (prerequisite for LMus)		£1 1s	£85.70
	Licentiate and Further Arts (if taken together)		£3 3s	£257.00
	Fellowship (in Composition only)		£6 6s	£514.00
	Performance:	1879		
	Intending teachers seeking validation of skills in practical subjects could sit for a 'Special Certificate'		£2 2s	£171.00
RCM	ARCM	1886	£5 5s	£428.00
RAM	LRAM	1882	£5 5s	£428.00

* www.measuringworth.com/ukcompare/, accessed 29 September 2010

candidates passed, a rate of 48%.[41] Thus the fact that the ARCM attracted so many candidates despite the hazard presented by the high standard and the significant 5 guinea fee (2½ guineas for a second attempt) is itself indicative of professional desirability. What helped establish the ARCM's reputation (as well as adding to the candidate's perils) was that its examiners were from 'the great and the good' of music. Nominations for the first examiners' panel of 1886 included the eminent pianists and teachers Ernest Pauer and Franklin Taylor, the violinist and conductor Henry Holmes, the redoubtable organist Walter Parratt, as well as Stanford, Parry, F. H. Cowen, Carl Rosa and A. C. Mackenzie (later Principal of the RAM). Out of thirty-six candidates entering the first ARCM, only ten were successful. Clearly the ARCM was designed to be impressive, with a reputation that would outgun anything being offered by any other body. Of the 850 passes in the period 1909–13, the overwhelming proportion were in the only two available teachers' diplomas: 535 in piano teaching and 42 in singing teaching; this is strong evidence of the candidates' purpose in taking these diplomas, and their belief that the significant financial and musical investment was professionally worth while.[42] All ARCM

[41] RCM Centre for Performance History, draft of the 1894 RCM Prospectus.
[42] RCMA, RCM *Annual Reports* for 1909 and 1913. The other diploma subjects were in performance.

candidates in those early days also had to pass a test of literary proficiency with an essay on a named musical subject, the equivalent of TCL's 'matriculation' paper, required in order to enhance the public's belief in the general educational standard of its diploma holders.

Candidate numbers reached by 1914 give a sense of just how astonishing the take-up of music exams had been. In that year TCL claimed that, annually, it now had over 30,000 entries for its exams worldwide at all levels (grades and diplomas), and that since 1879 a total figure of over 500,000 candidates had been examined at 500 centres in the UK and the Dominions.[43] The ABRSM Practical and Theoretical grade exams – despite the expense of the Local Centre Exams – had overtaken TCL and had 32,910 UK entries for the year ending 30 April 1914, and over 45,000 entries worldwide.[44] With the level of involvement these figures represent, it is not surprising that the ABRSM's and TCL's exams proved to be immensely influential in changing perceptions. The new professionalizing agenda being pushed by the music colleges fundamentally altered the nature of British musical training. Firstly, the spread of these grade and diploma exams was the most effective way possible of establishing the institutional 'brand' in the public's mind as a symbol of musical authority. Secondly, diplomas with their splendid array of post-nominal letters helped to dignify the music teaching profession in the eyes of the public and also in terms of the general teaching profession. Thirdly, the exam system played a considerable role in generating a new body of musically more proficient students, whose improved technical and musical skills at this earlier stage gave them much greater professional potential, so driving up musical standards all round. Fourthly, the grade examination market helped generate teaching opportunities for ex-music college students who would help produce the next generations of music college students. Finally, these examinations were a vehicle for institutions to offer patronage to their professors: an appointment as an examiner represented both prestige and also an additional income stream to the economically often hard-pressed staff of the music colleges. Indeed, the examiner's role added to the status of the music profession, not least because his incontrovertible judgements gave him a certain omniscience, and so created a new breed of musician – the virtuoso assessor.

Underpinning all this musical infrastructure were the fees from these examinations. They were to prove a crucial income-stream in keeping the music colleges afloat economically. In the face of insufficient government aid, restricted scholarship capital and without the space to admit all the fee-paying students necessary to cover operational costs, fees from grade and diploma examinations constituted an essential lifeline. TCL, sensitive to allegations that music exams were merely a money-making machine, disclosed at a Distribution of Certificates ceremony in October 1890 that in total TCL had received something like £60,000 from Local Exams since starting its scheme. Annual exam income was

[43] TCL *Calendar*, 1914, 21 (TCLA).

[44] *Twenty-fifth Annual Report of the Board* (1914), 14, 24. In stark contrast, the figures for the Society of Arts exams in 1914 (fifty-five years after the Society began its music exams) totalled only 836 entries: 342 for Rudiments, 245 for Harmony, and 249 for practical subjects.

£6,000–7,000, with one-third of that going to Local Centre expenses and much of the remainder to running the exams. TCL said that its total annual income came to some £10,000 a year, but that the fees of its enrolled students at Trinity did not cover its costs: for every £1 it received from its students, Trinity spent £1 8s 3d on its work. Yet the income from examination fees meant that TCL had also saved about £1,000 for its capital fund, which puts its exam income into perspective.[45]

Well might Ehrlich have dubbed the whole music exam venture a uniquely British enterprise. It was so for reasons that would have been unsustainable in another type of society. Combining a determined sense of free-market enterprise with strong assertions of musical authority, it was initially characterized by a diversity of exam boards and umpteen syllabuses. But out of this inchoate situation, the most respectable exam boards emerged with a national, indeed Empire-wide, reputation. They did so on the back of exams that were designed to achieve so much more than to turn a quick profit, although it will now be clear exactly why the income from these exams was vital to the colleges that ran them. Educational and musical integrity was present from the beginning in the work of the best boards, something that explains why these exams had such a strong professionalizing effect. From the 1880s there was a decisive shift as British music education and its achievements became something that mattered to the nation. And that is why it is not too much to claim that the sometimes strange, often controversial system of musical examinations – that very British invention – continued to be a significant factor in the astonishing transformation of British musical life in the twentieth century.

---

[45] *The Academic Gazette of Trinity College* 7/82 (November 1890), 162.

II The Board Established, 1889–1920

3 The ABRSM Idea and the First Exams, 1889–91

⁄⁄⁄ Setting up the Board: the exams in 1890 and 1891

O N 3 May 1889, six years after the founding of the Royal College of Music, its Director, Sir George Grove, was visited by Alexander Mackenzie, the newly appointed Principal of the Royal Academy of Music, and Thomas Threlfall, Chairman of the Academy's Board of Directors. It had been agreed beforehand that this informal meeting should also be confidential, which is understandable, given the controversial subject the Academy team wished to raise, and the very uneasy relations that existed between the RAM and the RCM. Mackenzie and Threlfall first referred to the rumour that the RCM were contemplating setting up their own extramural exam scheme, and then revealed the purpose of their visit, which was to propose that the two royal British music schools should bury their differences and combine to form a joint music examination board. Grove reported this meeting to the RCM's Finance and Executive Committee and secured their support to explore the idea further.[1] It took less than a year for the Associated Board of the Royal Schools of Music to be formally constituted and conduct its first exams at forty-two centres across the country. Despite very little warning and the very substantial two-guinea entry fee, these exams attracted 1,143 entries. That so many entered says much about the contemporary British enthusiasm for taking music exams, as well as about the assurance, and perhaps cachet, of exams conducted by an associated board of the two royal music schools. For not only were the Board's exams new, indeed unknown, experiences, but candidates' families were paying what in today's terms would be about £172 for the privilege – an amount that is more than double the £72.20 entry fee required to enter Grade 8 in 2010.[2] This chapter outlines the history of the Board's first two years. It relates how the Board came into being, and looks at the organizational and logistical aspects that had to be put into place in order to run the first two years of exams, in 1890 and 1891.[3]

The Associated Board was established in a remarkably short time when one considers the conceptual, administrative and operational challenges of the undertaking. Firstly, the RAM and the RCM had to reach an acceptable way of working together; given the level of institutional antagonism between them this cannot have been altogether easy. (It was helpful that Mackenzie and Grove both lived in Lower Sydenham and enjoyed a cordial, neighbourly relationship.) Secondly, the scheme of exams had to be settled upon, and the syllabus agreed, certainly an area with the potential for considerable dispute. Thirdly, and perhaps most sensitively, the organization and operation of the Board's exams had to be framed in such a way that distanced them from the corrupt and damaging

---

[1] RCMA, Minute Book of the Executive and Finance Committee, vol. 2, 285–6.

[2] www.measuringworth.com/ukcompare, accessed 29 September 2010.

[3] Much of the source material for this comes from the Board's first minute book (ABMB1), which covers the period from 17 June 1889 to 19 November 1890.

1 George Watson (seated, centre), the ABRSM's first Secretary and the organizing force behind its early success. Standing immediately behind him is the intrepid Frederic Cliffe, whose experiences as one of the Board's early overseas examiners are discussed in Chapter 5.

practices of the RAM's own first attempt, from 1881, to run Local Exams in music (discussed in Chapter 2). Mackenzie's realization of the discredit these exams had brought the Academy was the motivation in starting this new association with the RCM.

The bare bones of the setting-up process are recorded in a slim notebook titled simply 'Minute Book / Local Examinations'. There were two preliminary meetings of a founding committee with an equal representation of the two Schools on 17 June and 18 July, 1889. Chaired by Lord Charles Bruce of the RCM, they were held on the neutral ground of the Royal Institution in Albemarle Street. The venue was made available through one of the RAM's representatives, the distinguished scientist Professor (Sir) James Dewar. Dewar, the inventor of the thermos flask and cordite, among many other things, was a passionate music-lover and an amateur violinist who had rooms in the Royal Institution.[4] But Dewar was not the only distinguished outsider involved in the process. Representatives of the RCM included the very influential (Sir) Edward Hamilton, civil servant and diarist, at one time Gladstone's Downing Street Secretary and confidant, and since their Eton schooldays a close friend of Lord Rosebery.[5] Hamilton, who became one of the heads of the Treasury after periods advising successive Chancellors of the Exchequer, was a cousin of Hubert Parry, who was another of the RCM representatives, together with Sullivan, Stainer and the distinguished pianist Franklin Taylor.[6] The other RAM representatives were Thomas Threlfall (who was also a barrister, and chairman of his Liverpool family brewery), (Judge) Meadows White, Alberto Randegger (singing teacher at both institutions and a famous choral conductor) and Frederick Westlake (a piano professor at the Academy). The founding committee intended to issue a detailed scheme of exams by no later than January 1890. In fact such good progress was made that the whole scheme was announced in mid-November 1889, and this earlier notice boosted the number of candidates for the first exams. The speed with which the exam structure was framed owed much to the behind-the-scenes work of George Watson, the RCM's Registrar, who was formerly to be appointed the Board's Secretary at the November 1890 meeting.

George Watson is a rather shadowy figure (even his year of birth is uncertain), but the warmth and generosity of the praise showered on him at different times by the Board acknowledge that he was pivotal to the successful setting-up of the ABRSM project. Watson's death and funeral in February 1896 were both reported by *The Times*,[7] and the list of those attending his funeral is impressive testimony of the regard in which he was held. Watson came from Rochester, born into a

---

[4] H. M. Ross, 'Dewar, Sir James (1842–1923)', rev. Trevor I. Williams, *ODNB*.

[5] Dudley W. R. Bahlman, 'Hamilton, Sir Edward Walter (1847–1908)', *ODNB*; on his influence see references in H. C. G. Mathew, *Gladstone, 1809–1898* (Oxford: Clarendon Press, 1997) and Leo McKinstry, *Rosebery: Statesman in Turmoil* (London: John Murray, 2005).

[6] Franklin Taylor (1843–1919) had studied with Moscheles at the Leipzig Conservatoire at the same time as Sullivan and Grieg, and was a pupil of Clara Schumann in Paris. He was an enormously influential teacher.

[7] *The Times*, 18 February 1896 (unsigned obituary by George Grove); and 20 February 1896.

tradesman's family, and he managed the musically ambitious Rochester, Chatham and Strood Choral Society. From 1882 he worked with Grove on the founding of the RCM and became its Secretary, or chief administrator. Grove's obituary attested to Watson's gifts for organization and financial management, saying that much of the early success of both the RCM and the ABRSM derived from the solid administrative basis that Watson had established for them. This may explain the ease with which a draft agreement between the two institutions setting down the ABRSM's conceptual and operational framework was approved without amendment at the founding committee's second session on 18 July (just a month after its initial meeting, and only some two and a half months after Mackenzie's original visit to Grove with the idea of an Associated Board).[8] The first official meeting of the Associated Board (which until 1900 was called the Associated Board of the Royal Academy of Music and the Royal College of Music for Local Examinations in Music) was on 1 October 1889 (again at the Royal Institution). That meeting was presented with a draft syllabus, which was agreed with only a few amendments of musical detail. How had all the exam and syllabus framework come into being with such little apparent effort? When Mackenzie proposed Watson as the Secretary of the ABRSM at its second meeting on 28 October, he left little doubt that Watson was the organizing force behind the Board, expressing 'his own sense of the obligation and that of the Board for the invaluable services which Mr Watson had already rendered to the association, and for the time and attention he had devoted to organizing the same'.[9] The Annual Report for 1891 also records that, 'The Board have difficulty in finding terms in which they can adequately express how gratefully they appreciate the value of the services of their Secretary, Mr George Watson', and credits him with instigating the new scheme of 'School Exams' as providing a preparatory stage to the Local Exams, a vital innovation that was to secure the Board financially.[10] Unfortunately, Watson's time with the Board was to be brief, because he suffered a seizure in 1894, his long illness being noted in the Annual Report 'with extreme regret'.[11] Announcing his death, the 1896 report describes him as the 'respected Secretary and adviser for whom [the Board] entertained such feelings of high esteem and regard'.[12] Watson's name is now long forgotten, but his ability and drive and the considerable respect in which he was so clearly held explains much about the Board's seemingly effortless emergence as a mature operation.

The Board's first official meeting on 1 October (part of which was carried over to the next day to approve the revised proofs of the syllabus) was a very busy one. The matter of accommodation had become pressing, and the publisher Arthur Chappell had offered two rooms at 52 New Bond Street for a year's rental agreed at £84. The meeting sanctioned the appointment of a clerk at £112 10s and a messenger at 10s a week. Money was set aside for printing syllabuses and stationery (£100), advertising (also £100) and postage (£50) – the Board was dependent upon

[8] This Agreement, dated 24 October 1889, marks the ABRSM's legal identity.
[9] ABMB1: 28 October 1889.
[10] *Second Annual Report of the Board* (1891), 23.
[11] *Fifth Annual Report of the Board* (1894), 30.
[12] *Seventh Annual Report of the Board* (1896), 34.

the advances in communication offered by the post and the railway. The Academy and the College each advanced half of the £372 18s 9d necessary to meet all the estimated costs of setting up the Board and running its first exams.[13] The minutes record that a list of proposed examiners was presented to the Board on the basis that: 'Examiners shall consist of present members of the teaching staff of the RAM and the RCM.' Grove and Mackenzie were left to settle the matter of examiners' fees, and at the next meeting on 28 October, they recommended a two-tier system of remuneration that preserved the distinction between senior and junior professors. Senior (in some cases veteran) professors (including Parry, Stanford, Parratt, Randegger, Oscar Beringer, Ernest Pauer, Ebenezer Prout, Westlake and Franklin Taylor) were to be paid £7 10s for a six-hour day (25s an hour) exclusive of travel and hotel expenses, and junior professors (including the pianist Frederic Cliffe, the violinist Henry Holmes, the cellist Edward Howell and the organists F. E. Gladstone (cousin to William Gladstone) and C. H. Lloyd) would have 5 guineas, or 17s 6d per hour. The published syllabus included all the examiners' names, and the presence of so many highly regarded musicians added considerable weight to the impact of the Board's exams.

The Prince of Wales's agreement to become the Board's President certainly gave it a sense of national significance. Less helpful was his later intervention to propose changing the Board's name to 'The Royal National Institute of Music', because that title would have undermined the sense of the Board being an alliance between the Royal Schools.[14] However, seeing the opportunity to capitalize on its royal connection, the Board then proposed it be called 'The Royal Associated Board' – which would have added to the unwieldiness of an already awkward name. This idea was dropped because by then the title 'The Associated Board' had already gained some familiarity through the recruitment of Honorary Local Representatives (HLRs) at strategically placed centres in towns and cities across the country. HLRs were chosen for their professional or social standing in these communities, and to reflect the Board's integrity and seriousness of educational purpose. Grove had undertaken many trips all over the country in order to raise scholarship funds for the RCM during 1882–3, and so he was well placed to approach people who had lent their support to the RCM's cause. This is one reason why the initial set of HLRs was in place so quickly, and the network simply continued to expand. (As indicated in Chapter 1, the idea of HLRs – volunteers who were responsible for the examination arrangements in their locality – was borrowed from the Oxford and Cambridge Local Exam schemes.) Professional musicians or music teachers were not allowed to be HLRs, which carefully distanced the Board's new exam scheme from that of the RAM's earlier one. It also made the Board's administration of its exams very distinct from the way that TCL ran its operation. TCL's exams were organized by a local committee of three, led by the Local Secretary who forwarded the exam fees to Trinity, keeping back a 'capitation' element for each student which could be used to pay the Secretary or be put into a prize fund.[15] The ABRSM's Honorary Local Representatives

---

[13] RCMA, Minute Book of the Executive and Finance Committee, vol. 3, p. 21.

[14] ABMB1: 28 October 1889.

[15] TCL *Calendar, 1890–91,* 100 (TCLA).

remitted all of the fees they received from senior Local Centre Exam candidates directly to the Board and invoiced for expenses incurred in running the exams. (The administration of the more numerous junior School Centre Exams, including remitting the fees, was the responsibility of the schools or teachers involved and not done by the HLR.) Because many of these early HLRs were solicitors or other professionals, in practice it seems that the actual work was done by one of their office staff.

The HLRs were clearly essential to the success of the start-up process. The Board had to tread the delicate line of writing to its HLRs in a way that engaged their full co-operation in ensuring the efficient accomplishment of tasks that certainly some of them would have considered below their station in life. The letter the Board sent to its HLRs about the administration of the Preliminary Rudiments paper (which preceded the first Practical exams) neatly combines a respectful tone with a clear and comprehensive set of instructions. The HLRs were asked to do the following: ensure the necessary accommodation had been booked for the candidates to sit the exams on the due date and time; notify the Board of where the exam was to be held so that the Board could notify the candidates; ensure that there were sufficient supplies of scribbling paper, ink and pens. HLRs were reminded that the papers would be sent directly to them and that they should open the package in front of the candidates; that either they or a reliable deputy should be there in person throughout the Preliminary Exam; to return the completed papers to the Board by that night's post; to check for themselves or to send to the Board the birth certificates for Junior Grade candidates who should be between the ages of twelve and sixteen; to send the Board a cheque for the entrance fees received, together with a completed form detailing expenses incurred and disbursements made. On one level, all this is fairly mundane, but in the context of the careful class distinctions of Victorian society it was not easy to strike a balance between the necessary social consideration and the direction that needed to be given. Offending an HLR would have been damaging, but it was also important to ensure that the HLRs ran their operation efficiently. For in timetabling a compulsory written paper to be sat simultaneously across the country, the ABRSM was doing something none of the other music exam boards had ever attempted. Of course, a single exam sitting was the only way to minimize the possibility of cheating between centres and to demonstrate the integrity of the process (which is why it relied upon the HLRs performing their administrative tasks correctly). But it was also symbolic: by holding the Preliminary Exam simultaneously across the country, the ABRSM was announcing itself as a national exam board. There must therefore have been a degree of trepidation as the afternoon of 21 February 1890 (the date for the very first Preliminary Exam) approached. The Board was later very careful to emphasize its indebtedness to the HLRs for the success of the first year of exams.[16]

The Board's syllabus was widely distributed across the music profession, to schools and to music shops, and it was accompanied by a circular letter explaining the Board's aims and emphasizing that it was acting under the authority conferred by the royal charters of the Academy and the College. Interest had been stirred

---

[16] *First Annual Report of the Board* (1890), 1.

in advance because details of the scheme had been carefully 'leaked' to *The Musical Times*, music's trade paper, and the *MT* (doubtless with future advertising revenue in mind) obliged with two helpful articles. The first briefly summarized the current music exam situation, acknowledging TCL's pioneering role in offering different grades across the country, but casting doubt upon the uniformity of its examining standards. The *MT* explained the public's enthusiasm for music exams as meeting 'a great desire, which had before been neglected simply because it was inarticulate', and pointed out the dangers of a free-for-all that was open to abuse because profit could come at the expense of musical considerations. It argued that there were two possible safeguards for the public in the present situation. One being to cede musical authority to a centralized institution as was the practice in continental Europe, the other being an examination board whose musical weight and influence would set the gold standard for musical examinations. Given the British preference for a solution arrived at voluntarily rather than imposed centrally, the Associated Board represented a significant development and the *MT* anticipated its exams would be enthusiastically received.[17] The second article coyly 'ventured to anticipate' the contents of the syllabus and the 'probable' names of the examiners ('a formidable band ... including some of the best musical talent in the country'). Obviously carefully briefed, the *MT* opined that: 'Well-wishers to music all the country over will watch the enterprise now about to begin with interest and sympathy, desiring for it unqualified success as a stepping stone to still higher and better things.'[18] The carefully managed publicity for these exams (including notices in the local newspapers for each centre) was attracting the attention needed to ensure that, despite their cost and the shortness of notice, they would not flop. People also wrote in to propose their own town for a centre, and with this evidence of local support, it was decided to increase the number of centres as quickly as possible. A complaint received from the Headmistress of Cheltenham Ladies' College seems to have expressed one possibly common anxiety, in 'complaining generally of the rigorous nature of the Examinations'. She also voiced concern about 'the shortness of time to prepare for them', suggesting that there may have been some misunderstanding that these exams would be held only once; a perception that may have given the process an additional sense of urgency as some rushed to take advantage of the opportunity. At its meeting on 11 December the Board sanctioned the order for a further 10,000 copies of the syllabus.

Entry to the first exams had to be made by 7 February 1890,[19] and the compulsory Preliminary Rudiments paper was to be sat on 19 February. Candidates could take an exam in one of the three subject areas (Theory of Music; Practice of Instrumental Music; Practice of Vocal Music) at either the Junior or Senior Grade (except for Singing, where there was no Junior Grade). The syllabus informed candidates that the Rudiments paper would 'comprise questions in

[17] 'Musical Examinations', *MT* 30 (October 1889), 585–6; the *MT*'s endorsement of a market solution to drive out charlatan examining boards reflects the free-market attitude taken to these exams which was discussed in Chapter 1.

[18] 'Local Examinations in Music – R.A.M. and R.C.M.', *MT* 30 (November 1889), 649.

[19] *First Annual Report of the Board* (1890), 2.

Centre _____

Candidate's Name in full _____

N.B.—Candidates are to write their Names on this Paper as above.
All Answers are to be written on this Sheet.   No others will be accepted.

Associated Board of the Royal Academy of Music and the Royal College of Music

FOR

LOCAL EXAMINATIONS IN MUSIC.

PRELIMINARY EXAMINATION PAPER,

Referred to in Syllabus, page 8; to be worked on **FEBRUARY 19, 1890**, from 2 p.m. to 5 p.m.

1.—Write on the stave below a series of all the notes in common use, with their equivalent rests, commencing with the breve and ending with the demi-semi-quaver (one note and its rest in each bar).

2.—A. Explain the difference between simple and compound time.

B. Write a bar in $\frac{2}{8}$ time, commencing with a sound of the value of seven quavers, and fill up the remainder of the bar with rests.

C. Write a bar in $\frac{4}{4}$ time, commencing with a sound of the value of three quavers, and fill up the remainder of the bar with notes or rests.

3.—Put the time signatures to the following :

4.—Write two examples of syncopation (one in $\frac{4}{4}$ the other in $\frac{6}{8}$); two bars of each are required.

5.—Write the particular note known as the "Middle C."

6.—A. Write in the Treble Clef, on the staves below, the scales of A flat, F sharp, B flat minor, and E minor, and mark the semi-tones in each. The minor scales to be in the melodic form, ascending and descending.

2 Extract from the ABRSM's first examination paper. The blackletter typeface surmounted by the royal crest signals institutional authority. Candidates had to pass this written Preliminary Examination before they could proceed to take the Practical grade.

harmony, as far as the triads and their inversions, formed on the degrees of the major and minor scales', but there was no sample paper. Presumably those taking the Theory of Music exam would have felt reasonably sanguine about passing the Rudiments element, for the demands on them were searching: both Senior and Junior Grade Theory candidates had to do an analysis of a Beethoven piano sonata movement, and sit a twenty-minute viva which included playing from a figured bass; at the Senior grade, they had to realize the parts of a figured bass, harmonize a melody and write specimens of counterpoint, covering all species in up to three parts. Those who succeeded in passing the Rudiments paper then had a little more preparation time before their Practical exams, which were scheduled to begin from 10 March. The syllabus gave the exam requirements only for piano, organ, violin, cello and harp, already cast in the familiar pattern of scales and arpeggios, studies and pieces. The rubric stated that candidates in other instruments would be accepted, but that they should request their syllabus directly from the Board, a strong indication that such entries were considered unlikely to be received in numbers that justified the additional printing costs of including them in the syllabus itself. The next year's 1891 syllabus is more specific: it invites players of the viola, double bass and woodwind instruments to apply to the Board should they need syllabuses for their instruments; however, there is no reference to brass instruments at all, a reflection of how self-contained was the training provided by the brass band world.

The smooth progress of these preparations was disturbed by the news that a Dr Illiffe of Oxford was running a venture on his own account called 'Preparatory Local Examinations' designed to cover the same subjects being offered in the Board's exams. According to Illiffe's Prospectus, his own syllabus was 'drawn up to supply a need felt in several Local Centres, of a good Preparatory Examination, specially designed to lead Candidates on the way to the more difficult one of the Royal Academy and the Royal College of Music. Though not officially connected with them, it therefore follows as closely as possible – consistent with its preparatory nature – the lines indicated by that examination', and the examiner would be 'a London musician of eminence'. The entry fee was half a guinea, and the syllabus said that after expenses had been deducted, the proceeds would be handed over to the treasurer of the RCM. This presented the Board with a difficult situation. Their immediate response was to make it clear through the press that 'our Board desire to make it known that no local examinations, "preparatory" or otherwise, are authorised or recognised by us as being in anyway connected with our local examinations'.[20] Whether it is a historical legacy of Illiffe's initiative or not, even today the Oxford Music Service continues to offer its own music exams from Initial to Grade 5.[21]

Examiners had been asked to provide the Board with some feedback of their experiences of these first exams to guide the planning for the 1891 exams, which began at the Governing Body meeting on 11 June 1890. Responsibilities for setting the 1891 syllabus were quickly allocated: Mackenzie and Parry were to draw up the Theory syllabus, Taylor and Westlake do the same for the piano (so

---

[20] ABMB1: 4 February 1890.

[21] www.oxfordshire.gov.uk/cms/content/instrumental-exams, accessed 29 October 2011.

neatly pairing the Schools), Mackenzie the violin, Parratt the organ, Howell the cello, Randegger singing, and the famous harpist John Thomas to prepare the syllabus for that instrument. It is worth repeating the point that this selection of instruments makes very clear what the Board considered to be its candidate market. Planning continued at the meeting on 28 June, which heard that the cost of supplying 20,000 copies of the syllabus was £68 7s 6d, and the printers quoted a slightly reduced price if it made an order for a further 10,000 copies. The decision made was to order just the 20,000, and in this the Board was mistakenly cautious, as 22,500 were reported to have been distributed by November 1890 – an indication of the level of interest already being shown in these exams.[22] It was also decided to institute a new 'honours' category for candidates awarded 135 or higher out of the maximum of 150 marks, and in a fair-minded gesture, it was agreed to make this category apply retrospectively to the 1890 exams.[23]

The final results of the 1890 exams were reported to the Governing Body meeting on 28 June. Of the 1,141 entries (764 for the Senior grade, 377 for the Junior), sixty-three failed their Rudiments and so could not take the Local Exam itself, and 160 took advantage of the latitude the Board had introduced, because of the shortage of time, to allow those who had passed the Rudiments paper to postpone their Practical subject exam until the 1891 session, provided that they played pieces from the new, 1891 syllabus, and so would not gain the advantage of further preparation time. After absentees had been accounted for, 904 candidates actually sat the Local Exams, of whom 431 (48%) passed. Those fortunate candidates who had survived the arduous demands and passed the first exams enjoyed public acknowledgement of their achievement in the shape of Distribution of Certificates ceremonies, which over time came to be popular across the country and were valuable in raising the Board's profile. For several years, minor royalty would attend the London distributions, considerably increasing their cachet. Over time, however, these public distributions generated periodic turf-wars between HLRs and the Board, the usual points of contention being the format of these ceremonies, the question of whether the guest of honour should be a senior member of the Board or a local notable, and whether or not successful candidates should risk the reputation of all concerned by making a further attempt at their once well-practised pieces – successive minute books refer to unfortunate performances that cast considerable doubt about the validity of the certificate that a successful candidate was receiving.

Financially, things had also gone well, with the major costs being the examiners' fees (£809) and expenses (£178) and Local Centre expenses (£150). On the basis of the figures given in the minute book as listed above, the Board's income had been some £2,330, less start-up costs of £472 and the costs of running the exams of £1,137, leaving a balance of £721. The Board was therefore able to repay £100 each to the College and the Academy, and as a mark of appreciation it gave Watson a gift of £250 (a sizeable proportion of his likely annual salary), 'in recognition of the very great services rendered to the Board by Mr Watson during the twelve months

[22] ABMB1: 12 November 1890.
[23] Ibid.

that he has acted as their secretary'.[24] After the payment of expenses and the other disbursements, the Board was left with a balance of £271 that was available to set up and run the 1891 exams. These figures throw interesting light on exam board economics. Income is advanced from candidates paying for a service they will receive at a later date. Revenue before the real expenses fall due minimizes the need for capitalization (effectively limited to direct start-up costs), and as long as the candidate numbers are healthy and expenses are under control, there should be no cash-flow problems. The small proportion of capital investment to set against potential income helps explain why music exams could be such lucrative operations, and why they were especially attractive to bogus exam boards who could operate as a cottage industry on a very small scale. It was confirmed at the 28 June meeting that the Board's Annual General Meeting would be presided over by the Prince of Wales at his official residence, Marlborough House – further indication of royal involvement for the development of British musical education. A celebratory dinner was also arranged, for HLRs, examiners and Board members, though participants were required to pay for themselves.

Local School Examinations

P ROMPTED by Illiffe's scheme of preparatory exams, the Board decided to run its own in 1891, called 'Local School Examinations', for which a much lower entry fee would be charged than for the senior Local Centre Exams.[25] Local School candidates would not be required to pass a preliminary paperwork exam, and these 'School Examinations' would be conducted by a single examiner – an important point of distinction between them and the senior Local Centre Exams with their panel of two examiners. The name Local School Examinations was misleading (its purpose was to signify a junior learning stage), because it was not intended that these exams be confined to schools, but that they be available to private teachers too. The decision to set up these School Examinations transformed the educational effectiveness of the Board's work, and also revolutionized its economic potential. It immediately established a four-grade structure, a move which opened up the Board's scheme to a higher volume of entries from a wider level of accomplishment, and with the opportunity to expand further as more School Exam or Junior Grades were gradually instituted. A well-established characteristic of grade exams is that they consist of a large candidate base at the lower grades that gradually tapers away as the numbers taking the higher grades fall off. This explains why School Exam entries were to grow at a much greater pace than those for the Local Centre Exams. But in only its second year and with no market testing to guide it, the Board may not have anticipated this difference, nor foreseen its economic and logistical implications. Certainly the minutes of the meeting that set up these School Exams give no indication that the far-reaching effects of these Junior Grades were envisaged.

[24] ABMB1: 28 June 1890; this *ex gratia* payment reinforces the sense of Watson's vital role at the Board, a job he had been doing simultaneously with his own work at the RCM and his consultancy at the RAM.

[25] ABMB1: 11 June 1890.

As always under Watson, the immediate administrative process of School Exams was well thought through. Those wishing to enter pupils had first to pay an annual two-guinea registration fee (lowered the next year to one guinea) to the Board, a fee that helped offset the operational expenses in light of the lower entrance fee being charged to School Exam candidates. The registration process (a means by which the Board could decide whether to accept or decline entries) was also a logistical safeguard that allowed the Board to assess for itself the feasibility and cost of examiners' travel to each applicant location. (The fledgling organization was not yet in the position to commit to provide a fully national service, something that unconstrained acceptance of School Exam entries would have entailed.) The other safeguard was that a minimum number of ten entries was required from any one location before an examiner would be sent. In the event, 153 schools and thirty-seven teachers had registered for the first School Exams in 1891, and 1,812 candidates had entered, each paying a half-guinea fee, with 303 taking additional subjects at 5s each, making a total of 2,115 examinations to be carried out, and producing an income of over £1,400.[26] The School examiners were paid 5s. per candidate, plus travel and an out-of-London subsistence of £1. They came from the original list of examiners with some other illustrious additions, 'whose names and position in the Musical Profession afford the fullest guarantee for the thoroughness of the School Examinations'. Certainly the Board was offering a Rolls-Royce service, but – ominously – the Annual Report revealed that by July 1891 as many as 676 of these School Exam candidates still remained to be examined: the consequence of attracting a large number of candidates for examination by a small number of very prestigious examiners. The service the Board was providing was already very overstretched.

The success of the Board's first exams embedded two principles that in practice would prove restrictive and increasingly awkward. One was the requirement for a candidate to pass the Preliminary paper before proceeding to the Practical exam itself. This helps explain the high cost of these exams: entry in one musical subject was 2 guineas, plus a further guinea for any additional subject entered. If the candidate failed the Preliminary paper, then half the original fee (i.e. one guinea) would be returned and the candidate had to start from scratch again the following year. This linkage of Rudiments with Practical exams has remained a sometimes contentious issue that the Board has dealt with in different ways over its history without ever quite relinquishing the principle. As we shall see, the later attempt to introduce a voluntary Rudiments paper nearly fractured the Board. The second principle was to use two examiners for the Local Centre Exams. Originally, the Board did this as a powerful selling point, and in its introductory circular it stated that 'the presence of two Examiners at each Centre indicates the thoroughness with which it is intended they [the exams] shall be conducted'. Problems soon developed: one was that as entries to the Local Centre Exams increased, so did the logistical problems of securing two examiners for sufficient periods of time (indeed, two examiners were never provided for these grades when conducted overseas because it was simply not feasible); another was the cost burden that this provision imposed on the Board. Even so, the Board held to the two-examiner

[26] *Second Annual Report of the Board* (1891), 21.

principle for Local Centre Exams until 1933, when it was forced to rationalize its scheme.

In 1891 the *MT* wrote enthusiastically about the first two years of the ABRSM's activity. Though the *MT* had an advertising interest in the Board's success, the editorial is still interesting for how it saw the benefits of the ABRSM's scheme. It felt that exams by the Royal Schools would be perceived as carrying the weight of the university-conducted exams (i.e. the Oxford and Cambridge Local Exams) because of the RSMs' chartered status, by having two eminent examiners conducting each Local Centre Exam and because of the 'gentlemen of influence and position' who performed the role of HLRs. The *MT* saw the ABRSM's exams as a means for enabling parents 'at a very moderate cost' to discover 'if their children are obtaining good music lessons' and also an opportunity for heads of schools to be able to test 'the quality of the music teaching in their establishments'. This, the *MT* argued, was necessary because, 'notwithstanding our musical progress, incompetent and neglectful teachers may still be found in considerable numbers'.[27] The ABRSM's exams represented a benefit because they would help increase the provision of the sort of good-quality music teaching that was necessary to sustain what the *MT* saw as the changes and improvements in British musical life. Clearly the ABRSM's entry into the music examination field was considered to represent an advance for British musical life.

[27] *MT* 32 (December 1891), 717–18.

4 The Early History, 1892–1920

∥ The exams

A s far as the Board's work in the UK is concerned, the period 1892 until 1914 was essentially one of consolidation that saw only a cautious expansion of its scheme of exams. The success of its early exams created a demand for additional ones to cater for a wider gamut of musical levels and abilities, particularly at the earlier stages, but the Board seemed reluctant to extend the scope of its examination scheme much beyond what had originally been envisaged. It is worth emphasizing quite how limited the original scheme was. Tables 4.1 and 4.2 trace the development of the Practical and Written exam structure from 1890 until 1933. The first shows that the original two Local Centre Exams of 1890 were the equivalent of today's Grades 6 and 7, an advanced stage for which there was no opportunity to prepare. Even the first two 'School' exams (now Grades 4 and 5), instituted in response to requests for exams at a preparatory stage to the Local Centre Exams, were still relatively ambitious. But the Board did not respond very quickly in providing lower grade exams: Elementary (Grade 2) was introduced in 1897 and Primary (Grade 1) only in 1906. Unfortunately, the only record of developments between 1891 and 1905 is in the published Annual Reports; the minute books for these years, with their details of decisions and underlying debates, are missing. But it is reasonable to infer that it took the Board quite a long time to face up to the longer-term implications of its initial success. It could only provide a wider range of exams if it was ready to expand its administration, and an expanded ABRSM would have placed a significant additional responsibility upon the heads of the RAM and the RCM. In other words, it is likely that while the Schools had looked forward to the income they might expect from their exams, they had not anticipated what would be involved in satisfying market need and running a more comprehensive examination scheme. It was only after its reconstitution in 1985 that the ABRSM really began to invent itself in proper business terms, investing some of its profits in the research and development of a new product range. Until then it was essentially a reactive, unbusiness-like institution, relying exclusively on variants of its 1890 examination prototype, and with no sense of any need to do otherwise.

Given how ill-equipped the Board was to cope with the logistical pressures of even its UK context, it seems extraordinary that so early on it should have sought to export its exams to the Empire. But the impetus to do so originated from the responsibilities spelled out by the RCM's royal charter,[1] and this development was undertaken very much in the sense of fulfilling a cultural obligation. Making the Board's exams available in far-flung Empire communities (helping them retain a sense of cultural affinity with the mother country) was very much in keeping with the psychology underlining the idea of the 'British World'. So the muddling through which exporting these exams involved (discussed in Chapter 5) was more representative of heroic endeavour than an under-resourced commercial venture.

[1] As in the responsibility as an examining body to advance 'the encouragement and promotion of the cultivation of music as an art throughout Our Dominions'.

Table 4.1 Levels in ABRSM Practical Examinations, 1890–1933

Levels of Practical Exams, 1890–1932	Equivalent Levels in Practical Grades, 1932/3[‡]
Preliminary Division* (1929)	Preliminary Exam (abolished 1949)
Primary Division* (1906)	Grade 1 (Primary)
Elementary Division* (1897)	Grade 2 (Elementary)
—	Grade 3 (Transitional) [new exam in 1933]
Lower Division* (1890)	Grade 4 (Lower)
Higher Division* (1890)	Grade 5 (Higher)
Junior Grade[†] (1890) → Intermediate Grade (1904)	Grade 6 (Intermediate)
Senior Grade[†] (1890) → Advanced Grade (1904)	Grade 7 (Advanced)
Final Grade[†] (1922)	Grade 8 (Final)

Dates of introduction are shown in parentheses.

* 'Divisions' denoted School Exams (LSE)   † 'Grades' denoted Local Centre Exams (LCE)

‡ The single eight-grade exam series was instituted in 1933.

Notes: (1) From 1890 to 1903 no candidate below the age of twelve was accepted for examination; the Junior Grade was restricted to candidates aged twelve to fifteen; candidates aged sixteen and above could enter only for the Senior Grade, although there was no bar on younger candidates. When age restrictions were abolished in 1904, these grades were renamed 'Intermediate' and 'Advanced'.

(2) From the 1932/3 exams the 'Honours' category was replaced by 'Distinction'.

This spirit of cultural *noblesse oblige* was underlined by the fact that for many years the Colonial exams were run at a deficit, cross-subsidized by the UK income. In 1898/9 it was reported that running the Colonial exams had cost the Board some £1,400.[2]

The Board's UK income increased significantly when it added new lower Divisions (Elementary and Primary) to its School Exams; indeed, the Primary Division constituted 19% of all School Exam entries when it was first run in 1906. The dominant instrument, by far, of both the LCE and LSE categories was the piano, and only very occasionally was a flute, clarinet or oboe examined. The first thirty years of LCE exams (1890–1919) had entries from only two oboes, two clarinets, six flutes, two cornets, two trombones and six undefined 'other instruments'. Piano, stringed instruments, singing and harp confirm the Board's drawing-room cultural market, and organ its Anglican ethos. LCE entries for 1910 are indicative of this trend: piano 3,550; organ 34; violin 415; cello 20; viola 1; harp 7; oboe 1; singing 152. Initially LCEs were offered only once a year in the spring. From 1902 a second exam session was held in London during November/December, and because entry was not confined to a candidate's own geographical location, out-of-London candidates could enter in this second period. Winter exams were

---

[2] *Tenth Annual Report of the Board* (1899), 19.

Table 4.2 Levels in ABRSM Written Examinations, 1890–1933

Levels of written exams, 1890–1932	*Equivalent levels in Theory grade exams, 1933*
Grammar of Music	Grammar of Music (Theory)
Division I*	Grade 1
Division II*	Grade 2
Division III*	Grade 3
Rudiments of Music (1890–9)/ Elements of Music (1900)†	Grade 4

* 'Divisions' denoted School Exams (LSE)

† Prerequisite for the LCE Practical Exams

Note: From 1890 to 1899 the 'Rudiments of Music' was originally the prerequisite for either LCE Practical exam. In 1900 it was made voluntary and renamed 'Elements of Music', but from 1901 all Practical candidates had to sit it. Those who failed could still take the Practical, but would forfeit nine marks.

offered in the main provincial cities from 1907, and gradually their availability spread, until from 1924 they were offered at all UK centres. It was only after the 1933 reorganization of the exams into a single, eight-grade series that the higher grades could be taken three times a year, as now. This was because the 1933 reform abolished the two-examiner assessment of LCEs, a provision that had become a logistical nightmare. This change to a single examiner thus made it possible to hold the higher grades on the same basis as the others. The Theory exams were held in March and December in all centres from 1904. Initially LSEs were held on a flexible basis, with each school given four weeks' notice of the date the examiner would attend; during 1892–7 they were offered four times a year before settling into the familiar pattern of three exam periods a year: A (March–April), B (June–July), C (October–November). The Board first offered its Exhibitions (now Scholarships) in 1898, when two were offered, one at each RSM. They were tenable for two years and conditional upon an Honours pass in an LCE exam and a previous pass in an LSE, so tying aspirant scholars firmly into the ABRSM system. In 1889 the Exhibitions were increased to six (three at each RSM), and there was an award of a Gold Medal for the highest Honours marks in the Senior and Junior grades, and a Silver Medal to the second highest candidate. The Exhibitions were especially valuable awards, and good public relations for the Board and for the Schools, too. They ensured that the very best players could afford RSM training. (Occasionally a rich family exchanged a scholarship for a fee-paying place so that the scholarship could go to a poorer student; this act was acknowledged with the title 'Honorary Scholar'.)

From 1930, candidates were automatically sent a report with examiners' comments supporting the marks they awarded. Until then the Board's view was that:

Experience confirms the Board in their opinion that it is undesirable for Candidates to be made acquainted with the number of marks which they may have obtained; but, on payment of a small enquiry fee, information as

Table 4.3 Assessment criteria for Piano and Violin from 1896 Local Centre Exam syllabus

Piano	Violin
• Excellence of Scales and Arpeggios	• Posture – holding Violin and Bow
• Accuracy as to Notes, Rests, and Signs of Legato and Staccato	• Excellence of Scales and Arpeggios
	• Intonation
• Correctness of Fingering (there is no restriction as to fingering Technical Exercises)	• Accuracy as to Notes and Rests
	• Production of Tone (includes action of Bow and Firmness of Stop)
• Strictness of Time, and choice of Tempo (including use of Tempo Rubato where suitable)	• Dexterity of Fingering (includes Brilliancy and Velocity)
	• Facility in varied Bowing
• Observance of Phrasing and Accent	• Strictness of Time, and Choice of Tempo
• Accuracy of note-values in Part-playing	• Gradation of Tone
• Variety, Gradation and Balance of Tone	• Phrasing and Accent
• Quality of Touch	• Reading at Sight
• Discretion in use of Pedal	
• Reading at Sight	

to the causes of failure will be given on a form prepared for that purpose, showing under what heads the Candidates failed to satisfy the Examiners.[3]

An example of 'heads' can be seen in Table 4.3, which gives the assessment criteria for piano and violin for the 1896 LCE syllabus. The examiners noted a mark against each criterion, but all the candidate then received was a simple honours/pass/fail notification. Those seeking to improve their result after a fail could then send in the 2s 6d enquiry fee to discover under which criteria they had fallen below the pass level. Interestingly, these violin criteria omit any mention of vibrato. As Clive Brown points out, the turn of the century saw a division in playing styles between the German and the Franco-Belgian schools, with Kreisler and Ysaÿe of the latter both advocates of constant vibrato.[4] The influential tutor by Joachim and Moser recognized 'the steady tone as the ruling one', with vibrato only selectively used, and not as an inherent aspect of tone production. Interestingly, the School Primary and Elementary Divisions in 1906 specify technical exercises and a study from the Joachim and Moser *Violinschule* (1905). In the first ABRSM exams candidates and their teachers had been given little choice in the matter of music. Until 1898 there was a single piano list each year, after which three lists (each with three pieces and three studies) were published annually, which must have afforded some relief to piano teachers. Table 4.4 has the LCE piano lists (Junior and Senior grades) for 1901, which indicates the sort of repertoire selected for these exams and illustrates the Board's cultural outlook. It is beyond the scope of this book to attempt the systematic comparison of the repertory set for ABRSM grades necessary to assess its consistency of standards in setting exam pieces. And even then the question of the standards that examiners applied at any one time

[3] *Second Annual Report of the Board* (1891), 22.

[4] Clive Brown, *Classical & Romantic Performing Practice, 1750–1900* (Oxford: Oxford University Press, 1999), 534.

Table 4.4 Music prescribed for Piano Local Centre Examinations in 1901

Junior Grade

List A	List B	List C
Studies:	*Studies:*	*Studies:*
Bach, Two-part Invention no. 5 in E♭	Bach, Two-part Invention no. 4 in d	Bach, Prelude no. 2 in c
Paradies, Toccata in A	Czerny, Study in E, op. 299/33	Cramer, Study no. 9 in G
Heller, Study in g, op. 47/14	Cramer, Study no. 13 in A	Heller, Study in D, op. 46/12
Pieces:	*Pieces:*	*Pieces:*
Haydn, Sonata in F, 1st mvt (Peters 713B, no. 13)	Clementi, Sonata in f♯, 1st mvt	Goetz, Sonatina in F, 1st mvt
Mozart, Andante Cantabile, Sonata in C (Peters 486 no. 2)	Beethoven, Bagatelle in A, op. 33/4	Chopin, Valse in a, op. 34/2
Schubert, Momens musicals no. 3 in f, op. 94	Rubinstein, Romance in E♭, op. 44/1	Hiller, 'Ständchen' (*Albumblatt*)

Senior Grade

List A	List B	List C
Studies:	*Studies:*	*Studies:*
Bach, Three-part Invention no. 9 in f	Bach, Fugue in d (*48* Book I)	Clementi, Study in D, no. 8 of *Gradus*
Loeschhorn, Study in C, op. 118/1	Moscheles, Study in E♭, op. 70/11	Bennett, Study in c, op. 11/1
Mendelssohn, Prelude in b (no. 2 of Three Preludes)	Chopin, Study in B♭, op. 28/21	Heller, Study in d, op. 16/24
Pieces:	*Pieces:*	*Pieces:*
Hummel, Rondo in b, op. 109	Beethoven, Sonata in A♭, op. 26, 1st mvt	Bach, Sinfonie, *Partita* no. 2
Chopin, Polonaise in c, op. 40/2	Schumann, *Fantasiestücke*, op. 111/3	Raff, Valse 'L'Espiègle', op. 125/3
Jensen, 'Dryade', no. 4 of *Idylles*	Tchaikovsky, 'Feuillet d'Album' in D	Schumann, 'Novellette', *Bunte Blätter*, no. 9

remains speculative until we reach the point when the recording and videoing of performances for examiners' training seminars gives us the necessary evidence. But just for interest, five of these pieces in the 1901 Junior Grade – today's Grade 6 – have appeared in lists since 1971: Invention no. 4 at Grade 5, but the Mozart, Schubert, Paradies and Beethoven at Grade 6 (although in its most recent appearance, in 1999/2000, the Paradies was set for Grade 7).

Two educational facets long associated with the Board's exams are the theory element and aural tests. The requirement that Grade 5 Theory was the prerequisite for taking the higher Practical grades has long been a familiar hurdle on the grade landscape, and as we have seen, originally it was obligatory to pass a Rudiments paper before the Practical exam could be taken. In 1900 the Rudiments element was actually scrapped, only to be restored the next year in an amended form. From 1901 it was no longer conditional to *pass* the Theory in order to take the Practical. However, those who failed the Theory automatically forfeited nine marks from their Practical total. This penalty – which effectively put that candidate out of the running for an Honours award – reinforced the importance with which the Board viewed musical literacy. The public explanation for the Board's 1900/1901 change of mind over the Preliminary Rudiments exam (now called 'Elements of Music'), was that making the paper entirely voluntary was 'not proving conducive to the best interests of Musical Education'.[5] In fact there had been a power tussle within the Board. The loss of the minute books for the period makes some of this difficult to reconstruct, but what has survived is a partial account of the circumstances set out by the Honorary Secretary to the Board, Samuel Aitken.[6]

Little is known about Aitken, although a manuscript annotation in the proof score of Sullivan's *Golden Legend* suggests they were friends. Aitken was Honorary Treasurer of the Academy, on its Committee of Management and one of the Academy's Representatives on the ABRSM. In 1896 power within the ABRSM shifted from the College to the Academy as Aitken succeeded George Watson as Honorary Secretary (i.e. not salaried), and Thomas Threlfall, the Academy's Chairman, became ABRSM Chairman after the RCM's Lord Bruce died. The RAM's new dominance on the Board seems to have put the RCM's nose very much out of joint, for after Aitken's arrival, Parry seems to have taken a back seat, not speaking or making a report to the Board's dinners in 1897 and 1898. Aitken's financial grip and his commercial focus seem to have alienated Parry further, as Aitken's comment, 'It would not be a bad thing if some of our eminent musicians had a little less counterpoint and a little more commerce in their composition', seems to confirm.[7] The final break appears to have been caused by Aitken's impatience with what he felt was the way that the obligatory Preliminary Examination hampered the growth of LCE candidates, as well as the logistical difficulties it imposed on the Colonial exams. It seems, therefore, that Aitken pushed through the new, voluntary 'Elements of Music' theory exam against Parry's wishes. There then followed an acrimonious exchange, the upshot of which was that the Board preferred to lose its Secretary, for all the capacity he had demonstrated, rather than the RCM's Director for fear of the fracture that would cause. After Aitken's departure, compulsory sitting of 'Elements' returned from 1901. As Aitken averred in his pamphlet, 'it was nothing short of an attempt to re-introduce the preliminary examination'.[8]

Given the importance the Board attached to musical literacy, it is interesting that there was no compulsory aural testing element in the Practical exams until 1921. It was acknowledged that this was an innovation that 'may frighten some people very much … I think that it will be found that aural tests are not the "bogey" that they may at first be thought by some, and I am sure they will be approved

---

[5] *Eleventh Annual Report of the Board* (1900), 14.

[6] Samuel Aitken, *The Associated Board … and Its Honorary Secretary* (privately printed, 6 February 1900).

[7] Ibid., 15.

[8] Ibid., 4.

by all musicians who come into contact with the work of the Board.'[9] With the institution of compulsory aural tests, the framework of the Practical grades as we know them today was complete.

⁄⁄⁄ Examiners and complaints

T HE Board's examiners have always been complained about, but the way that complaints are received and treated tell us a great deal about the institutional culture prevailing at any time. As Chapter 12 discusses, today's complaints receive a very different sort of reaction from some of those from the past. For much of its history, the Board treated complaints on an *ad hominem* basis, according to the eminence or otherwise of the examiner or complainant involved. It seemed oblivious to the fact that distinguished musicians who undertook their examining activity only out of financial necessity might resent it, and so have been more prone to vent their frustration on a hapless or inadequate candidate than examiners who actually enjoyed the work. The fact was that the early ABRSM relied upon the distinction of its examining panel to establish its primacy, and from the outset it was resolute in holding to the line that its examiners' judgement and behaviour were beyond reproach. The semantic wriggles which this often involved are paralleled in today's essentially meaningless cliché that 'lessons have been learned'. Physical incapacity through drink, however, defied even the most elegant explanation, and the examiner was mostly dropped, but not always. So when a complaint was received that a Mr O'Leary was not physically fit to conduct the examination and that he had asked candidates to perform certain work not contained in the syllabus, it was decided not to use him for School Examinations again. At first sight, the implication might seem to be that the older LCE candidates would be better able to cope with a drunk examiner, but because LCEs were conducted by two examiners (School Exams had one), the Board's disinclination to sack O'Leary meant that the onus fell firmly on his co-examiner to keep him off the drink, or at least supine enough so that the exams could be conducted without further embarrassment. Trickier was a complaint against the eminent organist Dr Walter Alcock, who had seemingly unnerved a candidate by telling him to play a passage until it was correct. Parry undertook to speak to Alcock himself, and the explanation given to the complainant was that Alcock's intention 'had been merely with a view to encouraging the pupils to do better'. Sometimes the complaints built up so that, despite pressures to field sufficient examiners, the consequences were simply not worth it. Many complaints were received against a Dr Hoyte concerning his results in general and in particular that one School candidate had been made to play a scale from the top of the Piano. In reply, the complainant was told that the examiner had no recollection of the occurrence, that if such a mistake were made the Board regrets it, but does not consider it important enough to have prejudiced the result of the examination. Hoyte, however, was dropped from School examining.[10]

[9] *Thirty-first Annual Report of the Board* (1920), 17; Ear Training and Sight Singing had previously been available as a separate Practical subject.
[10] ABMB4: 29 May, 26 June 1906.

One of the Board's most celebrated, and most complained about, examiners was Frederic Cliffe (1857–1931), whose Australian exploits are discussed in Chapter 5. A man of immense personal resourcefulness, capacity and courage, it is possible that his frequent bouts of irascibility and bad temper reflected the frustrations of professional underachievement. Initially celebrated as a brilliant composer as well as a pianist, it had all seemed to come to nothing. His pupils, of whom Arthur Benjamin was the most celebrated, speak of him as inspiring in matters of interpretation, but sarcastically defensive and inadequate in his technical guidance.[11] In May 1911 it was decided to tell Cliffe of the range of complaints made about his manner of conducting examinations because they were bringing the Board into disrepute. In February 1913 a serious situation arose at a school, and a vote was taken as to whether Otto Beringer should be sent to 'test the complaints in situ'. The result was a draw, so Beringer did not go, but it was decided that Cliffe should not be used again for School Exams, and at the next meeting the Chairman, Sir William Bigge, reported that he had told Cliffe of 'the serious concern which is felt at the recurrence of complaints against him'. Evidently contrite, and realizing he had probably gone too far, Cliffe wrote a letter, which was read out at the next meeting, asking for reconsideration of his case, and it was decided to leave him in suspense before making any decision. In October 1914 two of Cliffe's RCM colleagues, Eaton Fanning and Stanford, proposed that he again be allowed to examine in School Exams. This was carried, seven to one, with four abstentions, and so Cliffe was reinstated; he was obviously relieved, because he sent the Board a letter of thanks.[12]

More unusually, a complaint was received from the Cape Department of Public Education in South Africa concerning the fact that a teacher had been dismissed from her teaching post because of the report of one of the Board's examiners. Here, the Board wrote back distancing itself from the examiner, who had 'exceeded his instructions', and expressing its extreme regret at the circumstances.[13] While ill temper and drink were usual causes for complaint, an examiner's morality was rarely questioned. One exception was a senior examiner, and later a member of the Board's Governing Body. He had been accused by the headmistress of a school in Somerset of molesting girl candidates, but it seems that the accusations had been modified after being first laid, and their seriousness then downplayed. The muddle was further compounded by the fact that the headmistress had then said that she would be prepared for this examiner to return and examine at the school again. This complaint, however, was treated very seriously indeed, and heard at a Special Meeting on 18 July 1913, with the full Governing Body in attendance. The minutes record:

> The charges now only amount to this, that [the examiner], from fatherly motives, and from a desire to put the Candidates at their ease, committed certain acts, the propriety of which was doubtful, but the motives for which were pure and right and absolutely free from all blame. How completely

[11] See Arthur Benjamin, 'A Student in Kensington', *Music & Letters* 31/3 (July 1950), 196–207; Howard Hadley, 'Frederic Cliffe', *RCM Magazine* 28/1 (1932), 21–2.

[12] ABMB4: 23 May 1911; ABMB5: 11 February 1913; 13 and 27 October 1914.

[13] ABMB4: 14 May 1907.

he is exonerated is shown by the desire which [the complainant] greatly emphasized he will examine her school again.

With no further knowledge of the case itself, additional comment is superfluous, but the Board's response in calling a fully attended Special Meeting shows that it was keenly aware of the reputational damage that could have been caused. And although the Board must have been very certain that the examiner was not guilty in terms of his intention before later accepting him on the Governing Body, the knowledge of his peers, and the phrase in the minute book, 'committed certain acts, the propriety of which was doubtful', is likely to have overshadowed him throughout his time there.

⁄⁄⁄ The organization

MUCH of the administrative detail noted in the surviving minute books of this period is relatively mundane, but there were some important changes. One was the Board's relocation from Hanover Square to 15 Bedford Square, its headquarters until 2000. This took place in 1907, and the first Governing Body meeting in the new offices was held on 15 October. The outlay required to secure the new building prompted the setting up of a sub-committee, 'The Committee on the General Working, Expenditure and Revenue of the Board', which included the financier Charles Rube, and the new Chairman, William (later, Sir William) Bigge. The Board was lucky in securing Bigge, who was the younger brother of Lord Stamfordham, Private Secretary to King George V and on the Council of the RCM. Rube and Bigge injected a new administrative efficiency into the Board and its finances. Not long after the Bedford Square move, Stanford reported to the Governing Body that Parry's doctor had insisted that he be relieved of all his Board responsibilities following a breakdown in health that caused him to resign his Oxford Professorship.[14] This presented the legal problem of whether, under the original Agreement of 1889 that constituted the Board, Parry could appoint a deputy on a permanent basis for the time he continued as the RCM's Director. In the event, Parry continued to attend the Board's meetings, but the situation underlined the need to consolidate the several existing agreements governing the Board's constitution into one comprehensive legal agreement defining its financial and operational basis. The revised agreement covered matters such as the constitution of the Board's Governing Body and the amount to be held in financial reserve before distribution between the College and the Academy; it also renewed the formal authorization (originally given in 1896) for the Board to pay the expenses incurred in holding its exams overseas (effectively covering members of the Board for any losses incurred in doing so). This revised Agreement, dated 12 January 1910, remained in force until the Board's reconstitution with a new partnership arrangement in 1985. Parry died in October 1918 and was succeeded as Director of the RCM by Hugh Allen, whose presence and forceful personality reinvigorated the Board to new purpose.

[14] See Jeremy Dibble, *C. Hubert H. Parry: His Life and Music* (Oxford: Oxford University Press, 1992), 422–4.

3 Bedford Square, London, where the ABRSM had its headquarters from 1907 to 2000. The boardroom was in no. 14, above the second front door from the left. In 1989 the lease of no. 13 was acquired (the third front door from the left). As the organization grew, the restrictions in access between the individual buildings rendered them increasingly impractical as offices.

⁊⁊ The First World War

G IVEN the appalling number of casualties in the First World War which affected nearly every British family, it seems perverse to suggest that in some respects civilian life was less disrupted during that time than it would be in the Second World War. But even though bombardment of coastal towns and Zeppelin raids demonstrated that 'civilian status no longer conferred immunity',[15] civilian society was not to experience the dislocating effects of widespread direct action, such as the air attacks on British cities, which made for the total involvement of the population in the Second World War. Table 4.5 shows a falling-off in candidates for the Board's LCEs during the war years, while the numbers for School Exams continued to grow. Peacetime, however, brought a very quick recovery in LCE numbers. What these figures suggest is that throughout the war the expansion of middle-class music tuition continued without check at the more junior levels; the decline was in the older age groups as the effects of war and the prospect of war service loomed, especially for the officer classes, for whom concentration on sport and fitness might have seemed more essential than acquiring skill in art music.[16] The class implications of the increase in candidates for the School Exams are all the more striking because it came at a time of wartime disruption to state educational provision, when unenforced school attendance orders allowed adolescent labour to be recruited into agriculture and industry.[17] On the other hand, attendance at grammar schools grew from 187,000 in 1914 to 337,000 in 1920.[18]

Interestingly, the observable effect on the Board's exams was less extreme in the First World War than it was to be in the Second, which saw a sudden increase in candidate numbers, as Table 7.1 shows. But that surge may also reflect an uptake in music lessons in consequence of the government's encouragement of the arts as a morale-boosting measure, as well as a general determination to resume the normal pattern of civilian life as quickly as possible. As we see from Table 4.5, the Board's financial position was safeguarded by the continuing expansion of School Exam entries. The Board's exams were hit by the 1918 flu epidemic, and it was agreed that a full refund of fees (less 10%) would be given to schools or teachers obliged to withdraw all of their candidates where the fee paid was £5 or more. But even with these demands, the Board's financial position throughout the war years remained surprisingly strong. The reduction we see in the dividends paid to the London Schools was caused by poor investment performance and the need to put money into reserves; another expense came with the acquisition of the lease of 14 Bedford Square in 1918 (the premium to acquire it was £800) and necessary alterations which cost £2,612 in that year – but the opportunity to acquire that

---

[15] G. R. Searle, *A New England?: Peace and War, 1886–1918* (Oxford: Oxford University Press, 2004), 751.

[16] On the other hand, popular music in the form of patriotic songs and music hall ditties acquired great significance. See Andrew Horrall, *Popular Culture in London, c. 1890– 1918* (Manchester: Manchester University Press, 2001), 192–7.

[17] Searle, *A New England?*, 778.

[18] Michael Sanderson, *Education and Economic Decline in Britain 1870 to the 1990s*, 2nd edn (Cambridge: Cambridge University Press, 1999), 55.

Table 4.5 Entries to ABRSM Local Centre and School Exams, 1912/13–1920/21*

Year	LCE Practical[†]	LCE Rudiments[‡]	LSEs[§]	UK income	To RAM/RCM
1912/13	4,552	3,074	23,196	£24,461	£4,976
1913/14	4,590	3,040	25,416	£25,912	£5,100
1914/15	4,429	2,900	24,653	£24,707	£6,084
1915/16	4,140	2,898	25,338	£24,602	£2,603
1916/17	3,785	2,654	26,911	£24,654	£3,852
1917/18	3,669	2,656	30,879	£26,426	£4,413
1918/19	3,707	2,816	34,040	£28,509	£3,752
1919/20	4,020	3,121	35,699	£30,647	£3,111
1920/21	4,601	3,635	41,692	£35,233	£5,148

* The Board's year ran from 1 May to 30 April.

† Practical includes the small number taking papers in Harmony and/or Counterpoint as distinct, separate, subjects.

‡ Officially called 'Elements of Music'

§ All Practical subjects and Theory

next-door lease was just too good to pass up. These lower dividends hurt, however, certainly in the College's case, because wartime saw its student numbers drop to 246 in 1916 and to only 215 in 1918; its fee income collapsed from £15,822 in 1914 to £8,375 in 1918. Yet it is indicative of the underlying vitality of the demand for musical training that not only did the Board's LCE numbers recover so quickly following the war, but so also did the College's student numbers, which reached 426 in September 1919 and 589 the following September.[19]

The effect of the First World War on the institutional life of the Board very much reflected the spirit of the times. The Annual Lunch and the public distribution of certificates were suspended until 1919, and the Board felt some of the effects of strong anti-German feeling. Two of its examiners, Oscar Beringer and Hans Wessely, both volunteered to step down as examiners, and this was agreed, although they continued to sit on the Governing Body and Beringer still examined in South Africa. They were reinstated in 1919. On the other hand, the Board was happy to accept Parry's recommendation that one of its Exhibitioners at the RCM, Hyman Grünbaum, should have his award extended.[20] The Board changed its publisher from Augener to the more British-sounding Joseph Williams, and on one occasion it avoided the obviously Germanic genre-label 'Phantasiestuck' by the expedient of using Woldemar Bargiel's less German-sounding surname, listing his piece simply as Bargiel, op. 32, no. 1; however, it rejected one patriotic appeal that its publications should change from the 'Continental' to the 'British' system of fingering.[21]

[19] H. C. Colles and John Cruft, *The Royal College of Music: A Centenary Record, 1883–1983* (London: Prince Consort Foundation, 1982), 43–5.

[20] ABMB5: 27 October 1914; 9 February 1915; 29 October 1919.

[21] 'British' fingering denoted the thumb by a + and numbered the fingers as 1–4; ABMB5, 8 December 1914; 4 May 1915; 11 December 1917.

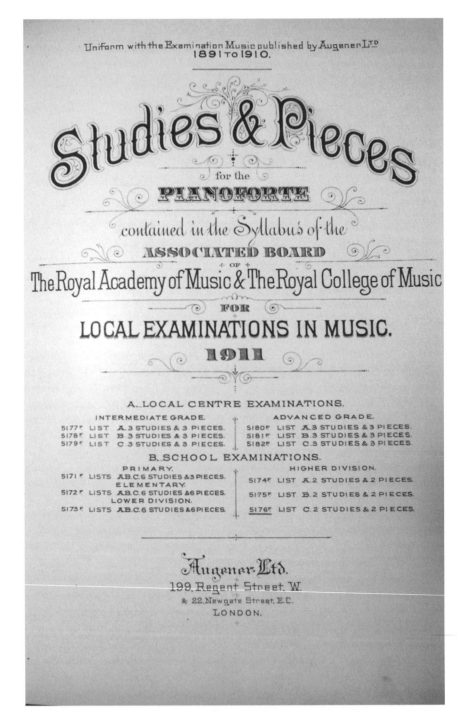

4 Difficulties with music publishers forced the ABRSM to establish its own publishing department in 1920. Augener was the Board's original publisher until 1914, when anti-German sentiment ended that relationship. Seemingly only the most extravagant potpourri of typefaces did justice to the ABRSM enterprise.

Meanwhile, the Board supported the war effort by buying War Loans and helping office staff on active service by making up the difference between their salary and the War Office allowance they received. However, in its treatment of its wounded Assistant Secretary, Mr Long, the Board was inexplicably harsh. Having originally promised Long that his job would be kept open, and despite a medical certificate and his wife's pleas, 'In view of the uncertainty of the date of Mr Long's return, it was decided to give him notice at once and to pay him six months' salary in lieu of notice.'[22] Inevitably, the Board was affected by the paper shortage. It discontinued publication of lists of successful candidates and their teachers (which had now become a very expensive exercise), which was very unpopular, and it reduced its piano list from six to five pieces. In 1918 it had to apply for a special concession from the Paper Controller for sufficient paper to produce exam music.[23]

The Board reflected in microcosm the broader social and economic effects of the war. From an all-male workforce at the outset of the conflict, the gender balance had shifted considerably, and new lavatory accommodation had to be provided for the rising number of female employees. Long, the Assistant Secretary, had been replaced by Miss Helen Benson, appointed on £150, half his salary. She was obviously impressive, for after four months her wage was increased to £200, 'in order that her salary should bear a proper relation to those of the staff generally'. When Miss Benson later had to take some months' medical leave, she was paid half her salary. By October 1916 there were at least eight female employees, and their pay was increased from 25 shillings per week to 30 shillings, which gave them parity with some of the male staff, an indication that they were valued.[24] The wage bill continued to rise because staff shortages pushed up salaries, and the Board struggled to retain its employees. In early 1916 the Board's Chairman, Sir William Bigge, made a survey of the employment conditions of clerical staff in other professional offices, and concluded that the pay and office hours of the Board's employees were in line, except in the matter of overtime. The pressures on the Board's staff at the peak exam periods had previously been met by consolidating the overtime that was worked into a 5% bonus on annual salary. However, wartime pressures increased the need for systematic overtime, and with the need to retain senior staff the bonus stood at 10% by the end of 1917, or double its pre-war level. As far as possible, the Board resisted putting temporary clerical staff ('extra clericals') on salaries, preferring to keep them on weekly payments and offering them a 'war bonus' as needed. By 1917 extra clericals alone were costing more than half the total amount paid in salaries before the war. Unsurprisingly, office working and salary levels are a regular feature of the minutes at this time.[25] Having gained more freedom, the office staff were naturally reluctant to relinquish it, and twenty-seven staff signed a memo requesting that office hours should end at 5 p.m. instead of 6 p.m. Attempting conciliation, the Chairman (now Ernest Mathews) met staff to ask if an additional summer holiday week would be acceptable as an alternative

[22] ABMB5: 26 October 1915; 13 February 1917; 18 February 1919.
[23] ABMB5: 16 May 1916; 9 January 1917; 14 May 1918.
[24] ABMB5: 16 November 1915; 14 March, 3 October 1916.
[25] ABMB5: 16 May, 20 June, 3 October 1916; 15 May, 30 October, 11 December 1917.

to the shortening of office hours, and this was agreed. However, in an attempt to regain control, a sub-committee was set up to 'consider the work and discipline of the office staff, and if necessary to interview Mr D. Garland, Chief Clerk, and to take such action as may be necessary'.[26]

The continuing growth in the numbers of School Exam candidates meant that by 1917 the Board was facing a serious shortage of examiners. Those who had applied to become examiners, such as W. H. Reed (Elgar's collaborator and Leader of the LSO), Ivor Atkins (Organist of Worcester Cathedral), George Dyson, Harold Samuel, Felix Swinstead and Colin Taylor (who taught and encouraged Philip Heseltine (Peter Warlock) at Eton), were offered the opportunity, on condition they would initially be prepared to undertake Colonial and School examining. But invitations also went out to cathedral organists such as Edward Bairstow (York), G. J. Bennett (Lincoln) and Herbert Brewer (Gloucester), as well as to the cellist William Squire to examine School Exams. Several (such as Atkins) refused to examine abroad, or (like G. J. Bennett) were so unenthusiastic in practice that their names were soon removed from the list. But it is difficult not to feel that there was some mismatch of expectations that tells us something about the status the Board felt it had accrued. The idea that the legendary Edward Bairstow (who commented that he had adjudicated at every music festival *once*) should have been prepared to be confined to examining only junior grades for the Board seems a very odd one, but the Board saw such work as a sort of rite of passage, 'in order to comply with the rule laid down by the Board as to the appointment of external Examiners [i.e. those not on the staff of the RAM and RCM]'. In other words, it felt that the chance to become a Board examiner was a valuable opportunity to those so invited, regardless of how eminent they were.[27] In 1919, for the first time, a committee was set up to sift the applications from would-be examiners, although staff at the Schools would be appointed by recommendation, as in the case of John Ireland, who was appointed in that year.[28] Wartime travel had made it very difficult to send examiners abroad. When one examiner had withdrawn from the hazardous journey of the Gibraltar and Malta tour in 1916, his successor was required to give a written assurance that he was undertaking the tour of his own free will. And in 1917 the difficulties of sending examiners to Australia and New Zealand were such that the examiners *in situ* were asked to stay on in readiness for the following year's examining, and most agreed to do so. Travel conditions remained difficult after the war, so when the University of South Africa requested seven examiners for the 1919 tour, this was agreed on condition that the University would defray examiners half their pay for any time wasted in securing their passage home.[29] The experience of the First World War had changed so much about British society, and in common with other institutions, the Board would find that the old certainties of pre-war life would no longer hold true. The ABRSM was fortunate that the new RCM Director, Hugh Allen, would be a leader of real energy who would give the organization the confidence to face the changed social conditions and new

[26] ABMB5: 18 March, 3 June 1919.

[27] ABMB5: 30 October 1917.

[28] ABMB5: 7 January, 11 February 1919.

[29] ABMB5: 18 March 1919.

technology of the inter-war years. Allen's huge personality tended to disguise the fact that he was no intellectual and had no real visionary sense, but underneath his drive was a pragmatism and decency that meant that his political wheeling and dealing would work very much to the RCM's and the Board's benefit.

5 The ABRSM and the 'British World'

⁄⁄ The 'British World' idea

THE ABRSM's exams contributed to the activity of cultural exchange that was constantly happening between Britain and its Empire. This chapter looks, albeit briefly, at some of what was involved with this aspect of the Board's history. Recent historiography has brought something of a sea change to explanations about the dynamics of Empire. Some historians have moved away from the traditional focus on nations and the history of regions to explore a more integrated view based on the idea of a community of Empire. The British Empire was characterized by the endless criss-crossing of its citizens, constantly on the move as they pursued mercantile, professional or jobbing interests, taking with them their cultural, social and religious views or values, shaping the perspectives of those they encountered along the way. Migration was another characteristic of Empire, with some motivated by the prospect of making new lives, and some by the hope of disappearing completely from their old ones. In other words, the everyday process of Empire involved the participation of ordinary people even more directly than it did the political wishes of a governing elite, something that has been referred to as 'globalization from below'. The ABRSM was very much part of this process of Empire, its examiners participating in this cavalcade of movement and exchange of networks that helped generate the cohesive force of what some historians have come to label the 'British World'.[1] We see from the Board's readiness to subsidize its Colonial exams out of UK-generated income that, as an institution, it was conscious that the RCM's founding charter effectively made the ABRSM an official participant in what John Darwin has so suggestively called 'The Empire Project'.[2] It is indicative that the accounts for the Australian exams over the thirty-one years (up to 1937/8) for which the figures are available show that the Board incurred deficits (ranging from £690 to £2,655) in eighteen out of the last nineteen of these years.

How can the British World idea be related to music education and learning instruments? The explanation is the influence exerted by the Board's syllabuses, its musical standards and the contacts between the examiners it sent out from London with local musicians and teachers. As well as this, the Board awarded Colonial Exhibitions to enable musicians from the Dominions to study in

---

[1] For a summary of this historiographical perspective, see Sarah Stockwell, 'Preface', in *The British Empire: Themes and Perspectives*, ed. Sarah Stockwell (Oxford: Blackwell Publishing, 2008), xi; Carl Bridge and Kent Fedorowich, 'Mapping the British World', in *The British World: Diaspora, Culture and Identity*, ed. Carl Bridge and Kent Fedorowich (London: Frank Cass, 2003), 6.

[2] See, *inter alia*, Richards, *Imperialism and Music*; Philip Buckner and R. Douglas Francis, *Rediscovering the British World* (Calgary: Calgary University Press, 2005); Andrew Thompson, *The Empire Strikes Back?: The Impact of Imperialism on Britain from the Mid-Nineteenth Century* (Harlow: Pearson Longman, 2005); John Darwin, *The Empire Project: The Rise and Fall of the British World-System, 1830–1970* (Cambridge: Cambridge University Press, 2009); I am most grateful to Andrew Dilley and Frank Bongiorno for encouraging me to explore this aspect.

London. The ABRSM's overseas exams – standing for the work of the London Royal Schools – were thus both a symbolic and practical means of keeping the musical communities of global British society in touch, despite daunting geographical distances, with the UK's musical world. And integral to this process – unifying in the more metaphysical sense – was the notion of the same exam pieces being learned and practised 'simultaneously' across the world; in the days before video-links and the other unifying capabilities of information and communication technology, this was perhaps the closest approximation there could be of an extended community united in a single form of common musical endeavour. Using the Board's syllabuses therefore put the pupil and teacher in direct contact with the musical values, teaching canon and technical stipulations advocated by the staff of the Royal Schools. They also meant having students independently assessed according to London, rather than local, standards; and the pass rates offered a chance for parents to see for themselves which teachers really did measure up to London expectations.

Parry was always very clear about the Board's potential to transmit cultural values across the world:

> to give people all over the Empire opportunities to be intimately acquainted with the finest kinds of musical art, and to maintain standards of interpretation and an attitude of thoroughness in connection with music which will enable it to be most fruitful of good.[3]

The ABRSM was conscious of having a musical obligation to Empire. But just as vital as its syllabuses were the more serendipitous benefits and consequent opportunities that came from contact with visiting examiners from London, such as spotting and encouraging local musical talent, the musical stimulus, and the help and encouragement some examiners gave to local teachers. The irony, however, was that the Board was so anxious about its examiners being seen to be impartial and separate from the local context, that it used to try to prevent them from engaging with teachers or from giving concerts. But such rulings were more regularly honoured in the breach rather than in their observance, not least because most examiners wished to help where they could, and because doing so helped combat the extreme loneliness of the early tours.

In 1893 the Board was approached by the University of the Cape of Good Hope (representing teachers in the colony) to hold music exams there. A special joint syllabus was agreed between the Board and the University, and the renowned Franklin Taylor examined 346 School Exams candidates at fifteen centres in August and September 1894. In 1897 the Board made a determined attempt to expand to other Dominions, sending letters written in the name of its President, the Prince of Wales, to a series of universities in Australia, New Zealand and Canada requesting their assistance to help the Board establish its exams. This was accompanied by the Board's new Colonial Syllabus, which enclosed a letter to be made available to teachers explaining what the Board was and its purpose in offering exams. The letter is explicit about the imperial purpose of these exams:

---

[3] From an address given to the RCM and subsequently quoted in ABRSM publications in the 1920s.

'By adopting the standards and Syllabus used in Great Britain throughout the Colonies, we shall unify the system of musical examination which is current in the Old Country, in all parts of the Empire.'[4]

The Prince of Wales's introductory letter was followed up by a visit from the Board's new Secretary, Samuel Aitken, accompanied by an examiner, C. Lee Williams, formerly Organist of Gloucester Cathedral. The University of Melbourne firmly declined to support the exams (as potentially detrimental to its own Conservatorium), while the Universities of Sydney and Adelaide agreed, although, as we shall see, in Adelaide the Board was being used as an honest broker in order to deal with its troublesome Professor of Music, Joshua Ives. In fact examinations had been going on in Australia at least since 1876, when they were instituted by the Musical Association of Victoria, followed by the arrival of TCL's exams in Melbourne in 1882.[5] Aitken's report back to the Board on his tour to Australia and Canada indicates the support which the Board received at the highest official levels. At Brisbane, certificates to the successful candidates were distributed by the acting premier, Sir Horace Tozer, while the Governors of New South Wales and of Victoria presented certificates in their respective territories. Aitken also moved quickly to recruit representatives independent of the universities and to set up centres (co-ordinated by a Resident Clerk sent out from London), and did the same in New Zealand.[6] Aitken then travelled to Canada, and again with support from the provincial governors set up a system of centres and representatives there, too. As we shall see, these (often attenuated) administrative networks did not always function very well, and although the tone of the Board's report of its ventures overseas suggests a settled, orderly expansion, the actuality was rather different and much more haphazard, particularly in the remoter areas, as Frederic Staton in New Zealand belatedly discovered: 'On three or four occasions, I arrived in a small town and rang up or sought the [HLR] printed in the syllabus to find he was dead, or at any rate had ceased his activities on behalf of the Board.'[7]

In both Australia and Canada the wish to establish local examination boards led to some determined resistance to both the presence of the Associated Board and to the other British music exam boards. The formation and subsequent growth of the Australian Music Examinations Board (AMEB) led to the gradual withdrawal of the ABRSM, which ended its 'British World' work there in 1951, after a period of co-operation with the AMEB. In Canada the Board's first exams, held in 1898, were marked by a tendentious exchange between Aitken, on behalf of the Board, and the self-styled 'Canadian Protesting Committee'. The so-called 'Canadian' protest boils down to a commercial spat initiated by three privately owned, non-chartered

---

[4] RCMA: *Associated Board: Syllabus; Local Centres and Schools, 1890–97.*

[5] Kieran Crichton, 'Resisting the Empire?: Public Music Examinations in Melbourne, 1896–1914', in *Music and Institutions*, ed. Paul Rodmell (Aldershot: Ashgate, forthcoming); see also Doreen Bridges, 'Some Historical Backgrounds to Australian Music Education', *The Australian Journal of Music Education*, first series vols. 10–15 (April 1972 – October 1975). I am grateful to Kieran Crichton for generously sharing aspects of his research-in-progress, especially information about the Board's entry into Australia from the Australian perspective.

[6] ABRSMA: 'Mr S. Aitken's Report on his Tour in Australia and Canada, 1897–98'.

[7] J. F. Staton, report on his New Zealand Tour, 1939 (ABRSMA}.

Canadian institutions, who then fanned their grievance with the Board into an appearance of a national campaign. It seems that the Toronto College of Music, the Toronto Conservatory and the Dominion College of Music (in Montreal) initially invited the Board to hold exams in Canada, but what they had in mind was that they should then act as the Board's exclusive agents for an initial five-year period. When Aitken replied that the Board could not agree to the terms being offered, and started to make separate arrangements (which were welcomed by teachers who saw the Board as offering independence from local musical factionalism), it was accused effectively of reneging on an agreement, and the 'Protest' began.[8]

The voluminous outpourings of accusation and counter-accusation are in themselves considerably less interesting than the 'British World' aspect, which came through the support given to the ABRSM's Canadian presence from no less a personage than the Governor-General. Although awkwardly placed, the Governor-General made the case for the Board, as an Empire-wide, trans-national endeavour, and while sympathizing with the wish for Canadian institutions to carry out their own exams, he felt that access to the Board's exams would presently do more for the development of Canadian music.[9] Aitken was also able to cite support for the ABRSM's exams from some significant national musical figures, including Charles Harriss. An aggravating factor in this protest was that the University of Trinity College in Toronto (with which Toronto Conservatory was associated) had been involved in an acrimonious (and sometimes farcical) dispute about that institution's right to confer degrees in Britain. The upshot was that in 1890 a petition had been addressed to the Secretary of State for the Colonies by the major British universities, together with the ABRSM, the College, the Academy and TCL, complaining about the importation of these Canadian degrees, hence Aitken's determined distancing of the Board from the Toronto grouping.[10] The pro-British sentiment that was so strongly evident in a near-contemporary event – the extended Canadian tour of the future George V in 1901 – suggests that the 'Protest' represented very much less the nationalist rejection of the British World ethos than its organizers wanted people to believe. And significantly, the Toronto *Globe* proclaimed that 'Canada is British because of the desire of its inhabitants to remain British.'[11] As in the case of Australia, gradually the ABRSM's position came to be displaced by local Canadian exam boards, primarily those of the now chartered Royal College of Music, Toronto, and the Western Board of Music;

---

[8] See *An Account of the Canadian Protest against the Introduction into Canada of Musical Examinations by Outside Musical Examining Bodies*, edited, compiled and published by order of the Canadian Protesting Committee (1899); Samuel Aitken, *The Case of the Associated Board* (Toronto: 29 March 1899); also 'Fight among Musicians: Mr Samuel Aitken Writes a Redhot Reply to the Strictures of the Toronto Professors', *Toronto World*, 10 March 1899.

[9] Aitken, *The Case of the Associated Board*.

[10] The petition is given in the TCL *Gazette* 7/75 (April 1890), 50–54; the Toronto controversy is briefly discussed in Scholes, *Mirror of Music*, vol. 2, 688–9.

[11] See Philip Buckner, 'Casting Daylight upon Magic: Deconstructing the Royal Tour of 1901 to Canada', in *British World*, ed. Bridge and Fedorowich, 159–89; the quotation is on p. 185.

accordingly the 'British World' phase of the Board's operations in Canada came to a natural close in 1953.

⫶ Examining in the British World

> ... the technique, as far as I can see, of an Examiner of the Board would be compounded of a talent for simple arithmetic, an elastic vocabulary, a synthetic memory, a decent handwriting, an unwearied patience, a ready power of description, a gentle demeanour, a sense of justice, solicitude for the weak, a taste for logic, a golden voice, and a bedside manner. These qualities together provide an undefeatable make-up of an Associated Board Examiner.[12]

HUGH Allen's listing of the desiderata for success as an ABRSM examiner was only partially ironic. These were indeed the qualities needed, but – quite apart from the striking omission of any musical attributes – Allen's list was not comprehensive. Examiners on the early Empire tours also needed sometimes astonishing levels of resourcefulness, courage, physical fitness and the ability to cope with isolation. They also needed the capacity to put up with physical discomfort; the social skills, diplomacy and tact necessary to rub along with people of very different cultural outlooks; to have the ability to keep systematic records of expenditure; sufficient empathy and understanding to appreciate what many candidates in remote places had achieved well against the odds; and to have the good luck not to lose all their financial records, reports and results in the process. It is hardly surprising that the minute books contain references to dealing with the consequences of mishaps, carelessness and malign fortune. For example, the letter of regret from the Board that had to be sent in 1919 to the Practical examinees of Malta after Benjamin Dale had lost all the results,[13] and the occasion when, because of an examiner's error, a Canadian candidate's name had appeared in the local press as having passed her exam when in fact she had not (the pass was allowed to stand and a certificate issued).[14] Examiners' reports back to the Board on their overseas tours frequently show real sensitivity to the issues presented by a local situation, and a true commitment to advancing the cause of music education where they can help to do so. They are often characterized by a generosity of spirit and a concern for individuals, and there are some heart-warming stories contained in the reports they made to the Board after each tour.

What sort of people were these examiners who were prepared to undertake long overseas tours? As Chapter 1 suggested, the richness of Victorian musical life and the new opportunities opened up by scholarship education meant that examiners came from more diverse social backgrounds and with a range of attitudes to professional life, Empire and travel. As with any specialist community they also brought with them the usual gamut of personalities with their share of fulfilled or disappointed personal and professional ambitions. The opportunity to travel to

[12] Sir Hugh Allen, *Forty-eighth Annual Report of the Board* (1937), 10.
[13] ABMB5: 18 March 1919.
[14] ABMB7: 29 September 1925.

far-off places at the Board's expense may well have represented a personal dream or the opportunity to cut free for a while, making the intense effort required by the examining itself a small price to pay. But as much as the anticipation of the arrival, there was the prospect of the excitement and enjoyment of getting there in the company of a truly cosmopolitan community of travellers, part of the procession of Empire. For travelling by ship was an essentially social process, and a gifted pianist would not have lacked for attention, no matter how much he may have come to tire of it. In the earlier days Board examiners were often treated as VIPs, hosted or entertained at British embassies or at the local Government House, but gradually this tailed off as British visitors became much more routine. However, it was sometimes very difficult to recruit examiners for these overseas tours because they required extended absence from professional and family commitments. Yet the exotic element of foreign travel remained a potent attraction for some until the days of mass tourism when long-haul journeys became more common.

Several examiners undertook tours to Australia and New Zealand for the chance to boost their financial position, some trading down the first-class ticket bought for them and pocketing the difference, or, as with Maurice Besley, undertaking two successive tours, not returning to England and claiming cash in lieu for the ticket they would otherwise have needed; Besley received £150 (some £6,600) in lieu of all fares and allowances he would have been due had he returned to England after his 1926 tour.[15] However, Besley's candid comments on Australia ('No musician should go to Australia except for health's sake; better to die of [musical] starvation than a broken heart') ended his ABRSM examining.[16] The composer William Alwyn seems to have been given his tour of Australia in 1932 as a favour by his former teacher and friend J. B. McEwen, the RAM's Principal, who seems to have thought it an opportunity to boost the Alwyn family finances. He certainly enjoyed the society on board ship, travelling first class in the company of the Duke of Buccleugh and Lord Rothermere, and meeting Captain Eckersley, a senior BBC executive. He also met the incoming Governor of Queensland, who as Governor of Bombay had hosted an ABRSM examiner, and who extended to Alwyn an invitation to Government House when he was examining in Brisbane. Alwyn worked each day with the famous Australian opera singer John Brownlee, a mutually enjoyable experience, and he happily played the piano for the ship's Sunday evening community singing ('very good fun'). On his arrival in Australia at the beginning of June, Alwyn was told by Arthur C. Hull, the Board's Australian Resident Secretary, that there would be nearly six months' examining, and that he would certainly not be leaving until the end of November. The prospect of this peripatetic existence must have seemed daunting to Alwyn as he faced the realities of life accompanied by three large suitcases, a small hand-case and vast amounts of paperwork. But Alwyn's motive in taking on this tour and leaving behind a wife and small son was very clear: 'The only thought that sustains me all the while is the financial security that this tour will give us – and this is really a very big thing in these times.' In fact he did not manage to make as much as he had hoped from this trip, because to console himself he began to spend heavily on drink and good

---

[15] ABMB6: 9 December 1924; ABMB7: 8 February 1927.

[16] Maurice Besley, 'Fresh Air and Variations', *The Sackbut* 8 (April 1928), 285–9.

meals: 'I should go completely mad out here if I did not have an occasional good dinner with a bottle of good wine, a good cigar and a good seat at the Theatre.'[17] That this had been cause for some contention is suggested by a letter written home from a trip to Canada in 1934: 'I am being much more careful over expenses on this tour ... Another thing, I cannot spend money on strong drink because there ain't any!'[18]

Drink was an occupational hazard for examiners, especially on long tours, with practical difficulties exacerbated by the loneliness and the monotony of examining the usual procession of low grades. As was the custom of the day, it was an issue usually ignored by all unless it reached a crisis point, as it did in the case of a Mr Rose, sent out to Australia as a supplementary examiner in October 1908. Almost on arrival in November the Sydney Representative cabled to report that Rose was drinking heavily and advising his recall. It then seems that he refused to return unless he received a further remittance, and the Board cabled, 'Pay Rose minimum to ensure return'. The matter rumbled on, because in June a Board meeting heard about a further claim being made by Rose. It was decided 'to ask Mr Rose to formulate his claim and if he does not demand more, to settle with him up to £80 19s 8d' (over £6,000), and it was reported at the following meeting that settlement had been reached and, not surprisingly, that there was unanimous agreement that he should no longer be asked to examine.[19] Given that the original cost of Rose's passage was around £123 (some £9,500), this had proved an expensive episode for the Board, who were determined to avoid any public admission of the human frailty of its examiners. The potential for boredom is well conveyed by Henry Moule, who recorded the details of his 1958 tour of New Zealand in letters to his sister:

> A soft gloom is about to descend on these letters ... for the agreeable gadding about that made the beginning of the work so pleasant in Kaitaia and Whangarei has decidedly ceased. For the last 2½ weeks I have been sitting in a Presbyterian Lounge from almost exactly 9.30 till 12.45 and from 2 till 4.45. [...] What is rather depressing is that this one-room life and with it the appalling regularity of hours, is not only going to have occupied five weeks here, but is quite likely to be repeated in Wellington for a month.[20]

Moule goes on to say that this period will be followed by days of correcting 1,100 Theory papers (it took him sixty-two hours) before contact with another examiner for a month of diploma examining. In fact Moule's mental constitution equipped him rather better than most to deal with the boredom without reliance on drink, for his quirky sense of humour enabled him to apply a wryly detached fascination in going about the most mundane of tasks – his meticulous time-and-motion study about the most efficient way of marking theory papers makes for bizarre entertainment in itself!

[17] Letter to Olive Pull, 14 September 1932.

[18] Letter to Olive Pull, 10 June 1934.

[19] ABMB4: 13 October, 2 and 24 November 1908; 8 June, 13 July 1909.

[20] *New Zealand Letters ... to Dorothy Bosanquet, 1958 & 1959.* I am most grateful to Mrs Lovedy Cornish for showing me this collection.

Frederic Cliffe interrupted his 1898 holiday in Switzerland for Australia at a few hours' notice, because the number of entries (744) had been unexpectedly high, and a second examiner was needed. His first challenge was a stint of joint examinations for Adelaide University with its notoriously difficult Professor of Music, Joshua Ives. Cliffe said that these exams 'were conducted in preposterous fashion, without any syllabus of pieces, with no method in examination, and with professor Ives's assurance that unless nearly all the candidates passed, as usual, the Examinations (and the receipts) of the University would be ruined'. Ives's incapacity enabled Cliffe to show the need for future exams to be conducted entirely on the syllabus of the Associated Board, as in England, and after negotiating the position, this the University accepted. The affair, however, had caused considerable public controversy. A special meeting of the University Council had to be convened to consider the protest mounted by teachers, and its outcome was reported at length.[21] Although the University was determined to save its face by declaring it had confidence in its own Professor of music, it was decided that he was not to conduct future public (as opposed to university) music exams, and Cliffe's handling of this furore cemented the wider perception of the ABRSM's integrity in the conduct of music exams.

Cliffe returned to Australia in 1909 for a trip that in several respects proved a nightmare of overwork and difficult travel. Because of the unreliability of communications, examiners visiting the more remote centres were not given an exact timetable, partly because travel was uncertain, and partly because the local secretaries had a habit of 'forgetting' about entries, as a way of enabling them to oblige friends with unofficial late entries. Thus the examiner was sent off to a rural centre with only the vaguest idea of what to expect in terms of numbers, and with a sense of obligation to fit them all in, regardless. Cliffe arrived in Western Australia with the expectation of two weeks' work, and found four. This he was able to clear only by working long days with no day off in order to meet the deadline of the steamer timetable, since failing to meet that would have jeopardized the scheduling of his New Zealand tour. The result was overwork, and Cliffe's report referred to the collapses of previous examiners. For one leg of his tour he travelled all night, arriving at 5.40 a.m. with instructions to look out for the HLR, who did not appear at all. Having waited until 10.00 a.m., he then travelled another four hours to the next centre, which he left at 5.28 p.m. for the next, which he reached at 7.50 p.m. He left that one at 8.25 p.m., reaching his base at 9.25 p.m. – the whole journey was to examine just four Primary students. Remarkably, the tone of Cliffe's report is neither resentful nor self-pitying. He is remarkably positive and understanding of the position of the local administration, and was anxious that the Board understand the complex logistics of running exams in such a vast area. He points out that the time taken travelling from Perth to Sydney is 'considerably greater and less "workable" than from [London] to New York', something only those who had experienced the vast spaces of Australia would be likely to understand. Again, one is left with the impression that this was a tremendous adventure in

---

[21] 'Musical Examinations: The Teachers' Protest Dismissed by the University', *The South Australian Register*, 14 December 1898.

which difficulties are par for the course. Cliffe's report tells us that the problems of timetabling in New Zealand were further compounded by the difficulties of travel:

> some steamers do not leave at all, some cannot land for 24 or 30 hours, and some leave 12 hours *earlier* than the time originally 'tabled'. Sometimes the coaches do not run – if the rivers are too flooded. Therefore it is only reasonable to *allow* a day occasionally for eventualities [...] Even if everything should go smoothly a couple of days' holiday for the examiner would not be *extravagant*, during 3 months of the most brain-fagging work there is.[22]

Thomas Dunhill's 1906 New Zealand and Australian tour was undertaken at the last minute, because the scheduled examiner was taken ill; Dunhill's story underlines the vulnerability of inexperienced examiners on these extended tours.[23] The offer to go to Australasia came without warning on 19 December 1905, and there was no hesitation in immediately clearing Dunhill from his teaching commitments at Eton and the RCM for a year, itself casting an interesting light on the respective musical networks involved. (Eton was closely connected to the ABRSM through its Precentor, or director of music, C. H. Lloyd, who was on the Governing Board, and through another music master, Colin Taylor (who inspired Peter Warlock), who was a prominent ABRSM examiner.) A flurry of activity followed to give Dunhill a crash course in examining, because he had never conducted an ABRSM exam before, and he practised on recent successful candidates in order to try to match the marks they had received. There were some memorable aspects of the tour, not least in 'discovering' the young Arthur Benjamin:

> Before he left Brisbane, Dunhill was brought to our house by a doctor friend (representative of the Associated Board in Brisbane) and he asked me to play and to improvise; and I showed him my first composition. Dunhill told my parents he hoped I should soon be able to go to study harmony and counterpoint with him. From that moment it was my burning ambition by hook or by crook to reach London.[24]

But things were turning sour. Dunhill's diary entry for 6 October reflects his acute sense of musical isolation, expressed in his reaction to attending an orchestral concert, his first in eight months, in a Tchaikovsky and Wagner programme: 'I enjoyed the mere fact of *hearing an orchestra* again beyond all description.' The diary does not make clear precisely what had gone wrong, but it seems that complaints had been cabled to the Board, and he was recalled to England to answer to Parry for the mountain of criticism his tour had generated.

As suggested earlier, one of the major impacts of the ABRSM exams came from the serendipitous benefits of contacts with examiners, especially when they engaged with the local situation and wanted to make a contribution of their own.

---

[22] Frederic Cliffe, draft of his report to the ABRSM (RCMp).

[23] This account is taken from Dunhill's diaries for 1905 and 1906 (RCMA).

[24] Arthur Benjamin, 'Schooldays in Brisbane', *Music Survey* 3/3 (March 1951), 171–2.

This comes to life in the account of Hildur Sanquist Eriksson, a teacher who hosted exams in her house in Lethbridge, Alberta, Canada.[25] In 1937 the very short-sighted Thomas Wood ('his nose rubbed along the paper when he wrote, but he did a wonderful job despite this handicap') arrived with a large number of photographs from various countries which he put out for the candidates to see in the hope of distracting their anxiety. He was so impressed by his experience of Australia as an ABRSM examiner that he had written a book about it, and wanted to do the same for Canada. In 1936 Mrs Eriksson's mother insisted that they offer Felix Swinstead lunch because it was so hot, and it would have been cruel for him to walk back into town. This was very much against Mrs Eriksson's own instincts because she feared that by offering him lunch, Swinstead would think she was trying to get more marks for her pupils; his humorous response to the invitation – that being given lunch would not produce any more marks – confirmed her unhappiness. Later Mrs Eriksson, travelling with some friends on a boat to Europe, discovered that Swinstead, returning from his tour, was one of the passengers. She turned the tables on him by reading out to her friends some of the remarks her pupils had made about Swinstead in front of him, much to his amusement. One of these friends had just finished a course in activating old people, and as Swinstead was unaccompanied, she thought she'd practise on him during the voyage and then dressed him up as a woman for the masked ball on the ship's last evening, which he again took in very good part. But Mrs Eriksson's favourite examiner was Harry Isaacs (1933), who, after he had finished a long day's examining, offered to return to play for her pupils. The house was full – she had invited other teachers and their pupils – and Isaacs gave a full recital. He then took requests, of which there were many. It was 'a long, marvellous evening', as Mrs Eriksson commented, and 'no one who was there would forget the wonderful experience'. The Swinstead story puts a human gloss on an otherwise remote ABRSM composer; Wood's account points up the rich experience that examiners accrued as they migrated between Dominions; but perhaps it is the treat that Isaacs gave that most satisfyingly captures what, at his best, the itinerant ABRSM examiner could offer to musicians across the global British community.

There are so many other examples of unselfconscious exchanges. (The unselfconsciousness is very much part of the point here.) During his tour of Ceylon in 1946 Richard Latham kept a diary which recounts his enjoyment of the country and its people as well as the wide-ranging conversations he had.[26] One incident, though nothing to do with music, gives a very different picture of an examiner's life:

> After examining ... I decided to have a bathe and asked two lads in bathing slips where it was safe to do so. They undertook to show me. As we walked along, these two kept talking in Sinhalese to everyone they saw and I noticed

[25] Mrs Eriksson, who was born in Canada of Swedish parents, moved to Sweden on her marriage after World War II. In her late seventies she became the Board's first HLR in Sweden; she narrated this account for the ABRSM when she was aged ninety-eight.

[26] This is Richard O. Latham (1906–80), who for many years was organist at St Paul's Knightsbridge, London, and a professor at the RCM; his son, Richard M. Latham, was also an ABRSM examiner.

that they all joined the cavalcade! By the time we got to the selected stretch of beach there were about 40 local people there to see the fun. In a few minutes a large inflated rubber raft was produced and I soon discovered that the great game was to tempt me onto one end of the raft when those holding the other end would let go which meant that I slipped off my end and went under the water! This was called 'Ducking Music Examiner' and all those on the beach had been brought to see the fun. There was great delight when music examiner started ducking them. Then everybody wanted to bathe but there weren't enough bathing slips to go round. So once in the water a bather would remove his slip, throw it on shore and someone else would put it on for the dash into the sea. ... All this because there were two or three maidens watching the fun! ... Later most of the lads who had bathed came and joined me and we had a long talk about England. They were all students and were amazingly well informed.[27]

In their different ways Isaacs's informal recital and Latham's enjoyment of the 'Ducking Music Examiner' game, with his readiness afterwards to talk with them all about England, would likely have stuck in the memories of at least some of those involved. And in their different ways, the very human interaction which these contrasting images of examiner participation represent make them engaging illustrations of the Board's involvement in the British World.

---

[27] Richard O. Latham, unpublished diary of his 1946 ABRSM tour to Ceylon; I am most grateful to Anthony Crossland for telling me of its existence, and to Mrs Gillian Agnew for allowing me to quote from her father's diary.

III The Institutional Culture, 1920–83

6 The Inter-War Years

⁂ The ABRSM's institutional identity

THE prominence of the ABRSM in the 1920s and 30s owed much to the persona of the RCM's Director, Sir Hugh Allen. His indefatigable energy, together with his qualities of leadership, made him something of a force of nature, and his assiduous politicking ensured that few major appointments in his spheres of influence were made without his knowledge or specific recommendation.[1] He was generally looked upon as the *de facto* leader of music in the educational and church spheres, a widely held view that was made explicit in Allen's obituary in *The Times*: 'He became for a time the acknowledged but unofficial head of the music profession in this country.'[2] Allen had strong views on everything. He was especially exercised about recording and radio damaging the world of amateur music: he feared that the too easy access to 'ready-made' music offered by this technology would discourage people from taking up instruments or singing in choirs, and he had the ear of *The Times* in which to air his opinions.

In 1931 Allen summarized the Associated Board and its work:

> The Associated Board *is* the Royal Academy of Music and the Royal College of Music, and the welfare of one is wrapped up in the welfare of the other. [...] Certain duties are laid upon us, backed by all the power of our Royal Charters, to do all we can for the advancement of music education. This is done in two ways. Firstly by the teaching of the two schools; secondly by the wider work of the Schools through the Associated Board. The Examinations which the Board controls are designed to spread the influence of the teaching and the prestige of the body of the Professors who form, in the two Schools, the most remarkable group of musicians and teachers of the day [...] so that all teachers in the country may receive by actual contact the guidance, encouragement and stimulus which can only come from such contact [...] with all the advantages that a common interest and companionship can give. It is only by *authority* that such work can be successful, and there can be no question as to the Board's authority.[3]

Allen's intention here was to stress the legitimacy of the Board's cultural and educational authority. He therefore belaboured the point that the Schools' royal charters gave the Board the prerogative to run music exams, and that these brought teachers and pupils into direct contact with the ethos and musical values of the

---

[1] For a summary of Allen's personality and achievements, see W. K. Stanton, 'Allen, Sir Hugh Percy (1869–1946)', rev., *ODNB*; more privately, Allen was someone about whom people speak with considerable affection for his practical support, including Douglas Fox (the virtuoso organist and legendary Director of Music at Clifton College) whom Allen encouraged to play again after the loss of his arm in World War I, Leon Goossens the oboist and Joseph Horovitz the composer.

[2] *The Times*, 21 February 1946; see also Cyril Bailey, *Hugh Percy Allen* (London: Oxford University Press, 1948), 104–5.

[3] Sir Hugh Allen, *Forty-second Annual Report of the Board* (1931), 32.

5 Sir Hugh Allen, whose energetic and no-nonsense approach reshaped the Board between the wars

Royal Schools and the eminent musicians teaching in them. Through its exams the Board was offering an authoritative programme of repertoire and technical progression that had been carefully structured by professors of the Royal Schools. By invoking the quality of 'companionship', Allen was representing the Board's system of exams as something of a transcendent force as well as the practical means of transmitting the cultural influence and pedagogic practice of the London Royal Schools all across the country. It amounted to no less an assertion that, together, these three institutions (the RAM, the RCM and the ABRSM) represented the collective interests of much of the British musical community. Certainly if we look at those whose musical lives were affected by this nexus of the RSMs and the Board – the professors/examiners employed, their student bodies, the music teachers and their pupils who came under the extramural influence of the ABRSM exams and the British composers who wrote music for them – this encompassed a huge constituency in the UK alone, leaving aside the Board's operations in the Empire. As Allen realized, the ABRSM was emblematic of the Royal Schools' shared educational purpose and cultural mission, and the means by which their work and musical values could be disseminated into the wider musical community in a more cohesive way than otherwise would have been possible.

To all intents and purposes, it can also be said that until the reconstitution of the Board in 1985, Allen's maxim 'The Associated Board *is* the Royal Academy of Music and the Royal College of Music' continued to hold true. The ABRSM's musical culture encapsulated the musical culture of the Academy and the College. The Board's examiners were still mainly recruited from the staff of the Academy and the College, and when increases in candidate numbers obliged the expansion of the examining body, recruitment was initially confined to those who had been students at the Royal Schools and so very much imbued with their ethos.[4] The specific College–Academy influence over the Board only became more dilute as increased candidate numbers forced the post-war expansion of the examining body to include staff from the RSAMD and the RMCM who had joined the Board as junior partners in 1947. But by then the ABRSM's culture had become so deeply formed that its ethos continued undisturbed.

Throughout the Associated Board's history the examiners have been the Board's primary workforce and have constituted its biggest resource. And because so many examiners taught or had studied at the Academy or the College, inevitably the ABRSM became an extension of the two Schools. Confirmation of this shared musical ethos was the joint 'graduate' diploma (the GRSM) introduced in 1930. The GRSM was both a product of the Associated Board experience and its logical further expansion. This three-year course, with its demanding practical keyboard skills, defined the general musicianship expertise which the Academy and the College considered necessary for success in grammar or public school music

---

[4] This association with the Royal Schools continued to be promoted as a unique selling point, despite there being a number of examiners occupying prominent musical positions who were not trained at either. Allen was therefore stretching a point when he said, 'Examiners are in actual fact members of the teaching staff of the Academy or College, or were trained in one or other of these Institutions.' *Fortieth Annual Report of the Board* (1929), 28.

teaching. In order to qualify for a GRSM the student also had to have passed either the ARCM, LRAM or LRSM (the Board's own diploma), and with this new qualification the RSMs were extending their musical authority, covering from the very earliest beginner stages, through the professional 'performer' and 'teacher' diplomas, to the 'graduate' level.

Now very secure in their collective position as the music training 'establishment', and as the major employers of musicians at this educational level, it is not surprising that the RAM, RCM and ABRSM had come to see themselves as the representative body speaking for much of the British music profession and responsible for furthering its interests. It was this proprietary attitude that led the colleges to contest the BBC's musical policy in the 1930s, as discussed later. But the point most needing to be emphasized here is that although the ABRSM was acknowledged in many respects as the single most significant agent in bringing about a general improvement of British musical attainment, its hidebound musical horizons coloured that achievement with a distinctly nineteenth-century hue – something that as the twentieth century progressed seemed increasingly reactionary and out of step. Thus the Board's domination of British musical education was to have significant consequences for British musical life more generally because it was so conservative in matters of repertoire and musical language.

It is clear from Allen's representation of the ABRSM that people were not encouraged to see it as an institution in its own right. Until the 1985 Reconstitution, the ABRSM had little independent weight or institutional substance, and this was for reasons that were bound up with its original purpose. As initially envisaged, the Board was the neutral ground constructed so that these two institutional rivals could meet to conduct examination business together, and the administrative vehicle to implement their decisions. Because the Board was conceived of as only the cipher of its two partners, all the significant decisions affecting it were taken by the heads of the Royal Schools and by their senior staff members to whom duties such as syllabus setting and examiner selection were delegated. It was understood that part of the job of being the College's Director or the Academy's Principal was to direct the affairs of the Associated Board. Throughout the 1920s and 30s, and continuing well after the war, the minute books show that it was the two heads of the Schools who allocated examiners' tours. They did this on the general principle of giving priority to the teaching staff of the two institutions, with preference given to the most senior; in all likelihood this practical form of patronage must have been welcomed as a useful means of exerting control over their staffs.[5] Usual practice seems to have been that the heads of the Schools and the Board's Secretary held weekly business meetings,[6] at either the College or the Academy, though no details of this arrangement have survived. Thus the sway of the two Royal Schools and their respective governing bodies over the ABRSM was absolute. Indeed, from 1939 to 1984 there was no independent Chairman of the Associated Board. Instead that role was fulfilled as necessary by the Principal of the Academy and the Director of the College acting in alternate years. (By contrast,

---

[5] ABMB7: 8 November 1927.
[6] ABMB8: 10 November 1931.

the early Chairmen had been well-connected figureheads from public life, who had had no involvement in any form of musical decision-making.)

The Board's nominal head was the Secretary, whose task was to ensure the efficiency of the actual examining process – given the ABRSM's then purely administrative role, nothing more was required. Indeed, the partner Schools clearly regarded this structure as the ideal hierarchical configuration, because when it came to the appointment of a new Secretary in 1934, it was decided that the person appointed should not be a professional musician.[7] That decision eliminated Reginald Thatcher, an examiner since 1924 and Director of Music at Harrow School, and secured the appointment for Hilary Macklin, then the Board's Resident Secretary in India.[8] The reason these arrangements changed after Macklin's retirement in 1962 was because the scope of the ABRSM's operations had come to extend well beyond the capacity of the Schools to exercise detailed oversight. The appointment of William Cole as the first professional musician-Secretary to succeed Macklin in 1962 was important because it marked the first transfer of substantial musical responsibility to the Board. Even so, it was not until the restructuring of the Board in 1985 (bringing full partnership to all four Royal Schools), when an independent Chairman was appointed and the Secretary's role had been redesigned as a Chief Executive's, that the ambiguity of the Board's own entity seemed to be resolved. Only from then could it be said that the ABRSM had attained the strategic responsibility of planning for its own future as a free-standing institution.[9]

⫸ Relating the Board to its market

ALLEN'S 1931 speech to the ABRSM's Annual Lunch also signalled a series of modernizing reforms that were put in place in the period 1931–3. They were implemented in an attempt to preserve the level (and income) of the Board's operation under very difficult economic circumstances in the wake of the Great Depression and the resulting slump. In 1928/9, candidate numbers reached a low of 51,895 and then stagnated, at a time when the Board's own costs were running out of control. As an economy, it was decided that, instead of the traditional Board lunch in July 1932, HLRs and examiners should be invited to tea instead, with HLRs given expenses for third-class rather than first-class rail travel, which must have been an unwelcome development that not even the decision to offer cigars and cigarettes with the tea was likely to assuage.[10] But the actual reduction

---

[7] ABMB8: 27 March 1934.

[8] In 1936 Thatcher moved to the BBC as Assistant Director of Music to Boult. He joined the Board's Governing Body in 1943 when he became the Warden of the RAM, and he succeeded Stanley Marchant as Principal of the RAM in 1949.

[9] This transfer of responsibility from the Schools to the Board was a gradual one. The two Secretaries who followed Macklin (William Cole and Philip Cranmer) and the first to be designated Chief Executive in 1983 (Ronald Smith) were professional musicians, but the Chief Executives appointed from 1993 (Richard Morris and Guy Perricone) are from the financial and business worlds.

[10] ABMB8: 23 February, 28 June 1932.

in candidates was not Allen's only anxiety. The Board was increasingly concerned about the potential damage of broadcasting and recording technology on the numbers of those learning to sing or play instruments. To meet these challenges the Board seems to have appreciated that it needed to revivify itself to increase its appeal to teachers – hence Allen's argument. This new mood had been reflected in the speeches given at the 1929 AGM. On that occasion the Chairman, Raymond Ffennell (a close personal friend of Allen's), said that the Board had 'determined that everything must be done to make our Examinations better known and more popular [...] and we have been busy in making preparations to widen and strengthen the foundations on which our operations rest'. For his part, Allen spoke darkly of facing 'a new set of circumstances, presented with a rapidity and force that leaves us almost breathless', a reference to his fears that technology would weaken the vigorous state of British amateur music-making.[11] The Board was also vulnerable to the consequences of an adverse economic climate; and given this combination of circumstances it could have been seriously enfeebled without Allen's dynamism in bringing about some much needed changes, and had not its new Secretary, Hilary Macklin, also improved the quality of its administration.

The first step in the process of sorting out the Board's operation was an adjustment to its title, which on 1 January 1932 became 'The Associated Board of the Royal Schools of Music, London (The Royal Academy of Music and the Royal College of Music)'. This change dropped the previous reference to 'Local Exams in Music in the British Empire' that had been part of the Board's title since 1900, although reference to Local Exams in the Empire continued to appear on the syllabuses for a time. In reality, the Board was experiencing tremendous difficulty in operating under the substantial losses incurred by its examining work in the colonies. The Colonial account showed a deficit of £2,443 in 1931 and £3,272 in 1932, a loss that had to be met through the Board's UK operation, which obviously reduced the income the Schools received from the Board.[12] In 1932 Allen, in a move agreed with the RAM, called upon the ageing Secretary, James Muir (who had been in post since 1900), to make a £1,000 reduction to the Board's operating costs, something that he was either unable or unwilling to do. In the end the Chairman, Raymond Ffennell, requested that Muir took retirement in the light of a situation in which 'we feel that some change of system is absolutely necessary and you that none but the present system is desirable'.[13]

Astonishing though it now seems, only after some forty years of existence, and in the face of an economic crisis, did the Board awake to the need to cultivate its market. From an attitude of olympian detachment towards those who used its services, it shifted to become slightly more responsive to the needs of teachers and

[11] *Fortieth Annual Report of the Board* (1929), 26, 29.

[12] In 1931/2 the 'moiety' (as it was called in the accounts) or share of profits paid to each School reached a new low point of £2,144, less than half the amount paid the previous year (ABMB8, meeting on 28 June 1932). Various 'robbing Peter to pay Paul' measures had subsequently to be taken in order to increase the level of money going to the Schools from the Board, such as withdrawing money from the Board's Colonial Examiners' Insurance Fund, and from the Working Fund (ibid.).

[13] Letter from Ffennell to Muir, dated 4 August 1933 (ABMB8, attached following the minutes of the meeting on 18 July 1933).

pupils. As part of this new departure, from 1930 candidates were sent an exam report with remarks by the examiner supporting the marks that had been awarded (as explained in Chapter 4, previously they had received only marks awarded under the headings of assessment set out in the syllabus). In its early days – with a roster of musical knights on its examining panel – the Board had a rather imperious sense of its own authority. It believed that the market would come to it, and that its operation could be run without any real regard to efficiency, opportunity or cost effectiveness. The restructuring of the system announced for 1932/3 marked the watershed. The unwieldy two-series system of Local Centre Exams and Local School Exams was simplified and merged into a single, eight-grade series (see Table 4.1), and the 'Honours' category was replaced by 'Distinction'. The Board also attempted to placate string and singing teachers by offering specialist examiners in these subjects once minimum candidate numbers had been reached at any centre. For the first time the Board recognized the stumbling block for senior grade candidates of having to take both the compulsory Theory paper and Practical exam at the same session, and it now allowed these to be sat in different exam periods. The decision to move to a single examiner for all exams enabled the senior grades to be offered at each of the three sessions, instead of twice a year. It also reduced costs significantly, saving a second examiner's fee for the 3,793 senior grade exams held in 1933/4 alone.

Another significant innovation, intended to foster loyalty to the Board and bring it a little closer to its teachers, was the founding of the 'Society of Corresponding Members'. This Society was intended to recognize those teachers who had entered candidates to the Board's exams regularly for at least three years with the title of 'corresponding members of the Royal Schools of Music', and for this recognition to be an incentive to other teachers. 'Corresponding members' were formed into local committees and encouraged to run lectures and discussions, sometimes given by visitors from the Board. The kudos for the teachers was that their names appeared in a Year Book, in company with the names of the Board's examiners and the staff lists of the two Royal Schools. Ffennell summarized the Board's new strategic purpose in the letter which appointed Hilary Macklin as Secretary:

> the work to be done outside in establishing and maintaining closer contact with Teachers, Schools, our own Local Representatives, our corresponding members, other examining bodies such as some of the Universities, Examiners, etc., etc., will be of the highest importance. [...] it is essential that we should commence a regular campaign at the earliest possible moment, to recover lost ground.[14]

▨ Teachers and candidates

ALTHOUGH in itself Allen's representation of the Board's authority was not a new argument, circumstances had made it necessary to restate the case for the Board's exams. Allen's argument was a cunning play to the market: how could

---

[14] Letter from Ffennell to Macklin, dated 27 April 1934 (ABMB8, attached following the minutes of the meeting on 17 July 1934).

responsible teachers fail to take the opportunity to be in 'actual contact' with the Royal Schools and all that they stood for? His message was calculated to bind existing teachers evermore securely to the Board's exams, as well as to appeal to new ones. The Board's exams had enjoyed a period of unchecked growth in the UK from their inception until the outbreak of the 1914 war. And as Table 4.5 shows, even during the course of that war, in 1916/17, numbers continued to grow because of the increase in candidates for the junior level exams. As suggested, it was a signal of how strongly in the nation's psyche these exams had come to stand as part of the pattern of life that candidate entries saw significant increases during and in the immediate aftermath of both the First and Second World Wars, as people determined to reassert peacetime values.[15] In the 1920s the UK music entries had peaked at 59,862 in 1923/4, after which came a steady decline that continued throughout the 1930s, annual entries averaging out at 50,376. (The lowest point was 47,427 candidates in 1936/7.)

In fact the fall in the Board's figures would have been greater but for a considerable piece of luck which came its way, for in 1926 the Incorporated Society of Musicians asked the Board to take over their music exams, which also had been declining since 1921. The ISM, however, also sought from the Board payment in compensation (around £300 a year for two or three years) to help it adjust to the loss of its exam income; this the Board refused to do, and the idea was dropped.[16] But examining was obviously draining the ISM's resources, and so an arrangement was reached that from 1929 the Board should take over and run the ISM's 'Primary' exam (renamed 'Preliminary'), as a preparatory step to its own 'Primary' exam. When the Board restructured its exams into the now familiar eight-grade pattern, this Preliminary Exam was retained as a pre-grade gateway. The ISM's offer was a real gift to the Board because it attracted a large new candidate market (by 1933 some additional 5,000 candidates) and brought more ISM teachers directly within the ABRSM ambit.

The ready access and diversity of music that broadcasting and the gramophone brought to people in their own homes made the inter-war period a pivotal one that changed cultural perspectives for ever. The influence of these media also led to taste becoming much more uniform across the country, usually at the expense of the often distinctive local repertoire patterns that had characterized concert life in different provincial musical centres.[17] Interestingly, the ambition to correct 'defective' musical taste had been one of the ABRSM's own objectives, as Parry made clear in his speech to the Board's 1895 Annual Dinner:

> By means of drawing up schemes which comprise first rate music, and nothing except what was good, whether studies or artistic works, you can

---

[15] In the last year unaffected by war, 1938, music entries were 50,269, near to the 1930s average; in 1944 they had risen to an astonishing 84,367.

[16] ABMB7: 9 March 1926.

[17] For a contextual perspective on broadcasting, see Ross McKibbin, *Classes and Cultures: England, 1918–1951* (Oxford: Oxford University Press, 1998). For a detailed account of the impact of the gramophone that goes well beyond the boundaries implied by its title, see James J. Nott, *Music for the People: Popular Music and Dance in Interwar Britain* (Oxford: Oxford University Press, 2002).

bring people from the ends of the land into contact with good things of which otherwise they might have remained in ignorance to the end of their days. [...] I had a sort of trepidation as to whether people in the outlaying parts of the British Islands would not be found hopelessly out of touch with the works of Schumann, Schubert, and the divine works of Bach [...] But our first experiences were enough to dispel any anxieties on that ground, and to assure us that we were taking the best policy.[18]

The Board's syllabuses did indeed bring about a greater conformity in repertoire and associated high art musical values across the country. But the ready home access to more popular music and jazz that the radio and gramophone brought, together with the reduction in domestic music-making, meant an inevitable dilution of the Board's own hold on musical taste. Even so, it is reasonable to assume that the Board's writ was still the dominant factor on those teachers involved with its exams during the inter-war period. The extent of the Board's influence was such that even in the 1930s, when entries were relatively flat, over 500,000 candidates took its exams.

But in this context it needs again to be emphasized that the 1930s Board had simply nothing like the musical range or broad candidate base of today's ABRSM. It was content to remain as it had been in the 1890s, and to examine a very narrow spread of instruments. In reality, therefore, its work and influence still affected a restricted – although culturally dominant – musical constituency. Orchestral wind and brass instruments were almost completely outside its sphere. For, incredible as it may seem, in the whole of the pre-war decade, 1929/30 to 1938/39, the Board examined only 20 flutes, 9 oboes, 6 clarinets, 2 horns and 2 trumpets. The main subjects were piano (398,277), violin (23,589), singing (5,451), cello (1,789) and organ (879); it also examined violas (211) and one double bass. This preponderance of drawing-room instruments shows that in some fifty years the Board had simply rooted itself in its middle-class identity without any attempt to broaden its musical appeal. The exam entry fee, for example, remained high. In 1933 Grade 1 cost 10s (£26.30 in today's RPI terms), Grade 5 cost one guinea (£55.30) and Grade 8 Practical cost £2 12s 6d (£138). However, Grade 4 Rudiments, which cost 10s 6d (£27.60), had to be passed by every candidate entering for Grades 6 to 8, and if a candidate was moving straight to Grade 8 without taking either Grades 6 or 7, the Rudiments exam pushed the cost of Grade 8 to £3 3s (£166). As earlier chapters have indicated, with exam fees at this level the musical worlds outside the middle classes, for example brass and wind bands, did not form the Board's natural market. However, the minute books do not suggest that the Board saw this situation as offering any real cause for concern; apart from inviting players of brass and woodwind instruments – presumably those learning at public schools – to write in for a syllabus (because they remained unpublished), it simply took no further action.

Despite the attempts to make the Board more attractive to its market, there seemed to be relatively little change in the numbers of teachers entering pupils in the 1930s. The fuzziness of the available data makes it impossible to be accurate about what proportion of UK music teachers were entering candidates for the

---

[18] C. H. H. Parry speaking at the ABRSM's Sixth Annual Dinner, 8 July 1895 (ABRSMA).

ABRSM exams at this time, but it is possible to suggest an indicative figure. The Board's statistics give the number of teachers entering pupils for each of the three annual exam periods, and certainly a proportion of teachers would have been entering pupils for more than one exam session. However, the Board published its teacher figures only on a cumulative basis, which, of course, magnified the impression of teacher support. In 1925/6 the number of teachers entering the Board's School Exams exceeded 16,000 for the first time, and during the 1930s there was an annual average of 16,980 teachers entering candidates.

However, breaking down these figures shows that the Board had a rather smaller UK teacher base than it liked to suggest, and reflects the restricted market for its exams. A more realistic gauge is to average the number of teachers entering candidates for the two most popular exam periods (the summer and winter sessions). In 1933/4, the year when the cumulative teacher total peaked at 18,297, averaging the teacher numbers for these two periods produces the much lower, but probably more realistic figure of 7,212. This seems to be corroborated by the membership of the Society of Corresponding Members, which in that year was 5,470. So 7,212 (which allows for entries by teachers who do not meet the three-year criterion to be a Corresponding Member) is probably a reasonable indication of the Board's teacher support in the UK at the time. The 1931 Census gives a total of 48,500 Musicians and Teachers in England and Wales, subtotalled into 22,600 Teachers, and 25,900 Musicians.[19] (However, the element of self-representation in completing the Census means that the 'teacher/musician' categorization has to be treated with some caution. Some may have thought that 'musician' carried more status than 'teacher' and so described themselves as such, and also a considerable number of those describing themselves as 'musicians' rather than 'music teachers' would nevertheless also undertake teaching as a means of boosting their income.) If we accept that around 7,212 teachers were entering candidates for the Board's exams in 1933/4, this is 32% of the 22,600 Teachers returned in the Census, a percentage that has a broad credibility, given the numbers of teachers who would be entering pupils for Trinity College exams, exams offered by other boards, or teachers who did not enter pupils for exams at all. If this calculation of about one-in-three teachers coming under the ABRSM's direct guidance is correct, the Board, because of its polarized market, clearly exerted considerable influence on the teaching of certain instruments, particularly the piano, as well as being more generally influential through its syllabus requirements for aural and theory.

In the context of the 1930s we also need to have in mind another aspect of the ABRSM's influence. The Board's syllabuses – because of their carefully structured approach – came the closest to teacher-training (in terms of practical guidance in repertoire and technical progression) that most private music teachers would have encountered. In the days before student grants opened up the opportunity for higher education more generally, many music teachers would simply themselves have progressed through the grades and then taken on pupils from their locality in their own turn as economic necessity and opportunity arose. Therefore from today's perspective, although now we are likely to be much more sensitive to

[19] Ehrlich, *The Music Profession in Britain*, table 1.

the fact that the Board's exam system was a manifestation of cultural authority, neither should we underestimate that there was a considerable educational *need* for the Board's exams to help teachers perform their role. The grade structure and exam contents gave a framework to teachers of limited experience; grades also supported those teachers of more musical sophistication, who could use them more selectively in conjunction with their own teaching methods as a means of external verification to reassure parents that the children were indeed on the correct musical path.

Finally, how seriously should we take Allen's claim that the ABRSM system was a means whereby 'all teachers in the country may receive by actual contact the guidance, encouragement and stimulus' of the work of the Royal Schools? In reality, the only personal form of 'actual contact' in the whole process took place when one of the Board's examiners examined and commented on the work of both teacher and pupil. In the print age the benefits of the Board's 'instruction', or 'guidance, encouragement and stimulus' which Allen cited had to be communicated through its prospectuses and published editions of music. But few teachers would have had difficulty in accepting the validity of Allen's claim that the Board's exam process represented 'actual contact' with the Royal Schools. This is because the carefully marked-up editions of exam music prepared by the Board belonged to a well-established tradition. Before the age of recording, the transmission of musical influence through the medium of personalized editions was the closest means of encountering the interpretations of famous players or teachers without actually studying with them or hearing them play in concert. Editions made by celebrated players or renowned teachers, like Busoni's edition of Bach's 48 Preludes and Fugues, were liberally marked up in an attempt to convey the essence of how they played or taught these works. With their own tempi, fingering, phrasing and textual amendments, these editions were the nineteenth-century print equivalent of making a recording. (Such editions are commonly derided in our Urtext age, because their didactic purpose is not always appreciated.) Thus the Board's way of making 'actual contact', through syllabuses and by means of celebrated editions of Bach and Beethoven, was nevertheless an effective means of transmitting guidance and influencing taste.[20]

⁂ Publishing

T HE Board decided to set up its own publishing company for essentially pragmatic reasons. It offered a solution to the perennial problems that had threatened the Board's autonomy in choosing music for its syllabuses, and it also offered greater security in the supply of exam music to teachers and candidates. A further benefit of being its own publisher was that the Board could control its prices and the market discounts it offered retailers. In the early part of the twentieth century, print music was still big business financially, and so the trade,

---

[20] This question of the degree of guidance represented by 'traditional' didactic editions was to resurface in an interesting way during internal discussions at the Board about the philosophy underlying the new Barry Cooper 'Beethoven' edition.

through the Music Publishers Association (MPA), carried considerable weight in stipulating conditions of production and sale. Initially the Board's main publishing focus was on music for its piano exams (the Board's prime market), which was the area causing it most difficulty. Until, as mentioned in Chapter 4, the First World War made it inadvisable to publish its music through a publisher with a German-sounding name, the Board had been dealing with Augener. But Augener had always been reluctant to secure the necessary permissions to publish music outside its own list, and as about 35% of the Board's Piano syllabus consisted of pieces still in copyright, Augener was able to levy a hefty premium for securing copyright agreement from other publishers. After wartime patriotism had forced Augener's expulsion from the MPA in 1914, the Board faced considerable difficulty in finding another publisher willing to issue their piano exam album for the same one shilling price that Augener had charged, and so approached the MPA for assistance. But the MPA made difficulties over the Board's wish to work on a long-term basis with a single publisher, calling it 'arbitrary and unnecessary', obviously hoping to broker deals with members on its own account on a Buggins' turn basis. So when the Board then approached the publisher Joseph Williams directly, the MPA applied pressure to secure retailers a profit of 33.5% on sales of exam albums. The Board appointed Joseph Williams to publish its exam albums (for violin as well as piano), on the basis that the Board could select up to ten pieces per syllabus whose copyright was with other publishers, and agreeing to offer an alternative where the copyright could not be negotiated. However, backing the MPA's restrictive practices, several of the major publishers refused permission for their works to be included in the Board's albums. In view of this boycott, the Board decided in March 1918 to become its own publisher and distributer of official editions of its piano and violin lists, and terminated its arrangement with Joseph Williams. Taken aback, the MPA tried to insist that the Board's terms of trade be on a strictly net basis, i.e. with no discount, but the Board refused, and offered the usual trade discount (33.3%) to shops undertaking to stock the complete range of the Board's music, otherwise it would offer a 25% discount. In January 1920 Jonathan Reeves was appointed to become 'Manager of the publication and sales of Examination Music' from 1 April 1920 on an annual salary of £400, plus 2% commission on net sales in the UK. He was appointed for three years, 'renewable for a further term of three years if reasonably successful', and with a guarantee of one year's salary if his contract was not renewed.[21]

Reeves was to make a financial success of this publishing venture. Very quickly he was urging the Board to expand its publishing scope beyond just the exam albums and other exam material, such as books of scales and sight-reading, into editions of the classics and modern teaching pieces. The Board agreed, and in January 1921 decided to ask Donald Tovey to make a new edition of Bach's *Well-Tempered Clavier*.[22] Initially all went well, and Tovey set down as guidelines for his edition that 'marks of expression, other than Bach's should be in brackets; that difficult passages should be fingered; that the mode of performance of ornaments should be printed over the text; and that permission should be obtained to make a

---

[21] ABMB5: *passim* 10 February 1914 – 3 June 1919; ABMB6: 12 January, 21 June 1920.
[22] ABMB6: 15 December 1920; 10 January 1921.

facsimile of the original title page'. Tovey proposed to submit one sample Prelude and Fugue to illustrate his approach, but after more than a year even Hugh Allen's forcefulness had not managed actually to wring anything out of him. In order to expedite the process it was decided to ask the eminent Bach pianist Harold Samuel to provide the fingering, whereupon Samuel and Tovey promptly fell out because of disagreements about Tovey's preface and editorial. Allen resolved that if they could not be induced to work together, he and Percy Buck would write the preface, 'combining the views of the chief authorities on Bach', and finalize the proofs. In the event, the edition ('Edited with Critical and Explanatory Notes to each Prelude and Fugue by Donald Francis Tovey' and 'Fingered by Harold Samuel') was published in 1924 and announced in that year's syllabus as an 'important new publication'. It proved a huge success as a teaching edition and the fees originally paid to Tovey and Samuel (£75 and £45, respectively) were subsequently doubled.[23]

Emboldened by this success, Reeves had suggested editions of the Bach *Inventions*, the Keyboard Partitas and the Beethoven and Mozart piano sonatas. Originally George Dyson and Harold Craxton were to act as editors for the Beethoven and Mozart sonatas, but first they both disagreed with the editing style specified by the Board's Editorial Committee, and then they turned down the financial terms being offered. By 1929 Tovey (with Craxton) had replaced Dyson on the Beethoven, and Aubyn Raymar had taken on the Mozart. With history repeating itself, the Mozart was being delayed 'owing to Mr Raymar failing to proceed with his part of the work'. Similar problems were hindering the Beethoven, and Tovey seemed to have vanished so completely that Allen was obliged to 'ascertain his whereabouts … so that if necessary the Board could send a messenger to him'. Eventually, though, Tovey started to make progress with his prefaces, but their scale had expanded far beyond what had been expected, and he was asked 'to omit the less important points of the prefaces so as to shorten them generally'. But in May 1930 the publication of the Beethoven was being held up 'by Mr Craxton's failure to deliver edited sonatas', and it was decided 'to press Mr Craxton continually for further Sonatas'. It was only when the Board threatened to bring someone else to take over from him that Craxton completed his editing.[24] In the end the project had so grown that in 1931 it had to be published in two parts. First came the sonatas themselves, as edited by Craxton and with brief introductions and performance notes by Tovey, and second came Tovey's now extensive analyses, published separately as *A Companion to Beethoven's Pianoforte Sonatas*.[25] The edition attained such legendary status, that, as discussed in Chapter 12, even after fifty years its fame was a deterrent to the making of a new critical Urtext edition. Indeed, even after the publication of Barry Cooper's critical edition in 2007, the Craxton/Tovey edition continues to be available.

As the inter-war period ended, the Publications Department was well established and making a significant contribution to the Board's profits. From

---

[23] ABMB6: *passim* 15 December 1920 – 9 January 1923.

[24] ABMB7: *passim* 14 December 1926 – 13 May 1930; ABMB8: 9 December 1930 – 27 January 1931.

[25] In 1998 the *Companion* was published by the ABRSM in a revised edition, edited by Barry Cooper.

6 Design reflecting musical attitudes: the title page of the ABRSM's famous 1931 'Craxton/ Tovey' Beethoven edition. Its layout emphasizes the importance of Beethoven's editorial intermediaries (including the heads of the RAM and the RCM) to symbolize the musical authority of the Associated Board.

May 1937 to April 1938 it had a turnover of £14,591 (the Board's exam income was £41,559), returning a balance of some £3,000 (the Board's exam balance was nearly £7,000).[26] In addition, the Board's reputation had been considerably enhanced by its Bach and Beethoven editions and a good turnover was ensured by a range of other piano repertoire, including Mendelssohn's *Songs without Words*, Schubert's *Impromptus* and *Moments Musicaux*, as well as works by Schumann and Scarlatti and the Mozart Sonatas. On top were the strong sales generated by a large selection of educational repertoire by ABRSM 'house' composers such as Thomas Dunhill and Felix Swinstead. Until the late 1940s the amounts of royalties paid to composers were noted in the minute books. However, these figures need to be treated cautiously, as no detail is given as to what the total covers, or what proportion of the figure represents royalties or covers single payments made for a particular task, such as sight-reading tests. But on an indicative basis these entries tell us who the most successful ABRSM composers were, and what level of financial reward it brought them. The first payment recorded was in 1925, to Thomas Dunhill, Felix Swinstead, Herbert Howells and Benjamin Dale, who each received between £23 and just over £25, or around £1,000 in today's terms. If we fast-forward to 1947, we see that Ernest Read was earning some £88 (approximately £2,560 today), Swinstead £85, Howells £68 and Basil Allchin (from his Aural test booklets) some £53. Dunhill had died in 1946 and his widow received royalties of £89. It is interesting to compare these figures with the royalties paid to editors of the Board's editions of the classics. Also in 1947 Tovey's widow was paid some £181 for royalties on his editions of the Beethoven Sonatas and the Bach *48*. The royalties paid to Craxton for his collaboration with Tovey on the Beethoven, were nearly £110 (some £3,200 in today's terms) for the same period. The ABRSM was a valuable patron to its composers and editors.

⁄⁄⁄ Technology

F OR all of Hugh Allen's seemingly high-minded harrumphing against the new media of broadcasting and recording, in reality the ABRSM's anti-technology agenda was driven by its market vulnerability. The Board's exams were dominated by the piano to such an overwhelming extent that a collapse in the number of piano candidates would have wiped out the Board's profits. In the nine-year period considered earlier (1929/30–1937/8), piano candidates constituted an astonishing 78% of the Board's Practical exams market. As explained, the Board had neither sought to develop nor diversify the instruments it covered, and it was now facing the consequences of its inertia. The 1920s and 1930s saw a significant diminution of the old piano-led music culture in favour of the new convenience, cheapness and expanding musical horizons made available by the radio and the gramophone. In the 'old technology' of traditional domestic music-making, the piano's sheer musical versatility ensured its dominance. It made obvious sense to invest in children's piano lessons – quite apart from the matters of individual fulfilment and social attainment – to enhance the household's capacity to entertain itself.

---

[26] ABRSM, Accounts and Balance Sheet for the Year ended 30 April 1938.

Contrast that with the 1930 report that 'more pianos are sold by householders to dealers than by dealers to householders',[27] and adverts such as the one for the Barker Department Store's 'Great Annual Stocktaking', which sets out the price of pianos – the cheapest at 29 guineas – against that of gramophones – the cheapest only 5 guineas.[28] In 1924 estimated consumer expenditure on musical instruments and sheet music was £9 million, as against £7 million for radios and gramophones; by 1935 that had been reversed – spending on instruments had dropped to £5 million, while for radios and gramophones it had risen to £27 million.[29]

Articles in *The Times* gave important support to these new media. There was general recognition that this technology would bring considerable change to the musical environment but that, as with other technological developments, people will adapt and that the substantial musical benefits to be gained will outweigh the disadvantages of change.[30] The Board's forlorn attempt to preserve its stance put it in a rather ridiculous position, as in the spat between Allen and Walford Davies. This was triggered by Allen's jeremiad on mechanical music in his 1930 Presidential address to the Incorporated Society of Musicians. Grudgingly admitting the potential for musical benefit, Allen also complained that where these media had 'filled many homes with the repellent, devastating and sordid noises of some of the worst forms of jazz and some of the cheapest forms of comic songs ... its influence is pernicious'.[31] Walford Davies, an RCM stalwart and (from 1926) a music adviser to the BBC whose broadcast music talks were enormously admired, rebuked Allen, arguing that 'wireless and gramophone are our born allies ... Already the pursuit of our art has been advanced by them on a scale hitherto unimagined and quite measureless.'[32]

Isolated in the pursuance of its own vested interest, the ABRSM's pronouncements put it very much out of step with the attitudes of other serious musical educators in the 'musical appreciation' movement. A notable figure who early on had grasped technology's potential was Percy Scholes, author of the innovative *The Columbia History of Music through Ear and Eye*, which combined written texts with recordings of the works discussed. And it is difficult not to relate to the enthusiastic reaction of a London schoolteacher: 'My first introduction to the Beethoven symphonies was in the form of pianoforte duets; my pupils are learning to appreciate their orchestral colour as well as their form and principal

[27] 'Music and Mechanism: Sir Hugh Allen's Address', *The Times*, 11 January 1930.

[28] *The Times*, 14 January 1926.

[29] Ehrlich, *The Piano*, 189.

[30] For example, see 'The Gramophone: Preserved Music and its Hearers', *The Times*, 26 January 1926; 'Wireless and the Gramophone: New Developments', *The Times*, 11 February, 1930; 'Novel History of Music: 50 Gramophone Records and series of Books [announcing the *Columbia History of Music through Ear and Eye*], *The Times*, 8 April 1930; 'From Ballad Concert to Wireless', *The Times*, 3 May 1935; also, 'Bringing the Proms to the Fireside', *Glasgow Herald*, [n.d.] September 1932.

[31] 'Music and Mechanism', *The Times*, 11 January 1930.

[32] 'A Mechanical Age: Gramophone and Wireless the Musicians' Allies', *The Times*, 7 January 1930.

themes by hearing excellent orchestral records.'[33] Instead, the Board pursued its minatory finger-wagging, well illustrated from one of the speeches given by Benjamin Dale as he went up and down the country representing the Board at Distribution of Certificate ceremonies:

> there is another danger lurking in Broadcasting … that some lovers of music might be tempted to give up some of their own personal efforts at music-making and to take a merely passive interest in the art. One can imagine such people putting this kind of question to themselves – 'why should I go on struggling with this complicated Fugue of Bach or that exacting Sonata of Beethoven when, by turning a knob, I can hear it played flawlessly by Myra Hess, or Backhaus or other famous 'stars'. And it is possible that some parents might, on similar grounds, be tempted to dispense with music lessons for their children. This, too, is a danger which we must do our best, by advice and precept, to check.[34]

The Board maintained its hostility to the medium by rejecting (if at all possible) offers to broadcast its examination repertoire, nor did it encourage recordings of it. As early as 1923 the Anglo-French Music Company (founded in 1916 by John McEwen, later the RAM's Principal, and Tobias Matthay, the RAM's celebrated piano teacher) had asked the Board if it had any objections to the company making 'a series of gramophone records reproducing the music set for the Pianoforte Examinations'. The Board made no objections, provided that its name was not associated with these recordings and so did not appear to endorse them.[35]

Even where broadcasting was being harnessed to a wider cultural purpose the Board's resistance remained implacable. In 1946 the BBC proposed to broadcast in India a series of programmes featuring works on the syllabuses of different examining bodies, in order to 'raise the standards of performance of Western Music in India'. The Board replied that while it had no objection to what was proposed, whether in broadcasting the music itself or in accompanying it with commentaries by eminent teachers ('who might happen to be Examiners to the Board'), it was felt 'inadvisable' for the Board to be involved in the proposal. A possible, but unspoken, concern may have been that the Board's sharing the platform with its rivals might have carried the implication to the audience that all exam boards were on a level with each other, something it would have been desperate to avoid.[36]

As late as the 1950s the Board was objecting to the BBC staff pianist Violet Carson (later famous as Ena Sharples of *Coronation Street*) broadcasting and commenting on its exam pieces in the BBC Northern Region's *Children's Hour*. It continued to resent recordings specifically made of its exam music because of the profit it brought others on the back of the Board's name, such as those made

---

[33] Joyce Herman, *The Sackbut*, May 1927, 293.

[34] Benjamin Dale, Speech at a Distribution of Certificates ceremony held in Gloucester during the early 1930s (ABRSMA: B. J. Dale Associated Board Addresses).

[35] ABMB6: 13 February 1923.

[36] ABMB9: 23 January 1945.

by James Ching in the 1950s.[37] In 1962 EMI proposed making 'Play-it-Yourself' recordings of the music set for Violin Grades 3 and 4, with complete performances on one side, and just the piano accompaniment on the other. The Board did not object to EMI doing this, but initially decided not to mention them in their syllabus. After strong representation from EMI that it would also benefit from the venture, the Board agreed to make a footnoted reference in the syllabus, but with the warning, 'the interpretation in these performances is not necessarily the only one acceptable to examiners'. Shortly after, EMI abandoned the series because it made a loss.[38] Old audio technology made this pioneering attempt clumsy to use. By contrast, a digital application called 'Speedshifter' (a download offered by the Board in 2009) has made the co-ordination of the learner's part with the recorded accompaniment very much more straightforward. Ironically, as soon as syllabuses were produced for less familiar instruments, such as the guitar, the issue of examiners' training arose; accordingly recordings were used to illustrate the points made in the briefing notes for examiners.[39] Today the Board treats recordings, downloads and podcasts as integral elements of its market presence and professional development strategies.

𝒲 The ABRSM's musical values

W E can retrace the ABRSM's musical ethos through its syllabuses. Their contents preserve for us the Board's musical attitudes and its aesthetic values, which are captured by the repertoire, technique-building processes and musical skills prescribed for its examinees. An obvious but important point to make about this documentary evidence is that if a piece, a technical requirement or a musical test is included in a syllabus, it is there because the syllabus-setters consider it to have a place in the Board's musical scheme of things. Thus these syllabuses are, in the original sense of the word, 'representative' of the Board's musical values. And for much of its history the Board's syllabuses were indeed drawn up by senior figures from the Academy or the College, who set the standards of expected musical accomplishment for each grade which were then left to be enforced by the Board's examiners.

There needed to be a tight musical match between the scope and requirements of the ABRSM's syllabuses, and the skills and mindset of those sent out to examine them. For clearly the Board could only offer exams that its examiners had the wish, credibility and musical capacity to assess. The examining process left no room for ambiguity, and much of the public's belief in the grade system was based on the predication that all the Board's examiners marked to a common standard. It was this symbiosis of the Board and its examiners in propounding a comprehensive set of musical values that made the ABRSM such a coherent musical force, and which established examiners' judgements and the Board's syllabuses as 'official' arbiters of musical correctness. Accordingly the Board's conservative musical

---

[37] ABMB10: 18 March 1952.
[38] ABMB10: 30 January, 27 March 1962; ABMB11: 22 March 1966.
[39] ABMB11: 14 June 1966.

ethos became the determinative musical experience of its candidates, imbibed by successive generations of musicians as they progressed through the grades. The grade process is such a formative influence because of the all-embracing way that it can shape learners' expectations, tastes and responses. This can be especially the case for pupils whose teachers have little musical breadth and so adhere very closely to the grade syllabus at all times; for many pupils in this position, their grade experience established or conditioned their musical preferences for life.

Even though the Associated Board has played such a major role in transforming British musical life into the world force that it has become, its significance in the cultural process of musical formation is seldom much discussed. Its system of musical grades was so effective in training musicians because of the quality of its syllabuses in staging the technical development of instrumentalists and singers, and because it offered a clearly defined structure or ladder of attainment that could be used more or less flexibly by teachers. But participation in these exams requires engagement – or at least acceptance – with the cultural perspectives they contain. This is the area in which the ABRSM's reputation for a conservative outlook that constrained musical adventure, particularly in matters of repertoire, has gathered more criticism. The negative consequences of the Board's musical leadership have been most felt in periods of its history when its cultural base was narrowly restricted to very traditional tonal idioms, and less musically conventional pieces were firmly eschewed.

Several commentators have remarked on the twentieth-century British unease with modernist music, from Arnold Whittall's observation that 'it might seem that British musical life, as well as British musical composition, has been characterized at least as much by a resistance to [twentieth-century modernism] as by an embrace of it',[40] to the critic Richard Toop, who diagnosed British resistance to avant-garde compositional styles as the consequence of a musical culture 'where 19th-century traditions of amateur music-making and all-purpose anti-intellectualism are still very much embedded in the collective psyche of the musical establishment'.[41] One explanation of this very British reluctance (equally evident among audiences, performers and composers alike) to accept contemporary idioms is that it was a consequence of the particular sort of musical conditioning imposed by the graded examination culture – a culture with strong nineteenth-century roots. On the basis of this argument, the powerfully formative musical experience exerted by the grade system carries at least some responsibility for the observable tension between modernist and traditionalist music cultures that has characterized twentieth-century British musical life.

The middle-class take-up of the Board's grade exams meant that the normative values of the ABRSM's musical culture (transmitted via its syllabuses) had defined the cultural expectations of many middle-class families well before the BBC began to influence taste through the music it programmed. And although most of the BBC's repertoire was drawn from the classical music mainstream, there were

---

[40] Arnold Whittall, 'British Music in the Modern World', in *The Blackwell History of Music in Britain*, vol. 6: *The Twentieth Century*, ed. Stephen Banfield (Oxford: Blackwell Publishing, 1995), 9–26; the quotation is on p. 11.

[41] Richard Toop, 'Four Facets of "The New Complexity"', *Contact* 32 (Spring 1988), 4.

some notable exceptions. During the late 1920s and 1930s its broadcasting of concerts of European modernist music by Berg (including *Wozzeck*), Schoenberg, Webern, Stravinsky and Hindemith made this radical repertoire accessible to many British listeners for the first time.[42] It is worth emphasizing that for most people such broadcasts would have been the first truly counter-cultural alternative to the conservative British musical diet on offer in the educational and concert hall spheres. In his biography of the conductor Adrian Boult, Michael Kennedy discusses the constraints on repertoire in the 1920s occasioned both by the limitations of orchestral playing and the unwillingness of audiences to pay for adventurous programmes: 'Compared with today, the 1920s in an English provincial city were a Stone Age musically. [...] We too easily forget that for public – and critics – in 1924 a Brahms symphony was still an adventure.'[43]

Until 1956, when women examiners were first appointed, an ABRSM examiner was male and nearly always primarily a keyboard player, often academically highly qualified, and usually traditional in musical outlook. For much of the Board's history, examiners were chosen on the basis of personal recommendation, and drawn from a restricted range of musical occupations, predominantly staff of the Royal Schools, cathedral organists and public school music staff.[44] Many were organists whose musical tastes and character had been formed by the preserved culture of the church music tradition. Recruiting such a narrowly based but well-connected group of examiners created an influential cadre of musicians all of similar musical values and cultural perspectives, whose own positions of musical authority made them disinclined to see challenges to their aesthetic values or musical mindset. Thus while examiners' individual attainments as players and in the paperwork skills of conventional harmony and counterpoint were highly developed, they were more likely to be antagonistic to, rather than interested in, musical innovation. This was particularly the case when it came to the radical techniques and the modernist musical idioms that were such a strong feature of contemporary European musical life. It is therefore not surprising that many progressive musicians should have felt that the Board had become something of a musical redoubt for the preservation and economic benefit of a particular sort of British music composition, because its music appeared so regularly on the Piano syllabus or in the Board's own publications. The Board's own 'contemporary' style was epitomized by composers such as John Ireland, Thomas Dunhill, Herbert Howells, Eric Thiman, George Dyson, Markham Lee and Felix Swinstead.

Perhaps the most celebrated illustration of the restricting creative environment produced by this form of musical conservatism is the case of Benjamin Britten.

[42] For a comprehensive account of the BBC dissemination of 'advanced' European contemporary music and the works that were broadcast, see Jenny Doctor, *The BBC and Ultra-Modern Music, 1922–1936: Shaping a Nation's Tastes* (Cambridge: Cambridge University Press, 1999).

[43] Michael Kennedy, *Adrian Boult* (London: Papermac, 1989), 133.

[44] In the early days the selection of examiners was done by a vote (so making it essential for an application to be supported by the personal recommendation of a Governing Body member), such as at the meeting that accepted H. D. Davan Whetton (proposed by Parry and Parratt) but rejected (without explanation) the application by Dr A. J. Silver, who did not have such a recommendation (ABMB5: 13 October 1914).

Britten had passed his ABRSM Advanced Certificate (i.e. Grade 7) in January 1927, aged thirteen, and later went for composition lessons with Frank Bridge, perhaps the most musically adventurous British composer of his generation. Bridge, who was decidedly *not* an ABRSM examiner, and whose enthusiasms included the music of Alban Berg, introduced Britten to an advanced harmonic world then only very rarely encountered in English musical life.[45] In 1930 Britten sat for his RCM composition scholarship in front of Vaughan Williams, John Ireland and Sydney P. Waddington. Ireland and Waddington were stalwart ABRSM examiners, and Waddington had been on its Governing Body since 1916. All three acknowledged Britten's brilliance, but Waddington (highly regarded by his contemporaries for his teaching and musicianship, and a close friend of Vaughan Williams) is reported to have said, 'What is an English public school boy doing writing music of this kind?'[46] Britten later attempted to study in Vienna with Berg on an RCM travelling scholarship (prompted by Frank Bridge's recommendation that he should 'leave England and experience a different musical climate'), but this gesture of independence was firmly quashed by the RCM, probably by Hugh Allen himself. As reported back to Britten by his mother, the refusal was on the grounds that Berg was 'not a good influence', leading Britten to comment that, 'There was at that time an almost moral prejudice against serial music.'[47]

To the twenty-first-century eye, all this must seem a very odd situation, not least because today's technology has given the individual freedom to explore an astonishing breadth of instantly accessible repertoire realized in performance – a world away from the situation when the only way to gain an impression of unfamiliar music was by reading and auralizing the score or by trying it out on the piano, unless it was given a BBC broadcast. In the 1930s, only a comparatively limited range of repertoire had been recorded because commercial pressures meant an emphasis on well-known works from the classical repertoire for which a market could be guaranteed. So for most people until the final quarter of the last century, music's cultural boundaries were quite tightly drawn between the limits of a recorded repertory that was largely defined by its market potential and the ideas of musical worth defined by an encompassing educational system. It is easy to see that in this circumstance the BBC played a hugely influential role in expanding the British musical experience.[48]

---

[45] Humphrey Carpenter, *Benjamin Britten: A Biography* (London: Faber & Faber, 1992), 14–19.

[46] Quoted in ibid., 37.

[47] For Britten's account of this, see *Letters from a Life: Selected Letters and Diaries of Benjamin Britten, 1913–1976*, vol. 1: *1923–1939*, ed. Donald Mitchell and Philip Reed (London: Faber & Faber, 1991), 394–5.

[48] For accounts of the BBC's music in its very different phases of radical and less adventurous music programming, see, *inter alia*, Nicholas Kenyon, *The BBC Symphony Orchestra: The First Fifty Years, 1930–1980* (London: BBC, 1981); William Glock, *Notes in Advance: An Autobiography in Music* (Oxford: Oxford University Press, 1991); Humphrey Carpenter, *The Envy of the World: Fifty Years of the BBC Third Programme and Radio 3* (London: Weidenfield & Nicholson, 1996); Alison Garnham, 'The BBC in Possession: 1945–59', in *The Proms*, ed. Doctor, Wright and Kenyon, 130–67.

⅍ The music college profession and the BBC: contesting musical culture

As suggested, the formative nature of the Board's exams mean that the conservative musical values its repertoire transmitted were influential in shaping British musical culture. This makes it difficult to dissociate the ABRSM's own guidance from the strange reception history of modernist and avant-garde music in Britain. Because the Board spoke for and employed a significant element of the British music profession, it has always had a strong nationalistic aspect to it. It is also important to remember that the Board was not alone in its suspicion of the BBC and its potential to be an independent musical force; it shared this attitude with concert promoters and orchestras who feared that broadcast music would destroy concert attendance.[49] Early signs of the Board's mistrust of both the BBC and of broadcasting came in 1923 when Allen reported that the BBC wished to broadcast the music set by the Board for its exams in 1924.[50] Yet far from seeing this as an opportunity, at the next meeting Allen reported that he had met the Director of the BBC (John Reith), 'and had explained that the Board could not give its approval to the broadcasting of its examination music though it had no power to prevent the music being broadcasted'.[51] When the next year the BBC renewed its offer, it elicited an even more negative response: not only did the Board not wish the broadcasting to appear to be done under its imprimatur, it did not wish for any of the Board's examiners be employed to play the pieces.[52]

The underlying antagonism came to a head during the 1930s in a jockeying for position between the traditional conservatism of the music college heads (as the music profession's 'establishment') and the rising new musical power of the BBC. This was the period when the BBC was developing a musical policy of its own to signal its independent role as a publicly funded broadcasting service. In his classic study *A Culture for Democracy*, D. L. LeMahieu draws attention to the BBC's careful use of classical music to construct and reflect its own cultural identity and sense of broadcasting mission.[53] The professional establishment was obviously anxious to push the BBC into a music policy that privileged national music interests. The profession's evident suspicion of the new technology of broadcasting, as well as the institution that controlled it, was shaped by experience: the arrival of the 'talkies' around 1928 had decimated musicians' employment, something still very much on the profession's mind. The British musical establishment resented the BBC's support of European composers and performers, and also disliked its championing of modernist idioms (as detrimental to 'core' musical values). The BBC felt that the founding charter laid upon it a rather wider remit than to champion national composers and performers if it was to fulfil adequately the Reithian-defined mission to 'educate, inform and entertain' in the sphere of

[49] See, for example, Kennedy, *Boult*, 137–43.
[50] ABMB6: 13 November 1923.
[51] ABMB6: 27 November 1923.
[52] ABMB6: 30 September 1924.
[53] D. L. LeMahieu, *A Culture for Democracy: Mass Communication and the Cultivated Mind in Britain between the Wars* (Oxford: Clarendon Press, 1998), 183–90.

serious music. These conflicting stances are highlighted in the evidence submitted to the 1935 Ullswater Committee, which Parliament had convened to review the work of the BBC as part of the charter renewal process. The evidence to Ullswater shows the sort of pressure that was being exerted by the nationalist, conservative axis of the British music colleges and the Associated Board in an attempt to mould the BBC to its way of thinking.

The music colleges had been given an official voice within the BBC in 1925, when Reith had created the Music Advisory Committee (MAC), which was chaired by Hugh Allen, with John McEwen (Principal of the RAM) and Landon Ronald (Principal of the Guildhall School) as prominent members. (Trinity was not represented.) As Nicholas Kenyon saw the situation: 'The Committee represented established interests, at the opposite pole from those of Reith's Music Department, and in the years to come it would attempt to interfere in artistic decisions, claiming that the BBC should support only British music and musicians at a time when [its programming was] most adventurously continental.'[54] In her history of the BBC's involvement with 'ultra-modern' music, Jenny Doctor chronicles some of the unedifyingly nationalistic battles (of the 'British music and British performers for British airwaves' variety) that followed.[55] As well as interfering in policy, the Advisory Committee sought to influence the selection of Music Department personnel (for example, blocking the appointment of the more modernist composer Arthur Bliss as Boult's senior colleague),[56] attempting to pack the newly constituted Music Programme Advisory Panel with College and Academy nominees; all seven names the MAC proposed taught at either the College or the Academy, and five of them were ABRSM examiners.[57]

It was Boult, the BBC's Director of Music, who bore the brunt of the Advisory Committee's pressure, and tensions came to a head at the Ullswater hearings. Boult's opinion of the Advisory Committee and its agenda was unequivocal:

> More often than not the members occupy their time at meetings trying to bully the Corporation into adopting courses of action which they think would be to the benefit of the music profession, but without due regard for the Corporation's programme standards, or for the interest of the listening public. That Committee has tried to insist on the Corporation broadcasting a far larger quota of British music than is merited by the quality and the quantity of that music.[58]

The verdict given by the Ullswater Committee powerfully vindicated the stance taken by Boult and the BBC. The Committee's adumbration of the difference between the immediate interests of the music profession and the responsibilities of

---

[54] Kenyon, *The BBC Symphony Orchestra*, 11.

[55] Doctor, *The BBC and Ultra-Modern Music*, 232–305.

[56] Ibid., 286; this cleared the way for the appointment of R. S. Thatcher as Deputy Music Director. Thatcher, Director of Music at Harrow, was a longtime ABRSM examiner, who had sought to become Secretary in succession to James Muir (1930). Thatcher became Principal of the RAM in 1949.

[57] Doctor, *The BBC and Ultra-Modern Music*, 238–40.

[58] Quoted in ibid., 304.

a nationally funded broadcasting corporation cleared the way for the Corporation's pursuit of its independent music policy: 'The purpose which a broadcasting organization should regard as paramount is that fine music, played under the best conditions, may be heard and appreciated over the whole country to the vast extent which broadcasting alone has made possible.'[59] Effectively, the confidence that the Ullswater Committee showed in the BBC's approach to music broadcasting brought to an end that phase of the attempt of the music college professionals to secure a significant element of control over the BBC's music policies. Very quickly the BBC became the dominant influence in British music, while the ABRSM and music college culture was firmly relegated to the educational sphere.

Of course, anti-modernist sentiment was not confined to music alone, but fed in to a very British type of creative aesthetic between the wars. As the artist Paul Nash expressed it:

> Whether it is possible to 'go modern' and still 'be British' is a question vexing a few people today […] The battle lines have been drawn up: internationalism versus an indigenous culture; renovation versus conservatism; the industrial versus the pastoral; the functional versus the futile.[60]

Nash offers here a very neat encapsulation of the tensions between modernist abstraction and traditional representation. But we would be missing the point if we saw the BBC/ABRSM–music profession spat as only (or even primarily) a cultural issue. It was a much cruder battle about power which saw the music college establishment seeking to dominate the parvenu BBC. For the Corporation it was a question of its institutional and broadcasting independence, while the music profession was seeking to maintain the position and cultural influence it had achieved for itself since the late nineteenth century. But the BBC's economic and broadcasting power soon put it into the ascendant. Not only did the BBC, with its prestige and fees, become the most significant patron of composers and the employer of choice for all musicians in the UK, but its broadcast output made it the pre-eminent arbiter of musical taste and standards of performance.

---

[59] Quoted in ibid., 305.

[60] Paul Nash, 'Going Modern and Being British', quoted in Alexandra Harris, *Romantic Moderns* (London: Thames & Hudson, 2010), 21.

7 The Board in Wartime

〽 Maintaining the exams

THE Second World War put considerable pressure on the Board's capacity to maintain its examining. As Table 7.1 shows, there was an astonishing 64% increase in the number of entries by the end of the war as people returned to peacetime life. The war involved the civilian population very directly. Disruption of the railway network, fuel shortages and the heavy German bombing of major urban centres caused considerable logistical dislocation, quite apart from the constant danger to civilians. So the determination of teachers, candidates and examiners from the very outset to continue the exams as far as was possible can be seen as an example of the British wartime spirit. The issues of sending examiners abroad also put the Board under very great difficulty. The continuation of overseas examining was indicative of the importance felt in maintaining cultural links between the home country and the rest of the British World during the conflict.

The Board began its planning for the war by constructing an air raid shelter in the basement of 15 Bedford Square and moving some of its records and stationery to the RCM so that it could work from there if Bedford Square was hit. The Board feared that the initial fall-off in candidates (see Table 7.1) would set the trend for the war, and so it moved swiftly to reduce examiners' fees and allowances in order to bolster the financial position. It also instituted severe staffing cutbacks, stopped the public Distribution of Certificates ceremonies, suspended the Society of Corresponding Members, and replaced gold medals with 'Certificates of Honour'.[1] All this helped to offset, but did not cover, the drop of some £6,000 of fee revenue experienced in the usually popular winter exam period.[2] And in addition, the Board had to take on expensive additional insurance for risks to examiners. Further financial pressure was caused by illness across the country with the abrupt withdrawal of over 700 candidates from the spring exams after the examiners' itineraries had been settled; most candidates were allowed to transfer to the summer exams.[3]

It is hard not to feel sympathy for the Board's examiners as they coped with wartime circumstances. Their fees were cut from 5 to 4 guineas, and allowances and travel conditions were also reduced. Third-class, rather than first-class rail travel, became the norm, something that must have added considerably to the discomfort and hardship of those wartime tours. The Board excused this cut in fees on the grounds that it reflected similar reductions being made to professors at the Academy and the College.[4] However, the reluctance the Board displayed in returning fees to 5 guineas – despite the huge upsurge in income from the increased candidate numbers – carries a whiff of opportunism. Restitution of the 5 guinea fee came only in the winter of 1944, after the Board's income had reached

[1] ABMB9: 10 October 1939.
[2] ABMB9: 21 November 1939.
[3] ABMB9: 19 March 1940.
[4] ABMB9: 23 July 1940.

unprecedented heights, when Harold Craxton asked, on behalf of the examiners, that the fee be increased to 6 guineas to reflect the Board's new prosperity. The Board refused, but offered the compromise of returning the examiners' first-class travel allowance.[5]

The Secretary reported that an unusually large number of examiners had refused tours, and that several had suffered from the bombing. Thornton Lofthouse had been bombed while examining in Plymouth in March 1941; he lost all his possessions and was extremely lucky to have escaped physically unscathed. He also lost all the results of his examining in Plymouth and Falmouth, and – unsurprisingly – he felt unable to examine as scheduled the following day. All the examined candidates were deemed to have passed! The Board expressed sympathy with Lofthouse's predicament, but also decided that it would not pay compensation to examiners for losses caused by enemy action while on tour.[6] When the Theory papers worked by candidates in Newport and Birmingham in the summer of 1943 were destroyed in an air raid, the candidates were given a resit in the winter period without further charge. The exams in that winter were again disrupted by a flu epidemic and the withdrawal of some 1,200 candidates. Under pressure, the Board suspended its usual requirements, offering a full refund with prior notification, and some refund for last-minute absences, and waived the need for a medical certificate. However, for any examiner suffering flu on tour and unable to return home, things were less generous: he had to plead a special case if he wanted his subsistence allowance to cover the additional time spent ill in bed. Wartime instructions to examiners asked them to be prepared to reorganize their local timetables in the event of disruptions caused by air raid warnings. And, because of the dislocation caused by school and family evacuations carried out without notice, examiners were also asked to be prepared to examine candidates who might present themselves without being timetabled. Exam centres were required to organize transport for examiners from the train station, but otherwise examiners were left to bear much of the practical brunt of wartime dislocation and discomfort on top of reduced fees, downgraded travel and little hope of a sympathetic response to illness or being bombed out. So, not surprisingly, the problem of securing sufficient examiners became acute. Even so, the Board still refused to appoint women to do the job.[7]

Overseas examining represented a considerable challenge, and sometimes the examiners themselves showed great ingenuity in securing tickets for very risky sea passages. Examining in Australia and New Zealand was kept going because of such determination, and some examiners stayed out for extended periods. Unsurprisingly, the exams in Malta were cancelled in 1941, but as early as 1943 the doughty Maltese Representative, Miss Briffa, despite the destruction of her own home, had written to urge their reinstatement. Astonishingly, given the conditions in the Mediterranean, the exams took place in 1944, using the 1940/1 syllabus; the examiner, Dr Thomas Fielden, was paid £180, rather above the usual rate for undertaking the trip. (Examiners' fees were then based, pro rata, on

[5] ABMB9: 24 October 1944; 15 May 1945.

[6] ABMB9: 29 April 1941.

[7] ABMB9: 10 November, 8 December 1942.

a salary of £800.) Both Fielden and Dr Frederick Staton (who had just returned from examining in the West Indies) were concerned at the quality of the wartime teaching they had encountered, and urged the Board to provide 'refresher courses' for teachers and summer schools for advanced pupils. Initially the Board seemed receptive to the idea of making such courses an integral part of its work overseas after the war; however, the idea was not pursued, and the Board's obstinate reluctance to allow its examiners to offer help to teachers abroad became a point of continuous frustration.[8]

The Board relaxed several of its exam regulations in the light of wartime conditions. In July 1940 examiners were asked 'to adopt an exceptionally sympathetic attitude towards candidates and to mark leniently in view of the difficulties under which they had been preparing and would be attending for examination'.[9] This was in response to the effects of bombing raids across the UK throughout the war, and later the V1 and V2 flying bomb attacks on London in 1944. Some 2,400 candidates withdrew from the 1944 summer exams (costing some £1,100 – nearly £36,000 today – in refunding three-quarters of the entry fee), and the Board's AGM was first postponed and then held in the most minimalist fashion, with no examiners or HLRs invited.[10] The regulation that required Grade 6–8 candidates to pass the Theory section before they qualified for the award was being pragmatically applied, and by January 1942 some 790 candidates had their Theory outstanding. The Board was also involved in other forms of morale boosting. The Red Cross applied for a prisoner of war in Stalag Luft VIII to take a diploma, and an LRSM in Theory was offered with no fee charged. As a result, the Red Cross requested, and the Board agreed, that Theory exams might be made more generally available to PoWs (eighty-one took Board exams in 1943), and this was followed up by offering a discount on Board publications purchased for PoWs.[11] In December 1942 it was agreed to allow an aircraftsman on active service to take the harmony grades on an accelerated basis in quick succession, the condition being that the Camp Education Officer be responsible for the exam arrangements. The Board continued to give PoWs and civilian internees repatriated from Germany free entry to written exams until November 1945.[12]

There are several examples of the Board behaving well to its office staff on active service, and its practice seems to have been to pay some sort of 'retaining allowance' for at least some of them. In the case of Robert Thomas, a cashier's assistant who had been confirmed as a prisoner of the Japanese, the Board decided to continue paying his mother the difference between his salary and army pay (£2 5s per week).[13] This had a happy ending, because Thomas survived his experience and returned to work in 1946. But, as was probably the case with most organizations, there was some injustice, too. One Mr Randall, a clerk in

[8] ABMB9: 26 October 1943; 16 May 1944.
[9] ABMB9: 23 July 1940.
[10] ABMB9: 27 June, 26 September 1944.
[11] ABMB9: 23 June, 29 September 1942; 25 May 1943.
[12] ABMB9: 15 May 1945.
[13] ABMB9: 22 June 1943.

the Publishing Department, found himself the victim of summary justice when he declared himself a conscientious objector. The Secretary, Hilary Macklin, and the Publishing Manager, Jonathan Reeves, considered his grounds for doing so insufficient, and decided that 'they could not recommend the continuance of his employment with the Board, when he should be engaged in national service'. Accordingly, he was sacked 'as a further measure of staff reduction'.[14] Paradoxically, the Board was harsh on women volunteers, telling one Miss Violet Dunkley that although the Board would not object to her volunteering, her employment would cease, and she would have to reapply to work again at the Board after demobilization.[15] As in the First World War, male conscription had made the Board very dependent on its female labour force. So consternation was caused when women staff were told to attend the Ministry of Labour and National Service with the possibility of their being required to undertake work of national importance. Hugh Allen made representations on the Board's behalf to secure their exemption and there was relief at the announcement that the Board's female office workers would be treated on the same basis as university administrative staff, and that women with special qualifications or in pivotal positions would not be withdrawn without prior substitution.[16]

Hilary Macklin himself had been offered the chance to enrol as a temporary Principal in the Ministry of Shipping. Macklin's secondment proved very successful; he was involved in running the North Atlantic convoys, was sent to Washington and then became principal private secretary to the Minister of War Transport. The Board was anxious that he should come back and not remain in Whitehall. Accordingly he returned in October 1944 to an enhanced salary of £1,200 plus 15% 'additional allowance' and on the express understanding that he should be able to retire on a full pension aged sixty. In post again, he reorganized the Board's administration along Civil Service lines, and his skills kept the operation running effectively despite the severe pressures it was to face after the war. Given the Board's resistance to appointing women examiners, surprisingly it appointed the female Assistant Secretary Miss J. L. Harding to deputize as Secretary in Macklin's absence. This arrangement had proved enormously successful, and on Macklin's return, Miss Harding was given three months' leave on full pay as a gesture of the Board's appreciation.[17]

Wartime brought some unexpected consequences. One was an astonishing increase in the Publishing Department's sales, reaching nearly £18,000 in 1941. This exceeded the previous highest sales of nearly £16,000 which the Department made as far back as 1924/5, shortly after it was established. An explanation of this odd-seeming situation is that the Publishing Department's potential had always been deliberately constrained by the Board's publishing policy which was not to compete with commercial music sellers, but instead to confine Board publications to material in connection with the examinations.[18] Presumably this policy was

---

[14] ABMB9: 19 March 1940.
[15] ABMB9: 19 May 1942.
[16] ABMB9: 20 January, 17 February 1942.
[17] ABMB9: 5 December 1944.
[18] ABMB9: 17 February 1942; 26 October 1943.

Table 7.1 UK music exam entries and ABRSM income, 1938–45

Year	UK music exam entries	Dividend taken by RAM/RCM	Profit available for distribution
1938	50,269	£4,036	n/a
1939	43,578	£4,181	n/a
1940	36,495	£975	n/a
1941	43,215	£1,721	n/a
1942	54,820	£3,022	n/a
1943	72,095	£4,000	£16,062
1944	84,367	£4,812	£20,793
1945	82,553	£5,127	£27,009

intended as a sweetener for when it came to negotiating the price of copyright permissions to reproduce other publishers' music in the Board's exam albums. In 1940 the Publishing Department's sales had been below £10,000,[19] and no explanation for the sudden surge is offered, but 1941 also saw a significant increase in candidates (see Table 7.1) which would have generated increased sales of the examination albums. The Board had also been building up its list of editions of the piano classics (considered to be exam repertoire and so not infringing its policy of avoiding direct competition with music publishers), and some of the sales increase would have come from these. However, wartime paper shortages began to bite: printed Annual Reports were shelved for the duration, only two lists were specified for each grade, and syllabuses were made to run for two or more years.[20] This was difficult for piano teachers, the Board's main income source, who faced three years (1942–4) of teaching to the same syllabus. In response to their complaints, candidates were allowed to play any study set for their grade in place of the first set piece.[21] In fact it was only possible to provide a new syllabus in 1945/6 because the Paper Controller granted a licence to the printers for the paper required.[22] The problem of achieving sufficient variety in the piano grades continued until the allocation of paper was relaxed in 1948. After that it was decided to give priority to the Board's own editions such as the Beethoven and Mozart sonatas, and Bach's 48; and instead of three lists of pieces for each grade, the wartime practice of two lists was maintained, with an option to substitute one Board-published classical piece to give more choice.[23]

Perhaps the biggest surprise of these war years was the enormous leap in candidate numbers, as Table 7.1 shows. The music entries for 1938 were close to the average, and then fell sharply as the war began to impact on the civilian population. Astonishingly, entries then surge in the successive war years 1942–4, when entries

[19] ABMB9: 29 April 1941.
[20] ABMB9: 19 November 1940; 15 July 1941.
[21] ABMB9: 22 June 1943.
[22] ABMB9: 18 January 1944.
[23] ABMB9: 20 March 1945.

grew to 67% above those for 1938. How should we interpret this wartime increase? One explanation is that it indicates the extent to which the Board exams had come to be emblematic of normal life for a segment of the middle-class population. But there were other aspects of wartime life that probably also contributed to the phenomenon. One, as Juliet Gardiner observes, was the unprecedented demand for something to read that the conditions of war had created, and Table 7.1 suggests that learning music was also one of the 'take-your-mind-off-things' activities that the war encouraged.[24] The BBC's audience for music and drama had doubled,[25] and concert audiences were very much on the increase, helped by the subsidies available to orchestras through the Council for the Encouragement of Music and the Arts, the forerunner of today's Arts Council.[26] It is likely that the sharp increase in music candidates reflects this wider picture, and especially the countrywide stimulus that many musical activities received for morale-boosting purposes through public subsidy to the arts.

This growth in entries put the Board in an extraordinarily cash-rich position. The Schools took a disciplined approach to this bonanza, taking only a proportion of the full dividend. This was only possible because, unexpectedly, the Schools had suddenly started to receive a significant increase in government support. Having had the notional £500 grant annually since Queen Victoria's reign, they received £8,000–10,000 in 1944 and some £17,000 in 1949.[27] It was extremely fortunate that the rest of the Board's new surplus was left in the business because, as we shall see, a series of astonishing misjudgements in late 1947 would so severely diminish the ABRSM operation that by 1953 these new reserves had been almost exhausted.

[24] Juliet Gardiner, *Wartime Britain* (London: Headline, 2004), 484–5.

[25] Peter Clarke, *Hope and Glory: Britain, 1900–2000*, 2nd edn (Harmondsworth: Penguin Books, 2004), 212.

[26] Perhaps the most comprehensive and statistically informed overview of British musical life at this time, with evidence of the growth of audiences and concert provision, is The Arts Enquiry, *Music: A Report on Musical Life in Britain Sponsored by the Dartington Hall Trustees* (London: Political and Economic Planning, 1949).

[27] Ibid., 182–4.

8 The Post-War Board

⅄ The new partners

T HE act that heralded a new phase in the Board's history – the expansion of the ABRSM partnership – came suddenly, and without formal consultation or prior warning to the Board's Governing Body. In November 1946 it was simply informed that the councils of the College and the Academy were inviting the Principals of the Royal Manchester College and the Royal Scottish Academy 'to become co-opted members of the Board so that those two Royal Schools might be identified with the Board's activities'.[1] This lack of prior involvement in such a major decision underlines the Board's position as only an administrative adjunct of the two London Royals. However, the involvement of the northern schools was offered only on a very circumscribed basis. The minutes specify that their co-option would not affect 'the constitutional position whereby the Board derived its authority from the governing bodies of the R.A.M. and the R.C.M., and the title of the Board would remain unchanged except for the omission of the word "London"'.[2] In other words, the 1910 Partnership Agreement remained operative. The composition of the Board's governing body retained five members for each senior partner and allocated only one each for the juniors. There was also a significant differential in the allocation of profits: in the 1948 distribution, the London Schools (the 'Partners') each received £8,461, while Manchester received £1,000 and the Scottish just £200. Over the years, as the Board's profits increased, so did the proportion taken out by the London Schools, while that given to the northerners remained very low, a situation that reflects the Londoners' continuing dependence upon their income from the Board, as Table 8.1 shows.

The Manchester College of Music's first petition for a royal charter in 1894 had been blocked by the London Royals. It had been a costly failure. So in 1923, when Manchester was preparing its new application, it had been careful to negotiate with the London Royal Schools the terms on which they would agree not to oppose its second petition. The condition extracted by the London Schools was that the terms of the Manchester charter should not empower it to offer a scheme of external exams or diplomas.[3] Having successfully ensured that Manchester would not encroach on its market, the ABRSM then simply ignored it, despite the anomaly in the Board's own title that Manchester's new status as a Royal School of Music had introduced. It was only in 1937 that Manchester's position was first referred to at the Board, when Hugh Allen questioned whether the ABRSM's position would be strengthened if someone from the RMCM was co-opted as a member; the minutes make it very clear that the possibility of a partnership was not being raised, and the idea was not taken further.[4] However, in 1944 a further complication had arisen because a royal charter had been granted

[1] ABMB9: 12 November 1946.

[2] Ibid.

[3] ABMB6: 27 September 1921; Kennedy, *History of the Royal Manchester College of Music*, 12, 66.

[4] ABMB9: 26 January 1937.

to the Scottish Academy of Music and Drama. On the face of it, the consequent offer to the northern Royals to join the ABRSM seemed a neat solution to what would have been the awkwardness of an 'Associated Board of the Royal Schools of Music' from which half of the nation's Royal Schools were clearly disassociated. Linking the Scotland and Manchester Schools would also be likely to play well with the northern exam market. But perhaps as much of a pressure behind this expansion of the Board was the Secretary's urgent need for an additional twelve examiners to meet demand. The minutes state: 'Members of the professorial staffs of the Schools at Manchester and Glasgow would be eligible for appointment by the Board as Examiners.'[5] Given that the Board was barely coping with the large increase in candidate numbers, participation by the northerners secured access to a new pool of *male* examiners.

Both northern institutions accepted the offer to join the ABRSM, though neither Principal – Robert Forbes of the RMCM and Ernest Bullock of the RSAMD – was present at their first invited meeting.[6] Both, though, attended the next meeting in March 1947, at which the return of the Annual Lunch was agreed, and the Board's President, HM Queen Mary, gave formal approval to the enlargement of the Board. By way of a welcome, it was again spelled out to the northerners that the 1910 Agreement was not open for amendment, and so their invitation to join the ABRSM conferred no legal rights on them, because the Board 'had no independent legal existence apart from the authority granted to it by the governing bodies of the parent Institutions which alone had the right to enter into contractual obligations or to alter the powers delegated to the Board as an external committee of the associated Schools'.[7] As the years went by, the northerners saw themselves very much in the position of distant country members of a London club that was being managed for the benefit of the metropolitans, and this rankled. And while it was resolved that future ABRSM scholars could choose to study in Manchester or Glasgow instead of London, this was a somewhat minimalist gesture.[8] For all the convenience that the 1947 expansion of the Board seemed to offer, it also introduced a fissure that was only resolved by the 1985 Reconstitution.

⁂ Entries, examiners and dividends

PERHAPS the most crucial post-war issue faced by the expanded Board was the vexed matter of examiners' remuneration. The Board's clumsy handling of this problem was to set the tone for the following years. Action had again been taken by Harold Craxton (the co-editor with Tovey of the Beethoven Sonatas), one of the Academy's members on the Board, a highly regarded and enormously influential teacher. Independent-minded, he gave notice at the November 1947 meeting that at the next meeting in December he would be raising the matter of examiners' fees. These, he felt, were now set far too low, given the Board's new level of income,

---

[5] ABMB9: 12 November 1946.
[6] ABMB9: 12 November 1946; ABMB10: 21 January 1947.
[7] ABMB10: 25 March 1947.
[8] ABMB10: 28 March 1948.

and were, in any case, inadequate to meet the current cost of living. The minuted discussion highlights the partners' dilemma. It was acknowledged that, as things stood, examiners on the staff of the RCM and RAM were at a disadvantage because term-time obligations prevented their being able to accept the longer, more remunerative overseas tours, and so other, non-Royal Schools examiners collected the bulk of the available fees. However, the Board was concerned that any serious increase in examiners' fees would require them to raise the entry fees. It feared that any substantial increase in fees would deter candidates, which would mean a reduced dividend for the London partners. It argued that a reduced dividend would damage the Academy and the College rather more that it would benefit the individual RAM/RCM examiners involved. So an alternative offer was made, whereby the London Schools themselves would pay an additional allowance to those Board examiners on their staffs in order to bump up their earnings, as a means to avoid the 'disproportionate' effect of raising all examiners' fees.[9] This shifty contrivance made the situation all the more difficult, and in 1949 a letter requesting an increase in fees was signed by thirty-seven examiners on the London Schools' staff. The Board reacted indignantly and chose to correct 'misconceptions' in this letter rather than addressing the issue itself. This ploy seems to have been given short shrift, and therefore, very reluctantly, in 1949 the Board was forced to increase its fees to examiners, from £5 5s to £6 10s.[10]

The 1948 tactic to subsidize some – but not all – examiners by paying a further (hidden) allowance to those employed by the RAM and RCM in order not to raise the fees of all their examiners does seem particularly cavalier. Employment conditions at the London Schools (considered in Chapter 9) were poor, and these deliberately covert arrangements over examiners (further compounded by the Board's approach to the issue of women examiners) casts the prevailing institutional ethos in a shabby light. Significantly, neither Manchester nor Scotland was present at this discussion; perhaps, given notice of Craxton's intention, they had been asked to stay away from what the partners evidently considered a private family dispute. But it was the case that the London Royals remained in a very difficult financial position despite their increased Treasury grant: Dyson was determined to maintain the RCM student population at not more than 450, rather than the 600 of Allen's day, because of implications for student quality and the College's physical limitations. The data in Table 8.1, which details the position in Ernest Bullock's Directorship (1953–60), shows the RCM's continuing financial dependence upon the ABRSM. As the RCM's Treasury grant was reduced by £4,000 between 1953 and 1960, its place was taken by the £5,000 increase in the ABRSM-generated income to the College. However, the economic pressure of rising costs meant that, as shown in the table, the RCM was again forced to increase its student numbers.

Craxton had cause to emphasize the new level of income the Board was now enjoying. The wartime increase in candidate numbers had continued, and income had been further increased by adjustments to the fees in 1948; there were reductions for the higher grades, Grades 6–8 (Grade 8 now stood at £2 2s) and

---

[9] ABMB10: 9 December 1947; 20 January 1948.
[10] ABMB10: 25 January, 1 March, 22 March 1949.

Table 8.1 Sources of RCM income, 1953–60

Academic year	No. of students	Student fee income*	Treasury grant	ABRSM income
1953	449	£31,325	£17,000	£4,000
1954	476	£31,365	£17,500	£4,000
1955	438	£31,988	£16,125	£5,000
1956	462	£32,407[†]	£14,125	£9,000
1957	457	£36,316	£13,250	£9,500
1958	468	£36,533[‡]	£13,000	£9,360
1959	472	£47,576	£13,000	£9,000
1960	510	£46,050	£13,000	£9,000

* Some students were admitted on Scholarships.

† Fees raised from £63 to £75 per year.

‡ Fees raised from £75 to £90 per year.

Source: Guy Warrack, *Royal College of Music, The First Eighty-Five Years, 1883–1968 and Beyond* (unpublished: RCM, 1977), vol. 2, 395a

increases for the lower ones, where the entries were traditionally more numerous. From 1949 Grade 5 Theory replaced Grade 4 as the prerequisite for the three highest Practical grades, although there would be exemption for those with a school certificate in music.[11] The notorious winter of 1946/7 had produced a temporary setback, with examiners facing snowdrifts, fuel cuts and floods, and large numbers of candidates withdrawing owing to missed lessons and lack of practice.[12] But 1948 saw the highest ever music entry (123,510), generating a dividend payment of £8,461 to each London partner.

However, the increased volume of entries had put the Board under such serious pressure that it was in danger of being overwhelmed. The 1947 winter exam entry required 283 examining weeks to accommodate; however, just fifty-six examiners were able (or willing) to work only a single-week tour and many others had declined to examine at all. This left sixty-six examiners to do 227 weeks' work, which had obliged over seventeen weeks' examining to be carried over into January. The November 1947 ABRSM meeting saw agreement to Dyson's proposal that the Board should now seek to control the number of entries accepted for any period, matching them to the availability of examiners, as 'an unlimited increase in the number of examiners would entail many more on the panel unconnected in any way with the Royal Schools'.[13] But instead of taking the obvious course of action and ameliorating the situation by appointing women examiners from the staffs of the Royal Schools, the Board at this meeting embarked upon an astonishing and short-sighted policy of deliberately making the exams less attractive to pupils and teachers in order to reduce demand. Accordingly, it was decided not to present

[11] ABMB10: 21 January 1947.

[12] ABMB10: 25 March 1947.

[13] ABMB10: 11 November 1947.

successful Grade 1–3 candidates with certificates, and to abolish the Preliminary exam and merge it into Grade 1. If these measures didn't reduce entries sufficiently, then other ideas included the return to making a pass in Theory the prerequisite for taking a Practical grade; holding exams during school holidays instead of term time; reducing the number of Grades; raising the fees; raising the standard; and, requiring each candidate to take additional musicianship tests. Finally the idea was mooted to confine entries to an approved list of schools and teachers.[14]

Had all these ideas been implemented, then it is difficult to imagine that the Associated Board scheme would have survived in its present form. That November 1947 Board meeting must rank as one of the lowest points in the ABRSM's institutional psyche. It brought the ABRSM very close to abandoning any idea of itself as a national force in music education, with the corresponding responsibilities this entailed. The lack of any sustaining strategic view reflects very poorly on the quality of its leadership under George Dyson and Stanley Marchant, for never has the Board displayed a more deleterious attitude to its market or less sense of its original educational purpose. It then added insult to injury by the hauteur of its explanation for ending certificates for the early grades: so that, 'these elementary examinations should not be invested with an exaggerated importance'.[15] The decision to abandon the Preliminary Exam lost the Board that segment of its market at 10s an entry, which was compounded by a drop in Grade 1 entries. In the three years 1946–8 the average entry for the Preliminary and Grade 1 exams together was some 39,000. After the Preliminary was abolished, Grade 1 fluctuated in a range from 27,966 (1949) to 19,709 (1952) before recovering at 26,328 (1955).

The Board had always defended the legitimacy of its work as an Empire-wide exam board by reference to the terms of the RCM's charter. But that charter's ideals for the furtherance of music and music teaching would have been early casualties of the proposal to restrict access to the Board's grades. We should also remember that this 1947 crisis was caused by an insufficiency of examiners and the Board had a ready-made solution, had it only moved to appoint women examiners. It did not reflect well on the Board that its corporate chauvinism (not shared, as became evident, by the staffs of the London Schools) was so strong that it was prepared to cause itself significant damage, rather than to bring women into this area of professional activity. The measures adopted at this November meeting did serious harm to the very revenue stream on which the London Schools were so heavily dependent. The direct result was to halve the London Schools' dividend, which fell from £8,461 in 1948 to £4,000 in 1953 and 1954 before it began to recover in 1955. Another measure, taken at a later meeting, was to wind up the Society of Corresponding Members, the society it had established to encourage teachers to enter their pupils and to bind them closely to the Board's brand – that was clearly superfluous to a Board now bent on reducing its number of candidates.[16]

A reason why the Board did not pursue its course of self-damage to quite the full extent aired at the November meeting may be due to its Secretary, Hilary

---

[14] ABMB10: 11 November 1947.

[15] *Fifty-ninth Annual Report* (1947).

[16] ABMB10: 13 May 1947.

Macklin, working behind the scenes to retrieve the situation. As the resentment about the decision to end certificates for the lower grades grew, Macklin and his staff must have been left in no doubt about the effect this decision was having across the country. Seemingly the enterprising Secretary of the Edinburgh ISM – who obviously understood something about children's psychology – had designed and produced his own early grade certificates so that ISM-member teachers could present them to their pupils! The Board was furious because it considered the design so close to its own as to represent a forgery, and it complained to the ISM's General Secretary about what was being done in Scotland. Meanwhile, the financial consequences of the decision to discourage the lowest grades were really beginning to bite in 1951 (Grade 1 entries fell by nearly 25%),[17] and the Board had to secure a bank loan of £12,000 in order to meet its summer exam costs.[18] Slowly, it began to dawn on the Board that over time the drop in Grade 1 entries could feed through into the higher ones. So the Board decided to pay attention to the complaints it had been receiving from teachers about the quality of the Grade 1 pieces and to reinstitute certificates from 1953.[19] But now other adverse financial circumstances were coming into play: as well as the considerable reduction in income it had brought upon itself, there was also a large deficit on its overseas operation and an enormous depreciation in its investments, with no prospect of a significant improvement in 1953. Meanwhile, costs were continuing to rise steeply, and in 1952 the Board needed a bank overdraft of £20,000 to run its winter exams.[20] Indeed, the only way that the Board could afford its smaller, 1953 dividend, was to draw down its reserves for the third year running. The 'Equalization Account' from which this money came had had £28,000 withdrawn from it in three years, and there was only £16,000 remaining.[21] Had the Board not cached its unexpected upsurge of wartime-generated profits, it would have been in an extremely vulnerable position. Numbers again began to rise later in the 1950s, and only then did the Board begin to recover from its self-inflicted wounds, as the dividend payments shown in Table 8.1 indicate.

⁄⁄⁄ Women examiners

IN 1956, sixty-six years after its founding, the Board agreed to appoint women as Practical music examiners. The Board's bar on women examiners until then had represented a significant professional disenfranchisement, given that there had long been a predominance of women students enrolling for a music college education – numbers that reflect the rapid increase in women musicians as a proportion of the population as a whole from the 1880s to the 1950s.[22] And certainly the distinction

[17] ABMB10: 20 March 1951.
[18] ABMB10: 19 June 1951.
[19] ABMB10: 13 November 1951.
[20] ABMB10: 17 June, 30 September, 11 November 1952.
[21] ABMB10: 16 June 1953.
[22] The Census figures for this period are given in Ehrlich, *The Music Profession in Britain*, table 1, 235.

of women performers in British musical life had already been recognized in all sorts of ways, not least by the employment of women on the staffs of the Royal Schools themselves. Over the period of the Board's history to date, there had been a gradual, but substantial, decrease in discrimination against women musicians in Britain. The breaking of barriers had been occasioned partly by wartime shortages (as in the case of women joining Wood's Queen's Hall Orchestra) and partly by the recognition of the talents of women players.[23] In the face of such developments, the Board's holding out against appointing women examiners for as long as it did appears a quite remarkable act of institutional misogyny. In 1945 thirty-five RCM and RAM professors petitioned the Board to appoint women examiners, 'as women function in all forms of musical life alongside their male colleagues', something that reinforced just how out of step the Board's attitude was within the profession.[24] In retrospect, the Board's extended professional and economic discrimination against women seems particularly unfair, as well as wrong, given the numbers on a professional parity with men and the eminence some had achieved. Given that the Board preferred to do itself considerable damage rather than to appoint women examiners, the degree of prejudice shown by its leadership seems especially reprehensible.

The first time the issue of women examiners seems to have been raised was in 1921, when Allen moved to allow women examiners for the Board's Elocution exams only, 'on the grounds that Elocution was a special branch of the Board's work & that their appointment for this work did not commit the Board to throw open to Women Examinership in music also'. On this basis the decision was made to appoint two women elocution examiners from each institution.[25] Whether or not this move was seen as an opportunity, at the next meeting it was reported that an application to be an examiner had been received from a Miss Gertrude Burnett, as well as from M[armaduke] Conway and V[ivian] Langrish. It was decided not to appoint Miss Gertrude Burnett while Conway was admitted to the waiting list and Langrish with two others received immediate appointment as examiners, 'subject to their being able to allot sufficient time to the purpose'.[26] Two years later the Norwich and District Branch of the Music Teachers' Association wrote to the Board asking 'that in the interests of musical education women should be represented on the Board and on its examining staff'. The Secretary was directed to acknowledge the communication, and Allen said that at a future meeting he would raise the question of the eligibility of women for appointment as Board members and examiners.[27] Not until 1936 do the minutes record that the heads of the Schools were to consider the idea of appointing women and younger men as

---

[23] For some examples of women fighting their way into the profession, see Ehrlich, *The Music Profession in Britain*, 156–61; Gillett, *Musical Women in England*, esp. chap. 7, 'Music as a Profession for Women', 190–227; and Leanne Langley '"Women in the Band": Music, Modernity and the Politics of Engagement, London 1913', work currently in progress, to be published in *Unlocking Classical Music: Queen's Hall and the Rise of Public Orchestral Culture in London, 1880–1930* (forthcoming).

[24] ABMB9: 4 December 1945.

[25] ABMB6: 12 July 1921.

[26] ABMB6: 1 November 1921.

[27] ABMB6: 10 July 1923.

examiners, but no further reference was made and the idea then seems just to have been quietly dropped.[28]

The next attempt to progress the idea of women examiners was the 1945 petition by members of the College and Academy staffs, which again was followed by silence. Then there was an intervention in 1948 by an outside body, the Society of Women Musicians, who sent a deputation to raise the issue with the Secretary. The Society's President was the renowned pianist Kathleen Long, herself an RCM professor (1920–64). The Governing Body minutes record that there was considerable discussion, leading to the statement that, 'whilst the Board was not averse in principle to the appointment of women, and while it already recognised their capacity to examine as specialists in certain subjects, e.g. Singing, it was in fact very unusual for women musicians to have sufficiently comprehensive qualifications to examine candidates in all subjects.'[29] A subsequent letter from the Women's Society prompted the Secretary, Hilary Macklin, to say to the Board that he had never experienced administrative difficulties caused by the work of women examiners on the Elocution panel.[30] The Society then sought to broaden the debate, and in a letter to the ISM, it pointed out the absurdity of the Board's stance when the 1949 Yearbook of the British Federation of [Music] Festivals listed nineteen women adjudicators, and women examined for the Academy's own LRAM diploma. The Society then asked for the ISM's support in this matter, it being of vital importance, 'not only to women musicians but to the music-teaching profession in general'. The reply reflected the conflicted position of the ISM, given that most of its officers and executive committee (one a woman) were Board examiners and that it had women members. Its Secretary demurred about the Board's attitude being based on 'mere prejudice', but confirmed that the ISM had written to the Board, asking that it should not discriminate against women examiners.[31] The Society of Women Musicians then approached the Music Teachers' Association, which also trod carefully, saying that it felt this was an administrative matter for the Board, but also that it had heard that parents preferred male examiners.[32] It took another six years – and more correspondence – before Macklin could write to the Society of Women Musicians to confirm that the Board had invited four women to become examiners. The reply (drafted on top of Macklin's own letter) expressed the Society's welcome of this step, while making the point that Kathleen Long, who had also been invited to become an ABRSM examiner, had declined because of her own professional commitments.[33]

[28] ABMB8: meeting on 17 November 1936.

[29] ABMB10: 5 October 1948.

[30] ABMB10: 14 December 1948.

[31] Letter from Kathleen Long (President of the Society of Women Musicians) to D. Brearley (Secretary of the ISM), 16 March 1950; reply from Brearley dated 23 May (Papers of the Society of Women Musicians, RCMA).

[32] Letter from Raymond Tobin (Music Teachers' Association) to Margaret Bissett (Society of Women Musicians) dated 13 November 1950 (Papers of the Society of Women Musicians, RCMA).

[33] Letter from Macklin to Katharine Eggar, Society of Women Musicians, dated 24 September 1956 (Papers of the Society of Women Musicians, RCMA).

The Board's decision to appoint women examiners on the same basis as men was a significant breakthrough that opened up an important source of work and income to women. It belatedly recognized the significance of the contribution by women to music education. Music teaching was one of the few areas in which a woman could achieve her own economic independence with minimal or no external qualifications, and it had been a lifeline for many. However, one consequence had been a poor generic image of local women music teachers, of cheap lessons and no real musical authority. And this issue of authority – both social and musical – perhaps explains the Music Teachers' Association's comment that parents preferred male examiners. The presence of women on the ABRSM's examining circuit therefore challenged, and so helped to correct, some of the instinctively negative perceptions about women's musical authority that had been entrenched in the attitudes of some parents.

9 Too Much Success: the 1960s and 1970s

⫸ The ABRSM 'house' composers

IN the post-war Britain of the 1940s and 1950s, many felt there was a sense of cultural suffocation about British life, despite the liberating, though demanding, cultural agenda of radio's Third Programme. The feeling of British insularity is tellingly captured by film producer Lindsay Anderson:

> coming back to Britain is also, in many respects, like going back to the nursery. The outside world, the dangerous world, is shut away: its sounds are muffled … Nanny lights the fire, and sits herself down with a nice cup of tea and yesterday's *Daily Express*; but she keeps half an eye on us too.[1]

Some felt that the ABRSM had cast itself in the role of the nation's musical nanny, keeping the dangers of the outside world away as though the musical revolutions in Europe and the USA had never occurred. What is now forgotten is that when William Glock began to bring a breath of fresh musical air to the Proms in 1960, it was enthusiastically welcomed, the age range of the Prommers suddenly dropped and their numbers increased.[2] In the 1960s and 1970s Glock and the new radio producers he had recruited reshaped the BBC's serious music output. Against this appearance of radical new music and the new vogue for 'authentic' historical performance, the Board's musical stance seemed even more outdated. Rather than commissioning a younger generation of composers to contribute to its syllabus, the Board stuck to its cultural last, and the sense of an anachronistic disjuncture between music in education and music elsewhere grew stronger.

It was hard to become an 'ABRSM composer'. After considering 180 pieces submitted by twenty-two composers in 1976, the Board's Selection Committee recommended just one for 'possible' use![3] There are many other such examples of the Board's wariness. In 1975 just four pieces were recommended for purchase, out of fifty-seven offered by thirty-one composers; in 1966, two had been recommended out of fifty-one submissions; in 1960, three (two by the same ABRSM examiner) had been recommended from 158 pieces. The propensity to reject rather than to accept teaching material for publication was long established, as we see from the difficulties Myers Foggin encountered in 1954 when trying to put together a fresh collection of graded teaching pieces, called *The Highway of Progress*. As the Board's practice was to publish only pieces for which they owned the copyright, Foggin faced a rather difficult task in compiling a satisfactory album of pieces, given that the Board had bought only ten new copyrights in the last five

---

[1] Lindsay Anderson, 'Get Out and Push!', in *Declaration*, ed. Tom Maschler (London: MacGibbon & Key, 1957), 155.

[2] The reception of contemporary music in the Proms is discussed in David Wright, 'Reinventing the Proms: The Glock and Ponsonby Eras, 1959–85', in *The Proms*, ed. Doctor, Wright and Kenyon, 168–209, and in respect of a specialist new music ensemble, in David Wright, 'The London Sinfonietta, 1968–2004: A Perspective', *Twentieth-Century Music* 2/1 (2005), 109–36.

[3] ABMB11: 29 June 1976.

years.[4] And when the Board sought to rectify the situation by inviting thirteen composers to submit pieces, its reputation among composers generally meant that the invitation was unenthusiastically received: five refused, one did not reply, four had agreed but sent no pieces, and three had submitted thirteen pieces between them. The Board had also received pieces from five uninvited composers. A further invitation was issued, as a result of which, four of the thirteen invited composers had sent twenty pieces – of which only four were accepted. Also taken were six of the twenty-one pieces from uninvited composers. But what is particularly telling about this whole process, is that it had produced no composers new to the Board.

Composing musically satisfying pieces that fit a specific grade of instrumental accomplishment is a challenging assignment. Some composers demonstrated a considerable facility to write such music, and the epithet of 'Associated Board composer' was not necessarily intended to flatter. Partly this was a criticism of the very straightforward tonal idiom the Board both expected and required of the pieces it published, an idiom that sounded more and more anachronistic as time went on; partly it reflected the fact that the tweeness of some of the titles to the pieces was dated (such as 'Where Rainbows Bloom', 'Dairymaids' Dance' and 'Sleepy Head'), which also contributed to make their purpose seem more condescending than was intended. The Board's determined adherence to its established musical formula suggests an analogy with some publishers of genre fiction, such as Mills & Boon. And dismissiveness by the composers the Board rejected could also have a touch of jealousy, because success as an 'AB composer' was a reliable source of royalty income. But as the success of ABRSM's recent *Spectrum* series (now covering a range of instruments and genres) has amply demonstrated, it is perfectly possible for contemporary composers to write in a stimulating and informed way for learners. The fact that the Board in the 1960s and 1970s was so restrictive is more indicative of an attitude that saw contemporary musical idioms as inimical to its educational and musical purpose. This is highlighted by the following curious juxtaposition in the minutes: the Governing Body only noted a request made by the Music Teachers' Association that it should include some 'modern idiom' pieces in its Piano syllabus, but agreed to the proposal to publish studies and character pieces by the early Romantic Stephen Heller (1813–88).[5]

The Board's consistent rejection of more contemporary musical idioms drew a variety of criticism. One instance is the correspondence initiated by a letter from Donald Mitchell in the *Daily Telegraph*. Mitchell had written that (as the minutes express it) 'something should and could be done in the interests of musical education to introduce the works of contemporary composers into the Board's examinations'. In discussion Thomas Armstrong, the Academy's Principal, asked whether in rejecting 98% of the original pieces offered to the Board, the Manuscripts Selection Committee 'might possibly be too unreceptive of new ideas'. In defence, Foggin and the renowned piano teacher Arthur Alexander argued that part of the problem facing the Committee was that the pieces they had rejected hadn't maintained 'an even grade throughout, so as to suit any particular grade'.

---

[4] ABMB10: 5 October 1954.
[5] ABMB10: 11 October 1960.

For his part, Herbert Howells 'considered that modern composers of eminence do not generally produce piano music suitable for very young students or for the average children who take the examinations', and neither did he consider that the pronouncements of Donald Mitchell made a serious contribution to musical education.[6] Armstrong returned to the issue later in the year, more diplomatically suggesting that one reason why the Board was being criticized for the conservatism of its musical tastes was in part because British publishers were themselves out of touch with much that was going on in Europe, and that this blinkered perspective had affected the Selection Committee. Armstrong felt that 'the Board should seek its material from less limited sources'. This suggestion was promptly kicked into touch, or as the minutes record, 'It was agreed to give further consideration to this interesting idea.'[7]

Armstrong's persistence had secured a concession, though, for in May 1961 it was agreed that it would be worth including modern idiom pieces in the piano lists – not so much to advance the 'cause' of modern music, but to inspire some of the teachers to consider new material. With no trace of irony the minutes record that: 'it was the Board's duty to lead, not to follow, the teachers and it should therefore provide modern material in order to encourage a more enterprising outlook among them.' Therefore it was resolved that a 'modern idiom' work should be offered as an optional alternative to the last piece in each piano list and included in the exam album for each grade, and that a note be kept of the number of candidates in each grade playing them.[8] Accordingly there was a wider choice of pieces selected for the 1963 piano lists, including Stravinsky, Kodály and Hindemith, and the young British composer Richard Rodney Bennett.[9] Originally four Bartók pieces had been proposed for the 1963 list, but the Bartók estate had refused to license the Board's use of them in their exam albums, so they had had to be replaced. (Permission to reprint Bartók's music in the Board's examination albums was eventually granted in 1964.)[10] At its October meeting the Board members sat through the performance of the 'Modern Idiom Pieces' for Grades 1–7, and 'Members raised no objections to any of them'. Determined to offer some justification for his previous reluctance, Foggin felt that some modern idiom pieces were insufficient in terms of performance indications regarding tempi, phrasing and dynamics. He argued that in such cases the copyright owner should be asked to allow the Board to vary existing marks or print alternatives. However, the Board 'in general took the view that composers' own directions could not be altered', and so the matter was settled.[11]

Of course, the Board's own conservatism was very much in accord with its market, and the statistics covering the spring and summer exam periods showed that the proportion of candidates playing a modern idiom piece was only 20% across seven grades. It would, of course, be some time before a larger number

[6] ABMB10: 12 January 1960.

[7] ABMB10: 15 November 1960.

[8] ABMB10: 2 May 1961.

[9] ABMB10: 13 June 1961.

[10] ABMB10: 10 October 1961; ABMB11: 10 November 1964.

[11] ABMB10: 10 October 1961.

Table 9.1 Composer representation in selected ABRSM Piano syllabuses, 1933–83

Composer category	Nos. of pieces				
	1933	*1953*	*1963*	*1973*	*1983*
'Canonic'	31	32	27	29	25
Non-British	27	20	37	33	32
British	31	38	28	25	3

of teachers would dip their toes into a more adventurous list, something that attested to the effect of the Board's prolonged conservatism. The situation is illustrated by Table 9.1, which breaks down into three composer categories the repertoire included in five Piano syllabuses spanning a fifty-year period. The first category covers composers generally typecast as the archetypal creators of the piano repertoire: mainly Austrians and Germans, such as Bach, Beethoven and Schumann, but also a few composers of other nationalities, such as Fauré. The second and third categories are pieces by composers who are not part of the piano 'canon' but who have written repertoire chosen for its didactic or imaginative value.[12] What the table shows is a gradual diminution in the number of British pieces represented in the syllabus. In the 1953 syllabus, when the British representation in this sample was at its highest level, Felix Swinstead had no fewer than seven pieces, Thomas Dunhill five, Markham Lee three, and George Dyson two. Other established 'ABRSM composers' whose music was either published by the Board in albums of teaching pieces or was regularly set by them included, among others, John Ireland (his regular appearances in Grade 8 lists helped generate a vogue for his piano writing), Ivor Forster, Swinstead, Dunhill and Jessie Furze. When measured against the established ABRSM tradition, the 'new idiom' pieces in the 1963 Piano syllabus (even though in reality they were conventionally neo-classical) mark something of a fresh departure.

⁂ Working more widely: brass, woodwind and others

M OST people assume that the Board has always provided exams for the full range of orchestral instruments and that there has always been a strong take-up of exams across this spectrum. However, as was explained in Chapter 6, in the 1930s the Board still continued to occupy the very narrow musical ground that it had done since 1890. Table 9.2 reveals how comparatively recent has been the invention of the Associated Board in the form that we know it today. It was only from the later 1960s that the Board's exams were widely taken up by orchestral instrumentalists. The clarinet illustrates this very clearly, with 5,861 examined in

---

[12] Definitions of 'canon' and repertory' are notoriously slippery. This discussion (which serves an indicative rather than a definitive purpose) is based on the idea of canonic composers as those who have written the core or exemplary element of the piano's music. This issue is helpfully discussed in Dorothy de Val and Cyril Ehrlich, 'Repertory and Canon', in *The Cambridge Companion to the Piano*, ed. David Rowland (Cambridge: Cambridge University Press, 1998), 117–34.

1970 alone as against only *six* in the whole of the 1930s! Only from the 1970s can it be claimed that the Board's exams really came to be a serious influence on the learning of orchestral instruments. The consequent rebalancing of instrumental entries underlines how striking this was. In 1950 the piano constituted an astonishing 93% of all Practical exams, thirty years later this proportion had fallen to just 54%.

What we also see from this turnaround in the UK examination profile demonstrated by Table 9.2 is that not until the 1960s did the work of the ABRSM really begin to mirror what was happening in British music education as a whole. Until then the Board had rested on its middle-class, keyboard-centric foundations. Suddenly, however, the Board's exams were being perceived to have potential relevance to a much broader range of instrumental training. But the astonishing thing is that this change did not occur because the ABRSM had itself seized the initiative to expand the musical reach of its exams. Instead, it happened because the educational context of school music was evolving around it, with the Board the surprised beneficiary of an opportunity that this altered market had put in its way – another indication of quite how blinkered the Board was. As we saw from the damage it did to itself by mishandling its market after the war, the Board's leadership had no real educational vision. To be fair, the post-war pressures on the London Schools had reached the stage where it was simply not viable (even had it been advisable) for their heads to continue to combine *de facto* leadership of the Board with ever-increasing institutional responsibilities. However, that issue was not to be fully grasped until after the 1985 Reconstitution when the Board gained the opportunity it needed to function as an independent educational provider, pursuing a successful market strategy. Until then, one of the Board's persistent problems was that it did not really conceive of itself as 'marketing' its exams. Instead, the Board tended to give the impression that to view its work in this way smacked of 'trade', a residue of British social snobbery. This helps to account for the Board's commercial passivity over much of its life. It operated on the expectation that because of the image its title projected the market would come to it, rather than vice versa – even though the funding of the College and the Academy was so heavily dependent upon the Board's commercial success.

So what explains the turnaround in the take-up of ABRSM exams by the orchestral teachers and learners who had previously ignored them so completely? The key here lies in what had been happening in the wider music and educational context. The post-war period had seen a decline in the didactic tradition whereby brass and woodwind instruments were taught within the brass and wind band communities. This reflected a falling-off in the popularity of playing in bands as society and its preferred entertainments changed. The excitement and anti-establishment appeal of youth pop culture – with its trademark electric guitars, cheap and portable plastic Dansette record players and transistor radio access to offshore pirate pop stations – had undermined the musical taste and personal commitment the old brass band culture demanded. Increasingly, therefore, it became more usual for these instruments to be taught within schools, and outside the band context, by peripatetic instrumental teachers (many themselves ex-military bandsmen) employed by the LEA-funded music services. The growth evident in the numbers of brass examinees in Table 9.2 for 1965, 1970 and 1975

Table 9.2 ABRSM UK examination trends in selected instruments and theory, 1950–85

Examined	1950	1955	1960	1965	1970	1975*	1980*	1985**
				Practical exams				
Piano†	69,396	72,182	81,219	72,732	92,653	105,229	139,594	145,079
Violin	3,230	4,193	6,539	9,486	15,454	24,539	36,071	33,051
Viola	75	182	401	576	985	1,611	2,200	1,796
Cello	301	592	1,252	1,689	3,553	5,704	9,011	8,462
Double bass	6	7	26	107	202	370	624	739
Flute	62	164	454	961	2,962	6,542	17,655	21,743
Oboe	36	80	229	460	1,346	2,596	4,124	3,744
Clarinet	51	265	814	2,029	5,861	12,784	20,468	18,430
Bassoon	2	11	44	74	285	594	933	1,037
Horn	5	27	78	161	613	1,737	2,008	1,581
Trumpet	20‡	52‡	195‡	412‡	1,826	4,491	7,308	5,293
Trombone	9	–	57	142	661	1,679	3,113	3,329
Other brass	–	19	2	22	944	2,885	7,092	5,683
Guitar	n/a	n/a	n/a	n/a	271	1,700	3,239	3,048
Total Practical§	74,624	79,422	93,397	91,768	131,174	176,021	258,157	258,200
Piano as % of Practical	93%	91%	87%	79%	71%	60%	54%	56%
				Theory exams				
Total Theory	17,579	17,847	25,017	25,529	33,602	50,032	68,226	60,642
Grade 5 Theory	7,604	5,811	7,879	8,450	10,775	16,593	23,652	23,132
Grade 5 Theory as % of Theory	43%	33%	31%	33%	32%	33%	35%	38%
				All exams				
Total exams	92,203	97,269	118,414	117,297	164,776	226,053	326,383	318,842

* Grades 1, 2 and 7 were not provided for double bass, guitar, brass or woodwind; Grade 1 was not provided for viola; guitar Grade 7 was offered in 1980.

** Neither Grade 1 nor Grade 2 was provided for brass or woodwind, and Grade 1 was not provided for viola, double bass or guitar.

† Solo piano, excludes piano duet

‡ Trumpet *or* Cornet

§ Total candidates examined for *all* Practical grade subjects

coincided with another significant development in the brass band world. This was the decision made in 1964 by the main makers of brass band instruments, Boosey & Hawkes and the Salvation Army, to cease building instruments at the 'high pitch' standard ($a' = 452$) traditionally used by brass bands. This decision meant that in due course all British brass bands would have to adopt the universal lower standard pitch ($a' = 440$). The significance of this for the ABRSM was that more brass instruments (as the new ones were bought) could perform with piano accompaniment straight away, without the need for expensive tuning-slides to adjust their pitch.[13] (Military bands had adopted standard pitch in 1929.)

Because public funds were involved, LEAs required their county music advisers to account for their budgets. This is where grade exams came into their own, because they offered a straightforward, easily understood and readily available form of external validation. The syllabuses ensured coherence in what was being covered in Practical and Theory lessons, while the standardization into grades measured teachers' efficiency and pupils' progress. Passing a particular grade could therefore be the threshold for moving into a more advanced ensemble or senior orchestra; to qualify for a better loan instrument; or for other privileges earned by merit, such as extended lessons. In other words, the beauty of the grade system was that it could be used to satisfy many administrative purposes while fulfilling a musical function, and the Associated Board was well placed to benefit because of its long-standing reputation and national coverage. And although it is difficult to imagine that many orchestral instrument teachers were pleased at the prospect of their pupils being examined by a cadre of keyboard-playing examiners, the grade exam structure won out over such considerations because of its sheer convenience.

A typical example of how a music service originated and functioned in this period is that of Bury Music Service, which, as its website tells us:

> was founded in September 1973 as a direct result of an instrumental course for young people, organized by Jeffrey Wynn Davies who had just been appointed the first Music Adviser to the former County Borough of Bury. Its first 'home' was the Mosses Community Centre in the heart of Bury. From the outset, young people from schools in Tottington, Ramsbottom, Radcliffe, Whitefield and Prestwich were encouraged to join their counterparts in Bury on Saturday mornings each week, and so a truly Metropolitan Centre came into being some seven months before the actual date of Local Government reorganization. As the Bury M[etropolitan] B[orough] C[ouncil] Instrumental Teaching Service we taught in all high schools and virtually every primary school until August 1993 when the Service was discontinued as part of Bury Council's financial policy.[14]

This passage illustrates the musical vitality of this type of scheme, very characteristic

---

[13] See Trevor Herbert, 'God's Perfect Minstrels', and Arnold Myers, 'Instruments and Instrumentation', in *The British Brass Band*, ed. Herbert, 213–15 and 183–4. I am grateful to Trevor Herbert for alerting me to the potential significance of this pitch change for grade brass entries.

[14] http://burymusic.co.uk/home/history, accessed 3 February 2011.

of the time, ensuring the wide availability of school-based instrumental lessons further supported by Saturday provision.[15]

Although there are no statistics to demonstrate this, it would be feasible to explain the low numbers of ABRSM brass and woodwind entries in the 1950s as mainly from the public schools with their CCF bands whose pupils were also likely to have been taught by ex-military bandsmen. With numbers at this level it is perhaps not surprising that costs were saved by not publishing woodwind and brass requirements in the Board's printed syllabus; they were available only as a cyclostyled sheet which had to be specially requested from Bedford Square. But this discouragement was to continue until 1967. There were only five woodwind grades (Grades 3–7),[16] and the Board's adviser, Guy Warrack, was asked to respond to requests and to add a Grade 8 to the woodwind syllabus. Warrack, however, was adamant that although a new Grade 8 would be appropriate, this meant that there would be no need for a Grade 7.[17] In 1963 it was agreed 'that players of brass band instruments such as euphonium, tenor cor, etc. be accepted as candidates for examination and be permitted to use the appropriate syllabus (as already prescribed for Trumpet, Horn etc.), making the necessary transpositions.'[18] The increased take-up of woodwind exams then generated a considerable amount of criticism from teachers about the quality of these syllabuses. So the Board set up an advisory committee for each instrument under Warrack with staff from the College and the Academy and (something of a first) other 'teachers who offered informed and constructive comment'.[19] In 1967 the Board finally published a composite syllabus for Wind Instruments (which included brass) and Double Bass, a surprisingly Varèsian combination.[20] Revised the next year, the 1968 syllabus for Wind Instruments and Double Bass saw an enormous expansion in the brass instruments it covered, grouped as 'Category 1' for orchestral brass, and 'Category 2' for brass band. As Table 9.2 shows, there was a significant increase in the 'other brass' category, which from twenty-two in 1965 peaked at 7,092 in 1980, figures that indicate that there was now a substantial number of brass band instrumentalists wanting to take the Board's exams.

Despite many requests, the Board had considerable reservations about instituting a Guitar syllabus, as its rather condescending letter to John Williams suggests. It asked Williams 'to advise on whether there was sufficient music of suitable quality to provide material for examinations and if so to submit draft syllabuses for Grades IV–VIII inclusive for consideration'.[21] Initially Williams agreed to write the syllabus himself, but then passed it to Hector Quine, and guitar exams were first offered in 1967. There was then the issue of training the

---

[15] After that phase ended in 1993 the music service was re-formed as a not-for-profit organization, continuing at the time of writing.

[16] Grades 1 and 2 for wind and brass instruments were not added until 1988.

[17] ABMB10: 17 June, 7 October 1958.

[18] ABMB11: 15 January 1963.

[19] ABMB11: 12 October 1965.

[20] Varèse's modernist work *Octandre* is scored for woodwind, brass and a double bass, but this is probably best understood as a coincidence rather than an influence.

[21] ABMB11: 23 March 1965.

examiners. To help them, Quine made a demonstration record for distribution to all examiners; he also gave hints on examining the Guitar syllabus to the examiners' meeting that preceded the 1966 Annual Lunch. Evidently this sort of event was considered a successful innovation, and training sessions for brass instruments followed in 1967. The inception of Recorder exams had a curious history. There had been many pleas for the Board to offer exams for the instrument, but it seems to have been a request from the East African Certificate of Education Authority in 1972 that prompted a request to David Munrow to prepare a syllabus.[22] He apparently declined, so instead Freda Dinn wrote it. This, however, was never published because the Board began to fear that the examining body might not be able to cope with the increased volume in entries that recorder exams were expected to generate.[23] There was a further debate at the meeting in March 1982, in which the Secretary, Philip Cranmer, was outspoken. While understanding the Board's concern to maximize revenue, 'he felt it was inappropriate for the Royal Schools of Music to advocate the introduction of new instrumental syllabuses primarily for the money they would earn. In point of fact there was a good musical reason for offering Recorder examinations ... and the Board should make this its primary concern.'[24] Recorder exams were introduced in 1986. The saxophone was another instrument for which exams had been requested well before they were introduced in 1985; evidence of the strong demand was that there were already 1,212 candidates in 1986. Again, it seems, a factor behind the Board's delay had been anxiety about how well its examiners would fare in examining the instrument.

⁄⁄⁄ Theory and theory exams

As we know from Chapter 3, the Board's early exams required candidates first to pass a Rudiments of Music paper before proceeding to take the Practical. Grade 4 Theory was later required as a prerequisite for taking Practical Grades 6 to 8, and in 1949 this was advanced to Grade 5 Theory. Millions of candidates are likely to recall the ubiquitous little red *Rudiments and Theory of Music Book* first published by the Board in 1958 (withdrawn from sale only in 1989), and many will also have been familiar with William Cole's work books *Questions and Exercises on Theory of Music*.[25] Although these manuals represented a new didactic initiative by the Board (taken only after much anxiety),[26] the Theory exams which they covered had been in place, without change, since 1948. In fact the original *Rudiments* book (which was not by Cole) caused the Board considerable embarrassment. It had sold some 14,000 copies before it was discovered that its 'Glossary of Musical Forms' was identical with corresponding paragraphs in Novello's Music Primer No. 130, which Cole had written! As the minutes record, 'The compiler of this section admitted that "he must thoughtlessly have copied these paragraphs". The

[22] ABMB11: 14 June 1972.

[23] ABMB12: 17 November 1981.

[24] ABMB12: 23 March 1982.

[25] William Cole was to become Secretary to the Board, 1962–74.

[26] ABMB10: 17 January 1956.

Board recorded its stern disapproval of this action.'[27] Novello retrospectively licensed the use of this section in the books that had been sold for the payment of 50 guineas, but required the Board to withdraw from sale the remaining unsold copies (about 9,000). So the Board decided to issue a second, revised, edition with the offending section completely rewritten and various errors corrected. By way of further amends for the expensive embarrassment this plagiarism had caused, J. A. Sowerbutts was to receive £100 for revising the offending *Rudiments and Theory of Music*, and an *ex gratia* payment of £100 was made to Cole 'in recognition of the continuing success' of his edited series, *Questions and Exercises on Theory of Music*.

The Board had been just as conservative about its Theory syllabus over these years as it had been in its choice of examination repertoire. In valedictory mood at his last meeting in 1960, Sir Ernest Bullock, Director of the RCM, encouraged the Board to review its Theory syllabus and question papers, particularly in the higher grades, 'in order to give candidates a more modern approach to musical idioms, especially cadences, analysis, etc., and a less stereotyped and abbreviated kind of general knowledge about composers and their works'.[28] In response, a review panel consisting of Sowerbutts (an examiner since 1925), William Lloyd Webber and Cole 'agreed unanimously that no change was desirable either in the syllabus or in the form of the questions'.[29] The panel's decision reflected the undoubted efficiency of the Board's current practice. The Board's approach to this Rudiments paper had been the musical equivalent of multiplication tables, something to be learned by rote, and which could be marked on the simple basis of correct or incorrect answers. And this had worked well in two essential respects. With English as the second language for many Theory candidates, it was important that understanding the questions and answering them adequately did not require a sophisticated command of the language itself; furthermore, the papers needed to be of a type that could be speedily marked on a production line basis – essential when this had to be done in the interstices of Practical examining on overseas tours. A further advantage was that candidates could glean all the knowledge they needed from a general theory book or a basic harmony tutor, without reference to other sources, or on a self-help basis. This all made for a very straightforward process. Table 9.3 underlines just what an important consideration it was to have a system that worked optimally abroad, because the proportion of Theory to Practical candidates was so much higher overseas than it was in the UK.

This was where matters rested for a further sixteen years, when in 1976 a Committee, made up of the Secretary (Philip Cranmer), John Gardner and Timothy Salter, was constituted to re-examine the issue in the light of 'modern developments in the teaching of harmony'.[30] Gardner and Salter approached the subject in a very different way and wrote a completely new textbook. Their initiative now put the Board in something of an uncomfortable position. Should it adopt the more imaginative approach of the Gardner–Salter book (which some

[27] ABMB10: 11 March 1958.
[28] ABMB10: 14 June 1960.
[29] ABMB10: 11 October 1960.
[30] ABMB11: 16 November 1976.

Table 9.3 Proportion of Theory to Practical grade exams in the UK and overseas

Year	UK			Overseas*		
	Theory	*Practical*	*Theory to Practical*	*Theory*	*Practical*	*Theory to Practical*
1950	17,579	74,624	24%	6,013	10,410	58%
1955	17,847	79,422	22%	8,419	13,769	61%
1960	25,017	93,397	27%	11,792	18,737	63%
1965	25,529	91,768	28%	16,201	21,306	76%
1970	33,602	131,174	26%	21,861	27,242	80%
1975	50,032	176,021	28%	30,458	36,446	84%
…	…	…	…	…	…	…
2009	43,598	271,842	16%	92,773	177,675	52%

* The data for 1950–75 is reported as totals, hence breakdown by individual grades is not possible.

Source: ABRSM Annual Reports; for 2009 www.abrsm.org/press/factfile/theoryStats.html

felt was 'too advanced and sophisticated') and face disruption to its existing theory market? Or, should it seek out another basis for dealing with Rudiments, one that was not so creatively demanding as to deter potential candidates (and their teachers), while yet representing some improvement on current practice? What determined the outcome was the context of the difficult financial circumstances in which the debate was taking place, with income being undermined by escalating costs. The last thing that could be risked was any diminution of the Board's Theory market. And because the statistics showed that 90% of Theory candidates entered for Grades 1–5, the Board's concern was that anything too sophisticated and expensive might frighten people off. It was also anxious that the range of reference in the Gardner–Salter book *Basic Musicianship* meant that 'it would not be possible to give it to a pupil to read for himself without guidance'; also, that its more comprehensive approach involved unquoted music examples likely to be beyond the facilities of the average school library. The Board briefly considered running two different types of Theory exams in parallel: retaining the current Rudiment-type exams for the existing market, and introducing a new Basic Musicianship exam ('for candidates who had been taught theory aurally rather than simply as a visual exercise'), using the Gardner–Salter book. However, this new exam would have required some considerable investment in a fresh syllabus and accompanying sets of questions and exercises, and the Board was loath to undertake that sort of financial commitment.[31] Thus the Gardner–Salter book, although considerably admired, was not adopted.

Table 9.3 illustrates some of the issues involved. It shows a much higher proportion of Theory to Practical candidates in the overseas market than there is in the UK. One explanation for this is differences in educational cultures. In the Far East more pupils progress steadily through the Theory grades, and this contributes

[31] ABMB12: 15 June, 9 November 1982; 18 January 1983.

Table 9.4 Grade 5 as a proportion of all Theory grade exams in the UK

Year	No. of Grade 5 Theory exams	Grade 5 as percentage of Theory
1950	7,604	43%
1955	5,811	33%
1960	7,879	31%
1965	8,450	33%
1970	10,775	32%
1975	16,593	33%
...	...	...
2009	22,026	51%

significantly to the much higher proportion of Theory to Practical exams taken overseas. Given the numbers involved, the Board's anxiety about making changes that risked undermining that overseas market is understandable, especially as the status quo then clearly worked – there was simply no incentive to make any change and every reason, in difficult economic times, not to do so. However, more recently, as Table 9.3 shows, there has been a significant decline in the overseas Theory market, where the proportion of Theory to Practical candidates fell from 84% in 1975 to 52% in 2009. There was a decline in the UK also, from 28% in 1975 to 16% in 2009.

Table 9.4 shows that in the UK this change was caused because Grade 5 (seen as a percentage of all grades) was not as dominant between 1955 and 1975 as it had become by 2009 – having leapt from 33% (1975) to 51% (2009). In other words, in 1975 more candidates were taking a wider range of Theory grades.

Table 9.5 analyses the 2009 Theory exams by grade in the UK and overseas. Although there is still a higher proportion of overseas to UK Theory candidates, the table indicates for both markets a sharp drop in Theory exams after Grade 5.

From these tables we can see how much Grade 5 has become more of an end in itself, with fewer candidates undertaking the preparatory step of earlier grades or following it up with the more demanding tasks set by the higher ones. In the UK the significant decline in entries for the higher grades (Grade 6 and above) seems to have become marked from 1991.[32] Two things may account for this. One is that in the UK the original purpose of the Board's higher Theory grades has been steadily eroded by other school-based exams such as A-levels. (Perhaps the slightly higher overseas take-up of Grade 8 indicates the lack of such convenient alternatives in some school systems.) The second is that in the UK, because of the heavy school pressures put on pupils today, the focus on Grade 5 suggests that people consider it a more efficient use of available time and effort to enter only for that single exam. The continuing drop in Theory entries probably also reflects the greater number of teachers and their pupils willing to challenge the ABRSM's educational principle of linking Practical performance subjects with Theory.

[32] ABMB14: 15 March 1994.

Table 9.5 Take-up of Theory exams by grade in 2009

Grade	UK	Overseas
1	17%	17%
2	12%	13%
3	11%	12%
4	6%	7%
5	51%	42%
6	2%	4%
7	0.5%	1%
8	0.8%	4%
TOTAL	43,598	92,773

Note: Figures above 1% are rounded to the nearest whole.

Source: www.abrsm.org/press/factfile/theoryStats.html, accessed 24 February 2011

As we have seen, this linkage of Theory and Practical has been an ABRSM tenet since its inception. More recently, however, the issue of a prerequisite Theory paper has become a differentiating factor in the exam market: Trinity–Guildhall's dropping of the Theory requirement for its own higher grades has made its exams an attractive alternative to candidates (or their teachers) with an aversion to Rudiments.

Although concern not to damage its market had motivated the Board's refusal of the Gardner–Salter book, it nevertheless realized that some new approach to its Theory exams was needed. So in 1984 it asked Professor Eric Taylor of Durham University to write a 'critical appraisal' of the existing Rudiments and Theory of Music books. The Board then accepted the subsequent recommendation to phase in new-look Theory grades over four years, based on two books (split at Grade 5) by Eric Taylor.[33] The new Theory syllabus was carefully trailed, and to mark its introduction Taylor conducted nine seminars in the Far East which were attended by 2,000 teachers. Even so, there was an initial drop in Theory entries, as in Singapore, which declined by some 2,000, although there was some dispute as to whether this reflected more the new Theory syllabus or an increase in entry fees.[34]

These Theory issues are so interesting because they reflect changing attitudes to musical literacy. For most of the Board's history there may have been grumbles about the linkage of Rudiments to Practical music, but no serious challenge. After 1990 the Board's determination to hold on to its Grade 5 requirement became increasingly controversial with teachers, and competitors saw it as a commercial vulnerability. The ABRSM was established in the print age, when literacy was an expected attribute. That applied as much to musical literacy as any other, and one of the striking aspects of musical life in the later nineteenth and earlier twentieth centuries was the enthusiasm for detailed programme notes, set with

[33] ABMB12: 27 March, 20 November 1984.
[34] ABMB14: 31 March 1992.

copious musical illustrations. Programme notes were shared across the country, as Christina Bashford has identified.[35] The Board's approach was very much within this music literacy context, and it was a given that a player should also be able to notate music without basic errors in musical grammar. Today computer software has changed general practice, affecting the skill-sets that individuals need in order to function. With music notation programmes such as 'Sibelius', composers are able to input music directly as printed notation, with all the instrumental parameters and the musical rudiments automatically formatted by the programme, without the user's intervention. In the same way that some composers may now struggle to notate from scratch an orchestral score in manuscript, so music software means correspondingly less pressure for performers to acquire a practical knowledge of rudiments. The Board's continuing insistence on Grade 5 Theory for its higher grades has therefore made this requirement very much a statement of educational principle.

%% The examiners from the London Royal Schools

I N 1978 the Gulbenkian Foundation commissioned a report into the training of professional musicians.[36] The result, *Training Musicians* (which caused a brief flurry of excitement but was soon forgotten), is less interesting for its recommendations than for its observations about the contemporary training environment. Dominated by music college and educational representatives, and lacking any real intellectual bite, the report's recommendations predictably favoured enhancing the status and funding of conservatoires well beyond the willingness of any government to pay. But some thirty years later one is struck by the report's portrayal of the gulf between the intellectual worlds of the university music department and the music college. One telling phrase describes the university experience as offering training 'in a wider environment than that of a music college', and another remarks that 'Performers of distinction have emerged from this kind of stimulating background.'[37] To put this in context, it was music-making in Cambridge that provided the impetus for the founding in 1968 of the London Sinfonietta, the specialist contemporary music ensemble.[38] And many pioneers of today's historical performance movement such as David Munrow and Christopher Hogwood were university-trained musicians.[39] Fresh musical thinking at that time was far more likely to be encountered in university music

[35] See Christina Bashford, 'Educating England: Networks of Programme-Note Provision in the Nineteenth Century', in Cowgill and Holman, *Music in the British Provinces*, 349–76.

[36] *Training Musicians: A Report to the Calouste Gulbenkian Foundation on the Training of Professional Musicians* (London: Calouste Gulbenkian Foundation, 1978).

[37] Ibid., paragraphs 164–5.

[38] See Wright, 'The London Sinfonietta, 1968–2004'.

[39] See, for example, Harry Haskell, *The Early Music Revival: A History* (New York: Dover, 1996), esp. chap. 8, 'The Early Music Subculture'; and Bernard D. Sherman, *Inside Early Music* (New York: Oxford University Press, 1997), especially Part II, with its suggestive title, 'The Renaissance, Oxbridge, and Italy'.

departments than in music colleges. Several such departments, working in the milieu of an interdisciplinary university environment, generated the intellectual impetus and critical freedom that encouraged young musicians to explore very different musical idioms from those they had grown up with.

In the music colleges of this time, more modern, let alone contemporary music, was very much a lonely field of endeavour. Bartók was still considered *outré* at the RAM in the 1950s, when Susan Bradshaw put on a pioneering student performance of the Sonata for Two Pianos and Percussion, causing something of a musical scandal.[40] And performing music of the post-war avant-garde was just as isolated (and isolating) an activity in the 1960s, 1970s and even the 1980s, emphasizing how much the conservatoire perspective remained stuck within traditional practice and thinking. Accordingly, those relatively few conservatoire champions of modern music and historical performance were characteristically 'outsider' figures, whose work, despite its impact in stimulating some outstanding students, was often perceived as controversial or marginal to the main work of the institution.[41] *Training Musicians* has several references to the antagonism of the conservatoire mentality to contemporary music: 'music college orchestras (and individuals) sometimes approach new music, including the new music of fellow students, with reluctance or even distaste – negative characteristics which are generally born of the performers' concern for their development as performers.'[42] Continuing into the 1980s, the *raison d'être* of a conservatoire was conventionally viewed as training students in the musical techniques necessary to perform the nineteenth-century or mainstream twentieth-century repertoire.

Another aspect preserved within *Training Musicians* is the harsh nature of the employment conditions for teachers at the London conservatoires. It was as late as 1980 that the Department of Education and Science (DES) agreed the implementation of the Burnham salary pay scales for the RCM's professors, which meant a very substantial increase from the College's own hourly rate. The move to Burnham resulted from far-reaching changes in government assistance for the RAM, RCM and TCM, which in 1975 had been moved from a simple Grant-in-Aid annual lump payment to Deficiency Grant Aid, or 'deficit funding'. Deficit funding was a more generous system of support, but it involved the Colleges ceding a significant degree of autonomy to the DES and its Inspectorate, who early on required more acceptable staff employment conditions (such as Staff Associations) and recognizable, committee-based, academic structures. As *Training Musicians* described the situation, the London music colleges were not really integrated into the public Higher Education sector.[43] One consequence of their anomalous

---

[40] Gerard McBurney, 'About Susan Bradshaw' (www.royalphilharmonicsociety.org.uk, accessed 8 February 2011).

[41] In a perhaps deliberately suggestive choice of words, the RCM's Twentieth Century Ensemble's influence was described as 'constructively explosive' in Colles and Cruft, *The Royal College of Music: A Centenary Record*; the Ensemble was founded in 1968, and while the RCM took considerable pride in its many concert and broadcast successes under Edwin Roxburgh it remained somewhat *sui generis* within the College's gamut.

[42] *Training Musicians*, paragraph 140.

[43] Ibid., 'Summary of conclusions and recommendations', paragraph 14.

situation was that conservatoire staff were significantly underpaid compared with their university equivalents. In its evidence the Academy's Teaching Staff Association said the fees paid to their members ranged from £2.90 to £4.75 per hour (£18.10 to £29.70 in today's terms), as against the contemporary university equivalent of £9.30 (£49.90).[44]

Another issue, as *Training Musicians* recognized, was the idiosyncratic academic structures of London conservatoires. At the time the report was written, virtually all of London's music college staff were on hourly-paid, annual contracts (only a very few senior administrators or teachers had salaries), whereas most university staff enjoyed salaried, permanent contracts. Thus teaching staff at the London conservatoires were not only considerably less well paid, but had none of the job security of their university counterparts – something that also carried implications for intellectual freedom. And no matter how individually illustrious, college staff were literally beholden to the patronage of the head of the institution or the director of studies for the renewal of their annual contracts. This explains the report's comment: 'We also felt that relationships between staff, principal and governing body in some of the music colleges still appeared to be rooted in the past and out of line with those prevailing in other academic institutions.'[45] It was a neat euphemism for a situation where no security of employment obliged individual professors to offer ready compliance with authority, aware that there were plenty of others who would welcome the chance to take their places. Under these circumstances, it is not surprising that ABRSM examining, no matter how poorly remunerated, was for some still a necessity. The dependence of some Royal Schools' staff upon examining to bring their incomes to a more acceptable level did not seem to have changed much since the time of Thornton Lofthouse, the celebrated harpsichordist. Lofthouse's 1924 earnings, which he itemized in his diary, put his income from RCM teaching at £202 18s 6d and his earnings in his second year as an ABRSM examiner at £140 15s. Lofthouse is probably a typical example of someone whose ABRSM examining formed a significant element of overall earnings at one point in his life (he was then aged twenty-nine) as part of a portfolio career, and certainly they brought him far more than he was earning as accompanist to the Bach Choir.[46] Even so, there had been a steady decline of Royal Schools' staff willing to examine for the Board; by 1979, out of 376 examiners offering their availability, only eighty-six (some 23%) were from the Royals.

Until the 1985 Reconstitution the strategy the controlling partners set down for the ABRSM was to run a demand-led operation. Their idea was that the best way to maximize the Board's income, and so its profits, was to minimize the Board's costs, while keeping the fees as low as possible in order to encourage candidates. The very tight rein kept on examiners' fees was an essential part of this strategy, and in 1978 examiners were paid at a daily rate of £27 for seven hours' examining, or £3.85 an hour (about the mid-point of the conservatoires' hourly pay rate), with a subsistence allowance set at £14 – an amount which examiners held to be insufficient to cover even basic hotel accommodation. Dissatisfaction

[44] Ibid., paragraph 148.
[45] Ibid.
[46] The Thornton Lofthouse Collection (RCMA).

at this state of things had been growing, but as no examiner dared speak out, the Incorporated Society of Musicians – the education profession's trade union – was asked to intervene. This produced something of a farcical situation, because Sir David Willcocks was both the RCM's Director and the ISM's President. Reporting to the Board's Governing Body on the 'amicable' meeting held with the ISM to discuss this issue, the RAM's Principal, Sir Anthony Lewis, 'thought that the [ISM] deputation had realized that the Board was sympathetic to the points which had been made on behalf primarily of certain members of the staff of the R.A.M. and the R.C.M.'.[47] However, as we shall see, the London Schools' ABRSM strategy was shortly to fall apart when a lethal combination of escalating costs, a resentfully under-rewarded body of examiners, insufficiency of business management capacity and inadequate financial reserves meant that in 1981 – for the first time in its history – there was no profit to distribute.

By the end of 1980 examiners' fees had been raised to £33 (£4.71 an hour) and subsistence increased to £18. But this still meant that such work was astonishingly poorly paid. Fee levels were not such an issue for the staff of the Manchester and Scottish Schools because (unlike examiners from the London Schools) they were more likely to be on salaries, which meant that examining fees came as a bonus. However, this was a source of real grievance to the northern Schools themselves; in releasing their own salaried staffs to examine for the Board, they were contributing more to the running costs of the Board than the distributions they received from it. So the northern Schools now asked that in consideration of the amount of examining work done by their full-time salaried staffs, the share they received of the Board's annual profits should be increased from the present token sum of £1,000.[48] This issue seems to have triggered their sense of grievance, and now the RNCM's and the RSAMD's hackles were raised. In view of continued resistance by the London Schools to increasing their share of the profits, the northern Schools employed institutional guerrilla tactics, and (without any warning) they sent the Board a bill to reimburse them for the accommodation expenses they had incurred by holding ABRSM exams in their premises.[49] No allowance for such a cost had been made in the financial estimates, so this additional bill of nearly £3,000 (timed when the Board was running a significant deficit for the financial year 1980/1) was intended to make a very big point indeed to the London Schools, who under the Board's constitution had unlimited financial liability.

Clearly the preparedness of two of the partners to take such action meant that the Board was at a crossroads. Somehow it had to deal with the organizational tension resulting from the inequalities inherent within the ABRSM's structure. But before it could do that, the partners first needed to resolve a more fundamental question. What exactly was the ABRSM's purpose? Was it a national musical educator running its operation with the degree of disinterested responsibility such a role required? Or was it primarily concerned with generating the profits needed to provide the RAM and the RCM with an income source? This debate had been initially aired in 1962, when questions were first raised about the proper use

[47] ABMB12: 23 January 1979.
[48] ABMB12: 1 July 1980.
[49] ABMB12: Finance Committee on 9 March 1981.

of the Board's profits, and (this in the context of the Cold War) whether 'instead of being used to subsidize the Institutions, [the profits] might more usefully be employed in sending visiting lecturers and teachers to overseas centres in order to combat the growing nationalistic tendencies in some areas and to counter the influence of teachers sent there from communist countries'.[50] Core to the ABRSM's Reconstitution was the question of whether it was proper for the Board as a national examining body to budget to achieve a profit for profit's sake, or whether it should budget conservatively, returning to the partners for charitable purposes any surplus made after operational, research and development costs had been met.[51] The decision by the Department of Education and Science to support the London music colleges as public Higher Education Institutions had fundamentally changed both the context and the Schools' dependence. No longer did the Board's strategy need to be focused so expressly on the profit generation needed to underwrite the survival of the London Schools.

▨ The 'new complexity': the business of managing growth

THE astonishing growth in candidate numbers that Table 9.2 reveals brought the Board huge problems that went to the heart of its operational nature. For the truth that the RAM–RCM partnership had never really faced was that in order to be effective in providing a good educational service, the Board had also to be an effective *business*. The failure to understand this and its strategic implications is a reflection on the leadership which the Board had received from the heads of the London Schools over the period covered by this chapter. Successive heads of the College and the Academy seemed content about having responsibility for a commercial operation (on whose success their institutions relied), even though their own, sometimes brilliant, musical careers did not equip them with either the perspective or the skills to meet the needs of directing an expanding business. Furthermore, the London partners gave the Board no latitude to invest sufficiently enough in itself to put its operation onto a sound business footing. On the contrary, there was every expectation that the Board would continue to minimize its operational costs in the interests of maximizing its distributions to the London partners. Consequently, the Board lacked the necessary in-house business skills required to cope successfully with handling growth on this scale.

Since its inception the Board's operation had been structured around the role of the Secretary, who was its administrative head, with the direction in all musical and examining policy matters being given by the heads of the College and the Academy. In Hilary Macklin (Secretary from 1937 until 1962) the Board had a greatly respected and very able general administrator. Macklin had been a choral scholar at Cambridge, where he had read English and Classics. As mentioned earlier, after a decade in India, where he combined his work for a shipping company with being the Board's Resident Secretary, Macklin was appointed Secretary. Macklin managed the Board rather like an old-fashioned Whitehall

---

[50] ABMB11: 19 June 1962.

[51] ABMB12: special meeting on 28 August 1984.

department and in a way that reflected his own wartime experience: policy was decided at the top and practical implementation was left to the executive sections. With the Board not yet really thinking of itself as a business, its operation, though intricate because of its logistical complexities, was relatively straightforward. So when Macklin retired in 1962, the Secretaryship was not advertised. Instead the London heads, Keith Falkner and Thomas Armstrong, proposed William Cole (an examiner since 1943) to replace him – indeed, Cole was present at the meeting at which Macklin's resignation was announced.[52] The choice of Cole signalled that more of the musical responsibility was to be transferred from the heads of the London Schools onto the Secretary. Cole was organist of the Queen's Chapel of the Savoy and on the staff of the Academy, where he had studied. With Cole in charge, it was felt, the examining process could safely be left to the Board to deal with. However, as we shall see, this was a decision which held longer-term implications. The Board's running and business efficiency – aspects which under Macklin had always been well managed – were about to face the serious operational challenge caused by an unprecedented expansion of its market.

Under Cole, the Board continued very much as usual. However, the even tenor was disturbed by a contentious issue that is revealing about the Board's relations with its examiners around the 1970s. In 1973 concern about examiners smoking in exams seems to have come to a head, because the customary cautionary letter was clearly not working: the complaints about smoking received after the 1972 winter exams were about examiners who had already received several warnings, and so it was decided to seek the opinion of the College and Academy staffs, saying that the Board was considering imposing a complete ban. Further complaints were received, and Cole had written again to two particular offenders. One promised not to smoke in exams, the other thought the complaint was unjustified. Meanwhile, in response to the consultation, the Academy staff felt that smoking, or not, was a matter for the individual examiner. The Board then withdrew its threatened ban. However, the RCM's Director, Keith Faulkner, felt that the Board should take a firm line and not leave it to individual examiners' discretion, pointing out that smoking had been banned in RCM exams,[53] and so a complete ban was decided on from 1974. This produced a demand from examiners who smoked that there should be a ten-minute smoking break in the morning and afternoon of each examining day. That was ruled 'quite impracticable even if it were desirable' because of the impact it would have had on the economics of the Board's operation. In fact such a break period would have destroyed the current economic basis of the operation: a previous time–cost analysis of examining produced by Cole had shown that even if just one minute were to be added to the duration of each exam, it would require an additional 500 days of additional examiner-time in a full year.[54] This smoking controversy is something of a period piece today, when the medical case makes fierce anti-smoking legislation uncontroversial. It is perhaps difficult now to imagine the strongly held opposition that there was on libertarian grounds to any

[52] ABMB10: 14 November 1961.

[53] An over-optimistic assessment: the author's page-turner for his ARCM in 1977 was a chain-smoking examiner! ABMB11: 23 January, 19 June, 13 November 1973.

[54] ABMB11: 22 January 1974.

attempt to curtail smoking when it was a very prevalent habit. Given that smoking was considered something of a solace at times of ennui, some examiners will have felt this complete ban represented a considerable worsening of their conditions. It was perhaps for this reason that the Board was so hesitant in implementing its policy.

Philip Cranmer became Secretary in September 1974. Cranmer was a musician of distinction, a brilliant organist and pianist, and an academic – he had been a popular Professor of Music at the Queen's University in Belfast and at Manchester. Unfortunately, there still was no clear appreciation of the Board's business complexity when he was appointed, and the Schools continued to think that the Board's primary need was for another musician-Secretary. As became increasingly clear, and should have been apparent much earlier on, the Board's current structure and in-house expertise were now very inadequate for the conditions it was facing. There had never been any doubt about the high quality of service that the Board's staff brought to their work, nor their capacity for sorting out difficult logistical situations, and they were esteemed wherever the Board's exams were held. Those skills in running the exams and coping with all the problems and practical difficulties associated with them would continue to be required. But the Board needed a whole new business and financial capacity, and this was the sphere that the new Secretary appointment had simply not addressed. So Cranmer's time was to be punctuated by bolted-on attempts to prop up the organization, while he continued to undertake with distinction the musical job he had been recruited to fulfil.

The issues mounting up across Cranmer's time were formidable. They included the Board's failure to secure sufficient examiners to cope with the rise in candidates; the financial pressures caused by the escalating costs of the late 1970s and early 1980s; the lack of sufficient financial forecasting, which left the Board without the ability to plan for the longer term; the necessity to computerize basic office systems in order to reduce staff costs and plan for new accommodation; the demand to devise new exams and materials or to revise older ones in order to satisfy market need and to meet educational expectations; the in-house tensions generated by the inequality of the partnership; and the emerging alternative views about the Board's mission. Some of these difficulties represented continuing and unresolved problems, while others that were surfacing would make the 1985 Reconstitution and the regeneration of the Board as welcome as it was necessary. The first task to be faced was to computerize the exam entries (part of the attempt to cut operational costs); the aim was to run tests of the computer systems in 1976. The computer went 'live' for Scottish and Irish entries of the 1976 summer exams, and then for the whole of the UK for the winter entries. The verdict was that the trial had been successful. Accordingly the 1977 syllabus contained a bright yellow insert giving detailed instructions for completing the new computerized entry forms, instructions which had to be strictly observed. The forms had to be completed in block capitals, one letter in each grid space, with the caution that 'A word or letter written outside the block will not be programmed.' There were numeric codes for days of the week, for the preferred week of examination and for the examination centre given in the syllabus. However, the costs of running the computer would exceed the estimate of £20,000 by some considerable margin, reaching nearly £35,000 per annum. Its potential for cost saving was clear, and Cranmer hoped that this would be covered by the savings of staff time that would be made.[55] But this magnitude of overrun evidently prompted the setting up of a separate Finance Committee of members from the London Schools to meet before each Governing Body meeting, an indication of mounting concern and the wish to return to closer oversight of the Board's costs.

Cranmer was very keen to go out to meet teachers, to learn of their concerns and to explain the Board's policy. Top of the list of the issues raised with him was that of specialist examiners, and he was keen to press the point that examining a candidate on the musicality of their playing was the best way of achieving parity of standards between instruments. The next most frequent concern was about the grading of wind instrument exams, and he recommended that the Syllabus Committee which had been dissolved in 1963 should be reconstituted.[56] Inconsistencies of standards had also prompted strong criticism of the Board's exams by LEA Music Advisers, and Cranmer pointed out to them that syllabuses for individual instruments had been devised with that specific instrument in mind and then 'co-ordinated' with those of the same family (strings, woodwind, brass), 'but they had not been moderated with an eye to uniformity of standard between all the subjects [instruments] offered'. Cranmer thought that the most constructive way of dealing with criticism about any apparent disparity in standards between instruments was to review and if necessary revise all the syllabuses on this basis, and so his proposal to reconvene the Syllabus Committee was approved.[57] Cranmer's willingness to engage with the Board's wider constituency of users was invaluable, and he recognized the Board's perceived vulnerabilities, not least those of orchestral instrument teachers who were uneasy about its mainly keyboard-based examiners.

Things became much more difficult when in 1978 – and seemingly out of the blue, certainly as far as Cranmer was concerned – the Board's Chairman, Anthony Lewis, announced the creation of the new post of Deputy Secretary for Administration. This had come at the instigation of the new Finance Committee, which had also recommended a full review into the Board's organization as well as a strengthening of the Finance Board itself. Although Cranmer supported the idea of a Deputy Secretary post, it was also clear that he resented the lack of prior consultation.[58] It was this review that was to set in train the long process that culminated in the 1985 Reconstitution. The minutes of the Special Meeting convened to consider the review's terms make clear that the review was considered necessary because 'the enormous success and consequent expansion of the Board's work in recent years had turned it into a very big concern and it seemed high time to take a comprehensive look at its internal organization and also at its relationship with the four Royal Schools'. Reference was made to the fact that the Board was still operating under its 1910 Deed, so there was a need to 'bring this up to date and to strengthen the organization'. Accordingly, it was decided to present the review

---

[55] ABMB11: 16 November 1976.

[56] ABMB11: 11 November 1975.

[57] ABMB11: 20 January 1976.

[58] ABMB12: 14 November 1978.

as a 're-appraisal' that needed to be undertaken as a matter of 'great urgency' and in 'private'. Ancillary to the review was a reinforced Finance Committee, which would advise the main board on administrative as well as financial aspects. The Finance Committee would be made up of the heads of the London Schools, and a further four members of the Board's Governing Body, two from the College and two from the Academy.[59] In other words, neither Manchester nor Scotland had a seat on this influential committee, which reinforced the privately expressed feeling that everything was sewn up by London.

The review was carried out by an external management consultant, and it was clear to all that with the Board's income now over £2 million there was the need for accountancy experience 'of the highest order', and that the new Deputy Secretary for Administration post was indeed needed. Another outcome was to put the Board's administrative staff on the University pay-scale structure, a decision that necessitated acceptance of the principle of annual increments and London Weighting, seen as necessary to retain staff. Therefore the priority for the new Deputy Secretary for Administration would be the necessary job evaluations for putting staff on the appropriate scales. R. J. R. Humphries was appointed to the post in June 1979. Despite several hefty increases in entry fees, the Board was now experiencing trouble in generating sufficient income to pay the expected dividend at the same time as maintaining sufficient reserves to cover contingencies. Indeed, the auditors had cautioned that the Board's reserves were already insufficient to cover contingencies, especially with the looming probability of the need to move premises.[60] The estimates covering the Board's operation in 1981 had been prepared on the basis of a 30% increase in Home fees, and the prediction of a 5% increase in candidate numbers. But even this hike was felt insufficient to generate the surplus necessary to cover both dividend and reserves, and so, instead, it was decided to raise fees by an extraordinary 35% in 1981,[61] a sign both of the security the Board now felt in its expanded market within the education authority context, and of its economic vulnerability. In fact the out-turn for the 1980 financial year was worse than expected, with a predicted deficit of £116,915 (among other things, staff costs had exceeded the estimate for the year by £53,000, and postage had increased by £14,000). The Board's ability for manœuvre was limited because even with the steep rise in entry fees, costs continued threatening to outstrip income.

The consternation felt at this situation, and the fact that the auditors had now moved to give the Associated Board formal warning that its reserves were insufficient to cover contingencies, was expressed by the Academy's Governing Body. Moving unilaterally, it required the Board to take measures 'to ensure not only the liquidation of the deficit made in 1980/81 but also the provision of adequate reserves during the ensuing 12 months'. The College, however, was taking a more realistic view and was prepared to consider remedial action taken over a longer timeframe, something that meant that the partners were no longer of the same mind in how best to deal with the Board's situation. The Deputy Secretary

---

[59] ABMB12: 28 November 1978.
[60] ABMB12: 1 July 1980.
[61] ABMB12: 18 March 1980.

indicated that he was pursuing possible savings of some £183,000 through reductions in staff costs, examiners' allowances (with travel reduced from first to second class) and computer development. The College, however, was concerned at the adverse consequences in the attitudes of both examiners and staff, hence its preference to see recovery over a longer period.[62] At the next Governing Body meeting, the Board was told to sort itself out and to trim as much as possible from the next annual estimates.[63] This was the very difficult context in which, with no warning, the northerners sent in bills totalling some £3,000 to reimburse them for their accommodation expenses in holding Board exams. The Finance Committee (drawn only from the London Schools) saw this for what it was, as something that reflected the constitutional position of the RNCM and the RSAMD, and so referred it to the Governing Body.[64] Thus there were no profits to distribute to the Schools in 1981. (However, the mutinous northerners had secured rather more than what would have been their usual share by their tactic of invoicing for exam accommodation!) Now anxious about making any diminution to the examiners' conditions, the subsistence allowance to them had actually been increased and first-class rail travel had been retained. The consequence was acknowledged by all: there would have to be a further substantial increase in candidates' fees in 1982.[65] What must have been a relief all round was that 1982 proved a turnaround, with a surplus of £271,857 on Home Exams and a surplus of £159,273 for the Publishing Division, all of which produced a balance of some £159,000.[66] In addition, the overseas market was looking healthy. Meanwhile, the Secretary announced that from 1982 the Board's syllabuses and regulations would be published in three booklets on a rotating basis, which was expected to save something like £18,000 from the current production costs of £54,000.

With the need to bring the Board's constitution up to date now recognized, in 1980 the northern Schools formally requested full and equal partnership in the ABRSM. This received the frosty reply that the 1910 Deed defined the partnership as being between the London partners, and that the northern Schools had been co-opted in 1946 with no financial liability. The northerners then requested a formal meeting of all the heads and the Secretary to discuss all these issues, to which the Chairman replied that it was up to the partners (i.e. the London Schools) to decide whether such a meeting should be called, and this was supported by the Governing Body.[67] In the midst of all this, Cranmer announced that he wished to retire in 1982. The advertisement was drawn up and the post attracted some eighty applicants – a mix of professional musicians with proven administrative ability, and professional administrators with a strong amateur interest in music. Clearly it was a difficult time to be making the Secretary appointment while issues of the Board's constitution were still to be resolved; and at the first of two special appointment meetings (at which the title 'Chief Executive' was first used),

---

[62] ABMB12: Finance Committee on 12 January 1981.

[63] ABMB12: 20 January 1981.

[64] ABMB12: Finance Committee on 9 March 1981.

[65] ABMB12: 24 March 1981.

[66] ABMB12: Finance Committee on 1 November 1982.

[67] ABMB12: 1 July 1980.

concern was expressed that the process of identifying a new Secretary had become unhelpfully interwoven with the process of determining the future constitution of the ABRSM itself. However, it was made clear that Ronald Smith, Music Adviser for the County of Avon and a former Vice-President of the International Society for Music Education (ISME), had been the selection committee's unanimous choice and that the other candidates had been stood down, and so a motion was passed to proceed to announce Smith's appointment without further delay.[68] After helping to induct his successor, Cranmer retired on 31 March 1983, and Smith, now designated 'Chief Executive and Director of Examinations', commenced his work on 1 April.[69]

---

[68] ABMB12: special meeting on 9 November 1982.
[69] ABMB12: 18 January, 16 March 1983.

IV The Board Revived, 1983–2009

10 The Reconstitution, 1983–5

◊ Reconstitution

TODAY'S ABRSM is a very different sort of institution from the one that entered the 1980s. Initiatives to develop its work in new directions have made the present Board a vigorous and vital force in music education, in striking contrast to the lethargic and routine body it had become. This chapter explains the reasons why and sets them into context. Key to this change has been that in the current phase of its history, since 1985, the Board has developed a very different and far more responsive attitude to its market. But breaking down some of the resentments of those with long memories of its customary peremptoriness has proved a hard task. The Board's high-handedness was partly the result of its long-time refusal to engage or seriously consult with teachers about their needs, or the practicalities of different teaching situations, and partly because of the heavy pressures on an under-resourced body that was barely able to cope with the volume of examinees that it already had. Periods of institutional transition and significant change are, by their very nature, far more interesting to study than long stretches of institutional inertia, although (*pace* the aphorism about 'interesting times') they are not necessarily comfortable for those living through them. In the case of the ABRSM, which had for so long been very firmly but largely unthinkingly set in its ways, modernizing to a changed market environment (which itself has been characterized by shifting cultural priorities and changed educational contexts) required a fundamental readjustment to its institutional mentality. In this sense the Board was extremely fortunate with the kick start it received from the 1985 Reconstitution. This event provided the impetus for the Board's rejuvenation, and gave it the incentive to reinvent itself to face modern, rather than early twentieth-century, circumstances.

The 1985 Reconstitution was the process that reconstructed the ABRSM partnership. It established a new senior structure within the Board itself, one of symbolic as well as practical significance. The role of Secretary (a designation implying a primarily administrative function) was discarded, and replaced by the more proactive-sounding position of Chief Executive. There was again to be an independent Chairman of the ABRSM (for the first time since 1939), and this new Chairman/Chief Executive structure strengthened the Board to take more of an initiative in its own development. At the same time, however, the Board had to be careful to maintain the best aspects of its identity, as well as the reputation it had for the quality of its examiners' assessments. In institutional terms, therefore, the ABRSM had to take to heart Lampedusa's celebrated dictum that in order for things to stay as they are, they have to change. And one characteristic of the Board's post-1985 development has been to pay much more attention to the needs of its market in order to avoid the trap of anachronism. The Board's recent thoroughness in researching the nature and identity of its market is evident in the expanded portfolio and musical scope of its exams, its online presence and its involvement in the area of teachers' professional development.

There are many observable differences between the state of the Board in 1983 (the point at which the last chapter concluded, with the appointment of Ronald Smith as the Board's first Chief Executive) and that in 2009 (when this history stops with the retirement of Richard Morris after seventeen years as its second Chief Executive). Firstly, the Board's non-executive structure has been completely reorganized so that each of the four constituent Royal Schools has parity. Secondly, the Board's focus has changed very considerably. From its original, self-limited concern with the process of examination – of setting syllabuses and assessment – the Board has now extended the spread of its educational services. New are the professional development initiatives for teachers, offering award-bearing courses, seminars and a wider range of diplomas. In publishing, where once the Board had deliberately constrained its activity in order to avoid direct competition with other music publishers, the post-1985 ABRSM publishing company has a new commercial freedom. This has produced a much wider portfolio of publications designed to complement and support across the range of the Board's work. It has also published an impressive series of significant performance editions of scholarly achievement. Outstanding has been the new Cooper edition of the Beethoven Piano Sonatas as well as Richard Jones's editions of Bach's *Well-Tempered Clavier* and *The Art of Fugue*.

Today's ABRSM has built itself up to fulfil a rather more inclusive educational mission than just grade examining because it has shouldered the more general responsibility of advocating the cause of classical music education in Britain today. It has published four invaluable research reports into the condition of music teaching, based on statistical data that sets out the environment of music teaching across the last two decades.[1] Successive governments have offered much motherhood and apple-pie preaching about the need to ensure that schools offer some musical experience to all children. But what the Board's research has identified is that it has become much more difficult than ever before to learn voice or instrumental skills to a high level, and that the music teachers' remit is becoming increasingly problematic in today's circumstances. As this chapter will suggest, if there was once a 'golden age' of British music education, in which learning an instrument was encouraged across state and private schools, and in which performance skills were additionally enhanced by a raft of LEA music activities, then that age lasted from the 1960s until the consequences of the 1988 Education Reform Act hit those very LEA music services. It needs to be remembered that it was politicians themselves who – through the agency of that 1988 Education Reform Act – created the conditions for making the serious learning of classical instruments an increasingly middle-class activity. The frequent linkage now made between classical music and cultural elitism would have been incomprehensible to our Victorian forebears, who could have pointed to the repertoires of enormous numbers of choral societies and brass bands countrywide as evidence of classical music's appeal regardless of its participants'

---

[1] *Making Music: The Associated Board Review of the Teaching, Learning and Playing of Musical Instruments in the United Kingdom* (London: ABRSM, 1994; 1997; 2000); *Research Report on Instrumental/Vocal Tuition in Private and State Schools* (London: ABRSM, 2006).

class.[2] In the post-1988 British musical condition, the ABRSM's involvement as an advocate for the importance of music learning has proved to be an important aspect of its institutional renewal.

⁄⁄⁄ Reconstitution: the context for renewal

T HE 1985 Reconstitution of the ABRSM was, in effect, its second founding. It resolved the ill will generated by the inequality between the northern and the London Schools which, as we have seen, had become a festering issue. It helped to clarify in all the partners' minds the fact that the Board was now simply too big to operate under their direct control and that, in order to provide a high quality of educational service, the ABRSM had to be successful as a business, and to be free to run itself as such. The lesson of the 1980 cash-flow crisis was still fresh in everyone's minds as a calamity that could happen again under difficult economic circumstances. Clearly, therefore, the best way to guard against that eventuality was for the Board to be able to run itself on a sound business footing, incorporating proper management controls and an effective market strategy. This required the Board to be able to develop its musical market on its own terms, independent of the operational direction of the Schools, and with sufficient financial leeway to invest properly in its strategy and services – although, as we shall see, being more hands-off has sometimes proved easier in principle than in practice. All these arguments for operational independence were to be underlined when the Board found itself facing the changed educational context following the 1988 Education Reform Act.[3] Chapter 9 explained the enormous gains that came to the Board from the widespread adoption of its grade exams by LEA music centres during the 1960s. Clearly, then, any serious change to LEA music provision would put this large and well-established market at risk. And that is what the 1988 Act did. Its financial measures prompted the dismantling of much LEA music provision in its then current form, which meant that most schools were no longer able to look to LEA music centres for the 'free' provision of peripatetic instrumental teachers. A consequence of devolved school budgeting was that instrumental teachers had to

---

[2] Among many other treatments illustrating this fundamental point, see Finnegan, *The Hidden Musicians*; Russell, *Popular Music in England*; Herbert, *The British Brass Band*; David Wright, 'Music and Performance: Histories in Disjunction?', in *The Cambridge History of Musical Performance*, ed. C. Lawson and R. Stowell (Cambridge: Cambridge University Press, 2012), 169–206. The social variety that was characteristic of the music college student body when this author was a student in the 1970s has since narrowed to such an extent that music colleges have come under criticism for their middle-class emphasis and lack of social diversity. The inevitability that classical music's social base would narrow because of the cost of music lessons and instrumental purchase following the withdrawal of LEA provision post-1988 was clearly flagged up by the three ABRSM *Making Music* reviews, and reinforced in its *Research Report on Instrumental/Vocal Tuition*.

[3] For a more widely drawn assessment of the significance of this Act, see the analysis prepared by the Public Studies Institute at www.psi.org.uk/publications/archivepdfs/recent/cenloc4.pdf.

be bought in, and therefore the facility to offer individual music lessons came into direct competition against other priorities of a school's budget. Chapter 12 looks in detail at some of the consequences for instrumental provision that this change has had, with teachers now working in circumstances that many perceive as being educationally less advantageous than before (raising issues of teacher/pupil access, contact time and restricted performance opportunities), and financially less supported (with implications for pupil take-up and for teachers' own employment).

The new independent Chair and Chief Executive structure signalled the Schools' awareness that if the Board was to prosper, then it had to be able to stand on its own. Even so, the relationship between the ABRSM and the Schools was, and is likely to remain, inherently delicate. Looking back at the events of Chapters 8 and 9, it is hard to argue that the heads of the London Schools really understood the nature of the ABRSM's work. As the Board's history shows, it can be misleading to argue too strong a symbiosis between the ABRSM and the Royal Schools. The central point of common interest – training musicians – can mask some important distinctions, such as the difference in the aspirations of the respective student or learner constituencies that each works with, and their distinctive needs and expectations.

In reality, the business of a conservatoire is very different from that of the Board, even though it is obviously complementary. As the earlier part of this history showed, an important rationale for the Board's work was the opportunity to increase the pool of prospective conservatoire students. It was a straightforward matter to design exams that helped pupils acquire the musical skills necessary for a professional-level training. Thus when the London Schools were in direct operational control of the ABRSM, there was always a sense that the Board's focus was on the Grade 8 outcome. In reality, those who achieve Grade 8 represent a tiny and distinctive component of the much broader educational market that the ABRSM deals with. Only very few progress to Grade 8 on any instrument, and most choose not to go beyond Grade 5; in 2009 UK and Ireland candidates for Grades 6 to 8 represented only 12% of the total Grades 1–8 entry. This small number indicates that people are using the grade exams for their own purposes, and that (for obvious reasons) for most people attaining Grade 8 is not the target. In other words, there is only a very limited overlap between the musical constituencies that the Board and the conservatoires serve. Arguably the most valuable aspect of the Board's work is the way it stimulates and fosters the general, rather than the specialist, musical interest of those who are sufficiently motivated to take its exams. And in today's cultural environment, that encouraging role has never been more important: not only for developing future audiences for music, but also in shaping people with musical sympathies who may go on in their turn to encourage their own children to take up music.

Another issue that had to be faced in the 1985 Reconstitution was that if the Board was left to run itself efficiently, then in the nature of things it would be very likely to turn a profit. As earlier recounted, much of the historical sensitivity about the Board's profits had been caused by the pressures of being an important income stream to the London Schools before they were funded within the Higher Education system. As commented on in Chapter 9, this explains the behaviour of the London partners in applying pressure to minimize the Board's operational expenditure, with examiners' fees (as its major cost element) always being very tightly controlled. Remarks in RCM Council meetings reflect awareness that the Board and the London Schools had indeed traded heavily on the goodwill and loyalty of these examiners; and that although this was a less than ideal practice, keeping examiners' fees as low as possible had been justified by them on a 'needs must' basis. All this may have fuelled a sense of unease about disclosing the size of the Board's profits too openly in case it fuelled a backlash from poorly paid examiners and the many unpaid volunteers on whom the Board relied so heavily.

In the context of the period, such sensitivities were understandable enough. But the mood of the times was changing, and the Thatcher government was clearly expecting that Higher Education institutions should no longer rely solely on government funding (which anyway was being significantly reduced), but should become entrepreneurial and generate more of their own income. This was an ethos driven by the ideological position of Sir Keith Joseph, who, as Secretary of State for Education, 'did not allow that education was solely a public good for it was also a highly desirable form of private consumption'.[4] The push for institutions to operate more on a business footing was so controversial because it was very much at odds with the outlook of a society used to perceiving the idea of higher education as a state-provided entitlement, with student grants available to all those who achieved the necessary entry qualifications. Today the higher education climate has completely changed, with society now accustomed to regarding tertiary education as a form of fee-based consumer choice, rather than as a free, entirely publicly funded, benefit. It is very much the expectation that universities should encompass significant business enterprises, making commercial use of their research expertise, and trading on their reputations to franchise courses, offer accreditation services, and, indeed, to levy student fees. This milieu means that it is now very much less likely that the Board's donations to the Royal Schools will be seen as the sensitive issue it was once felt to be. These donations, which enhance the specialist provision offered to students by each School, are the direct equivalent of the profits from university businesses to support their own institutions. Even at a historically much earlier stage, the Board's funding of the London Schools reflected well-established practice elsewhere, such as the contribution made by Oxford University Press to its University's income. It was just that such funding arrangements, though readily ascertainable from published accounts, were less openly acknowledged, which explains the sensitivity felt about finance as the Board was reconstituted.

The success of the Board's Reconstitution owed much to the financial and business advice that came from the RCM's Council. The ABRSM minutes suggest that RCM representatives and its Honorary Treasurer, one of the leading accountants of his generation, Sir Douglas Morpeth, were significant in formulating the new corporate structure. There seems to have been the view, as evidenced by the Board's 1980 cash-flow crisis, that the ABRSM was a tired and reactive operation with insufficient strategic direction of its own and impeded by the control exerted on it by the London Schools. It was felt, however, that with proper management it could be turned around and achieve its commercial

---

[4] Peter Jenkins, *Mrs Thatcher's Revolution*, 2nd edn (London: Pan Books, 1989), 182.

potential. Given the financially stringent approach of the government to higher education, the RCM Council would have been anxious about the funding implications for the College's future. What should also be remembered is that, for all the imposing grandeur of its physical appearance (the building was donated by the Victorian industrialist Samson Fox), the financial constraints under which the RCM had operated throughout its history meant that over the years there had been considerable underinvestment in developing its facilities. This situation helps explain the importance to the RCM of its Centenary Appeal, which provided the College with the on-site opera house it so badly needed for the productions that were a major feature of its performance training. In the more nakedly competitive educational environment of the 1980s, more finance would clearly be needed to improve the College further (including provision of dedicated student accommodation), if it was to attract the best national and international student talent. What was the case for the RCM was equally applicable to the other Schools, too. Well handled, the ABRSM's Reconstitution had the potential to unlock a major long-term asset of immense benefit to each of the Royal Schools. So the new ABRSM structure, with its deliberately easy buy-in terms for the new partners and the loosening of the Schools' reins, is best understood as an investment strategy devised to help secure the Royal Schools' collective future.

░ The refounding of the Board: the reconstitution process

FOR the reasons described towards the end of Chapter 9, a reconstitution of the Board had become the best way of resolving its internal issues. The DES's funding of the London Schools had alleviated their financial dependence on the Board's profits, and this new situation gave some latitude to resolve the philosophical basis of the Board's operation. Until the Reconstitution the Board was formally operating under the terms of the 1910 Agreement, with the RAM and the RCM as the Board's only legally constituted partners. But under the 1910 Agreement the London partners also had unlimited liability for the ABRSM, which meant that they carried financial responsibility for all debts the Board incurred beyond its resources, whether through financial failure or by the adverse consequences of any proceedings taken against it. And as the scale and financial complexity of the Board's operations grew, so this responsibility was causing the partners mounting unease.

But what was the ABRSM's economic rationale to be after its Reconstitution? As we have seen, the Board had a slightly problematic historical legacy in the matter of its profits. The image that had been so carefully cultivated (as in Hugh Allen's 1931 speech, discussed in Chapter 6) had emphasized the public benefit element of the Board's exams and its scholarships to the Schools, and had tended to disguise the Board's business element. Therefore, people tended to think of the Board's exams as priced to cover costs, rather than as intended to bring a return that would help to finance the London Schools. From the 1970s some members of the Board's Governing Body had been voicing their disquiet at the idea of planning to make a profit out of the exams, and questioning the appropriateness of the Board being run as a 'business' for its own sake. Instead, so that particular argument went, the Board's work should be more about educational service than increased profits. This debate was rekindled in 1984 by the Board's refusal, under its new Chairman, Sir Brian Young, to increase its fees for 1985/6.[5] In this, the last year of the old constitution, one voice on the Governing Body was raised in complaint because, although there had been an increase in the estimated operational costs submitted to the partners, the exam fees had not also automatically been raised to compensate for this. A compromise was reached whereby there would be no increase to the Board's fees for 1985, although it was agreed the Finance Committee would revisit the estimates of the Board's planned operating expenditure before the next meeting.[6] At that next meeting, held in November 1984, the issue of the Board's future purpose was again raised. A blunt alternative was thrown out: was the Board to be subordinate to the dictates of the London Royals; or was it to be independent, with a non-executive governing body advised by the Board's executive staff, run on a prudent cost-basis that would still allow for the return of a surplus to be donated to the four Royal Schools? All agreed that educational service was the Board's core purpose, but it was also pointed out that financial considerations had to be realistic if that objective were to be best achieved. And it was also acknowledged by all that the partners needed to be in agreement about the new constitution before the future of the Board could be more clearly defined.[7] This discussion, coming when it did in the lead-up to the Reconstitution, played an influential part in determining the nature of the Board's future. The inescapable fact was that, with each of the RSMs now being funded within the higher educational system, the Board's own economic *raison d'être* had fundamentally changed. It was agreed that the Reconstitution needed to give formal recognition of this new position by establishing the ABRSM as a charity to be run on a not-for-profit basis. It was following this November debate that the London Schools sent an explanatory memorandum to the DES, setting out the rationale for the proposed reconstitution of the ABRSM.

The Reconstitution of the Board now had two clear objectives: one was to change the Board's legal position so that it became a charitable company limited by guarantee (with its own Chairman); the other was to make the northern Schools full partners in the Board, with each of the four Royal Schools holding a quarter interest. There were, however, two complicating factors, and the procedure adopted to reconstitute the Board had to deal satisfactorily with each. First was the issue of expanding the partnership. And, given that the usual commercial practice was for new partners to buy their way into a partnership, this posed the question as to whether, or how, the northern Schools could raise the necessary capital to do so. Second was the issue of the Board's historical assets. Here the point was whether the government funding now received by the London Schools gave the DES a determining lien or hold over the Board's historically accumulated capital. Thus a scheme needed to be formulated that would release the ABRSM's historical assets and permit their use by the original London partners, but in a way that did not infringe the regulations that covered the government funding they were now

---

[5] ABMB12: special meeting on 28 August 1984.

[6] Ibid.

[7] ABMB12: 20 November 1984.

receiving. In the end the resolution of both these crucial issues came through an elegant and lucid structural formula that enabled the Reconstitution to proceed smoothly and on the basis of full agreement.

The DES's support of the Academy and the College had indeed given the Department a direct interest in the London Schools' finances. Under the rules governing their public funding, income received from other, non-government sources could trigger a corresponding reduction in the amount of the DES's annual grant. It was therefore essential that any future money that went from the Board to any of the Royal Schools should not be able to be categorized as income, but instead be defined as donations of capital sums for the benefit of music education. In order to achieve this distinction, it had to be clearly established that none of the partner Schools was directly participating in the work of the Board, otherwise it would be receiving income for work done. It was considered that the best way of making the distinction necessary to have transfers of money from the ABRSM to the Royal Schools classified as donations, and not income, was for the partnership interests in the Board to be held not directly by the Schools themselves, but instead by four music education charities on their behalf, with each School nominating its own charity. Thus any donations from the Board would go directly to the charity associated with each School, and not to the School itself. The four nominated charities were the Prince Consort Foundation (for the RCM), the Royal Academy of Music Foundation, the Royal Northern College of Music Endowment Fund, and the Royal Scottish Academy of Music and Drama Trust. As another part of this process of clarification, the Board's Music Publishing Department became a company in its own right as ABRSM (Publishing) Ltd, trading on its own account as a wholly owned subsidiary and donating its own profits to the ABRSM.

The proposed reconstitution of the Board was very carefully explained to the DES because, as indicated, Whitehall's prior agreement was critical to the whole process. In setting out their case the London partners emphasized the distinction between the purpose of the Associated Board as a music examining body, and that of the Royal Schools as teaching institutions. They also made clear to the DES that it was their intention that any proceeds generated by a realization of any of the Board's historical assets in the process of reconstitution, would be used for Academy and College projects for which DES grant support was not usually available, and student accommodation was put as top of their priorities. The DES agreed to accept the London Schools' case that the ABRSM represented a pre-1975 capital asset, thereby exempting the transfer of historically accumulated reserves from being set against current DES grant; the DES also agreed the principle that assets realized in the reconstruction process could be used to finance capital projects, as requested. The DES's acceptance of the basis of the reconstitution proposal thus cleared the way for it to proceed.[8] A blow-by-blow account of the technicalities of the reconstitution process would be likely to strain the patience of most readers. So what follows summarizes those aspects which, historically and institutionally, are most salient in terms of the Board's story. It is interesting that in all the contemporary documentation and in the minutes this process is called a

---

[8] Unless otherwise indicated, information about the reconstitution process comes from *The Associated Board, 1985 Reorganisation Documents* (ABRSMA).

'Reorganization', even though that does not convey how fundamental a change was being made to the ABRSM's constitutional position. For what was happening by the process was nothing less than the Associated Board's refounding. Accordingly, this account refers to the 'Reconstitution' rather than 'Reorganization'.

Although in the early 1980s the Board had been through a financial crisis, that was a cash-flow problem (caused by deficiencies of business planning) rather than a solvency issue, because over time it had built up sizeable capital reserves. So the principle that the Reconstitution followed was for the northern Schools to purchase their share of a newly constituted Board, while the London Schools, who as the original partners had built up the Board's position and had carried the financial risk, would benefit from a release of historic Board reserves. However, the College and the Academy undertook to leave sufficient working capital for the use of the newly constituted Board. As well as needing sufficient working capital, the Board was also having to face the issue of its future accommodation. Accordingly, some of the reserves transferred to the London Schools were to be earmarked for later use, if needed, to secure suitable new premises for the ABRSM.

The process of expanding the partnership went as follows. The northern Schools – through their nominated charities – would purchase their partnership by annual instalments over an agreed maximum of ten years. This arrangement was designed to avoid the need for the payment of a capital sum, which the northern Schools were not in a position to raise. Instead, the money for these instalments was to come from the annual donations the northern Schools – now in the position of full partners – would each receive from the Board; and the agreement was that, for the time it took to reach the purchase amount (either the full ten years or less than this), these donations would be remitted directly back to the College and the Academy.[9] So, in effect, this arrangement extended the time that the two London Schools continued to receive their traditional half-share of donations from the Board until the northern Schools had completed purchasing their share of the ABRSM partnership. A safeguard had been written into the agreement whereby if, after ten years, the northern Schools' repayments had not reached the full purchase amount (i.e. if the donations had fallen below the level projected for them), then the rest of the debt would be waived, and be deemed to have been discharged.

The price the northern Schools would pay for their respective quarter shares was based on the notional valuation of £9.1 million that had been put on the whole of the ABRSM. This amount represented the estimated total donations which it was projected the Board would generate over the next ten years – the duration which formed the maximum purchase period. After agreement on the process and the price with the northern Schools, the existing partners (the College and the Academy), transferred ownership of the Board to their nominated charities, respectively the Prince Consort Foundation and the Royal Academy of Music Foundation. These foundations then each transferred a proportion of their shares into the charities that the northern Schools had nominated, so that all four partners ended up with a quarter portion in the ABRSM. The rationale for extending such advantageous terms to the northern Schools was that had no

[9] ABMB12: 15 November 1983.

satisfactory arrangement been reached with them, and had they, in consequence, decided to withdraw from the ABRSM, then the Board's reputation and identity would have suffered the severest damage to its continued viability. Meanwhile, the whole process had been made more financially rational, because the historical monetary reserves had been taken off the books of the reconstituted ABRSM partnership and returned to the College and the Academy.

Even with what had been done to make the 1985 arrangement as financially rational as possible in order to suit the conditions of the day, clearly the northern Schools secured their full partnership on very favourable terms. As this account has argued, one of the strategic objectives of the 1985 Agreement was to preserve the Board's unified image; something felt to be quintessential to the ABRSM 'brand'. This meant that the prime concern was to arrive at a monetary valuation of the Board that the northerners could realize within an acceptable timeframe. And perhaps from the 1985 perspective, the London Schools had less cause to feel bullish about the Board's business potential than its development would subsequently prove. The combination of these two factors may explain why the partnership offer was made at a price well below what an independent business valuation of the Board may have been, given the Board's market potential and its existing market dominance. This point is an important one, because it may help us understand more clearly what the 1985 Reconstitution represented to those involved in drawing up the partnership scheme. Assessed purely from a business perspective, the sale of the Board on these terms could be portrayed as a considerable under-realization of their asset by the London partners, and as such a significant financial opportunity lost for these two institutions. But another way of looking at the 1985 Reconstitution is to see it as a pragmatic and, arguably, a far-sighted solution. It successfully secured the Board's new constitution on the basis of a financial settlement that was tailored to achieve as much as the circumstances permitted. That is likely to be the historian's judgement. The reality was that it would have been difficult for those involved in the 1985 Reconstitution to have foreseen the business success that the Board would achieve over the next twenty-five years, and even more difficult to have sold that vision of the Board's development to the northern Schools. It is therefore reasonable to assume that the view taken of the Board in 1985 was as the examination board that it had always been, rather than as the Board would become today: a broader-based education service provider whose diversification would in turn open up further significant areas of development and revenue-earning potential.

The last of the 'old' ABRSM governing body meetings was the 761st, held on 25 June 1985. And after the completion of the legal and audit processes necessary to close the accounts, the Unincorporated Association of the London Schools was formally dissolved on 20 June 1989. Coincidentally, the winding-up came virtually a hundred years after Alexander Mackenzie made that trip to the RCM in May 1889, with his request to bury the hatchet on the enmity between the London Schools by proposing the Associated Board, followed by the first exploratory meeting between the College and the Academy, held on 17 June.

11 Reconnecting with its Market: the Smith Years, 1983–92

∥ Evolving from the 'old' to the 'new' ABRSM

RONALD Smith brought a very different perspective to the ABRSM. His arrival as the Board's Chief Executive – jettisoning the historic title of 'Secretary' – seemed to signal that the ABRSM might, at last, be prepared to accept the need for change. There was a sense at the time that the Board was too much a bastion of the independent school sector, and so Smith's appointment from being an LEA county music adviser was all the more striking. Some saw it as a long-overdue recognition by the Board of the significance of state-school music in British music education. For the post-war development of LEA music provision had given new vitality to the training of young musicians, opening up opportunities through the development of networks of local youth orchestras, ensembles and choirs. The Leicestershire Schools Symphony Orchestra had shown just what could be achieved on a county basis, and its work with the composer Michael Tippett had been the inspiration for others. Meanwhile, there was powerful advocacy for the idea of moving classroom music away from the dominance of music 'appreciation' (usually delivered on a talk, chalk and listen basis), which in many children's experience usually entailed passive reception, and to make it a creative experience, involving pupils' own composition and performance. A big influence here was John Hosier, then a BBC producer, for his use of the BBC's resources to create inspiring music education programmes. His broadcast material adapted some of the approaches of Carl Orff and Zoltan Kodály, and by giving teachers a ready-made creative structure to use in their own classrooms, he encouraged their harnessing of pupils' participation in the projects he devised. Pioneers such as George Self and John Paynter – who with Peter Aston wrote the influential text *Sound and Silence* (1970) – had developed other innovative methods of classroom involvement.

All this had now put a very different kind of school music firmly on the map. The shift from music appreciation to music creation (encompassing a variety of musical idioms) and the possibilities of class music-making proved a transformative experience for many who encountered it. The idea that relatively unskilled but enthusiastic school children could begin to make music independently of any theoretical foundations was a very liberating one. It highlighted the contrast with conventional music education, something that in turn made the formal ABRSM parameters seem all the stuffier. When Hosier became the Inner London Education Authority's senior music inspector in 1973, he had the opportunity to achieve his ambition of integrating the work and example of professional musicians within the education of the young, both directly in teaching or coaching, and through concert-going schemes. The achievements of the London Schools Symphony Orchestra were built on the effective use of ILEA resources. Children were taught by peripatetic teachers working within schools and those with strong potential were encouraged to develop their talent and attend the specialist Saturday music centre at Pimlico School. Hosier also initiated the very influential Tower Hamlets

7 Ronald Smith, Chief Executive, 1983–1992, whose period changed the ABRSM in several important respects. An upbeat major triad would more truly have reflected his achievement than the minor one he strikes here.

string tuition project, which was run on the basis of group-teaching, an idea that was later extended to the piano. Ideas like this vitalized state music provision, and county music advisers had become powerful, and sometimes iconoclastic, figures in music education. By appointing Smith, the Board was consciously buying in to this stratum of expertise. And Smith's LEA experience meant that he came to the Board with a consumer's familiarity of the ABRSM's shortcomings.

Those who felt that the Board had stubbornly ignored the needs of many of its customers hoped there was now a realistic chance that Smith's own experience would bring about reform. And it was clear that changes needed to be as much concerned with institutional attitude as anything else. Prior to his arrival at the Board, Smith had shared with other music adviser colleagues their collective sense of frustration at the ABRSM's keyboard orientation, its reluctance to provide the complete range of grades in woodwind and brass, its failure to provide syllabuses for popular instruments such as the saxophone, and its old-fashioned Theory exams. The feeling was that if it was to serve music education properly, the Board needed to devise and offer exams for which there was a self-evident need. Smith had come to the Board at a formative time for consumer behaviour. The British economic and social environment was being reshaped by the policies of the post-1979 Thatcher government, and consumer attitudes were being changed by the experience of the privatization of the state monopolies in gas, electricity and telecoms. In particular, the extensive advertising of shares that accompanied these sell-offs raised the consciousness of consumers, and the subsequent drive by the newly privatized utility companies to attract more customers further encouraged consumers' expectations. Customers had long been conditioned into passivity by the dirigiste attitudes of the old nationalized industries, which supplied their captive markets entirely on their own terms and conditions. In its own sphere, the take-it-or-leave-it attitudes the Board had displayed to its customers seemed more characteristic of a nationalized monolith than a responsive educational service. It is against this background that Ronald Smith's two most notable accomplishments stand out. He first put the Board in a listening mode, more ready to respond to its market. For Smith realized that if the Board was to become more accountable to its customers, then it needed to make itself the service provider of choice (rather than necessity) through the relevance, as well as the quality, of the exams it was offering. Secondly, Smith worked to increase the transparency of the examining process itself and to improve the consistency of examiners' marking. A big step forward was to publish the examination criteria (which was done in the ABRSM booklet *These Music Exams*) so that teachers, candidates and parents could be given a clear sense of how the examiner was marking. Although such reforms were long overdue, in the context of the Board's established practice and historical culture, they undoubtedly took some determination and persistence to secure.

Despite some catching up of ground under Philip Cranmer, the Board was as much behind the times in its office administration as in its attitudes to consumers. Indicative was the practice of continuing to provide examiners with a detailed railway itinerary for their tours, whether or not they were travelling by train (and most by now were using a car); Smith said that this service to examiners should be put on a request-only basis, and the wasted effort that supplying train timetables had long represented was underlined because it was subsequently hardly ever asked for. As the 1980 cash-flow débâcle had demonstrated, the lack of investment in the Board's infrastructure had put its administration under considerable strain. However, the move to put the organization on a sounder operational footing (by implementing new office practices and computerization) was uncomfortable, prompting some internal resistance and high staff turnover. Additionally, Smith's first two years in post were made uneasy at times by the process of negotiation to put the new constitution of the four Royal Schools' partnership in place. Then followed a further period of adjustment as the Board's Executive and its Governing Body had to bed in the revised constitution and establish a new working relationship. Under the old partnership arrangement, decisions about the Board were taken by the London Schools acting bilaterally, and often simply presented as a *fait accompli* to the Governing Body. But if the post-1985 constitution, with its new independent Chairman/Chief Executive structure, was going to work, then a much more formalized governance committee structure needed to be implemented. Whereas the Board's Governing Body had previously been an executive board directing the Secretary, now it was having to adapt to the very different circumstances (and attitudes) of working more as a non-executive board, delegating operational responsibilities to the ABRSM's own Executive officers.

It may seem extraordinary to us now, but before the Reconstitution of the Board there had been no corporate plan, as such. The Board had simply been run continuously on a 'more-of-the-same' basis. And although care had been taken to build the financial reserves to a level that the auditors had thought prudent to cover the Board's operations, there had been no real planning to develop either its administrative capacity or its business function, or, indeed, strategic views about the future. Thus the formulation of a corporate plan, setting out the Board's ethos and mission, represented something of a radical departure. The process, however, did not happen immediately, and seemed to be initiated in 1987 by the discussion that followed Smith's own review to the Governing Body of his first years as Chief Executive. In the course of his presentation, one of the Schools' principals, responding to Smith's suggestion that candidate numbers had been adversely affected by Local Authority economies, asked if there needed to be a shift in the Board's policy in order to bring it and schools' needs into better alignment – the first time such a concern about the market had been expressed in quite this way. Such an exasperatingly po-faced statement must have been more than irritating to Smith, who had already put a considerable amount of effort into building up a better relationship between the Board and its market by widening its exams and improving its customer attitude.[1] All agreed that the Board's centenary was an appropriate time 'for the Board to improve its public relations image, and to adopt a more aggressive marketing approach'.[2] The corporate plan set out the Board's mission:

> We aim to provide an efficient and valued service to music education through graded examinations in all parts of the UK, and overseas where practicable, within a framework of financial objectives which provides

[1] ABMB13: 24 November 1987.
[2] Ibid.

for overall surpluses, to be applied by the Board to charitable educational purposes.

To this end we will:

(i) seek to encourage musicians of all ages without compromising standards;

(ii) train and moderate examiners to achieve greater uniformity in marking and provide constructive criticisms to improve standards of teaching and performance;

(iii) endeavour to develop still further the influence of the Associated Board throughout the world compatible with local needs and market opportunities.

Our publishing subsidiary will:

(i) support the Associated Board by providing a professional service for all examinations-related material required by the Board;

(ii) enhance the reputation of the Board and provide for the needs of musicians as well as examination candidates by publishing a wide repertory of scholarly, performing editions at reasonable prices, and albums which aim to educate to a better understanding of style and performance;

(iii) make money, through the sale of publications world-wide, with which the Associated Board can further its charitable objectives.[3]

This plan shows that the ABRSM had already travelled a certain philosophical distance from its pre-1985 state, because it now recognized that it was supplying an educational service within a market context. The Schools were also beginning to appreciate that the Board needed to be successful as a business if it was to fulfil its potential in the educational sphere. For on its commercial success depended the financing of the research and development of future initiatives, as well as the surpluses for charitable music education purposes expected by the Royal Schools.

Undoubtedly, the main achievement of Smith's decade as Chief Executive was to reawaken the Board from its debilitated state and to set about its reinvention. This meant that the Board went into its 1989 Centenary Year with greater cause for optimism than would have been realistic only a few years previously. As another first in the build-up to this event, the Board appointed an external agency, Lawrence Cheung, to review and advise it on marketing and public relations. The main Centenary event was the concert at the Royal Albert Hall on 29 October, when forces from all four Royal Schools and the choir of Tiffin School combined to give a performance of Mahler's Eighth Symphony, conducted by the Danish conductor Ole Schmidt (permanent guest conductor at the RNCM), to an audience that included the ABRSM's President, Queen Elizabeth, the Queen Mother. At the Centenary Lunch the guest of honour was the Earl of Harewood, the great-grandson of Edward VII, the Board's first President. Another element of the celebrations was the inception of the Centenary Travel Grant

---

[3] ABMB13: 24 January 1989.

scheme, designed to bring teachers from abroad to study for a term at one of the Royal Schools to help their professional development and to prepare to take the LRSM.

In this crucial transitional phase of the ABRSM's history, Smith's was certainly no easy assignment. What could not be doubted was the educational commitment and determination that he brought to his role, and there was admiration for his hard work as he slogged his way to effect the changes he thought essential for the Board to fulfil its potential and make a sustainable future. By sheer energy he made things happen, sometimes despite the discouragement he received from the Schools as he ventured to set the Board in new directions. Professional development initiatives (in the shape of teachers' seminars), for example, began cautiously, and though the idea took some time before becoming a major element of the Board's portfolio, these early events signalled a significant departure because they recast the ABRSM as an educational service that encompassed more than just exams and assessment. But at first this was all viewed warily and with a degree of reluctance by some of the Schools' Principals (not least because of the financial investment involved), and only later was it acknowledged that the move into helping teachers by offering professional support and development opportunities constituted a vitalizing strategy. Similarly, other initiatives, such as the expansion of the exam portfolio, more transparent examining processes and development of a new relationship with the Board's market, were also vindicated as candidate numbers continued to increase during Smith's time. Such growth was remarkable in the face of a less propitious market context – not least because the 1988 legislation had thrown the state sector music provision into flux. Despite the operational and financial constraints he faced, Smith's period as Chief Executive was notable for its advances. What is certain is that without Smith's spadework and his dogged resolve, Richard Morris's period as Chief Executive would have begun from an altogether weaker position.

※ Developing the exam portfolio

THE Schools were careful to put checks and balances on the new Executive. Committees covering the main areas of the ABRSM's activities were established, each chaired by one of the Schools' Principals and reporting formally to the Governing Body. Similarly, when working parties were set up to develop new syllabuses or consider new initiatives, so Schools representation was also included. The Examinations Board was one of the most significant of these committees because of the influence it exerted right across the ABRSM's work. Its terms of reference (drawn up in 1986) indicate the extent of its authority. Acting on its own account, the Examinations Board confirmed, or otherwise, the appointment of new examiners recommended by the Appointments Committee, and had responsibility for overseeing the training of examiners; it also implemented the retirement of examiners at the statutory age of sixty-seven (though it could recommend individual exceptions to the Governing Body). It also confirmed the awards of exam prizes and ABRSM scholarships to the Schools and agreed any proposed minor changes to existing exam syllabuses. The Examinations Board was the primary source of advice to the Governing Body about any exam matters that carried financial or strategic implications, the introduction of new syllabuses, any proposed major changes in exam policy or exam procedures or issues that affected the overseas exams. Under the Examinations Board's remit the Chief Executive was given more direct formal responsibility over individual examiners, and could take any immediate disciplinary action should it be necessary. He was also responsible for liaising with the publishing company on bringing out supporting publications for new syllabuses.[4] As these terms of reference indicate, the reality was that a great deal of practical control continued to reside with the Schools through the Governing Body, and certainly enough to tempt them to cross the usual corporate executive/non-executive divide. A striking illustration of this divide being crossed was the development of grade exams for the free bass accordion.

In the introduction of a grade syllabus for the free bass accordion, the Board's Executive – acting against its own wishes and better judgement – was being obliged to supply these exams, despite the lack of any market demand for them, because of pressure being brought by one of the constituent Schools. The RAM had instituted the teaching of the chromatic free bass accordion and, not surprisingly, it wanted to have its initiative complemented by the availability of grade exams. So in 1983 it began to press its request at Governing Body level. The Board's Executive, however, felt that the development of harpsichord and percussion exams should be given a higher priority, because of the demand for these subjects, and this it proceeded to do. The evident reluctance to develop an accordion syllabus generated strong protest, and so a compromise was reached with an assurance given by the Governing Body (rather than the Executive) that the accordion syllabus should be made a priority by the Board in its new, post-1985, guise. However, when the proposal went to the Examinations Board, that committee expressed major reservations about an accordion syllabus, and after an extended discussion, effectively suggested that the idea be dropped. It had two main concerns: first, that accordion grades might require specialist examiners (something that would drive a coach and horses through the Board's long-held, and staunchly maintained, principle that its examiners were marking on the musical qualities of a candidate's performance rather than the technical aspects of its production); second, there were reservations about prescribing a graded repertoire consisting mainly of transcriptions.

Given that the free bass accordion was still something of a rarity in the UK context, and that the RAM had only just instituted a three-year course for the instrument, the Examinations Board diplomatically suggested that instead of moving straight away to develop a grade syllabus, it might be more prudent to await a report on how the initiative was progressing. This recommendation was received at the Governing Body meeting in October 1986 and generated what might best be described as a frank discussion. Disquiet ranged between anxiety that any serious move by the Board to promote the accordion (which was also featuring in that year's Young Musician of the Year competition) might damage the take-up of more conventionally popular classical instruments, and the observation that the small number of players learning at the RAM (about six in any three-year

---

[4] ABMB13: 24 June 1986.

period) did not inspire confidence that there would be much of a demand for accordion grade exams. Essentially, the underlying concern was that the cost of developing an Accordion syllabus would be unlikely to be recouped. But in the awkwardness of the situation, with neither enthusiasm nor scepticism about these exams expressed decisively enough to carry the day, it was agreed to refer the matter back to the Examinations Board, asking it to reach a decision by the summer, but with an eye to implementing these exams in 1989. Much sooner than that, however, the Governing Body was again heavily lobbied. At its next meeting in February, three players came to demonstrate the instrument, after which a vote was again held about introducing accordion grades. This vote produced four in favour and seven abstentions, a result which, as the minutes described it, 'seemed to indicate a degree of uncertainty'. So it was again resolved to refer the matter back to the unfortunate Examinations Board. However, that decision was resisted by its Chairman because of the 'disproportionate' amount of time already taken up in discussing the accordion issue. At the following meeting of the Governing Body in June 1987, the proposition for accordion exams was again voted on. It attracted five votes in favour and four votes against, and so it was decided to implement accordion grades in 1990 at the same time as percussion grades. Four years later, in June 1994, it was reported to the governing body that despite the distribution of over 14,000 syllabuses, there had been a meagre total of twenty-one candidates for the accordion grades, and only four in 1993. Accordingly it was decided to terminate the syllabus from 31 December 1994, while allowing those who had started the grades to continue to proceed, using the current syllabus.[5]

This accordion controversy can be interpreted in several ways. The Academy wished to maximize the opportunities for an instrument whose cause it was promoting in the UK, and grade exams represented a good way of doing this. However, the Board's own reluctance to take the idea further showed that it was anxious to adopt a much more business-like attitude in the matter of developing new syllabuses, with all the associated costs of examiner training, publicity and printed materials. Essentially, the Board's future depended on its investing in and supplying exams that the market actually wanted or for which there was an overriding educational need. It was because percussion and harpsichord grades would clearly fulfil a perceived requirement that the Board's Executive wished to give priority to developing new syllabuses for these instruments and not for the accordion. The lesson of the accordion grades was that if the Board was to be successful, it could no longer afford to privilege one School's special but very restricted interest, especially when doing so flew in the face of advice from the ABRSM's own Executive (who knew their market), as well as from many of the non-executive directors. This episode showed that the Governing Body was not always finding it easy to adjust from its old executive role to its new non-executive one; neither had the Board's old partner institutions, the College and the Academy, entirely understood that under the new ABRSM constitution they could no longer just call the shots. In retrospect, and uncomfortable all round though it was, this accordion affair might well have been a cautionary but formative experience that

    [5] ABMB12: 15 November 1983; 25 June 1985; ABMB13: 21 October 1986; 17 February, 21 June 1988; ABMB14: 21 June 1994.

helped both the new partners and the Board's Executive to acclimatize to the realities of the post-1985 situation.

The ten years that Ronald Smith was in post saw several new syllabuses and a greater rationalization of the Board's exam portfolio. As mentioned in the previous chapter, the Board had been sniffy about introducing saxophone exams, despite the instrument's popularity in schools and many requests that the Board should offer them. There was a similar situation over the recorder. But whereas in previous years any move to include the saxophone had stalled because it was felt that examiners would be insufficiently acquainted with it (the implication seemed to be that it was too vulgar an instrument for them to have encountered), the concern over recorder exams was that entries might be so numerous as to exceed the Board's capacity to cope. Initially it was also difficult to gain support for percussion grade exams, the argument against being that these instruments were 'technical rather than musical' and that such exams could therefore only be conducted by specialists.[6] Oddly enough, it was the protracted debate over the accordion exams that seems to have unlocked the barrier to offering the percussion ones; presumably it was felt that if generalist examiners had to deal with examining the accordion, then they could certainly cope with something as conventional as percussion. The saxophone exams were introduced in 1985, followed by recorder exams in 1986; by 1990 there were already 4,160 saxophone candidates (nearly as many as for oboe at 4,333) compared with 3,224 recorder players and four free bass accordionists. Percussion exams started in 1990, the year that also saw the introduction of a new type of exam, the 'Preparatory Test', for pupils who had been learning for between six and nine months. The test was designed to give early and positive feedback directly to the pupil in the form of comments, rather than marks (there was no pass or fail judgement, so all candidates received a certificate), and as a helpful experience for taking grade exams in the future. Trialled in fifty selected centres, the Preparatory Test had 2,166 entries in its first year, and, now called the Prep Test, it has become very popular. These successes indicate that the UK market was developing very positively because the Board was becoming much more responsive to its users. There was now a scheme of 'special visits' whereby schools could arrange for exams to be conducted outside the normal exam periods. The Board had also benefited from hearing some uncomfortable truths about itself from the consultative committee which was established in 1986. Again something of a new departure, this widely based committee drew its members from a range of different teaching contexts (school, private and LEA), the DES music inspectorate, Higher Education, an LEA music adviser and an HLR.

There was a much less successful market response to the revised Theory grade exams. As Chapter 9 recounted, the Board was greatly concerned that the more involved and creative approach to theory which the Gardner–Salter *Basic Musicianship* represented might prove a disincentive to candidates and their teachers who had been conditioned for so long in the 'right or wrong' approach of the Board's traditional Theory exams. Because the Theory fees were a significant part of the Board's overall income, getting this decision wrong would be expensive, hence the reluctance to make too great a change. Even so, it was felt that some

---

[6] ABMB13: 21 October 1986.

updating was indeed necessary. The result appeared under the generic title *Music Theory in Practice*, chosen in order to make the exams sound as relevant as possible. Eric Taylor had rewritten the material for the first five grades (the market's most crucial ones), and Peter Aston with Julian Webb had written the books for the higher grades, requiring the four-part realization of figured bass, harmonization and some composition. The introduction of these new Theory exams (Grades 1 to 5 in 1991 and Grades 6 to 8 in 1992) was greeted by a big drop in candidate numbers, both in the UK and overseas. In the UK the number of Theory candidates fell from 68,304 in 1990 to 43,991 in 1991, an indication of the strength of the adverse reaction to them. The introduction of a new syllabus sometimes has the effect of initially depressing entries but is then usually followed by a recovery. However, in the case of these Theory exams, candidate numbers have never since returned to their pre-1991 levels, and the decline has been especially marked in Grades 6–8 (see Table 9.3). Some felt that too large a discrepancy had been introduced between the approach followed in the first five grades and that used for the higher ones (Table 9.4 indicates this fall-off). Only Grade 5, privileged as the prerequisite grade for entry to the higher-grade Practical exams, has been able to maintain its relative hold in the Board's Theory market. This revision of the Theory grades illustrates the Board's vulnerability to a serious and continuing adverse market reaction, even when the change it makes is motivated by the wish to secure an improved, or more enlightened, educational outcome. Sometimes, then, a good educational case for making substantial revisions can also constitute a sensitive commercial issue for the Board. Underlying this is the actual upfront cost of implementing a significant change (as in the case of Theory), which involves considerable financial investment in commissioning new syllabuses and issuing supporting publications, as well as the costs of publicity and guidance sessions for examiners and teachers.

The involvement of contemporary music in the Board's exams continued to be contentious. The issue came to a head again in 1988 during the planning for a new exam, the Advanced Certificate, which was to be an intermediate stage between Grade 8 and the LRSM diploma. The Governing Body meeting in November 1988 agreed that more contemporary music (defined for the purpose as 'works of composers still living') should be incorporated throughout the grade system as well as in the Advanced Certificate. At the next meeting in March it was reported that there were still issues about the inclusion of contemporary music, so it was decided that a list of 'contemporary' composers be provided to those compiling syllabuses. The recommendation was that the Board should commission new works where no suitable ones existed, and these should be published individually or in a compendium. It was agreed that the updating of the Corporate plan should also make specific reference to the place of contemporary music within the Board's exam syllabuses.[7] (This ambition for the Board to treat contemporary music much more seriously was later realized in 1996 by its publication of the first of the contemporary music *Spectrum* series.) Another idea mooted in 1988 was to explore the possibility of exams in non-Western music, but references to this in the minute books very soon dry up, and it is difficult to see how the Board would have demonstrated the necessary credibility to do this. This proposal reflected

---

[7] ABMB13: 15 November 1988; 14 March, 20 June 1989.

the strong development of interest in world musics at the time, particularly in the gamelan and in music from the Indian subcontinent, and its timing coincided with the development of music as a subject in the new National Curriculum.

⁄⁄⁄ Beginning a professional development role

IN June 1989 Smith gave a presentation to the Governing Body about possible future directions for the Board. One idea was for helping instrumental teachers with professional development. He proposed a scheme of ABRSM-produced videos to illustrate examples of good teaching practice, to prepare those taking the LRSM diploma, which Smith wanted to make an internationally respected teaching qualification. Other ideas included an advisory service for non-state schools and regional centres for teaching gifted children. (As we shall see, in 1990 Smith took the opportunity to roll forward some of these ideas into the broader scope of a schools' advisory service.) But there was some reluctance to commit to the necessary investment, so when Smith added the teaching-video production costs of £60,000 to the 1990/91 financial estimates, this was resisted, and its priority against other things was questioned. But in the context of these proposals for teachers' professional development, the decision that the RAM made around this time to stop offering its LRAM diploma to external candidates from 1990 was obviously significant for the Board, because it opened up the possibility for expanding its work at diploma level; and from July 1990, the LRSM (which in order to preserve the British market for the London Schools' own diplomas had previously not been available in the UK) was to be offered in Britain. The RCM continued to examine its ARCM diploma until July 2000, though some subjects, such as School Music, had been phased out earlier than this. So the way was now open for the Board to promote its LRSM as a UK music qualification linked to teachers' professional development. (The new ABRSM diploma strand, with a structure of three tiers of professional diplomas, was completed in 2001.)

The professional development initiatives, a series of one-day seminars for piano teachers, began in earnest in the autumn of 1990 – a hundred years after the Board's first exams. In retrospect it seems strange that only now was the ABRSM seeking to interact directly with the teachers who used its exams. But because it marked such a departure, there was likely to have been a certain amount of anxiety in Bedford Square about how these seminars would be received. What actually happened was a very high level of enrolment for these seminars (applications from teachers exceeded the available places), which demonstrated that they fulfilled a real need. Initially this enthusiasm was a surprise to the Board, and only later did research reveal the reason why these seminars were so appealing. Through its research reports, such as *Making Music* (launched in 1994), the Board came to realize the professional and musical isolation that characterized the circumstances of so many private teachers.[8] (The *Making Music* reports are discussed in Chapter

---

[8] The teachers' statistics in this 1994 report are based on a self-completion survey of 5,000 sent to a random selection of teachers who entered pupils for AB exams, from whom 1,867 responses were received.

12.) The reality was that events such as these teachers' seminars (and later the CT (Certificate of Teaching) ABRSM courses) held out valuable professional (as well as personal) musical lifelines to many instrumental teachers. They also offered rare opportunities for them to enhance their skills in a significant way while maintaining their core economic activity.

The pioneering 1990 seminars, held on Sundays, took place in Glasgow, London, Manchester and Birmingham. Their aim was 'to provide information about preparing candidates for the Board's piano examinations and also, for those of you who would be interested in a professional qualification, preparing yourself for the LRSM'. Accordingly, the programme focused on the issue of examiner standards, the 1991 Piano syllabus, the new Preparatory Test, Theory exams, the post-Grade 8 Advanced Certificate and the LRSM – a neat means of introducing teachers to new exams and offering them professional assistance. Those attending would be given supporting notes on the areas being covered and a copy of the introductory booklet *These Music Exams*. The tone in which these seminars are described is strikingly different from the Board's traditionally authoritarian manner, being more friendly and inclusive, and inviting not only experienced teachers, but also 'those who may not have a great deal of experience or any professional qualifications'. These seminars certainly proved popular, and the four originally planned had to be expanded to six, attended by over 1,800 teachers. Indicative of the enthusiasm they had engendered, more than 1,500 of these teachers then returned a questionnaire, giving their opinion about the events and what future events they would welcome. Their undoubted success was important. These seminars had proved that teachers had both an appetite and a need for interaction with the Board; that seminars provided a good medium for the Board to acquaint teachers with new exams and to offer them help with syllabus revisions involving repertoire that might feature some less familiar musical styles; and this involvement with teachers and their development showed that the Board was keen to use its expertise to put something back into the educational process. The idea of an Associated Board offering routes to professional enhancement was philosophically rather more attractive to the late twentieth-century mood than the idea of a Board that just examined but otherwise chose to maintain an olympian distance from the educational hurly-burly.

It was in this sense of wanting the Board to become more practically involved that Smith was also keen to explore the possibility of developing a consultancy role in music education. In 1990 he had informed the Governing Body that music services in some LEAs were 'in turmoil' following the devolved school management introduced by the 1988 Education Reform Act. This was followed up by the Governing Body in early 1991, under the agenda item 'Future of Music Teaching', when Smith reported that in some areas local authorities were dismantling the highly successful process of music teaching which had been built up over many years. This discussion was given further impetus by a conference called 'Music in Crisis' (held at the RNCM), at which two resolutions had been passed. The first expressed its concern at the threat to LEA music services, and the second urged the DES to ensure that coherent planning took place at government level in order to provide for the regional structures necessary to safeguard the continuation of instrumental teaching and other forms of music-making. Fully realizing the adverse consequences that diminished music provision would have for its own work, the Board asked Smith to write a paper advising what representations the ABRSM should make to government ministers, and how the Board might ally itself to other bodies with the same concerns about the damage being done to music teaching. This was the first time that the ABRSM had considered taking up advocacy on behalf of music education in any wider political sense. Smith was also asked to consider whether there was any action which the Board might take to supplement the services which were being withdrawn in order to safeguard its own future.

Smith responded with a proposal that the Board should consider undertaking a consultancy role. He suggested setting up an advisory service to schools in both the state and private sectors, to be run commercially. This, he argued, should offer school music inspections, curriculum guidance and advice on teaching appointments. He also proposed Board involvement in additional musical activities such as area or regional youth orchestras. Smith's plan was enthusiastically received, and he was asked to develop these ideas further. At the next meeting, in November, permission was given to flesh out ideas for the schools' advisory service, subject to there being no adverse tax implications.[9] Less enthusiastically received, however, was Smith's scheme for a network of regional centres to teach musically gifted children, run in conjunction with the Schools' own Junior Departments. It is obvious that Smith thought this plan would appeal to the Schools because of its potential to benefit their student entry. However, in order to keep their fees as low as possible, the Schools' Junior Departments were run on a financially tight rein, and setting up any regional satellites would have involved a considerable amount of pump-priming and administration costs. Therefore, the long-term financial commitment required by Smith's scheme for musically gifted children either would have fallen directly on the Schools themselves, or, if it were financed out of Board income, would have meant smaller donations to the Schools in the future.

Although in principle the Board was enthusiastic to avail itself of the opportunity to take up some of the slack of displaced LEA provision, it simply was not a realistic ambition. The sort of consultancy scheme that Smith was outlining would have demanded a significant level of investment to set up, as well as requiring financial commitment on a sustained basis to meet staff and running costs until it could start to pay its own way. Ultimately, as suggested, that sort of financial exposure could well have been at the expense of the size of donations to the Schools. Once an appreciation of this had sunk in, the consultancy idea in the form Smith had proposed was quietly shelved. What had become evident was a degree of muddle in the respective ambitions of the Executive and the Schools. As we shall see, later initiatives to develop the ABRSM's role would be expressed in a more focused and financially controllable way. Meanwhile, the Board was learning that, for all the reputation it had as an assessment body, it did not have the capacity – nor the backing of the Schools – to run a music service franchise. And just as in the post-1985 age the Schools were having to learn to give the Executive more freedom to develop its market, so the Executive was also having to learn the limits of prudent ambition.

---

[9] ABMB13: 13 November 1990; 12 March, 18 June, 12 November 1991.

⁄⁄⁄ Examiners

T HE rationale for the new post of Chief Executive was that the Board should take greater responsibility over running its operations. But this change had wider implications for the organizational structure, and it was quickly realized that a designated Chief Examiner post was also needed. It was initially decided to appoint a senior professor from one of the Schools on a two-year secondment, which was another way of maintaining the Schools' influence on the Board's new Executive. The first Chief Examiner (commencing in autumn 1983) was Jean Harvey, a professor at the RAM who had the unusual distinction of appearing in each half of the same Prom concert as a soloist on two different instruments.[10] In fact the title 'Chief Examiner' marked a significant historical change. This is because the label clearly signalled that now full responsibility for the examining process lay completely within the ABRSM, whereas throughout the Board's existence there had been scope for ambiguity. The administrative title of 'Secretary', even when held by the professional musicians William Cole and Philip Cranmer, had done nothing to convey to the outside world where responsibility for the judgements of the Board's examiners lay – or indeed that anyone in the Board's organization specifically held such a function. As we have seen, successive Secretaries (whether professional musicians or not) 'standardized' examiners by comparing the averages of their results. The names of those examiners whose marking deviated significantly from the norm were then reported to the Governing Body, and seemingly no independence of action resided with the Executive of the Board itself, either in issues of standardization or in matters of examiners' discipline. But now the Chief Examiner label clearly established who it was within the Board that examiners reported to, and who had responsibility for the oversight of their training, moderation and development. The designation of a Chief Examiner was therefore integral to the process of shifting responsibility onto the Board itself for all aspects of its examinations, from syllabus setting to examiner training.

Ronald Smith had come to the Board feeling that there needed to be a major overhaul of the process of examination assessment and the standardization of marking between examiners. He also believed that the basis of assessment should be made much more transparent, and that the marking criteria should be publicly available to teachers and examinees. Publishing the examination criteria in the Board's booklet *These Music Exams* also placed a greater onus on the Board to ensure more effective standardization and moderation of its examiners.[11] One of the most often-voiced complaints by teachers concerned perceived variations in marking, and Smith's concern was that the passive method of statistical monitoring traditionally used by the Board to identify anomalies in marking patterns

[10] On 24 August 1957, with the BBC Concert Orchestra and Vilem Tausky. Harvey was the violin soloist in Bruch's First Violin Concerto and piano soloist in the Scherzo of Litolff's *Concerto symphonique* no. 4.

[11] *These Music Exams*, originally written by Pam Harwood (later revised by Jean Harvey), was an attempt to make the examining process a more human and approachable one. It has been periodically updated and the current edition has the name of Clara Taylor, Harvey's successor.

between examiners could not itself ensure the necessary parity of approach. He felt the Board was vulnerable unless its examiners could deliver a greater level of consistency as evidence to its customers of an inherent stability of standards. This was something he believed could only be attained through careful training and continuous development at examiner seminars.

Accordingly, the old system of selecting and training examiners that had held sway for so long in the Board was replaced by a much more thorough exercise. Jean Harvey gave a detailed description of the new training process, partly to demystify it, and partly to show the improvements that had been made.[12] The Board received some 150 examiner applications a year, and, on the basis of musical and teaching experience (it was preferred that applicants had done some adjudication and worked with young children), these CVs were sifted down to about twenty-five who were selected for interview. Typically around eight to twelve were then selected for training, and this stage was initiated by an informal session where videos of exams were used to illustrate the process and to develop discussion of the musical standards that were being applied. Then followed what was colloquially known as the 'guinea pig' day, when volunteer candidates were examined by the trainees under the eye of the Chief Examiner. (As Harvey used to remark, it was never certain as to whether the candidate or the trainee examiner was the guinea pig in question.) Only those applicants who passed this were invited to proceed to the next stage, which was to spend a series of exam days with different supervising examiners. Gradually the trainee would take-over more of the running of the exams, and Harvey commented that it was in this part of the training that the novice examiner gained real experience in applying standards and administering the exams properly. Whenever possible, the final day of training was spent with the Chief Examiner, who made the decision whether or not to pass the applicant to examine by themselves. The new examiner then spent two examining sessions on probation, when all their mark forms were read and assessed by a Readers' Panel before being issued. (The Readers' Panel now also carried out random checks on established examiners' reports.) The stages after training had also been changed. The old written form of moderation was now replaced with an interactive process of discussion between the moderator and examiner. Another innovation was a follow-up process of standardization and professional development in regional seminars, again often using videos of exams to facilitate discussion.

This long and thorough training process, now strongly focused on quality assurance and continuing professional development, meant that relatively few made it to the examining panel. This explains why the Board regularly found itself short of examiners, even with some 580 examiners on the roster at this time. But Smith and Harvey believed that the Board's reputation for its standards and consistency of assessment depended upon this degree of selectivity and training, particularly at a time when the composition of the examining body itself was changing considerably. Where once the push had been for examiners from the staff of the Royal Schools, increasingly the Schools were refusing to release their

[12] Jean Harvey, 'The Selection and Training of Examiners', in *News and Chairman's Report* (ABRSM: August, 1985).

salaried staffs during term time. This therefore obliged the Board to cast wider for its examiners (there was astonishment when it began advertising for applications), and over time this resulted in an examining body with a more broadly drawn professional profile than was ever the case before. This more variegated body of examiners (including jazz musicians after these exams started in 1999), helped by the selection of experienced but younger professionals, has also had a positive effect in projecting a more inclusive image within an increasingly diverse music education sphere.

Smith recognized the need to remunerate examiners properly in order to retain experienced examiners and to secure new applicants' commitment to this strenuous training process and later development. His experience as an ABRSM customer caused him to approach the issue of examiners and examining with considerable energy. It was not all plain sailing, however. Though, on the good side, Smith was able to report as early as June 1984 that the numbers of complaints about examiners was beginning to fall 'quite dramatically', he also protested to the Governing Body about the attitude of some of the examiners. The fact that the minutes read 'alleged attitude' is probably indicative of some tension being generated by the new broom.[13] By the time Smith retired he had brought about considerable change. The training process was well established and the inception of a formal complaints procedure had been announced in the 1993 Exam Regulations, with a paragraph headed 'Practical Examination Review and Complaints Procedure'. However, the old tension about examiners' fees remained unresolved. It continued to be argued by the Schools that because examiners represented so much of the operational cost of running the exams, so increases in their fees should be covered by a corresponding increase in exam entry fees. But a catch-up was needed if new examiners were to be attracted, and working from the very low daily base of £42 (with £29 subsistence) in 1984, it was planned to increase fees from £55 in 1987 to £70 in 1989, complemented by increases in the expenses they were given (from £38 to £42).[14] Although it was accepted that this level of increase would require some rise in exam fees, there was considerable concern by the Executive as to the effect this would have on candidate numbers. However, in 1988 the Board went through one of its periodic crises in mustering sufficient examiners, and as an emergency measure, retired examiners had to be recalled. The lesson was clear, the Board simply had to reward its examiners sufficiently if it was to operate effectively, even if some of those costs had to be absorbed by the Board. But prudence also pointed to the need to establish a reserve panel of examiners who could be called upon up to three years after retirement.

In 1993, and for the first time in its history, the Board signalled that it was prepared to deal with complaints levied against its exams; and not only about the result of an exam, but also about the way an exam had been conducted. This was a bold move. Previously the only complaints recorded in the Governing Body

---

[13] ABMB12: 26 June 1984.

[14] However, in such an inflationary period, this increase is less than the 67% suggested by these bald figures; taking their worth on the 2009 RPI indicator, they stand respectively at £101, £115 and £130 (www.measuringworth).

minutes tended to be from people – such as headmasters – whose positions had given them sufficient authority to ensure their representation was heard at that level. Now the Board was letting it be known to its ordinary users not only that its examiners could make mistakes, but that it was open to those who felt sufficiently justified in doing so to inform them of the fact. Even the fee charged (returned if the appeal was successful) was a moderate £5 (or some £7.50 today). This development marked an important change in the relationship between the Board and its market, because it added a new, and more reciprocal, dimension. The very existence of a formal appeals process also impacted on examiners themselves, as a 'checks and balance' measure that perhaps discouraged cavalier attitudes in some. From the managerial perspective, though, the serious investment now being made in training and developing examiners could be seen as a direct cost benefit if it resulted in fewer complaints and a smaller number of exam fees being returned or free exam entries being allowed. But the real advantage was more likely to have been that this measure encouraged its customers to believe that the Board wished to be seen to be acting fairly in correcting or acknowledging mistakes. Probably to the Board's great relief, complaints as a proportion to the numbers examined were in fact very low indeed. In the three examination sessions of 1993 (the first year that the Appeals procedure was operated) it ran at 0.3%, with 622 formal complaints (involving 844 candidates) made out of a total of 273,245 examinees. Less satisfactory, however, from the Board's perspective, was the fact that while this proportion was gratifyingly low, complaints made against the number of examiners working during that year averaged 30%, underlining the importance of enforcing a constant process of examiner training. Complaints came predominantly from the candidate's teacher (93% of those received) and only very rarely from the parent or the candidate. The Board categorized these complaints under three headings, with most being about 'Marking' (averaging 52% of complaints), followed by 'Method/ Procedure' (35%) and 'Examiner's Manner' (10%); only 3% of examiners were complained against on more than a single category. The fiduciary principle, or the ability to be able to take on trust the assessment made by the Board's examiners, went right to the heart of the ABRSM's work. Smith was very clear that in the modern context examiners' training and the consistency of marking standards had to be given the highest corporate priority. Subsequent years have seen the Board devoting considerable financial resources and very sophisticated monitoring to this area in order to seek to lend substance to its claim that ABRSM exams set the standard for the sector.

Exam fees

THE Governing Body agreed to implement in 1989 the first in what was to be a series of large, above-inflation fee hikes. The increase of around 20%, for both Home and Overseas exams, took the cost of a Grade 5 Practical from £11.20 to £13.50 and Grade 8 from £17 to £20. By June 1990, however, the Board was facing a projected loss of some £80,000 in UK fees, and this fuelled concern among the Executive that although the new level of entry fees might not produce much of a margin after operational costs had been met, even so they may already be priced too highly for their market; there was also a threat that some LEAs would introduce their own grade schemes because of the high cost of the Board's exams. Nevertheless, a 25% increase overall was decided on for UK Exams in 1991 (15% for Overseas), putting Grade 5 up to £18 and Grade 8 to £26.50. The Governing Body then decided to implement another 12.5% increase in Home fees on top of this for 1992, taking Grade 5 to £20 and Grade 8 to £30. The Executive resisted this decision strongly, feeling that this would result in a significant drop in entries, and they were proved correct. UK entries for Practical grades in 1993 saw a drop of nearly 11% from those of 1992. Concern over the level of fees had also prompted a suggestion to the Governing Body for some sort of remission of fees scheme to assist poorer families, but this was not voted through. These above-inflation increases generated considerable resentment and ill feeling from parents and teachers at a time when inflation in the wider economy was already putting great pressures on individuals. Teachers spoke of feeling 'embarrassed' by the amounts when collecting exam fees from pupils' parents, and Smith must have felt the irony of having to defend a level of increase that he had so strenuously resisted at Governing Body. Some of the letters the Board received certainly made for uncomfortable reading, with accusations that such a rise in fees epitomized the ABRSM's 'greedy approach' and risked alienating teachers and losing their goodwill. Smith was very concerned to explain the situation as far as he could, pointing out the increases the Board was facing in running its exams in terms of its rent on Bedford Square (up by 100%), the hire of public examination venues (which had risen three or fourfold in some cases), postage, examiners' fees and expenses. He was able to say that through efficiency savings the Board had been able to reduce its own administrative costs by the equivalent of 5% per candidate. In some cases Smith pointed out that the expense of the Board's exams was accentuated by some teachers charging well below the usual rates. Complaints about the costs of the Board's exams have been a constant bone of contention, and as we shall see, Richard Morris was also in his turn to face the resentment of teachers and candidates' parents. Looking back, it is remarkable that UK Practical candidate numbers remained as buoyant as they did during Smith's time as Chief Executive, despite the effects of inflation, significant entry fee increases and the disruption to the LEA music services. Undoubtedly this reflected the new exams (especially saxophone and recorder) that had been introduced, but Smith's efforts to make the Board more responsive had paid off too. There had been a demonstrable improvement in the Board's customer relations and also in the transparency and consistency of examiners' judgements. But what did remain a cause of friction between the Board's Executive and the Governing Body, as tellingly underlined by the complaint about fees, was the issue of whether or not ABRSM exams represented sufficient value for money to customers – especially when fees were still being set at a level designed to maintain an expected level of donations to the Schools.

The tension between the Executive and the Governing Body over the cost of entering the exams underlined a significant weakness in the reconstituted Board. This was that the Governing Body contained no truly independent members with sufficiently varied professional expertise to act as a balance between the respective interests of the Schools and the ABRSM Executive. Naturally enough, the Schools'

Principals came to the table determined to fulfil their institutional responsibilities by growing (or at least preserving) the levels of the annual donations they received from the Board. At a time of shrinking government grants to the Schools, the Board's donations were vital in enhancing the educational experience their students received. But when it came to planning for the ABRSM's future, the weight of the Schools' own interests was more likely to encourage shorter-term thinking than longer-term investment. This underlined the telling absence of disinterested members who had no institutional allegiance but who would have brought an abundance of business or wider educational expertise to the Board's Governing Body. It impeded the formulation of, and subsequent adherence to, a longer strategic perspective for the ABRSM. In this situation, the lack of non-aligned perspectives inevitably meant that financial and strategic decision-making between the Schools and the Executive could be a tense process.

⁄⁄⁄ Bedford Square administration

Aᴌᴛʜᴏᴜɢʜ the ABRSM that Smith joined was administratively very old-fashioned, and so under great pressure to manage the volume of candidate numbers, several of the administrative staff had acquired legendary reputations among generations of examiners. Philip Cranmer himself still arranged examiners for all the UK tours, working with Pamela Harwood, one of two Assistant Secretaries, on what had become a dauntingly complex task that now took several days to complete. Harwood, who had joined the Board in 1949, had later been responsible for the examiners and dealing with the complaints made about the exam process. Jean (Jenny) Jones, the other Assistant Secretary, headed the Overseas Department from 1967 until her retirement in 1987. Jones was another of the several staff who had been at the Board for most of their working lives. She also had joined the ABRSM in 1949, as PA to the Assistant Secretary, Christopher Thorman. Thorman had worked in Calcutta for the trading company James Finlay & Co, and had become friends with Hilary Macklin. When Macklin returned to England as the Board's Secretary in 1935 Thorman succeeded him as the ABRSM's Resident Secretary for India. Thorman himself then joined the Board's London headquarters in 1949. When Thorman retired in 1967 his role was split, and out of the blue, as it seemed to them, William Cole asked Jenny Jones to head the Overseas Department, and her colleague, Pam Harwood, the Home Exams. At that time there were only six administering the Overseas operation. Every examiner was individually briefed in preparation for an overseas tour and then debriefed, until the numbers involved necessitated briefings being held in groups. In the late 1960s and 1970s, a time when comparatively few travelled outside Europe, overseas tours were considered exotic. Communications were still difficult, with airmail letters the most reliable medium, though the seven days they took to arrive meant an exchange would take at least a fortnight. Because the examiners were so reliant upon the Board's International Representatives, and with communications taking such time, detailed briefings were important and Jones ran her operation with great thoroughness. By the end of her time, communications were improving, although telephone calls were sometimes difficult to arrange and very costly.

Jones was succeeded in 1987 by Philip Mundey (who had joined the Board after a period as Head of the Nairobi Conservatoire), and with the expansion in the number of countries now running Board exams, the title of the overseas operation was changed to International Division in 1991.

The retirement of such significant institutional figures as Pam Harwood (in 1983) and Jenny Jones (in 1987) opened the opportunity for a complete restructuring of the Board's administration, which by now had become very necessary. In the Board's new structure, announced early in 1991, there were three divisional heads reporting to the Chief Executive: Richard Humphries (Director of Finance and Administration) had responsibility for the three senior administrators now running the exams in the UK and internationally; Philip Mundey (moved from the International Division to become Director of Examinations) was responsible for the work of the Chief Examiner (Jean Harvey) and the Syllabus Secretary (Martin Teale); and Lynne Butler (Head of Planning and Development) was in charge of public relations and marketing, professional development seminars and the computerization process. All this was fully detailed in the *Bedford Square News* (then the current house journal) with the intention of facilitating communications between Bedford Square, the HLRs and, through them, the Board's customers. There were also photographs of those listed, presumably in an attempt to encourage the more sceptical to think of the Board as a human organization. This new administrative structure was intended to streamline the Board's work and to improve its efficiency as candidate numbers continued to increase. One important change was to unblock decision-making and to make clear who had specific responsibilities for customer-focused tasks. Thus, although Penny Taylor and Anthony Hocking both undertook the allocation of examiners to UK tours, it was the former who dealt with queries about assessment and the conduct of the exams, so the publication of her name gave teachers someone they could contact directly. The most amorphous brief was that allocated to Planning and Development, with its heterogeneous mix of corporate ambition and concrete tasks. Paradoxically, it eloquently made the point that despite the length of time that the Board had been in existence, as an organization it was, in many respects, really only just beginning to find its feet.

Gradually there began to be a new confidence in the Board's administration as it became better equipped with the information technology it needed to conduct its operations more efficiently. A major computerization scheme, costing some £90,000, was implemented in January 1985, and brought the installation of an IBM system to deal with accounts, word processing, database needs, stock control and sales invoicing. IT technology was now appreciated as essential to the cost-effective running of the Board, and in 1990 there was a further significant two-stage investment. The first (costing some £36,000) added another eight terminals to the six now in place in the Home Exams Department, and facilitated communication with the Board's mainframe computer agency in Southend. Then followed the second stage, a process of rewriting software programmes and the involvement of more sophisticated systems for which a provision of some £200,000 was to be made in the budget over the next three years.[15] These days,

[15] ABMB12: 20 November 1984; ABMB13: 20 March 1990.

when so much programming power resides within a single personal computer, it is easy to forget the time and labour that until only decades ago was required for relatively simple programming tasks. At that time the most cost-effective way to gain access to the computing power that the Board needed was through an off-site mainframe agency. This necessitated much couriering of material to and fro; for example, all the computer-generated certificates had to be transported from Southend to the Board for onward distribution to successful candidates. All this need for investment in the Board's operational capacity created some further tension with the Schools. And certainly some of the Board's reputation for its poor customer-relations in matters such as rearranging exams was a reflection of its being considerably under-resourced given the volume of work it had to deal with. As late as the mid-1980s Home Exams had very few phones, with one extension shared between several users, and at the very busy exam times it could be very difficult even to make contact with the relevant person. Not surprisingly, most communications with the Board were still being done by letter. Making any change to the examination schedules was itself a laborious process that had first to be entered manually. Then the change had to be forwarded to the computer agency for the paperwork to be generated and sent back to Bedford Square to be transmitted to the candidate and exam centre. Even so, when the Executive urged the establishment of an operational reserve to give it more flexibility when it came to dealing with administration pressures, the Schools were not yet willing to secede this level of control to the Board, and the request was refused.[16]

The publishing company

As mentioned, one element of the 1985 Reconstitution process was that the old Music Publishing Department became ABRSM (Publishing) Ltd, a company operating in its own right as a wholly owned subsidiary of the ABRSM to which it donated all of its profits. The constitution of its Board of Directors was made up of a Chair who was a member of the Associated Board's Governing Body, two Directors nominated by the Principals of the four Schools and a third Director nominated by the Governing Body itself. In April 1987 Julian Hodgson was recruited to be the Company's first managing director, joining Alan Jones, the publishing manager. Since its beginning in 1921 the publishing operation had always managed the distribution of its publications through its in-house Trade Department from Bedford Square. By 1988, with the expansion of the list to some 500 titles, and with some 120 new titles either planned or in preparation, the problem of managing the distribution had become a significant issue. By 1988 the Company's sales revenue had reached nearly £1.3 million, an overall increase of some 15% on the previous year. However, it was felt that further publishing expansion would be severely compromised by the restrictions imposed by the Bedford Square capacity, and the expense of maintaining a storage and distribution centre on a prime central London site. Therefore, it became a priority to find a better solution to the issue of distribution.

[16] ABMB13: 14 November 1989.

The Board was faced with a stark choice. It could either continue to run its own distribution independently from larger premises (in which case it faced the very hefty capital costs of establishing new warehouse facilities and the necessary computerization of stock), or it could contract for another publisher to manage the distribution process on the Board's behalf. For obvious reasons there was little appetite among the Governing Body for making such a major investment in further infrastructure. The solution reached was to appoint Oxford University Press the exclusive worldwide distributor of the Board's publications. The agreement with OUP was signed in May 1989 by Sir David Lumsden, the Publishing Company's Chairman, and it took effect in July. But successful and effective though that decision was to prove, it was neither cost-free nor an easy option to implement, because it meant that the twelve staff in the Trade Department were made redundant. The association with OUP was to prove extremely helpful in trading overseas. The popularity of the Board's publications in the Far East had made them a tempting target for pirate editions, and in 1992 it was agreed by the Governing Body that OUP's Malaysian company should be granted sole distribution for the Board's publications in Malaysia and Singapore. As the minutes explain, 'Piracy, instability in pricing policy of rival groups of dealers, and periodic shortages of dated examination pieces made it essential that a well-established, neutral agency should attempt to control the market if it is not to be damaged irretrievably.'[17] Now freed by its independence to make its own publishing judgements and to set its own commercial strategy, the publishing company responded to the enthusiasm for early music to produce a series of well-edited volumes of Baroque music as well as increasing its range of scholarly editions. The 'Signature' series was established to offer authoritative texts of standard keyboard works, prepared by leading scholars from original sources, with explanatory introductions and notes on performance. Richard Jones's editions of Bach set very high standards in this field; they included the *Two Part Inventions* (1990), and his new edition of *Das Wohltemperierte Klavier* won the 1994 Music Retailers Association's Standard Publication Award.

⁂ The international market

RONALD Smith's involvement in the International Society of Music Education (ISME) made him enthusiastic to see the Board develop internationally. But the truth was that the Board's very heavy reliance upon its traditional Asian market – which accounted for some 80% of its overseas exams – had made it very vulnerable to any adverse circumstances there. A 1989 assessment of the international position had shown that the traditional markets of New Zealand and South Africa were static, and Canada (where exams had been restarted in 1985 in response to requests by teachers) was being very slow to develop. Furthermore, although there had been a series of new initiatives in European countries (with a view to the Maastricht Treaty negotiations ushering in the European Union), entries there were coming from international schools rather than expanding

[17] ABMB14: 10 November 1992.

through the private teachers' market, meaning that growth was still very limited. The Governing Body asked that international development be given high priority, especially for the establishment of the Board's exams in the USA. It also put pressure on Smith for the Board to develop ideas for exams in communication skills which it felt would be attractive in Europe, as a more marketable alternative to the speech and drama exams the Board was in the process of phasing out. Smith demurred, saying that a study into feasibility and costs should be undertaken before throwing resources into such a new venture; it was agreed that a working party should be formed to look into the idea, but the proposal was not pursued.[18]

Smith had already been working hard to develop the efficiency of the Board's work overseas, as well as to expand its market. In particular he was keen to integrate ABRSM exams as far as possible into the local context and to ensure their acceptance within national education schemes, for if the Board's exams were not so recognized then clearly their attractiveness would be diminished. This concern for closer integration was behind the initiative that New Zealand Theory exams should be marked by New Zealand musicians, something he negotiated on a visit there in 1984. This also resolved what had been a bugbear for Board examiners, which was having to trail around New Zealand carrying Theory papers which had to be marked between Practical sessions. (In 1990 the scheme was extended by training some resident New Zealanders as Practical examiners.) In 1985 Smith followed up his visit to New Zealand with a wider Far East tour, taking in Hong Kong (where an arrangement for the local marking of Theory papers was also made), Taiwan, Japan (where arrangements had been made with the Japanese Arts and Culture Association to establish exams using the system followed in Hong Kong) and Australia, before returning to New Zealand. The reports sent back to the Board by those involved in developing the overseas markets, Ronald Smith, Philip Mundey and Jean Harvey, fascinatingly reveal how very personal it all was. So much depended upon individual contacts as a way of breaking down barriers and coping with different expectations and sometimes difficult situations.

Something of what they had to deal with comes across in the report written by Harvey of her 1988 visit to Malaysia. She conducted two extended seminars for teachers on ten well-known Mozart sonatas, and concentrated on discussing the pianistic and musical problems that usually caused difficulties in learning and performing them. Harvey emphasized that she welcomed questions at any stage, but had been warned by the local representative that there would be considerable reluctance by the teachers to ask any, in case doing so indicated a lack of knowledge on their part and so caused them to lose face with their colleagues. All the teachers had supper with Harvey between the seminars, and when at the beginning of the second seminar one of the senior teachers asked about the pedalling of a passage, the dam burst and questions flowed, and the seminar continued until 11 p.m. Harvey was also conducting auditions for the Centenary Travel Grants to bring teachers over to the UK for a term's study at one of the Royal Schools to prepare for the LRSM. Just before starting these auditions Harvey received an anonymous phone call to warn her that one of the applicants she was about to audition already

---

[18] ABMB13: 14 November 1989.

had his LRSM! Harvey's report is a rich account of varied activities and different sorts of encounters, musical and administrative. What comes across from this report was the warmth of the reception that Harvey received from those she worked with, her own enjoyment of the opportunity to work with teachers, and her wish to return to do more with them.

These reports on overseas visits also underline the political and cultural sensitivities involved in promoting the Board's work. The details they give quickly dispel any perception that the Board was continuing to operate as of right, as it were, or in a heavy-handed, residually colonialist manner. Things were now very different, and the Board was having carefully to negotiate its position in the light of the political situations of fiercely independent countries. One report by Philip Mundey, dated November 1989, identified, with considerable tact, the causes of some of the difficult issues encountered in one of the Board's Far Eastern market countries, recommending ways in which the Board could invest in teachers' professional development to help the musical circumstances there. It is indicative that the language of this report speaks of responsibilities, rather than profits, and goes out of its way to make clear its sympathy for the difficult situation local music education faced. Reading these reports also underlines how much there was about the process of holding the Board's exams in these countries that was sensitive within local society, in matters ranging from the choice of exam studios to hotel accommodation. Mundey's report identifies the benefits that there would be for the Board if it moved to a more quasi-autonomous administrative and Theory marking operation in all its major, well-established markets, such as Hong Kong. Not only would this be seen to reflect confidence in the quality of what was being done on the Board's behalf by its local representatives, but also the practicalities of local administration of the exams were being increasingly facilitated by the new communications and data transfer technologies that the computer age was opening up.

For much of its history the ABRSM's overseas market was dominated by the British Commonwealth. Gradually it expanded to other countries, sometimes to serve international schools such as Switzerland (1961), or schools teaching children of British Forces Overseas, as in West Germany (1965). In the 1980s the Board made a determined effort to break into the USA market, but with very limited success, achieving considerably fewer than 1,000 candidates in 1989 and 1990. In the USA, ABRSM exams were only taken up in comparatively self-contained communities with teachers or parents who had experienced the Board's exams in the Far East before moving to the USA. Reports written by Ronald Smith and Philip Mundey in 1988 and 1989 illustrate some of the difficulties the Board faced in trying to establish itself. One problem was simply that of the difficulties experienced in securing examination music, with examples of teachers withdrawing candidates because the music had simply not arrived, despite time and money wasted in transatlantic phone calls. Despite the contacts that both Smith and Mundey made with important national networks, such as the Music Teachers National Association and what is now the National Guild for Community Arts Education, and the responses to the Board's work by their presentations at various educational exhibitions, it remained very difficult to translate such interest into actual candidates.

As mentioned, the Board's crucial overseas markets were in the Far East. In 1990, entries in Malaysia had reached a total of 67,830 candidates, Hong Kong had 43,453 entries and Singapore entered 37,755. The piano was by far the most popular subject, but interestingly the numbers taking Theory exams in Malaysia and Singapore nearly matched those taking the Practical subjects. Various explanations have been offered to account for such a take-up of ABRSM exams, and these range from the cultural value that Chinese communities traditionally place on systematic educational achievement, to rather more sinister post-colonial interpretations of cultural power.[19] But the cultural status of the piano on mainland China (as reflected in Lang Lang's performance at the opening of the Beijing Olympics), and the very large numbers of Chinese learners, shows that enthusiasm for the piano in the Far East is completely independent of the Associated Board. Continuing this view of candidate entries in the rest of the ABRSM's world markets in 1990, New Zealand (with 11,533 candidates) continued to be important, followed by Malaysia [Sarawak] (8,088), Taiwan (2,809), Sri Lanka (2,605) and Malaysia [Sabah] (2,407). The Board remained popular in the Caribbean, led by Trinidad and Tobago (1,551) and Jamaica (1,505). In Africa, the largest candidate numbers were in South Africa (5,963), Kenya (4,250) and Zimbabwe (1,158). However, of the mainland European countries, only in Germany did candidates reach 500; interestingly, the largest European take-up of Board exams was in the long-established markets of Malta (3,348) – something that reflects the enthusiasm of some very committed Representatives – and Cyprus (1,554), though both islands also had important British military bases. There are also some interesting differences to be observed in the ratio of Theory to Practical exams between countries. In Malaysia there were only 328 fewer candidates in Theory than for Practical subjects, which seems remarkable, given the volume of numbers involved. In Taiwan there were actually more candidates for Theory than for Practical. In Kenya there were some five times as many Theory candidates as Practical ones, and in Trinidad and Tobago there were twice as many. Jordan, Brunei, Sri Lanka and New Zealand were other countries where Theory candidates exceeded Practical subjects, and in Malta these two branches very nearly balanced. Overall, the proportion of Theory to Practical candidates in 1990 was at the high level of 75%. This may reflect different factors. In some countries it may also have reflected the relative feasibilities of taking paperwork Theory exams rather than attending in person to do the Practical exams. But in some areas it may also indicate the significance of an externally validated qualification. The advantage of a Theory pass – and the certificate to show for it – is that it can take its place alongside other school exam qualifications in testifying to the individual's achievement in their studies.

Table 11.1 shows the change in the ratio of Overseas to UK candidates between 1983 (the year Ronald Smith arrived as Chief Executive) and 2009 (when Richard Morris retired). The growth in the proportion of Overseas candidates from 29%

---

[19] Roe-Min Kok, 'Music for a Postcolonial Child: Theorizing Malaysian Memories', in *Musical Childhoods & the Cultures of Youth*, ed. Susan Boynton and Roe-Min Kok (Middletown, CT: Wesleyan University Press, 2006), 89–104.

Table 11.1 Ratio of Overseas to UK candidates in 1983 and 2009

Year	Overseas GME			UK GME		
	Practical	Theory	Total	Practical	Theory	Total
1983 (candidates entered)	81,218	60,062	141,280	n/a	n/a	343,389
1983 (candidates examined)	n/a	n/a	n/a	264,280	64,599	328,879
2009 (candidates examined)	177,765	92,773	270,448	271,842	43,598	315,440

Sources: 1983 Annual Report; ABRSM website, accessed 11 May 2011

of total candidates in 1983, to 46% in 2009, points to the significance that the International market now has for the Board.[20]

But embedded within the table are some more cautionary indicators. Despite the expansion of its exam portfolio, there has been a less than 3% growth in UK Practical candidates between 1983 and 2009, and a 33% decline in Theory. This raises the question of whether a saturation point has been reached for the Board's exams within the UK market itself. The position has not been helped by the harm done to classical music by the elitist image it has been saddled with in recent years through its portrayal as a middle-class activity, something which is a direct consequence of the reduced access to instrumental tuition to children of poorer parents since the late 1980s. The information in Table 11.1 also highlights a striking decline in the proportion of Theory to Practical exams in both UK and Overseas markets between 1983 and 2009. Overseas Theory numbers fell from 74% to 52% of total candidates, and in the UK they fell from 24% to 16%. The decline caused by the introduction of new Theory exams and a seemingly unpopular text book for the higher Theory grades has, it would appear, discouraged significant numbers of candidates from taking the Board's Theory exams after the 'obligatory' Grade 5, which continues to hold its privileged position as the gateway to taking the higher Practical grades. But other factors may have also affected this decline. Given the pressures put on people by their school courses, many will find it a more efficient use of time to take music as an A-level course and so bypass the higher Theory grades altogether. There is perhaps also a more significant cultural factor at play here. Musical attitudes have been fundamentally realigned by a digital musical culture that is now so much based on performance and the experience of music as sound. In the early days of the Board, individual musical literacy was almost a given, which made written errors in musical grammar an embarrassing solecism. Now it is questionable how much sense of that remains, as more people have come to doubt the value of the laborious acquisition of the 'nuts and bolts' of written music as the prerequisite to the process of playing it. It is indicative that students are now

---

[20] This percentage is calculated by taking the total for 1983 as 484,669 and for 2009 as 585,888. The availability of the data for this table means that the proportion of Theory to Practical subjects cannot be given without some mixing of gross (candidates entered) and net (candidates examined) figures. However, the typical difference between the gross and net figures is a very small one.

admitted to music degrees on both conservatoire and university courses in the UK with very much less of a grasp of the harmony and counterpoint requirements than used to be demanded for such courses. No matter how much some may regret this trend, the pragmatics of attracting the best players and filling course places have made it more prudent to offer remedial help once students are admitted, than to continue to enforce these skills as a prerequisite for entry. However, the Board's own continuing adherence to maintaining the linkage of Theory and performance in its regulations seems to be hard-wired into the ABRSM's cultural DNA.

Ronald Smith's experience of the Board before his appointment as Chief Executive had conditioned his view of it. He came to the post with a clear sense of the ways in which the Board needed to improve and ideas of some of the directions in which it could develop. What he set in train was the realignment of the organization in ways that helped to give the Board a sustainable future and a basis for expansion. He encouraged the ABRSM staff to achieve a new relationship with the Board's customers, he rationalized and expanded the ABRSM exam portfolio, drove more international development and reorganized the administration. With his LEA music adviser background he was quick to see the implications for music of the 1988 Education Reform Act, and he moved the Board towards recognizing the dangers and opportunities which this presented. Indeed, the changes that have taken place in British music education since then have accelerated the pressure on the ABRSM to redefine itself and its role. The Board had to change, and the 1985 Reconstitution provided the catalyst for it to change significantly. Carrying on in the way that it was doing before 1985 was simply not viable if the Board was to continue to fulfil any substantive educational purpose. Smith's response to these challenges made his time in post an important springboard for the ABRSM.

8 Richard Morris, Chief Executive, 1993–2009, in the period-decorated splendour of the Bedford Square Boardroom. Morris modernized the ABRSM and set it in new strategic directions.

12 Redefining its Role:
the Morris Years, 1993–2009

%% Continuing themes

ONE of the problems in bringing the Board's institutional story into the present is the loss of a satisfactory historical perspective. Time's distance gives more of a chance to gain a handle on events, the better to evaluate and assess them for the positive or negative significance they might have as components of the Board's overall history. Clearly some of the initiatives that Richard Morris instigated in his time as Chief Executive have major implications for the Board's future, although it is too early to sense their impact. A good illustration is the decision of the ABRSM to invest in developing the Chinese market. The attractions of seeking to export grade exams to a country with some six million pianists are obvious enough, but the complexity of the process to be permitted to work there has represented a major challenge. It has taken considerable time and effort to gain a foothold, and it will be years before the outcome as a return on the investment of research and materials becomes clear. There is a further complication in writing about the recent institutional past, which is that commercial or other sensitivities sometimes preclude making anything other than tangential reference to source material. This account of the ABRSM in Morris's time is therefore more of a commentary on history-in-progress than a clear-cut interpretation arrived at from the comparative safety of a distanced perspective. Yet what is striking about this period is the extent to which its challenges correspond to those that have faced the ABRSM in the past, despite enormous differences in its circumstances. Even in recent events we continue to see things patterning themselves around the four central themes that have shaped the Board's development in its earlier phases. These are: first, the relationship between the Board and the Royal Schools; second, the tensions sometimes generated as a consequence of the Board's symbiosis of educational service and commercial enterprise; third, the 'supply and demand' balance between the Board and its market; fourth, the pressures that have been generated as the circumstances of that market and its customer expectations have changed. The continuing relevance of these underlying historical themes gives the context for how the ABRSM has developed in this recent phase.

It may help to set these historical themes in their 1993–2009 context before detailing the events of these years in detail. The first historical theme, the relationship between the ABRSM and the Royal Schools, has two dimensions. One is bound up with the issue of governance in relation to the autonomy the Board enjoys to fulfil its purpose as a registered charity. Prior to the 2006 Charities Act, just stating that 'the advancement of education' was the charitable objective was sufficient to qualify as a public benefit. Part of the purpose of the 2006 Act was to strengthen the public benefit criteria that had to be satisfied in order to qualify for charitable status. Thus to keep their status, existing charities (including the Board) faced a stiffer test of the public benefit they delivered in relation to the purposes they were set up to achieve. What was potentially sensitive in the

Board's case was that throughout Morris's time its Governing Body had only one member (the Chairman) who was independent of the Royal Schools. Effectively, then, this situation amounted to there being very little difference in the level of direct institutional interest between the pre- and post-1985 Board, despite the technicality that it was the Schools' associated charities who were represented on the Governing Body, rather than the Schools themselves. Looking back on this period, the question was whether the weight of the Schools' institutional interest against the lack of a sufficient counterbalance of independent membership placed too much of a constraint on the Executive's freedom to invest in the Board's development. The heralding of the public benefit test emphasized the importance of the Board demonstrating (proportionate to its income and resources) that it was indeed satisfying this requirement. And one way that it could do this was by investing in and supporting new products designed to meet the changing needs and conditions of music education. The issue here, though, was that all the research and start-up costs of new initiatives had to be funded out of surpluses that would otherwise have gone to the Royal Schools as charitable donations. All this, as discussed in Chapter 11, had the potential to make for a very difficult situation between the Board and the Royal Schools. The other dimension that comes into play is that the Board's volume market (i.e. learners up to Grade 5) lies outside the Royal Schools' own specialist expertise of training professional musicians. How well, then, did the Royal Schools – in controlling the Governing Body – understand the particular nature of the Board's work in terms of the expectations and requirements of its market? Certainly some of the Board's activity is closely compatible with that of the Royal Schools – the initiation of the new diploma programme in 2000 is a good example – but in other respects the differences between the focus of the work of the Royal Schools and the Board do not make for a close mutuality or even like-mindedness.

The second historical theme is the commercial success of the Board's exams and the resentments which this sometimes provokes. By nature the Board represents a symbiosis of educational service and commercial enterprise. And although in this the ABRSM is no different from other examination boards running GCSE and A-level exams in the schools sector, the direct expense of grade fees (experienced on top of the other direct costs of lessons, music and instruments) has generated resentment, especially among UK users. This was especially so in years that entry fees rose – sometimes very significantly – above inflation. Those increases were perceived to have worked to the particular disadvantage of lower income families who found it increasingly difficult to afford the cost of exams as well as the music lessons themselves. On several occasions the Governing Body insisted upon a level of increase against the advice of the Executive. The Executive's concern was that such fee rises would damage the Board's image as well as harming its market, and reflected its understanding that many parents had now to shoulder more of the direct costs of learning an instrument that formerly would have been alleviated by school provision; many letters to the Chief Executive highlighted the difficulties being faced. In Richard Morris's time the issue became more a question of whether or not the Board's exams offered value for money. Increasingly, teachers and parents have felt freer to apply a wider variety of value criteria in judging this. Not only did the calibre of the overall educational and musical experience (as in the repertoire set out by the syllabuses as well as the manner and quality of its examiners' assessment) now come into play, but also the delivery of the service too, such as the administrative convenience offered by the online exam service and the atmosphere of the examination centre.

Something that further complicated the question of how the Board priced its exams during this period was its market dominance. It had to take care not to abuse this position, something that could have threatened investigation by the competition authorities. On the other hand, the very heavy investment that the Board has made in researching and implementing its new exams simply would not have been possible without its business success. Examples here are the development of its Jazz syllabus and the new 'Music Medals' exam concept, both of which involved enormous start-up costs in syllabuses and training as well as the commissioning and publishing of a very extensive range of support materials. The Music Medals scheme (discussed later in detail) was designed to enable the growing number of group-taught pupils to take music exams within their group situation, and its innovative approach involved the Board in an investment of well over £1 million. But despite this evidence of heavy reinvestment back into music education, some have been concerned that virtually all of the charitable donations generated by the Board's commercial success were going to the Royal Schools. And given the almost exclusive representation the Royal Schools had on the Board's Governing Body, this did not necessarily sit well. Some have argued that the Board should develop a more disinterested charitable profile by spreading its donations more widely across the field of music education, particularly in areas more relevant to the majority of its market. The issues of the Board's relationship with the Royal Schools and the benefits of its commercial success therefore became very much more complex during Morris's time.

The third historical theme, the 'supply and demand' balance between the Board and its market, has similarly become much more interesting in this period. It is useful to cannibalize this economic concept here in order to express two contrasting modes of market behaviour by the Board. In the mode of supplying its grade music exams, the Board continues to be resolutely prescriptive, determining what is educationally 'good' for its market and refusing to shift from this, even in the face of declining entries in some areas of its work. But in Morris's time there became another side to the Board, concerned to design new types of exams and services in response to the market's changed circumstances. What the Board has supplied in this second mode has been offered only after very considerable market research and testing on groups of pilot users. For much of its history, as we have seen, the ABRSM had only one market to consider. There was a strong musical consensus around the repertoire and technical requirements it prescribed for the piano, strings and singing (its most popular subjects by far) and general acceptance of the Theory prerequisites it established. Given the locus the RAM and the RCM enjoyed in the nation's music, the Board was simply expected to 'know' and to prescribe the best repertoire and technical requirements to facilitate progression on voice and instrument. So in matters of cultural and technical formation the Board simply took the lead, and what it determined in matters of syllabus and standards, the market, with very few exceptions, followed. And until very recently, in terms of the sort of repertoire and technical expectations (though not necessarily in terms of standards and fees), there continued to be much common ground between all the examining boards. But recent decades have seen the fragmentation of music education as cultural values (affecting repertory), popularity of instruments, access to tuition and methods of delivering it have all significantly changed. No longer does music education work within a single cultural currency, as it were, but instead it now reflects a multiplicity of idioms and traditions.

The extent to which the Board chose to meet these changed circumstances in Morris's time was also indicative of its embedded institutional culture. Where it saw a threat to core musical values and skills it simply dug in. And in this the Board was also reflecting pressure from part of its market not to 'dumb down' in either the scope or extent of the musical requirements its exams demanded, and, above all, not to compromise its standards. Yet at the same time, in another element of its market, more and more teachers working through the state sector were struggling in the face of reduced teaching time to cover the full grade syllabus with their pupils. Under Morris, the Board has been resolute in offering a very British, very rounded model of music training, combining performance with searching aural tests (involving sung responses), scales, sight-reading and the requirement to pass a Theory or musicianship exam in order to progress to the higher grades.[1] One strong motivation for continuing to do this was that some higher education music courses continued to stipulate an ABRSM Grade 8 as an entry qualification, because it offered the assurance that all the relevant skills at this level had been covered. This British music exam model is widely supported across the world but there are exceptions. In the USA, for example, singing and sight-reading are not usual constituents of learning an instrument and the cultural attitudes regarding examination success and failure are expressed in ways that make the stark 'pass' or 'fail' polarization an uncongenial one. And so the Board's penetration of the USA market was only really successful in cities where a strong Far Eastern community had previous experience of the Board's exams. But in the UK the grade music landscape was beginning to shift. For the first time competing exam boards began to diverge from a common grade template in response to the changing candidate market. Some now adopted very different syllabuses, dropping theory as a prerequisite for higher grades, or dispensing with scales, so putting all or most of the focus on the performance element. But while the Board continued to hold to its traditional format of musically rounded grade exams, there have been other aspects in which it has been very much a leader. Historically, the ABRSM saw itself as only an examination and assessment board, saying that offering any guidance at all to teachers (even recommending study texts) would compromise its impartiality. A new strategic direction was begun when the Board made the decision to turn itself into a serious provider of professional development services to teachers, offering a range of seminars and workshops and restructured diploma exams. This involvement with teachers and their professional needs, just as much as its decision to develop the new exam format of 'Music Medals', signalled that the Board wished to reorientate itself in

---

[1] As an alternative to a written theory exam, Grade 5 in either General Musicianship or Jazz are now accepted as prerequisites to the higher grades.

relation to its market. Morris also led the Board in other initiatives that marked its claim to new territory. One was participation in the interactive web-based *SoundJunction*, a multi-award-winning resource for learning about music, exploring musical instruments and composing that covered popular as well as classical idioms. Another was the Board's development of its own sophisticated website as an interactive resource hosting teacher forums about all aspects of music education. In various ways, Morris's time as Chief Executive changed the Board for good.

The Board's priority to relate to different elements within the classical music market leads on directly to the fourth historical theme, which is the changing circumstances affecting and sometimes redefining those markets. Morris's years at the Board may be looked on as a very unsettled time for music education, as new, politically driven initiatives attempted to retrieve something that had been lost in the wake of the 1988 Education Reform Act. But at the same time, politicians were conflicted, anxious about the unattractive image that classical music now had among many of the electorate whose votes they relied upon, not least as a consequence of New Labour's populist – and popularizing – agenda. So while Blair's New Labour administration promulgated much high-minded talk about the benefits of every child having access to a formative musical experience at school, it was not entirely clear what sort of experience or musical idiom was intended by this. And while large amounts of money were going to resource successive initiatives, now largely forgotten, such as *Music for the Millennium* and the *Music Manifesto*, such schemes clearly did not have the scope to carry children through the long process of learning to play an instrument even to the lower grades. The intended effect of these schemes was further compromised by politicians and officials failing either to address or take account of two new realities that now affected music education. One was about attitudes to musical achievement that increasingly were being shaped or conditioned by digital technology and the immediate and professional-sounding results that could be obtained by even low-skilled users of ingenious music software packages. Few decision-makers seem fully to appreciate that the instant results available through music technology are antithetical to the 'slow burn' that is inherent in the process of learning to sing or to play an instrument even reasonably well.

The second reality was the deleterious attitude among children to classical music, which had been influenced by the 'cool Britannia' agenda. Its effects are well illustrated by London Underground's decision to play classical music at some of its stations in order to discourage loitering by young people. The theory was that classical music was now so 'uncool' to the younger generation that its sound could be deployed as an effective form of cultural deterrent. According to these representations, classical music was no longer popular – or even middlebrow – in the way it traditionally had been, and its ability to communicate across class or region (as in practice it had done so conspicuously well among state-educated instrumental learners until a decade or so ago) was apparently also diminishing. The transformation of music in ways the media variously described as elitist and middle-class had unwelcome implications. The ABRSM found itself having to deal with the consequences of music's new marginalization for much of Morris's leadership. Another issue already touched on is the pressures that many music teachers faced in the last decade of the old century and the first of the new. Grade music exams had been devised in a time when individual music lessons were the norm, and the sorts of skills needed to pass the aural tests could be built up through practice. However, the situation that many music teachers in the state sector had to face – reduced contact time and group teaching – made it very difficult to cover properly all the different elements of the Board's syllabuses, and it was becoming ever more problematic to develop aural skills and theory knowledge to the necessary standard. These cultural and musical pressures presented the Board with issues that it had never previously encountered, let alone had to deal with. It helps to explain Morris's positioning of the ABRSM to take a lead in the cause of music teaching. For the first time in its history, therefore, the ABRSM was to enter the politics of music education.

⅛ The modern ABRSM: governance, organization and profile

T o most in the music world, Richard Morris's appointment to lead the ABRSM seemed a very strange one. Many thought it axiomatic that the person in charge of the Board needed to be a musician with a long professional understanding of the minutiae of music education. Seventeen years later, with the Board offering an expanded and more varied portfolio of educational services in addition to its grade exams, and transformed as a business, Morris's appointment could be seen as both shrewd and forward-looking. Morris had trained as a solicitor, and had been a banker before joining the publishers Hodder & Stoughton, where he became joint managing director. His wide range of business and general educational experience had given him a very different perspective and trained him to be looking for new business opportunities; his was a very different mentality and approach from that of music educationalists. In his relations with the heads of the Royal Schools, Morris had the advantage of professional expertise in three areas that they did not – law, finance and business. He had an early passion for music, especially opera. He had had training as a singer and his musical enthusiasm gave a strong focus to his wider educational and academic publishing experience.

The ABRSM that Morris joined in 1993 was a trim, though narrowly based, organization, increasingly effective in developing its market and wanting to seek out other opportunities but with many constraints that impeded sustained development in new directions. Essentially focused on the process of examining, the Board, as we have seen, was becoming more responsive to the professional needs of teachers, and more customer-friendly in other respects. The Publishing Company, then managed by Alan Jones, provided examination materials and a steady additional output of core repertoire (such as Howard Ferguson's editions of Schubert piano music), and it won awards for graphic excellence. The Board's established position and its qualities therefore gave Morris a strong foundation on which to build. But in his first year he also came to believe that the Board was an underexploited resource. After a period of settling in and developing his understanding of the Board's market, Morris identified his strategic priorities. These were: to build the Board's involvement in teachers' professional development; to expand and develop the range of the Board's publications; to develop the potential of the Board's markets overseas. Success in these areas also depended upon the Board continuing to develop and refresh its existing portfolio of exams on a regular basis. It also required the Board to be seen to be speaking with a degree of disinterested authority as an advocate for instrumental and vocal teaching as a whole, and not exclusively for its own users. These set impressive targets for the Board to achieve. And it may be wondered whether such ambition was in the air when Morris was appointed. As we have seen, the institutional make-up of the ABRSM's Governing Body gave it not only every incentive but also very considerable potential to exercise tight control over the Executive. When Morris was appointed, it is probably fair to say that for some on the Governing Body his attraction was that he could be expected to use his business skills to run the Board on the basis of what it presently did, but doing that while operating ever more efficiently, in order to generate larger donations for the Schools. School representatives would see it as their institutional duty to ensure that as little money as possible was diverted from donations to the Royal Schools, and as far as possible would resist requests from the Executive for research and development funding. And so it proved. However, as a registered charity, the Governing Body's obligation was to act in the ABRSM's rather than in members' own institutional interest, so presenting something of a governance tightrope.

Morris's crucial relationship at Governing Body level was with the Chairman, who as the only independent member was the point of mediation between the Schools and the Executive. The Chairman when Morris arrived was a distinguished former civil servant and Director of the British Council, Sir John Burgh, who was also President of Trinity College, Oxford. It is not clear that the Royal Schools had actually expected the independent Chairman to be also independently minded. But both Burgh and his predecessor, Sir Brian Young, the former Headmaster of Charterhouse and Director General of the Independent Broadcasting Authority (who only served one term as Chairman), certainly seem to have been so. The appointment of Burgh's successor was thus a matter of great significance to Morris. The draft in-house guidance for the post argued that the new Chair should be able to represent the Associated Board at home and abroad and at the highest levels in politics, music and education; in other words, to be familiar with current education affairs and their impact for instrumental teaching and learning. The expectation was that the Chairman would have a public profile and be chosen through an open selection process steered by head-hunters. In the event, head-hunters were not used, and seemingly one idea in the air at one time was that since Morris was not a professional musician, the new Chair might be. Had this happened, it could obviously have made for a very difficult situation between the Executive and the Governing Body. In fact the person selected, Sir Peter Marychurch, was not an obvious choice for Chairman. Given that Marychurch's entire career had been at the Government Communications Headquarters (GCHQ) at Cheltenham, great professional care had been taken to ensure that he had no public profile whatsoever. After retirement, Marychurch became Chairman of the Cheltenham International Music Festival (for which Sir John Manduell, Principal of the RNCM, was Programme Director), and then Chairman of Cheltenham Arts Festivals (of which Manduell became a Vice-President). Marychurch was the ABRSM's Chairman from 1994 to 2000 and was succeeded by Sir John Baker (2000–2006), who had been the first Chief Executive of National Power and also Chairman of English National Opera. Having managed the transition of the former nationalized Central Electricity Board into the private National Power, Baker brought a strong business perspective to the ABRSM. In 2006 Baker was succeeded by another strong Chairman, former Vice-Chancellor of London University, Chief Inspector of Schools and Chairman of a Royal Commission on the long-term care of the elderly, Lord Sutherland of Houndwood. The post of independent Chairman as part of the 1985 Reconstitution was warmly welcomed by those working at the Board as someone who would be there to fight the ABRSM's own corner. Given the individual circumstance of the ABRSM's Governing Body, the most essential duty that lay with the Chairman was to continue to argue the case that the good corporate governance which was expected of a registered charity required the Governing Body to operate in the best interests of the ABRSM itself, rather than in the interests of the Royal Schools. In the nature of things, this was not always an easy message to put across.

In fact the Royal Schools' influence over the Board went wider than the Governing Body itself, because staff members from the Schools were placed as advisers on the main sub-committees reporting to the Governing Body and on the working parties that were set up to research and develop new ideas. After he had joined the Board, Morris had expressed concern that some aspects which usually formed part of the Executive's responsibility seemed to have strayed within the remit of committees such as the Finance and General Purposes Committee (F&GP) and the Examinations Board. In the latter case, Morris was concerned that its membership did not always have expertise in some of the areas (such as the lower grade exams and contacts with teachers) that formed a major part of the Board's own work. In 1996 Morris was asked to review the Board's committee structure (which then consisted of Finance and General Purposes, Examinations Board, the Publishing Company Board and the Professional Development Committee; the more *ad hoc* working parties were not reviewed) and report back to the Governing Body. Morris's report (dated March 1997) indicates how his strategic thinking had developed. It identifies his structural concept of the Board as now consisting of three 'divisions', namely Examinations, Publishing and Professional Development. His review identified some continuing confusion of Executive and Non-Executive functions in the Examinations Board (which had three representatives from each School), with the result that this committee appeared to see its role as offering the Executive ideas and suggestions instead of testing out the researched proposals that the Executive put to it. What had become more difficult for the Executive in respect of the Examinations Board was the way that carefully researched initiatives were being assessed by people whose thinking and experience were primarily shaped by a conservatoire music education agenda rather than the educational fields the ABRSM was working in. Morris's report included a radical proposal that went to the heart of the Board's governance issue, but one which he must have known risked alienating members of the Governing Body. He suggested that the Governing Body should recruit independent non-executives from commerce, education and public administration in order to widen the Governing Body's expertise to support the new ventures he envisaged. In the event, a compromise was reached that accepted in principle the wisdom of what Morris proposed. It was agreed that when making Governing Body appointments, the Schools would seek to provide people with wider experience from their own boards. What this represented was a very strong concern on the part of the Royal Schools not to dilute their influence on the ABRSM. This was to remain the position throughout Morris's time in office.

The issue of fee increases driven by the hawkish attitude of the F&GP continued to provide another point of tension between the Governing Body and the Executive. Morris wanted there to be no fee increase in 1995, making the case that to keep goodwill, the Board should step back from its position of imposing above-inflation rises; he felt that he could still deliver 5% growth in the Board's income while keeping fees at a standstill, and this was accepted. In 1996 Morris sought a 4.5% overall increase, rather than the 7.5% the F&GP was demanding. He pointed to the letters of complaint received after previous above-inflation fee increases, with the danger that another such increase would be seen as breaking faith with the public, and especially resented by the entries received through the work of the music services. But the 7.5% increase was insisted upon, and the cost of a Grade 1 Practical went up from £15 to £16, and Grade 5 up from £23 to £24.50. It was the reaction against the increase in costs for these lower grades that was most significant for the Board's market, as the increase in Grade 8 from £34.50 to £37.50 affected relatively few candidates. Similarly, for the Theory exams it was the 'compulsory' Grade 5 that had real consequence for the Board, and in 1996 this rose from £13.75 to £14.75. But the market position was to prove less clear cut than Morris predicted. While the 1992 fee hike (discussed in Chapter 11) had produced a drop of nearly 34,000 candidates for the Practical exams, the 1996 increase produced a drop of only some 4,500, and, of course, this muted reaction weakened the force of Morris's argument with the F&GP. But taking the longer view, his concern was justified because UK entries, for reasons that will be discussed below, seemed to have reached something of a ceiling. In reality, the situation of music education in the UK meant that it was no longer a propitious market for candidate growth, despite the very considerable investment that was continuing to be made in new types of exams such as 'Music Medals'.

Looking back now on Morris's period as Chief Executive, the strategic directions he was pursuing and having to sell to the Governing Body are clearer. Certainly the Governing Body was always happier when it was being told about expanding markets, and as we shall see, the development of the ABRSM's markets in the Far East was something it was very happy to support. Arguably, the Board's success in the international field gave Morris the credit he needed with the Governing Body to underwrite what in some ways was a much less enthusiastically received UK strategy. What the Board had to face was that the UK market needed substantial investment in new exams and new kinds of ABRSM services to provide for some now very changed circumstances, whereas the Far Eastern market continued to value the Board's traditional grade exams. The uncomfortable truth was that the Governing Body's insistence on pricing the UK grade exams as profitably as possible had produced an adverse reaction. Morris was able to answer a growing sense that the Board had become too greedy for its market by pointing to the very substantial level of investment being made in Music Medals, the new Jazz syllabuses, professional development services, examiner training, the website and more effective and customer-friendly administrative processes. Undoubtedly this heavy investment protected against accusations that the Board was in danger of abusing its market dominance (in 2007 it was estimated that the Board had 80% of the UK exams market). Clearly the Board's commercial success also brought with it responsibilities for reinvestment in its products, but there were also occasions when Governing Body resentment was voiced at the amount going to researching and developing new services at a time of declining UK grade exam entries; the underlying concern was that the ABRSM's cost base was rising too fast in relation to the level of donations.

In fact Morris was running a very tight financial ship, with surpluses being achieved on the Board's operations against very small administrative cost increases, something that proved a very effective defence against Governing Body grumbling. His approach was vindicated by a business review of the Board carried out in 1998, which the Governing Body set up as an independent review of expenditure. The review found no opportunity for substantial savings in costs, and it considered that the main issue that had impacted on recent levels of donations had been the Board's vulnerability to exchange-level fluctuations as its Far East market had expanded. What this underlined was the increasing complexity of the ABRSM's business, and the inadvisability of its Governing Body to seek to control it by attempts to chip away at its operational cost base. For whatever the cavils expressed or doubts raised, when Morris retired in 2009 he had positioned the ABRSM into the best strategic and commercial situation it had ever been in. Donations to the Royal Schools at the end of Morris's first year at the Board were £3 million, and in his final year they reached £5.4 million.

The ABRSM organization

Morris had inherited a very small senior management team that had to cope with a wide range of responsibilities. This would clearly not serve his ambition to grow the ABRSM, and so he began to expand it in order to create stronger expertise in the teams running different aspects of the Board's operations. Philip Mundey retained his core role as Director of Examinations, and others were brought in at senior level. Julian Hodgson joined ABRSM (Publishing) as its first Managing Director in 1987, and under his development the company showed its potential to go well beyond its exam focus and to build up its list in ways that furthered music education through good editorial practice and the sophistication of its editions. Leslie East succeeded Hodgson in 1999 as Director of Publishing, in a realignment that saw Morris become Chief Executive of both the ABRSM and the publishing company, an arrangement that better integrated the organizational structure of the two companies. In 1998 Tim Leates succeeded Richard Humphries as Director of Finance and Administration, and he and Leslie East provided the immediate senior management underpinning for Morris. When Mundey retired in 2007 after twenty years at the Board some reorganization was needed and a new Directorate level was established. This consisted of Tim Arnold (International Operations), Richard Crozier (Director of Professional Development), Penny Milsom (UK Operations), Eugene O'Donnell (IT), Nigel

Scaife (Syllabus) Ben Selby (Publishing) and Clara Taylor (Chief Examiner); Leslie East took on an expanded role as Executive Director: Syllabus and Publishing, with responsibility for syllabus research and development.

A major symbolic change was the Board's relocation to Portland Place. The Board had originally moved into 15 Bedford Square in 1907, having outgrown its previous accommodation in Hanover Square, and in 1918 it acquired the lease of number 14, next door. The Board additionally rented 33 Bedford Square in 1979, and it relinquished this when number 13 became available in 1989 (a previous opportunity to acquire it in 1978 had had to be shelved because the necessary refurbishment was judged too expensive). Attractive and elegant though this contiguous block undoubtedly was, it made for a cumbersome circulation of staff as they negotiated three houses and three sets of stairs. Even so, the leases had been renewed until 2000, and although attempts had been made to locate new premises, it appears that the Board might have stayed put in Bedford Square had not 24 Portland Place become available. Situated to the north of the now renovated Broadcasting House, the newly refurbished building combined open-plan office accommodation with some very attractive individual rooms. The decision was made to relocate and the move took place in September 2000.

There had been another symbolic change when in August 1999 Prince Charles became President of the ABRSM in succession to his grandmother, Queen Elizabeth the Queen Mother, who had been the Board's President for forty-six years. This ensured the continued involvement of the Royal Family with the ABRSM that had originated from the time when the future Edward VII was President of the RCM. The Queen Mother had been the RCM's President from 1952, and she became President Emerita of both institutions.

The new reality: the 1990s and 2000s

THERE can be relatively few organizations who over a hundred years of existence have had to do so little to their merchandising as the ABRSM. Updating and introducing new subjects apart, the original grade exam concept proved remarkably enduring. But the cultural consensus and the stable pattern of educational provision that had sustained a propitious operating environment was to be severely shaken in the 1990s, and the Board had to wake up to a series of new realities. Thus, much of Richard Morris's time as Chief Executive was, to use the now classic phrase, about managing change, and repositioning the Board to take advantage of new opportunities, but also to minimize the dangers of some of the threats it now faced. Table 12.1 sets out the sequence of new initiatives that the Board undertook in his time. For the first time in its existence, the Board felt the need to invent a grade exam alternative, the 'Music Medals' exams, which it conceived in response to the increased use of group teaching by LEA or independently run music services. A second initiative was collaboration with the Department of Culture, Media and Sport to provide the culturally diverse *SoundJunction*, an innovative educational website facilitating individual exploration of musical processes and structures. Thirdly, the Board undertook three valuable research reports called *Making Music* (briefly referred

9 24 Portland Place, the ABRSM's headquarters from 2000, where it faces the redeveloped Broadcasting House headquarters of its old BBC rival. The Post Office Tower looks on benignly.

to in Chapter 11), investigating the condition of instrumental music tuition in the UK.[2] Fourthly, the ABRSM undertook sponsorship on its own account of 'Music for Youth' (an organization which ran over forty regional festivals involving some 50,000 children) and the Federation of Music Services (the umbrella association for the music centres that had emerged out of the LEAs' traditional pattern of music provision). Finally, and on the strength of some of these other initiatives, the Board began to position itself as a representative voice of instrumental teaching in the political debates about music provision in schools.

To appreciate the context driving many of the initiatives shown in Table 12.1, we need first to understand some of the practical consequences impacting on the Board's exams in consequence of the 1988 Educational Reform Act.[3] There was perennial confusion in many people's minds (including some politicians) about the distinctions that need to be made between two different categories of music lessons. People frequently muddled music lessons in the classroom (provided as part of the school curriculum) with instrumental and vocal tuition provided on school premises – and often in school time – by specialist, peripatetic teachers employed by the LEAs or the newer music services (which were not part of the National Curriculum). The generic label 'music lessons' can make them appear synonymous activities. Estelle Morris (the Parliamentary under-secretary for school standards) illustrated this in a letter to Michael Wearne, Chairman of the Federation of Music Services, on the matter of instrumental tuition, 'which declared her regard for "the place of music within the national curriculum", which has nothing to do with instrumental tuition'.[4] For although the 1988 Act established the National Curriculum framework in which music was one of the subjects designated to be taught in all maintained primary and secondary schools up to the age of fourteen, instrumental tuition (although by implication encouraged) remained, as was historically the case, a non-statutory provision. The reason that practical musical activity seemed to be implied by the National Curriculum was because the attainment targets for music specified 'Performing and Composing' alongside 'Listening and Appraising'. It is perhaps an interesting comment on the situation of instrumental tuition that none of the five invitees (politicians and civil servants) from the Department of Education attended the launch of the ABRSM's *Making Music* (1994), an event that attracted wide representation from music education as well as print and broadcast media.

As outlined in Chapter 9, LEA-supported music services had reshaped the instrumental teaching market in Britain after the Second World War, and their adoption of the Board's grade exams had transformed the ABRSM's own reach and scope.[5] The upheaval to these music services caused by the Education Reform Act

[2] To avoid the cumbersome 'instrumental/vocal', in this section vocal teaching is implied within references to instrumental teaching.

[3] For a discussion of the wider issues affecting music education in the 1980s and 1990s, see the supplementary chapters by Gordon Cox in Part II of Bernarr Rainbow, *Music in Educational Thought and Practice*, 2nd edn (Woodbridge: Boydell Press, 2006), 345–85.

[4] 'Child's play?' *The Guardian*, 7 November 1997.

[5] There are two very helpful texts which summarize the provision of the music services at different stages. Shirley Cleave and Karen Dust, *A Sound Start: The Schools'*

Table 12.1 Major new ABRSM initiatives (excluding publishing), 1993–2009

Initiative	Research/ development began	Available
Making Music (research)	1993	1994
Professional Development courses	1994	Oct 1995
Music exams in China	1993	Dec 1996
Making Music (research)	1996	1997
Website	1996	1997
Jazz syllabuses	*c.* 1994	Jan 1999 (piano) 2003 (ensembles)
Higher awards (diplomas)	1996	Dec 2000
Making Music (research)	1999	2000
Accreditation of ABRSM grades (National Qualifications Framework)		2000
NQF accreditation of ABRSM diplomas		2003
New website featuring open access forums		2003
Music Medals	1999	Sept 2004
SoundJunction (online learning resource)	*c.* 2003	Oct 2005
Customer service statement		2006
Instrumental/vocal tuition in private and state schools (research), with MMA	2006	2006
First series of podcast discussions		2008

obviously affected the Board very seriously. Central government's requirement for Local Authorities to delegate funds to schools had reduced the education resource pot from which music funding came, which made money very much tighter for all music services than it had been before 1988, when they had been fully funded (and – just as importantly – been administratively supported) by LEAs. Music services were now having to charge for what they provided according to the individual circumstances of their region. Some were still partly funded by LEAs or Local Authorities (LAs), but others were now operating as independent entities, drawing their income from three sources, the LAs, schools and parents. The 1988 Act (and the following 1996 Education Act) had opened the way for music services to charge for instrumental lessons they provided on school premises. (In 1981 there had been a celebrated ruling against the Hereford and Worcester LEA who had levied a £10 fee on parents for individual instrumental tuition taught in a school. This ruling

Instrumental Music Service (Windsor: NFER-Nelson, 1989) traces the growth of LEA music services and presents the position as it was before the effects of the 1988 Education Reform Act took hold; Susan Hallam and Vanessa Prince, *Research into Instrumental Music Services* (London: DfEE, 2000) shows how these services changed during the 1990s.

effectively obliged LEA music services to absorb all tuition costs fully.)[6] In the past LEAs had often also met pupils' grade fees, but now that charge was being passed directly to parents. Concern over the worsening state of instrumental teaching provision nationally was highlighted in several reports.[7] As Table 12.1 shows, the planning for several of the major ABRSM initiatives – conceived as a response to these new circumstances – began in the 1990s, as the fallout on music services really began to bite. Some relief came with the DfEE consultation *Fair Funding: Improving Delegation to Schools* (1998), which recognized the vulnerability of the Instrumental Music Services and acknowledged the need to treat them as a special case for national funding. This resulted in the 'Music Standards Funds', which the Department made available from 1999. Richard Morris was involved in discussions following this consultation, and his profile in music politics grew when in July 1998 he became Chair of the Music Education Council, a pressure group representing a wide range of organizations and institutions that had been formed to promote government and public awareness of UK music education issues.

Research carried out by Susan Hallam for the DfEE in 1999 summarizes the position of music services then. 59% of music services (which the report called 'Instrumental Music Services') were embedded in some way within Local Authorities, 33% were independent (operating as charitable trusts, co-operatives, businesses, agencies) but contracted by LAs to provide services, and 8% of music services had no links with LAs.[8] Hallam also showed that as well as the expected difference in fee levels between individual and group tuition, there were significant differences across the country between what respective music services charged individuals and groups.[9] Another new income source for music services was to charge for the hire of the instruments they supplied. The obvious deterrent this posed was further exacerbated by differentiating costs between instrumental families, such as £13 per term for strings, but £21 for brass and woodwind.[10] This contrasts with the earlier practice of the largely free loan of instruments.[11] Hallam's report had been commissioned as a baseline from which to monitor the effect of the DfEE's 'Standards Funds' grants in ring-fencing existing LEA music services funding and expanding the provision beyond its current levels. As such it provided as comprehensive a survey of the 1999 situation as it was possible to achieve, given the variable responses (between 49% and 66%) received to the different questionnaires sent out to the heads of Instrumental Services, LEAs, parents and teachers. Subsequent surveys carried out by Hallam and her Institute

[6] Cox in Rainbow, *Music in Educational Thought and Practice*, 355–6.

[7] These included *Times Educational Supplement*, Music Survey, 30 June 1995; Performing Right Society/Pricewaterhouse Coopers and MORI, *Musical Instrument Tuition in Schools – Survey* (London, 1999).

[8] Hallam and Prince, *Research into Instrumental Music Services*, 32; ten categories of music service were listed in 'The Funding and Structure of Music Services', *ISM Music Journal*, September 1988, 128.

[9] Hallam and Prince, *Research into Instrumental Music Services*, 39.

[10] Ibid., 38.

[11] Cleave and Dust, *A Sound Start*, 44–7.

of Education colleagues in 2002, 2005 and 2007 received much higher response rates, indicative of more stable organizational structures.

The adverse implications for the ABRSM were underlined by another area of Hallam's report. This emphasized the extent to which 'financial rather than educational priorities have driven the development of the services and the ways in which they now operate'.[12] The drive to minimize costs necessitated reductions in staffing, by redundancies or by a diminution of the terms and conditions on which contracts were offered. It also prompted some music services to abandon external music grade exams and to run their own instead. Hallam had reported that 34% of music services were now operating their own examination or assessment schemes. The advantage of doing so was that these exams were 'free' and could be used more flexibly; as well as being less stressful to the individual pupil they could take account of smaller steps in progress (and so perhaps were more sensitive to group learning) and be framed more positively, so that 'try again' could be used instead of 'fail'.[13] Another approach adopted by music services was to reduce lesson times and/or increase the size of tuition groups. Group teaching, especially at the early stages of learning, was an obvious way of reducing direct teaching costs, and this pattern was soon well established.[14] It was the marked reduction of individual lessons in favour of group tuition that motivated the ABRSM to invest so heavily in the development of its new Music Medals concept. In 2005, one year after the introduction of Music Medals, Hallam reported that 24% of pupils were being taught individually, 64% had tuition in groups of between two and four, 7% in groups of five to ten and 10% in groups of above ten pupils.[15]

Hallam's report emphasized the arbitrary and uneven nature of the instrumental learning provision for state-educated pupils across the country, with all its scope for missing musical talent entirely, or leaving it badly underdeveloped. Differences in fees, the lack of uniformity in policies about the remission of fees, and a variety of imposed associated charges all meant, as Hallam observed, that 'nationally, there was great inequality of opportunity to learn an instrument'.[16] The chance to learn an instrument increasingly depended upon the means to pay for music lessons, and this had significantly adverse impact on expensive and less immediately attractive instruments such as the bassoon, double bass and tuba. In fact it wasn't just these three instruments for which ABRSM exam entries between 1993 and 1999 tracked a marked decline. Also affected were 'mainstream' instruments such as the oboe, horn and viola. As Morris expressed the position in launching the 2000 *Making Music*, while this period (1993–9) saw a 4.6% increase in candidates for the Practical grades overall, there was a 20.6% drop in these

---

[12] Hallam and Prince, *Research into Instrumental Music Services*, 8.

[13] Ibid., 30.

[14] As Cleave and Dust, *A Sound Start* identifies, group teaching had previously been fairly common practice at the early learning stages (p. 113), but it was then used more flexibly, and pupils 'graduated' to individual lessons once they reached a certain level of ability, and especially if learning one of the more specialist instruments (p. 116).

[15] Susan Hallam, Lynne Rogers and Andrea Creech, *Survey of Local Authority Music Services, 2005* (London: DES, 2005), 6. (These are the percentages as given.)

[16] Ibid., 4.

specific instruments. Opportunities for making music with others in orchestras, ensembles, bands and choirs were also declining, and as music educators well know, the opportunity to play with others is one of the great motivators that stimulates and sustains an individual in persevering with the effort needed to learn to play, especially instruments that do not have a great musical repertoire of their own.

Two aspects made it difficult to gain political support for the situation facing the instrumental and vocal music education sector, apart from its minority interest, that is. One was the very diverse nature of its musical, instrumental and vocal cultures, and the second was that much of the work of instrumental teachers is hidden or unofficial, either because it takes place in private homes or is not logged as part of any school curriculum. This makes it very difficult to quantify or measure the activity in statistical terms. We see this by the difficulties over comprehensive coverage that Hallam encountered in preparing her 2000 report – and hers was a survey of official service organizations. The most comprehensive database of classical instrumental learning trends was the ABRSM's own database of exam entries and results, listed by instrument, grade and region, and gathered from the 350,000 or so UK candidates being entered annually by over 50,000 teachers. When Morris arrived at the Board in 1993 he was amazed to discover that the Board had always worked on the assumption that it knew all that it needed to know about its UK market, and so it had never actually conducted a survey into the circumstances of its client teachers and their pupils. He therefore initiated the three *Making Music* surveys of 1994, 1997 and 2000 which offer some fascinating insights into the condition of the teaching, learning and playing of instruments in the UK in this unsettled decade.

On the basis of a representative sample of 859 children aged five to fourteen, and 1,915 aged fifteen and above, the 1994 report highlighted a major decline in piano playing by children, with 30% playing the electronic keyboard as opposed to only 18% playing the piano. It indicated that the number of children learning an instrument peaked at the age of nine years (59%), after which there was a marked fall-off down to 42% at the age of fourteen. The survey indicated that 84% of all teachers did at least some of their work from home (emphasizing the private nature of the activity). 70% of teachers had piano as their main instrument and 60% taught more than one instrument. Especially significant to the Board was that this research confirmed that there was a market for teachers' professional development. With 84% of teachers being home based, clearly those who were not tapped into other professional music or educational circles, or who were not musically active on their own account within their locality, were likely to find it hard to step outside what were effectively the confines of their own home. What such an isolated context usually means is a limited teaching repertoire, and little – if any – incentive to explore new teaching materials or methods, all of which works to disadvantage pupils. The situation in which some teachers can find themselves has therefore serious educational implications all round. Interestingly, 18% of teachers in the 1994 *Making Music* report did not teach beyond Grade 5. Almost 50% of established teachers in the 1994 report said they would be interested in a course of study were the ABRSM to run one, and this figure rose to a remarkable 77% among teachers with less than five years' experience. This latter percentage suggests there was a real absence of professional training for instrumental teaching (as opposed to the usual PGCE classroom training). Yet this was something the conservatoires now claimed to be doing, and the Governing Body was to be suspicious of the ABRSM's move into professional development as threatening to encroach on their territory.

The 1997 survey had a sample size of 783 children aged five to fourteen and 2,027 aged over fourteen. It showed a further decline in the numbers of children playing instruments, falling from 45% to 41%, with the percentage of boys declining from 39% to 33%. Because this reduction was evident in the five to ten-years age range, it meant that the learning base was eroding at its most crucial stage, and would produce a progressive decline in the older age range as this cohort worked its way through. Significantly, given the turmoil in the music services, this reduction was confined to the social grades C1 and C2 (junior managerial and skilled manual workers), down 10% and 6% respectively, while the social grades AB fell by only 1%. The survey also showed that there was a marked reduction in the likelihood of children learning an instrument as they passed the age of ten years, with only 10% of eleven-year-olds and a mere 2% of fourteen-year-olds likely to start learning. The 2000 survey, unfortunately the last in this triennial series, indicated no further decline in the proportion of children playing since 1997, a result seen to indicate a 'stabilization' in the number of children playing musical instruments. However, the press release accompanying this survey pointed out that the 4% decline in the numbers of children playing instruments identified between 1994 and 1997 meant that 'nearly 300,000 young people have almost certainly lost the opportunity of playing a musical instrument'.

These three *Making Music* surveys showed the importance of giving five-to-ten-year-olds the chance to begin on an instrument, because of the diminution of interest likely to be shown at a later age. This was obviously an alarm call for the ABRSM, and in conjunction with the Federation of Music Services it argued that to halt further erosion instrumental teaching provision needed to be supported by properly funded music service centres, and not be dependent upon individual schools. The trouble was that well-intentioned government initiatives had not really succeeded in addressing the underlying issues. Government funding to music services injected through the 'Music Standards Fund' had been negated because many LAs clawed back a corresponding reduction in the funding they had previously been providing to their music services, so there was little, if any, direct benefit. Pledges for every child to have the opportunity to learn to play a musical instrument, made by David Blunkett, the Minister for Education in 2001, and pilot schemes for whole classes to have the chance to gain experience of playing, just withered, because there was not the necessary funding to help talented pupils to take their enthusiasm to the next stage of learning in smaller groups. It was therefore inevitable that the 2006 *Research Report on Instrumental/Vocal Tuition in Private and State Schools* published by the ABRSM in conjunction with the Music Masters and Mistresses Association should have highlighted the gulf in instrumental learning between the private and state sector. A very striking aspect concerned the delivery of tuition: in private schools 93% of pupils had individual tuition, compared with 23% in state schools, while only 7% in private schools had group tuition as against 77% in state schools.

The ABRSM's own story is so much bound up with the condition of music education in the 1990s and the early part of the new century. The vicissitudes of the music services situation helps to explain the uneven performance of the Board's UK market in Morris's period. For although Morris was always able to point to an annual worldwide increase of ABRSM candidates in his time, the UK entries for Practical grade exams were never to exceed the highpoint of 307,018 achieved under his predecessor in 1992 – the highest UK figure in Morris's time was 303,658. This underlines Morris's wisdom in going for growth in the international market, especially in the Far East, while diversifying the Board's products and services in the UK. What can be argued is that without the resources that Morris secured in the 1990s to research, develop and implement new initiatives in the UK, it is likely that there would have been a considerable decline in UK candidates and every temptation for the Board to retreat more into the private sector market of traditional classical music. This would have been a significant disservice to music education nationally. Although by musical nature Morris was very much a traditionalist, his previous experience in educational publishing had also taught him the value of developing a broad portfolio, and this was the route he set down and pursued for the Board. He also understood, in a way that the Governing Body had never quite grasped, the potential of the ABRSM to provide a focal point to help rally the cause of children's instrumental education, and he had the energy and enthusiasm to muster the Board's weight and resources into this new role. The ABRSM's efforts in lobbying for better instrumental music provision within the UK had also transmitted an important signal about its broader educational commitment.

⌇ The UK market

PERHAPS a sense of the injustice prompted Morris to send an example of a complaint about fees to one of the hawks on the Governing Body who habitually pressed strongly for large fee increases. A teacher had written to remonstrate about the Board's habit of increasing its exam fees well above the rate of inflation. She pointed out that the rise in the 1999 fees was about double that of inflation, which she thought meant that either the Board was profiteering or that its administrative costs were out of control; either way, the exams were becoming so expensive that she was reconsidering her usual position of recommending pupils to take them. Caught firmly in the middle, Morris argued that the Board was offering an improved service in terms of its exams and their administration, and that such improvements were costly to make. Reinforcing the point to this member of the Governing Body, Morris included his response and asked, possibly tongue in cheek, whether they could offer any further ammunition to use in such a reply. Whereupon his correspondent replied that while Morris's letter was admirable, any follow up could be more 'aggressive', specifically relating ABRSM fees to other items of household expenditure and referring to the teacher's own fees as the major element of the cost of learning music.

What this exchange revealed was the very limited understanding of at least some members of the Governing Body about the modern circumstances affecting those who constituted the Board's customer base. One of the fundamentals of the Board's business was that a parent's decision to start a child to learn a musical instrument is not in itself an economically 'rational' decision. Parents have always been prepared to make sacrifices in order to raise the money for music lessons, wanting their children to play and listen to music for its life-enhancing quality, regardless of how proficient they ultimately become. And what the Board's own staff understood was that the early grades were as much about building the process of musical engagement and generating an enjoyment of music, as they were about rigorous standards. It is after the Grade 5 stage that the process needs to become more professionally objective, because this is the catchment from which future performers and teachers emerge. This two-stage characteristic of the Board's role and its market was not something that the Governing Body always showed itself willing to appreciate. Some members preferred instead to view the cost as a straightforward investment in a teleological process, in which the Board's role in fostering the future audience for classical music seemed to play little part.

From the letters they received, those working at the Board were well aware of the problems caused by the sizeable fee increases. One teacher complained that he had pupils who were never entered for exams because parents cannot afford the fees: 'In recent years there has been a welcome diffusion of music into all parts of society, but it seems to me that tide has turned, and I fear that music may once again become the exclusive prerogative of the better-off.' The real human issue underlying the position many faced was expressed by another teacher in response to a comment in the ABRSM's magazine, *Libretto*, saying that the Board was listening to teachers. Accordingly, she just wished to air her problem and represent her sense of frustration about the situation of an eleven-year-old pianist with clear potential. This pupil came from a single, unemployed parental home which could not afford to pay exam fees. The bind in this particular case was that passing a particular grade exam would secure the pupil's entry to a school with a strong and supportive music department. The teacher had already arranged for the pupil to practise at a local church with a good piano and had also allowed the parent to pay off the exam fee to her in easy stages because the LEA no longer supported such cases. Those involved with music education will know that such acts of kindness to help a pupil are far from rare. But for many at the Board there must have been frustration in seeing some of the effect of the aggressive pricing of the Board's exams on hard-pressed families, knowing that the policy was being implemented (against advice) at the express instruction of the Governing Body.

What Morris tried to put across to complainants was that so much more was involved in the cost base of grade exams than the usual direct equation made between rising entry fees and examiners' fees. And in 1999 the need for raising entry fees reflected substantial improvement in the Board's administration and information technology, and in the expansion of its services. As already noted, this period had seen substantial investment in syllabus development with new subjects such as Jazz and Choral Singing, the new Music Medals exams, as well as more extensive investment in examiners' training and their professional development. Interestingly, though, the pricing of music exam entry fees for 2000 shows that, compared with its rivals, Trinity and Guildhall, the ABRSM was in the middle. For

Grade 1, its fee of £19.90 compared with Guildhall's £20.25 and Trinity's £18.75; for Grade 8, the ABRSM's fee of £46.20 compared with Guildhall's £51 and Trinity's £43.35. And in Grade 5 Theory, the ABRSM was the cheapest, at £18.30 against Guildhall's £19.50 and Trinity's £18.50. The danger for the Board, however, was that its customers felt that fee increases were habitually above inflation and not specifically linked to a readily identifiable area of product development. This is reflected by a survey of teacher attitudes carried out in association with the Board's research report *Making Music* 2000. Some aspects of this small and to some extent self-selecting survey (with some 1,850 returns from 5,000 music teachers contacted) had a positive message for the Board. Of the respondents, 88% expressed themselves as either 'very' or 'fairly' satisfied with the Board's overall standard of service. Also scoring in the 80% range was satisfaction with the Board's exam administration, its syllabuses and the way examiners conducted the examinations. Against this was a lower degree of satisfaction expressed with the consistency of results: 69% of respondents in 2000 expressed themselves either 'very' or 'fairly' satisfied, as against 63% when the poll had been carried out in 1997, and 61% in 1994. (This 'consistency' aspect is notoriously tricky, because it rests on the largely subjective reaction of teachers' assessment of their own pupils, and no indication was given of the extent of any overlap between teachers in 2000 and those returning surveys in the earlier years.) The warning came in the two questions about the value for money the exams represented, and the level of the entry fee. In terms of value for money, 46% were satisfied, 26% were dissatisfied, and 25% were in between. Commenting on the level of the entry fee, 45% were satisfied, 29% were dissatisfied, with 22% in between. Broken down further, only 9% were 'very' satisfied in respect of value, with merely 7% 'very' satisfied at the cost charged for the exams. What this survey suggests is that the ABRSM had turned itself around in terms of the quality of the service it provided its customers, but not in perceptions of the value for money it was offering. Of course, in a sample like this it is difficult to be precise about what services these teachers were accessing, but the survey date indicates responses were focused on music grades. The Jazz syllabus (with its raft of supporting materials) had commenced in 1999 and Music Medals did not begin until 2004, and it is not known whether any of these teachers had experienced one of the professional development seminars or workshops. In other words, when people talked about the ABRSM in terms of value for money in this survey, it was the grade exams they were referring to.

The results of such teacher surveys (part of the new priority now being given to its consumer strategy) reinforced to the Board the importance of its HLR network and the benefits of doing more about communicating with them and increasing their sense of involvement. Thus began the *HLR News* and the running of HLR Seminars across the country to explain the changes the Board was making to its exams and services. As the review of its HLR Panel in 2001 recognized, 'encountering a supportive and efficient HLR in person can sometimes do more for the Board's good reputation [...] than any number of standard written communications from our London offices.' This captures the significance of the HLR as the Board's local contact point and administrative support, the person in whose hands the smooth running of the exams often rests, as they deal with the last-minute practical difficulties that inevitably arise. The long tradition of the role being an honorary, or voluntary, form of service (receiving expenses rather than a salary) continues, but the original ban on professional musicians being HLRs no longer applies. In 2006 the Board first set out and published its Customer Service Statement, or what effectively amounted to the Board's first ever customer charter. The published document was accompanied by an internal administrative schedule setting out detailed response times for queries and complaints for each stage of the exam process. This codified many of the advances the Board had made to its consumer practice, but it was also required as a condition of the Quality and Curriculum Authority's accreditation of the Board's exams within the new Qualifications Framework.

%%% Appeals and standards

CHAPTER 11 gave the context for Ronald Smith's institution of a formal appeals process in 1993, something that Morris inherited. Table 12.2 presents a snapshot of the complaints made over the first four years that the process was run. The number of complaints against examiners was proportionately very low, and fewer of these complaints were pursued as appeals. It is important to appreciate that some complaints concerned more than one candidate, which explains the difference between the number of complaints and the number of candidates involved.

It is not easy to run an effective grade appeals process. For one thing, what goes on in the exam itself is not recorded; for another, an appeal made against marks is essentially a reaction to the fact that the examiner's assessment has not corresponded to the hopes and expectations of the candidate, parent or teacher. In some cases the complainant is getting something off their chest, which explains the difference between the number of complaints made, and the appeals that are lodged. Very sensibly, a distinction was made from the beginning between appeals made in respect of (1) the examination process (such as the examiner making a procedural error, or a complaint about an examiner's manner which was thought to have affected the candidate), and this needed to be lodged within seven days of the exam; and (2) the examiner's judgement, which originally had a twenty-eight-day decision period. As Table 12.2 shows, appeals about process and judgement divide about equally. Where the examiner's judgement is at issue, the first stage was to check the correlation of marks and comments, and if they matched, then a letter was sent explaining why this was so. If they diverged, then the appeal was upheld and a re-entry voucher was issued to the candidate and the appeal fee was returned. (A later development was that if the exam report was ambiguous in some way, then the Board might request a cassette of the candidate playing their exam pieces and scales to give a sense of the candidate's playing, which was used to reach a more confident decision.) Occasionally an immediate re-examination was held by a Moderator (a senior examiner who moderated other examiners) which did or did not confirm the substance of the appeal. In every case the statistical record of the examiner concerned was checked to see if there is a pattern of appeals that has been made against them. This essentially is the appeal format in current use, except that an appeal against the outcome of an exam

Table 12.2 Complaints and appeals against examiners
in the summer exam periods, 1993–6

	1993	1994	1995	1996
Candidates	103,764	113,157	108,048	107,457
Candidates involved in complaints	313 (0.3%)	423 (0.4%)	416 (0.4%)	317 (0.3%)
Communications received	264	292	424	378
Complaints pursued as appeals	201	224	334	331
Appeals against:				
Marking	100 (50%)	110 (49%)	181 (54%)	132 (40%)
Method/Procedure	59 (29%)	62 (28%)	78 (23%)	75 (23%)
Examiner's manner	33 (16%)	31 (14%)	19 (6%)	54 (16%)
Examiner's comments	not categorized	16 (7%)	31 (9%)	19 (6%)
Time-keeping	not categorized	0	2 (1%)	4 (1%)
Handwriting	not categorized	0	1 (0.3%)	10 (3%)
More than one issue	9 (4%)	5 (2%)	22 (7%)	37 (11%)
Examiners	470	481	480	459
Examiners' work appealed	123 (26%)	141 (29%)	184 (38%)	176 (38%)
Complainants:				
Teacher/Professional musician	187 (93%)	206 (92%)	298 (89%)	280 (85%)
Parent	11 (5%)	15 (7%)	25 (7%)	41 (12%)
Candidate	3 (1%)	3 (1%)	11 (3%)	10 (3%)

has to be made within fourteen days (with the possibility of appealing the Chief Examiner's verdict), and a complaint may also be made against any shortcomings of the exam venue.

There are some interesting features about how this appeals process operates and what it tells us about the reciprocal relationship that governs the interaction between the Board, its examiners and its customers. Essentially the process was designed to deal with a situation in which establishing the relative rights or wrongs of the examiner's action and the complainant's reaction can be something of a compromise, and in which there are sometimes very good reasons for not taking a clinically 'judicial' attitude. This element of uncertainty can make it difficult to find a satisfactory resolution between the need to support the examiner's professional judgement and to satisfy the complainant's sense that the examiner has been unfair – particularly when that sense of unfairness is exacerbated perhaps more by a perceived affront to the teacher's own reputation than to the candidate. Taking into account the examiner's previous work, and (as is now done) also the candidate's previous exam record, is an attempt to be fair to both sides.

There are benefits to the Board, too, from what can be a time-consuming process. Careful regular monitoring of an examiner's work safeguards all sides, and the seriousness with which appeals are treated by the Board also gives it more control over its examiners, not least by reinforcing the need for attendance at examiners' development events. An examiner with a track record of appeals is in a vulnerable position, and there is the Damocles sword that being removed from the ABRSM's panel of examiners is a significant slur on a professional reputation, especially given the gossipy nature of musical networks. There is also a financial cost to the Board in operating this appeals process. The usual practice is to give either a full refund (where the evidence conclusively supports the complaint), or (where it is less conclusive) to issue a voucher to the value of the original entry fee that can be used for a free retake of that exam or set against the cost of a higher grade if taken within a year. This means a financial loss to the Board in terms of fees forgone, as well as the cost of staff and additional examiners' time involved in investigating the complaint and reaching a decision. It is difficult to gauge from the statistics exactly how many appeals were upheld because the Board felt the examiner was at fault. The early years of the appeals process signalled the Board's willingness to have concerns communicated to it, so making it part of a dialogue that helped to establish greater involvement with teachers and their concerns. Occasionally, therefore, where a re-entry voucher was issued, this was done more as a goodwill gesture than a signal that the Board believed the examiner's judgement was faulty.

The Board always faces the temptation to raise the appeals barrier, which it can rationalize to itself as the most efficient way of ensuring that only 'serious' appeals are lodged. The danger here is that by doing this the Board devalues some of the positive aspects that it accrues from the appeals process. For raising the barrier, either by increasing the investigation fee to a dauntingly high level (thereby effectively disenfranchising poorer customers from pursuing an appeal) or by making the process more complicated or demanding a higher level of evidence, can be construed by customers as smacking more of administrative convenience than the preparedness to get things as right as possible. In 1998 there was a revision to the appeals procedure that doubled the fee from £5 to £10 and halved the period for an appeal being made against the examiner's judgement from twenty-eight to fourteen days. What changed, and arguably stiffened, the Board's attitudes was the intimation it received of the favourable outcome of the statistical study of its examiners' marking carried out by Professor David Hargreaves and Dr Adrian North of Leicester University. This study (discussed below), with its evidence drawn from a database of 1,088,361 exam results, demonstrated that there was in fact a very high degree of consistency and reliability shown by the Board's examiners. At the time of writing, the appeal fee stands at £20. There is perhaps an obvious question, which is why does the Board not record all its exams (especially given the facility offered by digital technology) so that it has the evidence of what actually happened in case of an appeal? It may be that at a future time the decision is taken to record all grade exams. But from the historian's perspective, such a course of action would signal the end to the fiduciary principle, or the taking on trust of a professional service, that is at the heart of the ABRSM's work.

If we take the longer view, we can see that setting up an appeals process, though it probably appeared a radical and risky departure in 1993, is not quite the disjuncture with the Board's past that it might have seemed then. As was argued in the Introduction, the relationship between the Board, its customers and examiners is considerably less one-sided and much more a matter for negotiation than is sometimes understood. This is because each of these three parties depends one upon the other, both educationally and commercially, and so patterns and boundaries in their relationship adjust over time as social, educational and musical attitudes themselves change. In its earlier history, the ABRSM could afford to be autocratic, but as its market changed – for example, as more LEAs took up its grades – it had to adapt and become more accountable and to consult more with its customers. The interesting thing about the Board's appeals procedure is that, from necessity, it operates on the basis of some acknowledged compromises, enabling decisions to be reached on the weight of extant evidence such as the past record of the examiner and candidate involved. Certainly there are different degrees of certainty within the spectrum of appeal decisions, but the guidelines governing the appeals 'contract' between the Board and the complainant make clear that if an appeal is carried, then the outcome will reflect the weight of the available evidence.[17] It is this underlying principle that makes an appeal an essentially negotiated process between the Board, the examiner and the complainant.

The Hargreaves and North report into the consistency (in effect the reliability) of the assessments made by ABRSM examiners was to prove a powerful vindication of the Board's training and moderation of its examiners.[18] The research, funded with a £7,875 grant from the Board, reflected the ABRSM's appreciation that its reputation was largely in the hands of its examiners. This study may partly have been prompted by the new appeals process, because the need to provide satisfactory responses had underlined to the Board that it had comparatively little objective evidence on which to assert the consistency of its examiners' judgement. The internally generated sampling of examiners' results, which it used to assess the effectiveness of its selection, training and moderating processes, was relatively unsophisticated in its statistical techniques. Commissioning the Hargreaves and North study put to the test the Board's claims to be 'setting the standard' in its work, and it is much to its credit that it risked asking an external body to undertake this analysis. For their part, the lead authors, academics working in the social psychology of music, had the unique research opportunity to investigate a huge database of over a million examinations covering the full range of classical instruments across the spread of age and musical talent.

What the Hargreaves and North analysis of the UK and Ireland exam dataset unexpectedly revealed was the existence of a mean (or average) mark of 115.5 that applied across all grade exams, irrespective of instrumental family, grade level or its geographical location. The overall standard deviation (or spread of marks) from this mean was 11.12 marks, and the standard error, or the variability of marks from this average spread, was as little as 0.011. Further analysis of the data showed some interesting aspects. Examiners in specialist subject areas where they

[17] ABRSM, *Guidelines for UK Feedback/Appeal* (ABRSM website, accessed 27 July 2011).
[18] David J. Hargreaves, Adrian C. North and Ruth M. Hatcher, *Establishing Benchmarks and Reliability of Assessments in the ABRSM Examinations* (Music Research Group, Department of Psychology, University of Leicester, 1998).

felt less secure (such as singing) tended to play safe, especially in subjects (such as percussion) which they encountered only occasionally. (The ABRSM's own, in-house, commentary on the Hargreaves and North report noted this reflected the frequent lack of consensus about assessing singing grades in the examiner seminars.) Marks for piano tended to be lower than for other instruments, and there was more variability when it came to marks awarded for the higher piano grades (Grades 6 to 8). (The commentary observed that this finding matched the Board's own long experience that standards in piano teaching across the country were generally more uneven than for other instruments.) Hargreaves and North also looked at the perennially vexatious issue of marking differences between specialist and non-specialist in grade exams. This is an area that teachers find contentious, and there are considerable differences of opinion about the Board's policy of using generalist examiners to assess the musicality of the playing rather than its technical achievement. The Hargreaves and North analysis revealed that when these generalist examiners were marking their own instruments, they tended to give lower marks at the higher grades. (The exception was percussionist examiners, who awarded lower marks across all the grades.) But, interestingly, brass examiners showed *less* variability in their brass marking than non-brass players, while string examiners showed *more* variability in their string assessments than non-specialists. Another interesting aspect highlighted by the study was that those with intermediate service as examiners (usually aged between forty-six and fifty-five) tended to award lower marks overall than examiners with either shorter or longer periods of service. (Again this matched the Board's own experience that older examiners with longer service tended to be more comfortable than others with awarding a wider spread of marks, more frequently using the higher (above 140) or the lower (below 90) ranges.) Potentially the most contentious subject of the study's findings was about gender, though in terms of the exam outcome its effect was minimal: the variability amounted to no more than one mark over the entire examination. Overall, female candidates tended to gain higher marks than male candidates, and female examiners awarded higher marks than their male counterparts. (Female examiners tended to award higher marks to male candidates, while the converse applied to male examiners.) Unexpectedly, marks given for exams involving non-gender-stereotyped instruments tended to be higher than those for instruments which had accrued traditional gender stereotypes. But of the stereotyped instruments, it appeared that male ones (percussion, trumpet, guitar) were marked higher than female ones (flute, violin, piano). Again, this gender effect produced only the variability of a single mark across the exams. But because the Board operated a policy of 'forbidden' marks at category borderlines (the two threshold marks to Pass and the threshold mark to Merit and Distinction, respectively), this safeguarded against the statistical variability affecting an individual exam result so significantly as to move a candidate up to either a pass, merit or distinction category. As the in-house response pointed out, the gender aspect was clearly a complicated issue that needed careful treatment at examiners' seminars, because a bald statement, rather than a nuanced response, could easily produce a cautionary overreaction.

The Hargreaves and North study was clearly valued by the Board. Importantly, its findings allowed examiners' training and moderating processes to be refined in order to take account of the causes of marking variables that the study had identified, even though when translated into marks the margins themselves were comparatively slim. Another benefit was that the research gave the Board a firmer, more objective basis from which to respond to appeals made against the results of its exams. With the Hargreaves and North study behind it, the appeals process became perhaps less of the negotiated dialogue it had been at its inception in 1993, and initiated a more formal investigatory stance on the Board's part.

The exams portfolio

B ECAUSE most teachers and parents familiar with the system continued to see the grade exam format as representing something of the gold standard in instrumental testing, there was every disincentive for the Board to undertake a major revision of its exam portfolio. A small innovation (recalling the historical 'Primary' renamed 'Preliminary' exam that the Board took over from the ISM in 1929 and abandoned in 1947) was the Prep Test mentioned in Chapter 11. This was introduced in 1990 and had attracted over 30,000 candidates by 1997. The Prep Test (which included simple aural responses to pitch and rhythm) was intended for those in their first year of learning an instrument as an introduction to the experience of taking a grade exam. No marks were awarded, and so there was no pass or fail, but instead the examiner gave the pupil a certificate and an encouraging report. It was aimed at five- to ten-year-olds and covered a range of instruments, though, perhaps predictably, the biggest take-up by far was in the piano (86% of the 5,894 entries in 1995), followed by violin (5%) and singing (4%). Entries to the Prep Test in 2009 were over 15,000.

The Board's restructuring of its diplomas was intended to place its post-Grade 8 work on a more satisfactory basis. Its LRSM diploma in either performing or teaching had been established as the overseas equivalent of the LRAM and ARCM. The 'Advanced Certificate' had been introduced as an interim stage between Grade 8 and diploma. The Board's CT ABRSM (from 1995) was intended to help experienced teachers develop their skills further, and was aimed at practical music teachers for whom there was no other similar qualification. This move into professional development precipitated some rethinking about what the Board should be offering in terms of other vocational qualifications, especially given that the College and the Academy were no longer marketing their diplomas. This was a major opportunity for the Board, because diploma qualifications remained a potent shorthand by which an individual could signal their musical expertise to a potential employer, whether that employer was an institution or a parent seeking to distinguish one teacher from another. In the consultation paper of April 1998 which set out the proposals and the rationale for its new diploma structure, the Board had emphasized that its scheme was designed to reflect the standing the ABRSM had established for itself in the field of exams and assessment, but that it was also a response to 'the changing and developing structures of musical education'. Indeed, in *A Sound Start* attention had been drawn to the unsatisfactory provision of in-service training that was available to music services staff, and by implication the paucity of assistance on offer to help them gain further qualifications.[19] The Board therefore saw its development of the CT ABRSM and a new diploma structure as responses to what teachers now needed. The diplomas were to be offered at three ascending levels (DipABRSM, LRSM and FRSM), each with three subject lines, now called Music Direction, Music Performance and Instrumental/Vocal Teaching, and all candidates for these exams would be required to perform satisfactorily, according to the respective level of the award. In addition, it was stipulated that candidates would need to pass a *viva voce* and other specified tests in their specialist area and submit written programme notes. As currently placed on the framework for Higher Education qualifications, the demands of the DipABRSM correspond to the attainment level of a certificate of higher education, the LRSM to an undergraduate degree and the FRSM to a postgraduate degree. In April 2007 it was reported that these diplomas were attracting some 3,000 candidates annually, a 50% higher entry than before the new scheme was introduced. The scheme also plugged something of a gap in post-Grade 8 provision with its rival Trinity, which for most of its time had offered a three diploma structure at Associateship, Licentiate and Fellowship levels.

It was the new areas of the Jazz syllabus and Music Medals that showed a more innovative and creative approach from the Board. In particular they demonstrated the Board's capacity to harness a range of in-house and external expertise to produce an integrated package of exams and supporting materials that no other music examination board could have managed. The investment in the start-up costs that each required was daunting, quite apart from the staff time needed to co-ordinate each venture. Traditionally the Board had cultivated its prestige on the basis of its higher grade exams and diplomas, but looked at another way, much of its real impact lies in the work it does in its earlier grades. It is in this area that the Board needs to be creative in the way that it engages both pupils as well as teachers, and here the quality and imagination of its publications can be a significant stimulus to its users. Both its Jazz syllabus (Grades 1 to 5) and Music Medals were directed at early grade users, and both required considerable persuasion at Governing Body level.

Philip Mundey began thinking about an ABRSM Jazz syllabus after becoming Director of Examinations in 1991, and work began under the title 'creative keyboard'. The idea posed several immediate difficulties, not least the issue of the Board's credibility of working in this area. To sceptics this probably smacked either of tokenism, or of commercial opportunism, neither reflecting much credit on the Board. But Mundey was careful to recruit specialist jazz advisers, such as Michael Garrick, Eddie Harvey, Richard Michael, Stan Barker and Charlie Beale, in order to ensure that the planning was in genuine jazz territory. Another aspect of the Board's credibility was bound up in the question of who would examine the syllabus. Mundey was very clear that there could be no question of just using the main panel of classical ABRSM examiners. He realized that if the exams were to have any credence in the jazz community then jazz musicians would be needed as examiners, or at the very least musicians who actively participated in jazz. Advertising attracted a number of jazz musicians who were interested in the project, and Mundey also circulated the main examiners' panel and chose several

---

[19] Cleave and Dust, *A Sound Start*, 37.

who sent back promising responses. Both groups were offered initial training, the jazz musicians in examining skills and the main panel members in jazz techniques, and then they were brought together for further, joint training. The aim was to build up a team of dual-trained examiners, as the only realistic way of offering jazz exams to candidates without imposing limits on numbers because of an inadequate number of examiners. What soon became evident was that some jazz specialists turned out to be excellent all-round examiners, while (with help from a small team of jazz moderators) a sufficient number of classically trained examiners were able to demonstrate they had the necessary jazz skills to sound convincing giving the aural and quick study tests at the piano, and also to write up the mark forms with an idiomatic use of jazz language. The idea was to introduce the Jazz syllabus in two stages, beginning with Jazz Piano, to be followed by other instruments. In October 1996 the Jazz Piano syllabus had its initial field testing by eighty teachers who had agreed to try out the syllabus and the accompanying materials (graded anthologies, specimen quick study and aural tests, a 'how-to' book and a cassette), and to give their reactions by the end of the year. Further testing then took place in the summer of 1997, and much depended on the detailed feedback that was received; it was only when this stage was judged a success that commissioning the full production of all the materials (fifteen books and CDs) went ahead. In March 1998 the Jazz Piano and Jazz Ensemble syllabuses and supporting publications were launched at the South Bank's Purcell Room, followed by further launch events across the country, attended by some 1,500 teachers. The new Jazz Piano exams themselves were launched in 1999, in conjunction with twenty-one workshops that attracted 600 teachers. In 2000 a jazz development programme was launched, offering ten workshops or short residential courses which attracted 250 teachers, and there was an expansion of the Jazz syllabuses under the generic label 'Jazz Horns', opening up jazz exams to a range of woodwind and brass instruments.

It is worth relating this process in some detail because it illustrates both the considerable planning and also the commitment on the part of the Board as it moved into what was, for it, uncharted territory. The issue of its credibility in offering these exams was central, and much rested upon its jazz advisers and the level of support and continued advocacy of these exams within the Board itself. Just as the jazz planning was at its height, the Board had been approached to see if it was interested in participating in the development of Rock and Pop exams, initially for lead and bass guitar. The commercial temptations were obvious in a field which had such high levels of media coverage, and in which market research data showed very high levels of take-up, translated into instruments sold and music industry employment. But it was an area in which repertoire and fashions are in continuous flux, and there were significant obstacles to the credibility of ABRSM involvement in it. In the way that the Board took advice and adapted to the jazz idiom in the way that it did, arguably it built on, rather than undermined, its musical integrity when it developed its Jazz syllabuses. The rationale for taking on exams in the idioms of Rock and Pop would have been more difficult to justify. For despite their stylistic differences, there is very common ground between jazz and classical idioms in the musicianship and skills involved. The Board's serious acceptance of the music skills jazz represents is illustrated by the fact that Grade 5 Jazz (along with Grade 5 Practical Musicianship) is accepted as an alternative to

Theory as the prerequisite to entry to the higher Practical grades. The reception of the Jazz exams is interesting, and the 2009 statistics show that take-up of Jazz Piano, for example, has not advanced beyond the nearly 2,000 candidates of its first years. UK jazz exams had just over 4,000 candidates, which represented a much stronger take-up than in the rest of the world. So, viewed only in terms of candidate numbers, the Jazz syllabuses might be said to represent a disappointing return on investment and effort. On the other hand, their availability and the quality of their supporting materials have made them an important learning resource for teachers and pupils. Sales of the materials published to support the Jazz syllabus (CDs, aural tests, studies and pieces) reached nearly 190,000 units in the first five years. However, the question of the commercial viability of these jazz exams at the higher levels, as well as the feasibility of the increased specialization these would require, suggest why the syllabus has never advanced beyond Grade 5. But judging this jazz initiative only on the basis of its commercial viability is arguably to miss much of its point. And this is where the ABRSM's status as a registered charity becomes relevant in balancing its commercial success by demonstrating that it is also operating in the public benefit by doing things that are musically very beneficial but not in themselves profitable. Arguably the development of the Jazz syllabus and its associated materials falls into this category, and the investment in its development rested upon commercial success in other areas. If one agrees with the view that the early grades are as much about the idea of musical encouragement and exploration as about anything else, then the Board's broadening of its exam portfolio to include jazz, supported as it is by good-quality publications, is serving an important educational purpose. Interestingly, an internal review of these exams included a comment on the HLRs' reactions to them: 'almost universally [HLRs] say that candidates find them more fun and there is a different atmosphere to that at the [other] graded exams.'

Undoubtedly the single boldest step taken in the Morris years, and perhaps the single most innovative thing the Board had done since the grades themselves, was to create Music Medals. This assessment scheme (originally care was taken to avoid calling it an exam) was designed for pupils learning instruments through group tuition. It was radical in its educational philosophy and in its assessment processes, as well as in its administration and delivery. Its five-year development period saw considerable investment in specially written ensemble material, with a suite of twenty-four books for violin, flute, clarinet and the treble-clef brass instruments, and its syllabuses and administrative systems were carefully piloted with music services in two stages (involving 180 teachers and 1,000 pupils) before its launch in 2004. There was every educational reason for the Board to develop the Music Medals scheme as an imaginative and creative resource for music services and others involved in group teaching to use. What it had not predicted was the level of resistance to Music Medals by teachers whose patterns and habits of thought had been very strongly conditioned by the grade exam system itself. For the underlying issue was that many teachers involved in group teaching were doing so under sufferance, in consequence of the financial pressure on music services. Not all teachers find group instruction a natural medium. In the hands of a teacher committed to the idea of group tuition, it has many advantages, with pupils supporting each other and benefiting from a high integration of learning and playing across the group. But if the process is not well integrated, group learning can be no more than a succession of spots focused on individuals – and the lack of shared involvement can have a dispiriting effect. Much can depend on the mentoring of staff in the philosophy and techniques of group teaching, and in the ILEA-run Tower Hamlets Project, pioneering violin and piano group-teaching schemes led by Sheila Nelson and Yvonne Enoch trained teams of teachers to use the group situation effectively. But this was not usual, and many teachers were simply precipitated into group teaching in response to financial pressure on a take-it-or-leave-it basis. The feedback that the Board commissioned after the launch of Music Medals revealed the various pressures music teachers were having to deal with that encroached on their time and resources, as well as their teaching situations. For music teachers having to make enforced adjustments to their teaching in difficult circumstances, the new demands of learning to use Music Medals, no matter how useful and creative, were just too much to deal with. This would likely have been the case especially with those teachers who had strongly opposed the implementation of group teaching on ideological and musical grounds. Perhaps not surprisingly, therefore, as with the Jazz syllabuses, the initial years of Music Medals saw a greater take-up of the high-quality published learning materials than of the exams themselves. The reception of Music Medals brings the sometimes perilous condition of British instrumental teaching into sharp focus.

The idea behind Music Medals was to accommodate the different ways that group teaching was being done across the UK, and also, through the tests it set and the learning materials it supplied, to help promote good teaching practice. The Board was careful to point out that Music Medals was an assessment scheme, and not a curriculum, and also that Music Medals assessed the musical outcomes of the playing, and not its technical proficiency. This established that there was no difference in the principle of assessment between Music Medals and grade exams, because in both, the focus was firmly on the musical quality rather than the technical accomplishment – the essence of the Board's examining by generalists. Music Medals were intended to be done without disrupting the normal group experience. The usual mix of abilities within groups was catered for by the different Music Medals attainment levels (progressing from copper, bronze, silver, gold to platinum), and the Board's own Music Medals ensemble books combined parts written at different levels of ability in music covering a wide variety of idioms. Only one pupil per medal was assessed in any one assessment. Each medal had three assessment elements: Ensemble (capacity for playing with others); Solo (either unaccompanied or with backing); and Option. Option encouraged the early development of musicianship skills including improvisation and aural awareness, with the pupil choosing from 'Call & Response' (responding to a given phrase); 'Make a Tune' (using a given rhythm); 'Question and Answer' (playing a given phrase and improvising an answer); 'Sight-Reading'. The assessment avoided the idea of fail, and the categories were 'Excellent', 'Pass' and 'Working Towards'.

Statistics for the first four years of Music Medals show that the violin dominated, followed by flute, clarinet and guitar (34%, 15%, 12%, 10% respectively), and that nearly 75% of entries were at copper and bronze levels, with a very large proportion of these being teacher–pupil duets. In other words, teachers were using Music

Medals outside the genuine group teaching context, and this reinforced earlier concern that the take-up of Music Medals might be at the expense of Grade 1, even though care had been taken to avoid any direct comparison between these different forms of assessment. The problem for the Board was that in Music Medals, the Prep Test and Grade 1, it was now offering a choice of early-stage assessments, and effective marketing was needed in order to communicate their respective purposes and distinctions to avoid what internally was called the 'cannibalization' of Grade 1.

It was not just the new group assessment aspects of Music Medals that seemed to deter some teachers – originally the assessment process itself seemed dauntingly elaborate, the very opposite of what the Board had intended when setting it up. What had been envisaged was that Music Medals could be assessed locally, by the teachers themselves, taking place at the teachers' and pupils' convenience within the span of the normal group lesson. Concerned to protect the integrity of its assessments, the Board designed some safeguards into the process, insisting upon the training of the Teacher-Assessors (not examiners) who carried out the assessment locally and the videoing of the exams to provide a record of the occasion which could then be moderated by the Board's own moderators. Now that videoing can be done by commonly available miniature devices, this requirement presents little difficulty, but in 2004 it was much more of an issue. Because the Board envisaged that the music services would form the bulk of the Music Medals market, it was thought that everyone would have ready access to the necessary technology (the Option tests and report forms were delivered via the internet), and free video cameras were offered to music services guaranteeing a particular number of candidates. In reality, there was less initial commitment by music services to Music Medals than the market research had indicated. In consequence, the take-up of Music Medals was hampered by the difficulties in accelerating the number of Teacher-Assessors. Facing a muted response to its heavy investment, the Board carried out a review of Music Medals in 2007 for which it commissioned research into teachers' attitudes to the scheme; further research followed in 2009. These surveys showed that although teachers acknowledged the value of Music Medals as an aid to teaching and learning, resistance to the training and technology that were required reflected the hard realities of a peripatetic music teacher's life. It is hard not to be sympathetic, especially to the position of hourly paid teachers, visiting many different schools and always on the move with little sense of 'belonging'. The long hours in making a living and poor remuneration deterred their use of expensive personal IT resources and personal time to service Music Medals and to administer the assessments, and even to train as a Teacher-Assessor, especially if their music service was itself not supportive of Music Medals. Furthermore, there was resistance by parents to paying for these new assessments in preference to the gold-standard grade music exams they were familiar with. Market research suggested that parents considered the grade equivalents to the three higher Music Medals levels a better investment, even though they were very different types of assessment. This represented the Board with a paradoxical situation. Not only was educational innovation coming from a Board that was routinely accused of being very conservative, but the biggest obstacle to its initiative was coming from the fact that its own grade exams were so firmly embedded within teachers' and parents' consciousness. Clearly the new Music Medals approach would require time to gain the confidence of the market. And in the relatively brief period that Music Medals have been available, entries show a gradual but increasing acceptance of the new approach, having risen from 2,648 in 2005 to 9,358 in 2010.

In terms of commercial expediency, there had been no real imperative for the Board to invest in the development of Music Medals. It could have continued to sell its grade exams on the basis of accepting a certain amount of decline in the UK, compensated by growing its international market. That strategy would have allowed it to retreat from engagement with the challenges of public-sector instrumental teaching. But the pressures on the UK market had as much to do with the Board's institutional philosophy as its commercial judgement. Clearly grade exams no longer met pupils' and teachers' needs in the way they did when individual instruction was the norm. This presented the Board with a choice. Either it could take the line of least resistance and reconcile itself to a diminishing UK market, or it could use its resources and expertise to try a new formulation that would encourage the learning and teaching of instruments under these more difficult circumstances. The fact that it chose the course of educational integrity is significant. The Board believes that in time the many virtues this form of assessment represents will win Music Medals much greater acceptance. The innovative use of technology to facilitate delivery of exam materials and the moderating of assessment standards, as well as the flexibility of timing the assessment, may well have implications for the future development and delivery of music grades themselves.

Although *SoundJunction*[20] is an online learning resource rather than part of the exam portfolio, it represents another aspect of the Board's recent engagement with information and communication technology, and a further broadening of its musical base. The government wished to promote online learning (funded through the Department of Culture, Media and Sport) in a digitalization programme to enrich the National Curriculum with imaginative materials that children could return to at home. With all the research in the UK emphasizing the very uneven quality of the sort of formative music teaching and infrastructural learning support necessary to bring on a new generation of players, amateur as well as professional, it was clear that a central resource which offered something that people could plug into would be a good music training investment. *SoundJunction* was envisaged as a way of both whetting people's curiosity and satisfying it, and acting as a sort of surrogate community for those in situations where there was little ready access to musical mentors. As we saw from the Victorian context in Chapter 1, Britain has a long and very honourable tradition of musical autodidacticism, and *SoundJunction* offered a way of helping individuals to explore music for themselves. The Board's executive knew that music education software had huge potential to introduce people to musical processes through sequencing and visualization, and that by exploring textures and the ways in which compositions were put together it could provide imaginative introductions to musical repertoire of all kinds. Thus the Board's decision to involve itself with *SoundJunction* reflected the spirit of wanting

[20] www.soundjunction.org

to address a wider constituency of learners – the basis on which it undertook the Jazz syllabus, Music Medals and its website discussion forums. *SoundJunction*'s objectives emphasized the aim of encouraging and motivating interest in music by involving learners in a more interactive experience of how music actually works and relating this to the actuality of musicians' lives and work. The result was a practice-based website that offered the user the chance to witness a piece gradually unfolding as instruments were added (giving the chance to focus on individual lines or groups of instruments), to try to compose music and to explore some of the nuts and bolts of music and musical instruments using different sorts of popular idioms (jazz, hip-hop), world musics and classical works. In conjunction the Board published a series of Learning Activity packs which included practical performing activities for classroom use linked to the website. *SoundJunction* won a range of prizes for the creativity and the expertise with which it used multimedia resources to encourage users to investigate musical processes. It is difficult to estimate *SoundJunction*'s actual impact on individuals, as opposed to the statistics about its use. Up to August 2007 there was an average of 35,000 visits a month, but we gain a stronger sense of the impact it has made on individuals from some of the enthusiastic and admiring feedback left on the website from teenage users and teachers alike.

⁂ Professional development

W ITHIN six months of his arrival Richard Morris felt there was a very important educational need and a sound business case for the Board to move into providing training and qualifications for music teachers. In July 1993 he tabled papers to the Examinations Board seeking clearance to proceed with market research into the professional development needs of established instrumental teachers and to recruit a consultant to advise on the project. (Morris's original thinking was that professional development could be provided using RSM staff.) At its next November meeting the Governing Body gave formal agreement for a £50,000 budget to research the proposal and prepare a detailed business plan, and in January Richard Hickman, Principal of the Berkshire Young Musicians Trust (the county's former music service), was recruited on a part-time consultancy basis. Meanwhile, there occurred in December 1993 another event that was influential in setting the instrumental teachers' development agenda. This was the European String Teachers Association (ESTA) conference held at the RNCM under the title 'String Training 2000: Setting the Standards'. The conference was the brainchild of Rodney Slatford, then Head of Strings at the RNCM and Chairman of British ESTA, who was concerned to achieve a greater dialogue between the conservatoire teachers working with aspirant professionals and those doing the vital role at grass roots level. (At the RNCM Slatford founded the Junior Strings Project, a teacher-training scheme involving local children that led to a postgraduate instrumental and vocal teaching course at the College.) Themes from the ESTA conference reflected the need for the best quality of string teaching to be readily available at all levels, but also the feeling that this aim had been impeded by the damage being done to skilled string teaching because of the disruption to music services. There was also anxiety that the traditional 'Art of Teaching' classes offered by conservatoires to their students as preparation for the actual teaching experience was essentially outmoded. The conference reinforced to Morris his sense of the opportunity that there was for the Board to build up a professional development arm, while also making it clear that the Board's purpose in running development courses would not be best served by looking to the RSMs to deliver the instruction. Clearly the proposal had to be formulated in such a way that the Board would be free to recruit and control its own tutors, and the selection of the right kind of tutors was essential. Morris's view that the Board should carry out its own professional development work on its own terms generated a degree of tension with at least some of the Governing Body members at the March 1994 meeting, as evident when one School expressed its wish that no further funds should be committed to the project that might otherwise form part of the distributable surplus. It is not entirely clear how wholehearted were the RSM Principals in the matter of the ABRSM entering the professional development field. Certainly the Board's indication at the outset that its courses would operate from a position of independence from the RSMs, though facilities and staff would be used as appropriate, raised some hackles. But the Schools' own provision was very mixed, and they could not demonstrate that they had been able even to influence the professional development of their own instrumental and vocal teaching staff, as was clear from a report the conservatoires produced in 2003.[21]

Market research further reinforced Morris's view. A series of focus group meetings with teachers that were held at a conference at Eynsham Hall, near Oxford, in April 1994 indicated that teachers would welcome help. At least 90% of attendees had not received any professional training in teaching instruments or singing; indeed, those who had been professionally trained considered they were no better off in this respect than those who had not done higher-education study in music. There was a significant number for whom passing either Grade 7 or 8 represented their only 'qualification'. Those with teaching diplomas said they had passed them on the basis of reading rather than supervised training, and 80% said they had based their teaching methods on those used by their own teacher. The findings indicated that teachers would welcome professional development courses that enabled them to observe other teachers, and to have the opportunity to meet and discuss their work with other teachers and mentors as a way of countering the professional isolation they were experiencing in their work. The chance to develop personal musical skills was also seen as important. Most of the Eynsham attendees said they would prefer courses to be held away from the RSMs themselves, and some said they found the Schools 'daunting and intimidating'; most felt that professional development courses should be very practical and not 'academic' in their tone. What was good news for the Board was that there was very strong support for the ABRSM to provide such courses because of its established status and reputation. Some of these focus group findings may well surprise readers,

[21] Federation of British Conservatoires, *Teaching Performance: The Employment of Musical Instrument Teaching Specialists*, HEFCE Good Management Practice Project, 41 (2003).

because they reveal the gap between the regulation by qualification of school teachers and the absence of regulation for those teaching instruments and voice, not all of whom have a music diploma, let alone Qualified Teacher Status. The following situation, of a teacher who had entered many for ABRSM exams, is therefore far from untypical. This lady, who had learned the piano as a child, though not to the highest grades, had been asked to teach friends' children because there was no easy access to a piano teacher from the village where she lived. Her success as a teacher prompted her to renew her study (aged over fifty) to add more Practical and Theory grades to the ones she had passed as a school girl. Unfortunately, when it came to Grade 8, the need to care for her incapacitated mother limited her time, so she did not pass it. She had found teaching the piano a very fulfilling activity, and had always encouraged her pupils also to work at Theory to improve their understanding of what they were playing. The needs of this sort of extremely well-intentioned teacher, who was without realistic opportunities to develop her own teaching skills and take her musical abilities further, were just as significant in shaping the Board's professional development ideas as were those of teachers with formal musical qualifications. Accordingly, in May, Morris felt justified in putting forward detailed proposals to the Governing Body's Finance Committee. He did so on two grounds: firstly, that there was a shortage in the provision of instrumental/vocal teachers and that the Board was exceptionally well placed to fill this market need; and secondly, that in doing so the Board would be making a major contribution to music educational needs in a way that reflected its charitable objectives.

The irony was that the twentieth-century drive to degrees and professional qualifications had produced a bewildering plethora of diploma and degree-holding musicians whose qualifications had very little reference to instrumental and vocal teaching skills. The Board realized from feedback at the free seminars it was running for teachers in the autumn of 1994 as well as from its teaching seminars (for which a fee was charged) that there was a market for teachers' professional development. Research for *Making Music* 1994 had a very high percentage of questioned teachers saying they were either very or fairly interested in a development course leading to a teaching qualification (69% among teachers below thirty-five, and 77% of teachers in their first five years of teaching). With the unsettled state of the instrumental teaching market, teachers realized that it was becoming more urgent to obtain a readily understood teaching qualification from a recognized authority. The Board faced two competitors who had just entered the professional development field. One was a 'Practical Training Course for Private Instrumental and Singing Teachers' set up by the ISM in conjunction with Reading University, and the other was the work being done by the Music Education Department that Trinity College had established under John Stephens (the former ILEA Inspector for Music) which offered a range of music education courses at different levels, from Certificate to MA. But the focus of the Board's own work was to design and market professional development courses that could be delivered in such a way as to make them a feasible proposition for private instrumental teachers for whom a prolonged period of learning away from their teaching was simply not possible. Morris's proposals gained Governing Body approval at the meeting in June 1994, and an additional £20,000 in development costs for advertising a course in November 1994 to be run in the autumn of 1995. The finalizing of the structure and course content was done after a consultative, 'think tank'-style conference held in conjunction with a range of interested organizations (including TCM), again at Eynsham, in October 1994. With the 1995 course now announced, the profile of teachers enquiring about it revealed that 47% had no qualifications at all and 12% had one qualification, either a degree of a diploma. Of all enquirers, 40% worked in the south of England and 72% taught piano, and the majority entered candidates for Practical Grades 1–6 and Theory Grades 1, 2 and 5.

The person appointed to direct the Board's new professional development department, Richard Crozier, was not an archetypal ABRSM figure. He came to the Board from a career as head of music at secondary schools and as Music Inspector for Bedfordshire. Importantly he had considerable experience as an OFSTED Inspector and in delivering in-service training for instrumental and classroom teachers. He brought with him all this knowledge and his contacts in the field, one reason why the new CT ABRSM course was up and running so quickly. The course was open to all above the age of twenty-one (twenty-five for singers) with regular teaching experience; it had an emphasis on teaching skills for Grades 1–5 and was not concerned with performing ability *per se* except in the teaching context. Students worked together for thirteen days at their regional base (an initial week, followed by four residential weekends spread across the year) and completed a portfolio based on their teaching work plus three assignments and two projects. In addition, specialist mentors observed each student's teaching on four occasions at their school, home or studio. The first course was run at five regional centres, Bedford, Bristol, Glasgow, London and Manchester, each with an experienced course leader responsible for the students enrolled there. On the first course there were 117 successful students out of 120, each paying a course fee of £1,475. Keeping course fees to a minimum was something of a battle, and it was a relief when the course received sponsorship from British Reserve Insurance Co. (a major insurer of musical instruments). In its first ten years some 1,600 students successfully completed the course, and there have been variants of the basic structure, such as the 'Fast Track' residential course, with the teaching focused over six months rather than a year and lesson observations done through videoing, which has made it feasible for a more international student body; and the more recent CT ABRSM 'Plus', which is combined with the Principles of Teaching diploma (DipABRSM). In 1998 the CT course was first offered in Singapore, followed in 1999 in Hong Kong and Indonesia in 2008. There was a total of 2,347 successful completions in the fourteen years the CT ran between 1995 and 2009.

Although in some respects the CT ABRSM remains the flagship professional development course, the Board has continued to offer other sorts of teachers' workshops. In June 2004 the Board ran a Professional Development Research Symposium, reviewing the CT course and considering the need for other short development courses and training. At the time of writing, two new types of courses have been added to the Board's professional development portfolio, 'An Introduction to Instrumental and Vocal Teaching', intended to cover some of the main issues a musician needs to have in mind before starting a teaching career, and 'Teaching Music Effectively', combining study days and distance learning for those who have recently started teaching and wish to develop more methods and strategies. From the initial research begun in 1993 to Morris's retirement in 2009, the ABRSM has established itself as a major provider of training for instrumental and vocal teachers. Its success in this new area has been characterized by the practical nature of the courses it has developed, the effectiveness of those it appointed as student mentors and its understanding of the situation of individual instrumental and vocal teachers. What can make professional life so difficult for these teachers is not just the danger of professional isolation, but also the lack of a defined career structure, something that makes it very hard for the individual to assess or appreciate what they have achieved in their work. The networking that these ABRSM courses has opened up has given teachers something that many have found personally sustaining in addition to the stated professional aims and objectives of these courses. As one teacher remarked recently:

> My own working situation as a peripatetic music teacher is constantly changing. I find myself teaching in schools and privately, giving individual and group lessons, and working in teams and on my own, all the time striving to keep on top of the latest directives, technologies and pedagogical theories. It can be a lot to cope with![22]

China

D URING Richard Morris's time the Far East markets of Hong Kong, Singapore and Malaysia became the Board's biggest area of growth. A good illustration of the change of scale was that over fifty years the Board's operations in Malaysia went from the 1948 position of one examiner staying for a week or so, to the 1998 position of around forty centres with some thirty examiners working for almost three months. In Hong Kong – despite anxieties about how things would continue after the British withdrawal in 1997 – candidate numbers grew from 44,739 in 1993 to 85,004 in 2009. In the same period, by contrast, the traditional New Zealand market had contracted slightly from 9,355 to 8,474. This growth underlines the attraction of grade music exams within the Chinese diaspora, and so the desirability of establishing China itself as a market. The opportunity it presented explains the considerable efforts that Morris made to secure permission for the Board to hold its exams there. This account traces the difficult three-year process that led to the first grades being held on mainland China in December 1996.

The first contact came in a letter, dated 29 November 1990, from the Wuhan Conservatory of Music in the central China province of Hubei, via the Grimsby HLR Anne Holmes.[23] The letter indicated the Conservatory's interest in acting as

[22] Fiona Lau, 'Teacher's friend', *Music Teacher* 89/12 (December 2010), 42–3.

[23] The story behind this connection is itself fascinating, and involves the ambition of a Wuhan student, Cao Qun, to enter the Grimsby International Singing Competition, and the determined efforts made by its administrator, Anne Holmes, despite considerable practical difficulties, to help him achieve it. Cao Qun won the Bass-Baritone section of the 1986 Competition, and so the link with Wuhan was established.

an agent for the Board to facilitate the holding of ABRSM exams on mainland China. On its receipt at the Board, the letter was passed on to Ronald Smith with the comment, 'Dare we?', to which Smith added his marginal note, 'No harm in finding out!' The context for this enquiry was the resumption of the Chinese enthusiasm for Western music, something which had been badly disrupted by the Cultural Revolution (1966–76), when Chinese musicians and teachers had been an obvious focus for anti-Western sentiment, and fifteen of the staff at the Shanghai Conservatory had been killed or committed suicide. After Mao Zedong's death and the jailing of the Gang of Four brought political stabilization under Deng Xiaoping, teaching Western instruments in the main musical institutions restarted around 1978, and Western musicians were again welcomed in China.[24] One consequence of this resumption was that the Association of Chinese Musicians and the Central Conservatory of Beijing each began to offer graded music exams, heavily influenced by the Associated Board exams in Hong Kong, and these were beginning to attract support. (In 1993 there were some 3,000 candidates for the Central Conservatory's exams.) Thus the invitation from the Wuhun Conservatory may have been in riposte to these Beijing developments, and an attempt by a provincial music school to go one better by securing the Board itself as its partner. Another indication that the Board might be welcomed in China was that in 1993 the Royal Academy of Dance had received an invitation from the Chinese Cultural Ministry in association with the Beijing Academy of Dancing to examine in Beijing.

In October 1992 Wuhan Conservatory followed up their initial letter with an invitation to Ronald Smith to write a report on the teaching work at pre-conservatoire level and to explore the possibility of the Conservatory using the Board's exams. Following correspondence, Richard Morris arranged with Smith to carry out the visit in September 1993, and its success established co-operation with Wuhan. The Conservatory obtained the permission of the Hubei Provincial Government to hold the Board's exams, but such an important cultural exchange also required Central Government approval because of its foreign policy implications. In the event, that permission was not forthcoming, but in the light of this enquiry the Board began more systematically to investigate the possibility of examining in China and to ascertain the complexities involved.

A delegation from Wuhan Conservatory, including its President and Vice President, attended the next Competition in 1989, and Anne Holmes's discussion of her work as an HLR may have prompted them to make this approach to the Board in a letter using her name. In the course of researching this episode, it turned out that Anne Holmes was unaware of the contents of this letter, and – presumably in case pride was damaged if the proposal was turned down – Wuhan did not inform her of it. Not only, however, was she an unknowing intermediary, but amazingly the ABRSM itself failed to realize that the Anne Holmes who forwarded the letter was their own HLR, and thereby lost the opportunity to glean some valuable background information from her.

[24] Richard Curt Kraus, *Pianos and Politics in China: Middle-Class Ambitions and the Struggle over Western Music* (New York: Oxford University Press, 1989); Cui Shi-guang, 'Three Centuries of Cultural Interfacing: A History of Western Music in China', *American Music Teacher*, April/May 1990, 14–17, 51; Teresa Poole, 'China's elite music school starts a pop revolution', *Independent on Sunday*, 14 March 1993.

With a prospective market of (according to some estimates) six million pianists, the incentive was clear, and China was becoming more open to the idea of internationally recognized exams. By 1993 the University of Cambridge Local Exam Syndicate (UCLES) and City and Guilds had begun working with Chinese institutions. So despite the costs and practical difficulties of venturing into China, the Board could not afford to pass up the chance. And at first, all seemed to be progressing smoothly. Morris and Philip Mundey visited Beijing in September 1993 and held a successful presentation of the Board's exams and meetings with the Chinese National Educational Examinations Authority (NEEA) and the State Education Commission (SEC). (The SEC was responsible for all music education in China other than for the thirty-one specialist music conservatoires, and so advised NEEA on music education policy.) Morris received a positive initial response after these meetings, and NEEA held out the possibility of holding ABRSM exams in some major cities during July 1994. But NEEA needed to consult countrywide and would in due course give their considered response. In the event, the necessary permissions to hold exams were not forthcoming, but, helpfully, in August 1994 a meeting was facilitated between Morris and NEEA officials who were in Britain, visiting Cambridge to sign an agreement with UCLES for a major joint educational venture to be housed in Beijing. At this meeting Morris discovered more about the complex workings of Chinese bureaucracy that had put a temporary block on the Board's exams. It turned out that the Ministry of Culture (responsible to the SEC), which had not sanctioned the original Wuhan exams, had also originally advised against Morris and Mundey being allowed to make their 1993 visit to Beijing. SEC, though, had overturned that advice and issued the invitation. However, during the process of the subsequent consultation, some 'distinguished musical experts' had in their turn poured cold water on the idea of holding ABRSM exams, and so the SEC had forbidden NEEA's granting the necessary permissions. It was not stated whether the interests of the recently established Chinese grade exams had influenced this reversal. The NEEA officials advised patience, saying that the NEEA/UCLES arrangements had been protracted, taking some five years. But an opening was left, as Morris was advised to seek to try to change the minds of the 'distinguished experts'.

The next stage was a visit made to Beijing in November 1994 which was intended to explore the possibilities of a joint venture with the Central Conservatory. As on earlier visits, British Council officials were very helpful in offering assistance and interpreting the situation; support also came from the British Embassy, including the personal involvement of successive ambassadors – an indication of the potential trade and cultural significance of an ABRSM presence in China. Morris spelled out that the benefits of having ABRSM exams in China would include access to international standards (promoting perceptions of Chinese talent) and representation for Chinese teachers, scholarships and exchanges to the UK conservatoires, including professional development opportunities for teachers. However, the involvement of a foreign organization involved sensitivity over issues of cultural sovereignty and this remained a sticking point. While in Beijing, Morris also received an indirect approach from Shanghai; direct contact was then made and he visited the city in March 1995. It was clear that, despite the obstacles, there was still enthusiasm for the Board's exams, but much depended on achieving the appropriate Chinese partner in order to unlock the opportunity. The breakthrough came in December 1995 when in a visit to Guangzhou (formerly Canton) Morris completed negotiations with the Guangdong Culture Dispersion Department and the Guangdong Musicians Association. They had been given permission by Beijing to act as the Board's agents for the Guangdong Province, for the 'cultural benefit and enrichment of the Chinese people'. The agreement with the newly formed Guangdong Society for International Musical Development was signed in August 1996 and an opening ceremony was held in October. The first exams were to be held in Shenzhen in December 1996, and in other places in 1997, and in the practical arrangements for these the Board was very well supported by its Hong Kong Regional Consultants, David and Shirley Gwilt. David Gwilt had been an ABRSM examiner before emigrating to Hong Kong to join the Chinese University there. His wife was born in Hong Kong and had studied at the RSAMD before returning there and becoming head of the music section of the Education Department. Their joint appointment in 1995 as the Hong Kong consultants to the Board gave a new dimension to the Board's presence there, supervising the increase in Board materials available in Chinese translation and increasing the range of educational support for teachers through workshops and seminars.[25]

The advantage of Shenzhen for the first Board exams was its proximity to Hong Kong itself and its being accustomed to foreign investment as the first of China's Special Economic Zones. The two examiners were Angus Watson and David Robinson – helpfully, the former had been Dean of Music at the Hong Kong Academy of Performing Arts and had conducted the Shenzhen Symphony Orchestra. The atmosphere of the exams was somewhat *en fête*, as Watson remarked in his report, with enthusiastic parents and children seeming to spend the whole day at the centre and peering in to the exam room, and was marked by great courtesy and kindness shown to the examiners. Distinctions were awarded by both examiners and Watson remarked that three violin candidates were outstanding, and reflected the highest quality of teaching. However, one difference between the music education cultures was a general weakness in responding to the aural tests, as aural skills were evidently not systematically taught. The day had clearly been a memorable one, leaving those involved in assessing these twenty-five initial candidates very sure about the potential of the Board's exams to benefit Chinese music education. It confirmed the ABRSM in its view that pursuing the development of its exams in China was a feasible strategy and one it should continue to invest in.

---

[25] The Board had been seeking to improve the quality of the teaching for its exams in Malaysia, Singapore and Hong Kong by developing an Educational Support Programme of seminars and workshops for each country. These had proved very popular and had attracted substantial numbers of teachers – 1,300 teachers had attended the 1993 programme in Malaysia and Singapore. More extended professional development opportunities were introduced later; these included the CT ABRSM in Singapore and Hong Kong.

⫻ Publishing

FOR a long time the Board's publishing arm had offered a comparatively restricted list. The catalogue for 1968 shows an almost exclusive focus on editions of the piano canon and didactic piano pieces at different levels, and a very few items for voice and stringed instruments. By 1984/5 the range had expanded a little, with pieces offered for some woodwind and brass instruments and saxophone, but it was still comparatively limited. The big opportunity came with the establishment of ABRSM (Publishing) Ltd, as a company in its own right, as part of the 1985 Reconstitution. Julian Hodgson joined as its Managing Director in 1987 and oversaw the first real expansion of the list, and in 1999 he was succeeded as Director of Publishing by Leslie East. East felt that what the publishing firm produced should encompass and symbolize the range of the Board's educational and musical philosophy, so as well as producing authoritative editions and music fulfilling an obvious teaching purpose, it should also move into publications that helped move people towards a better understanding of style, performance and theory. An example of this thinking has been the *Performer's Guide* series, offering a clearly presented encapsulation of the salient stylistic issues in the playing of the Baroque, Classical and Romantic repertoires, illustrated by an accompanying CD. Another break from the Board's conventional past is the series *An Extraordinary Life*, which includes some provocatively revisionist accounts of composers' lives related to their social and cultural contexts. The list continues to build on the publication of scholarly editions, such as Richard Jones's new edition of Bach's *Well-Tempered Clavier* (1994), published seventy years after Tovey's celebrated edition, and Barry Cooper's new Beethoven edition (2007), but it also began to introduce a more diverse range of new music especially written for learners across the range of musical styles and idioms.

A pioneering venture was the *Spectrum* series of contemporary compositions by contemporary composers, the idea of Thalia Myers, to encourage music for learners in an attempt to break down the traditional barrier surrounding contemporary music. Originally for piano, *Spectrum*'s success has generated music for other instruments and for string quartet. Another new approach was to initiate a series of albums in more popular styles to meet the needs of beginners and learners in the Board's prime constituency of up to Grade 5, reflecting a much greater musical diversity presented in a friendly and contemporary manner that is a world away from the Board's rather more staid publishing past. The publishing company has invested heavily in commissioning and producing a wealth of new repertoire and learning material to support new syllabuses, and, as discussed elsewhere, the Jazz syllabuses and Music Medals assessments are good examples of this. In establishing its online presence in 2001 the publishing company had to reconcile its historical past with modern trading conditions. Clearly, online availability helped to open up its market, especially in areas of the world where retail access is difficult. But it was reluctant to abandon the value of a physical retail presence, and it still supports local music sellers. As Chapter 3 explained, one reason for the Board's early success was the role played by music shops, which, as the hubs of local teacher networks, were an effective means of spreading word about the Board's exams. Local music shops still have an unofficial or an actual representative role (some retailers are HLRs) within a locality, and so the Board has been very reluctant to relinquish entirely such a well-established resource. The commercial success of ABRSM (Publishing) and the significance of its contribution to the work of the Board as a whole is illustrated by 2009 sales figures of over £5.5 million, with a gift aid payment to the ABRSM of nearly £1.5 million.[26]

✇ The new Beethoven Edition

T HE Board's seminal Tovey/Craxton edition hung, in the Coleridge sense, as something of an albatross around its neck. Approaches to textual musicology and ideas about historical performance practice had developed considerably since its 1931 publication, not least because of the impetus given by the quest for 'authenticity' from the 1960s as a countercultural force to the contemporary avant-garde. Although the Tovey edition's shortcomings and errors were often commented on, the problem the Board faced was how to replace such a legendary edition and what exactly to replace it with. It was important for the Board's reputation that its imprimatur on any new Beethoven edition should represent no diminution in terms of scholarship, but that posed a difficult achievement requiring considerable financial investment. One short-term financial disincentive was that Tovey's edition continued to sell. The 1986 sales were 6,895 for the three volumes (both hard and paperbound), and 23,530 for the separately published sonatas. In the five years 1995–2000, sales of the volumes were 26,280, with popular individual sonatas such as the 'Pathétique' and the 'Moonlight' selling 11,075 and 25,775 respectively. However, Urtext editions from other publishers were encroaching on the Tovey, even though they did not offer the guidance to performers and teachers that was one of its established strengths. The potential of this performance/teaching market made the commercial case for publishing a new Beethoven edition. The files indicate that some thirty-two years elapsed from the first serious consideration of a replacement for the Tovey and the publication of the new Barry Cooper critical edition in 2007. During this time a variety of approaches and solutions were considered and discarded, but in retrospect it could be argued that the delay was ultimately beneficial in terms of the result. The project had three phases. The first involved the idea of an edition by the eminent pianist and teacher Kendall Taylor, which was considered from 1975 to 1982, followed by a period of abeyance; the second (1987 to 1991) was the proposal for an edition from the Mozart scholar Stanley Sadie (Sadie had, with the pianist Denis Matthews, produced the Board's new edition of the Mozart piano sonatas); and finally came the involvement of Barry Cooper, which began in 1994, then dragged before Leslie East took over the project in 1999 and made it a publishing priority.

The Kendall Taylor proposal was essentially for a corrected revision of the 1931 edition, retaining Tovey's prefaces virtually as they stood, but adjusting editorial slurs and pedal indications and correcting textual inaccuracies. There was some concern on the Governing Body about balancing Taylor's practical expertise

---

[26] *ABRSM Reports and Accounts for the Year Ended 31 January 2010*, 5.

ABRSM

BEETHOVEN

The 35 Piano Sonatas

Volumes 1–3

Die 35 Klaviersonaten

Bände 1–3

Edited by/Herausgegeben von

BARRY COOPER

10 Design reflecting musical attitudes: the cover of the ABRSM's 2007 Barry Cooper Beethoven edition. Cooper's concern to retrieve Beethoven's original text, and his historical performance focus, puts the composer unambiguously back at the centre, as the signature on the cover symbolizes.

with that of an established Beethoven scholar. Increasingly, though, the idea of a limited updating of the Tovey was being challenged because of a growing corpus of thought that, as a monument of its kind, it should remain untouched. Alan Tyson, the leading authority in the study of Beethoven sketches, was asked for his opinion, but his reply intimated he would not undertake any actual editorial involvement, which was obviously what had been hoped for. Whatever animation this project had accrued was then suspended, and in November 1982 Taylor withdrew and instead prepared an edition with detailed notes on performance that was published by the Australian publisher Allan's. Then, seemingly, Stanley Sadie proposed himself as editor of the Board's new Beethoven edition, with Joyce Rathbone, a fortepianist as well as an admired piano teacher, to provide the fingering. However, Taylor's performance commentaries were making his Allan's Beethoven edition very popular, and as a defensive measure, the Board suggested that a noted Beethoven performer should work with Sadie on interpretative matters. Various ambitious proposals were made, and Alfred Brendel, who was planning to record his third cycle of the complete sonatas, was approached to write detailed notes on their performance. Although the idea was not turned down out of hand, it was clear that the timing of Brendel's recording and the project schedule did not align, and Brendel was considering the possibility of a book, so the idea was dropped. Meanwhile, all was not proceeding smoothly between the Board and Sadie, and after consideration of a sample sonata, and with considerable pressure on the publishing company from other commitments, the Board decided to withdraw temporarily from the project.

The Board had asked the Beethoven scholar Barry Cooper to prepare a revised edition of Tovey's *Companion* to the sonatas, and in 1994, after some reassessment of whether to proceed with a new Beethoven edition, David Blackwell (the new Senior Music Editor) asked whether he would be interested in editing it. Cooper responded with a detailed proposal and a sample sonata (ironically, and unknowingly, the same that Sadie had submitted). The Board's reaction was positive, and it sought the opinion of a range of scholars, players and music teachers. But by now overwhelmed by the demands of producing the extensive publications to support the new Jazz Piano syllabus, the project did not advance further until the arrival of Leslie East, as Blackwell's successor in April 1998. East carried out a thorough review of the project and its implications. He was very clear about the need for a new edition with modern editing methodology and scholarly apparatus as well as guidance on performance and teaching aspects, and on this basis he agreed with Cooper the principles the edition should encapsulate. Key was the understanding that there should be symbiosis in matters of scholarship and performance, and that the commentaries should reflect scholarly thinking on general issues of interpretation, such as slurs, dynamics, realization of trills, staccato markings, pedalling, the beaming of notes and the significance for today's performer of the differences between the historical and the modern piano. Each sonata should have a detailed commentary of its own, identifying the specific textual and performance features presented by that work. It was agreed that the edition should contain suggested fingerings and that Cooper should write about the interpretative elements of his commentaries in conjunction with a specialist performer. In the event this went well, and there was a happy and productive collaboration with David Ward, a professor of piano and fortepiano at the RCM who had considerable teaching experience. An ingenious solution was found to accommodate the individual sonata commentaries, which totalled some 150,000 words, by presenting them as a separate pull-out within each volume, so facilitating the alignment of commentary with the relevant musical page. Each volume also has a CD illustrating a range of performance problems affecting passages from its constituent sonatas. Cooper decided that the edition should include the three sonatas Beethoven composed at the age of twelve, so it contains thirty-five sonatas rather than the traditional canon of thirty-two. Present circumstances mean that very few music publishers would have the resources to support such a major editing project. What was key in bringing about the ABRSM's new Beethoven edition was its propitious mix of commercial interest, didactic purpose and scholarly achievement.

Conclusion

T HE distance between the social and cultural environment in which the ABRSM originally flourished and the one in which it competes today is so great that the difference evokes the metaphor of the past as a foreign country.[27] But as we have seen, throughout its history the Board has been constantly preoccupied with the set of themes identified at the beginning of this chapter. These involve the relationship between the ABRSM and the Royal Schools; the complications sometimes caused on account of the Board's commercial success; and the need for the exams and services the Board offers to represent a workable synthesis of educational integrity and practicality. These all link to the issue that was outlined in the Introduction, about who was being scrutinized by the music exam process: the candidate, the teacher or the examiner? That triangle symbolizes the different power relationships at play within the music exam process. Little in that relationship is 'fixed' and much is a matter for negotiation; across the Board's history we have seen the different ways in which this interaction has been handled, according to the context and conventions of the time.

The ABRSM that Guy Perricone joined as Chief Executive in 2010 was, in important ways, very different from the organization that Morris had entered. For what Morris had very quickly realized was that unless he could develop the Board strategically as a business, its educational influence would be restricted to what it had always been: selling grade exams to those who could afford them. In today's cultural and technological climate that would have been tantamount to accepting the Board's gradual decline. New thinking had to be put in place if the Board was to retain either its relevance or its wider significance as an educational force. The ABRSM's commercial success was the *sine qua non* for the Board to develop Music Medals, its Jazz syllabus and its professional development programme, because

---

[27] The phrase coined by the novelist L. P. Hartley in *The Go-Between* was taken up by the historian David Lowenthal, *The Past is a Foreign Country* (Cambridge: Cambridge University Press, 1985).

these initiatives each required very substantial financial investment and the continued generation of a sufficient level of income over the lead time before a return could be expected on these new products. But the jury is obviously still out on the question of how much of a commercial success some of these recent initiatives will prove to be.

In recent years the Board has, for the first time in its history, been championing the importance of classical music education and the interests of instrumental and singing teachers. For as the cultural landscape has shifted, it is no longer a given that the cause of classical music will be properly understood, let alone respected, across society. This makes things very challenging for music education. Undoubtedly, much will change for music exams and the way they are delivered as society and technology, culture and concepts of musical authority move on. But whatever these changes may represent, maintaining the usefulness and value of music exams will continue to depend upon a continuing quality of engagement between candidates, teachers and the examining body. This helps to explain something about the ABRSM's institutional durability and why it has continued to be so influential for so long. For despite the indifference shown to its customers in some phases of its history, at watershed moments the ABRSM has also revealed its capacity to understand that a negotiated candidate–teacher–examiner relationship is pivotal to the educational success of its work.

Appendix 1 Speech and Drama Examinations

IN 1922 the ABRSM began to offer Elocution exams in the UK. (The Elocution exams were called 'Grades' in order to distinguish them from the Local Centre and Local School Exams in music; in 1933 'Grade' was the term adopted to distinguish the individual steps of the newly restructured music exams.) There were five Elocution grades, and, as in the case of the earliest music exams, candidates had first to pass a Qualifying Examination before they could take the Elocution exam itself. The Qualifying Examination required knowledge of musical notation, and its four tests were Pitch, Rhythm without Words, Rhythm with Words and Reciting to Music, clearly chosen to emphasize the complementarity of the disciplines of music and speech. The entry fee for the highest or Fifth Grade was £1 11s 6d (some £63.70 in today's RPI value), which made it an expensive exam. The candidate was required to give three recitations chosen from a prescribed list, to read at sight a poem and a prose extract, and to answer questions 'on the interpretation and significance of Selections, and general technique'. In the first complete year, although 226 candidates took the Qualifying Examination, only 134 proceeded to the Elocution exam, which suggests that the standards at the preliminary stage were set high. The Qualifying Examination was abandoned in 1926 and replaced with a written exam. Although women were not made examiners in music until 1956, in the case of the Elocution exams, women were appointed from the very beginning, but only 'on the grounds that Elocution was a special branch of the Board's work and that their appointment for this work did not commit the Board to throw open to Women Examinership in music also'.[1]

In the inter-war years the number of Elocution candidates remained low, never reaching the thousand mark. Despite requests for the Elocution syllabus to be examined abroad, the costs and logistics of doing so were simply not viable, and it continued to be offered only in Britain. As with music (see Chapter 7), the war brought about a surprising increase in the popularity of the ABRSM exams in general, and in 1945/6 there were 4,384 entries for Elocution. In 1948 the syllabus was overhauled into six grades, and from 1949 the title of the exams was changed to 'Speech and Drama'. Exams in less formal aspects of Spoken English were introduced in 1955, but this failed to stop the decline in entries, and from 1965 concern grew about the long-term viability of Speech exams, and whether it was appropriate for the ABRSM to continue offering them. Even so, 1986 saw another attempt to broaden their appeal, with the introduction of exams in Solo Acting, Group Acting and English as a Second Language. But Speech and Drama entries continued to diminish: in 1968 there had been 5,741 candidates and in 1989 numbers had reduced to 4,377. There seemed to be no real national purpose to these exams, because unlike the conservatoire situation, where Grade 8 in music was seen as an entry benchmark, there seemed to be little enthusiasm by the drama schools to view the Speech exams in a similar way. With the low candidate numbers involved, the economies of scale that applied to the music exams did not

---

[1] ABMB6: 12 July 1921.

work for Speech, where the fees were now falling well short of costs. Accordingly the Governing Body took the decision that in 1990 the ABRSM would discontinue its Speech exams.[2]

---

[2] ABMB13: 20 June 1989.

Appendix 2 ABRSM Personalia, 1889–2010

/// Chairmen

Lord Charles Bruce, 1889–96
Thomas Threlfall, 1897–1907
Sir William Bigge, 1907–16
Ernest Mathews CVO, 1917–28
Raymond Ffennell, 1928–38
(From 1939 to 1983 there was no independent Chairman;
instead the post rotated annually between the Director of
the RCM and the Principal of the RAM.)
Sir Brian Young, 1984–7
Sir John Burgh, 1987–94
Sir Peter Marychurch, 1994–2000
Sir John Baker, 2000–2006
Lord Sutherland of Houndwood, 2006–

/// Secretaries

George Watson, 1889–96
Samuel Aitken, 1896–1900 (Hon. Sec.)
James Muir, 1900–1933
Hilary Macklin, 1934–62
William Cole, 1962–74
Philip Cranmer, 1974–83

/// Chief Executives

Ronald Smith, 1983–92
Richard Morris, 1993–2009
Guy Perricone, 2010–

/// Principals of the RAM

Sir Alexander Mackenzie, 1888
Sir John B. McEwen, 1924
Sir Stanley Marchant, 1936
Reginald Thatcher, 1949
Sir Thomas Armstrong, 1955
Sir Anthony Lewis, 1968
Sir David Lumsden, 1982

Lynn Harrell, 1993
Sir Curtis Price, 1995
Jonathan Freeman-Attwood, 2008

Directors of the RCM

Sir George Grove, 1883
Sir Hubert Parry, 1895
Sir Hugh Allen, 1919
Sir George Dyson, 1938
Sir Ernest Bullock, 1953
Sir Keith Falkner, 1960
Sir David Willcocks, 1974
Michael Gough Matthews, 1985
Dame Janet Ritterman, 1993
Colin Lawson, 2005

Directors of the RNCM (following 1985 Reconstitution)

Sir John Manduell, 1971
Edward Gregson, 1996
Jonty Stockdale, 2008

Directors of the RSAMD [now RCS] (following 1985 Reconstitution)

Sir Philip Ledger, 1982
John Wallace, 2002

Select Bibliography

ABRSM, *Making Music: The Associated Board Review of the Teaching, Learning and Playing of Musical Instruments in the United Kingdom* (London: ABRSM, 1994; 1997; 2000)
—— *Research Report on Instrumental/Vocal Tuition in Private and State Schools* (London: ABRSM, 2006)
An Account of the Canadian protest against the introduction into Canada of musical examinations by outside musical examining bodies, edited, compiled and published by order of the Canadian Protesting Committee (1899)
Aitken, S., *The Case of the Associated Board* (Toronto: 29 March 1899)
—— *The Associated Board ... and Its Honorary Secretary* (privately printed, 1900)
Arts Enquiry, The, *Music: A Report on Musical Life in Britain Sponsored by the Dartington Hall Trustees* (London: Political and Economic Planning, 1949)
Bahlman, D. W. R., 'Hamilton, Sir Edward Walter (1847–1908)', *ODNB*
Baigent, E., 'Haweis, Hugh Reginald (1838–1901)', *ODNB*
Bailey, C., *Hugh Percy Allen* (London: Oxford University Press, 1948)
Banfield, S. (ed.), *The Blackwell History of Music in Britain*, vol. 6: *The Twentieth Century* (Oxford: Blackwell Publishing, 1995)
Bashford, C., *The Pursuit of High Culture: John Ella and Chamber Music in Victorian London* (Woodbridge: Boydell Press, 2007)
Bashford, C., and L. Langley (eds.), *Music and British Culture 1785–1914: Essays in Honour of Cyril Ehrlich* (Oxford: Oxford University Press, 2000)
Benjamin, A., 'A Student in Kensington', *Music & Letters* 31/3 (July 1950), 196–207
—— 'Schooldays in Brisbane', *Music Survey*, 3/3 (March 1951), 171–2
Besley, M., 'Fresh Air and Variations', *The Sackbut* 8 (April 1928), 285–9
Blake, A., *The Land without Music: Music, Culture and Society in Twentieth-Century Britain* (Manchester: Manchester University Press, 1997)
Boynton, S., and R.-M. Kok (eds.), *Musical Childhoods & the Cultures of Youth* (Middletown, CT: Wesleyan University Press, 2006)
Bridge C., and K. Fedorowich (eds.), *The British World: Diaspora, Culture and Identity* (London: Frank Cass, 2003)
Bridges, D., 'Some Historical Backgrounds to Australian Music Education', *The Australian Journal of Music Education*, first series, vols. 10–15 (April 1972 – October 1975)
Brown, C., *Classical & Romantic Performing Practice, 1750–1900* (Oxford: Oxford University Press, 1999)
Brown J. D., and S. S. Stratton, 'Preface', *British Musical Biography: A Dictionary of Musical Artists, Authors and Composers* (Birmingham: S. S. Stratton, 1897)
Buckner, P., and R. D. Francis, *Rediscovering the British World* (Calgary: Calgary University Press, 2005)
Carpenter, H., *Benjamin Britten: A Biography* (London: Faber & Faber, 1992)
—— *The Envy of the World: Fifty Years of the BBC Third Programme and Radio 3* (London: Weidenfield & Nicholson, 1996)
Carr-Saunders, A. M., and P. A. Wilson, *The Professions* (Oxford: Clarendon Press, 1933)

Clarke, P., *Hope and Glory: Britain, 1900–2000*, 2nd edn (Harmondsworth: Penguin Books, 2004)

Cleave, S., and K. Dust, *A Sound Start: The Schools' Instrumental Music Service* (Windsor: NFER-Nelson, 1989)

Colles, H. C., and J. Cruft, *The Royal College of Music: A Centenary Record, 1883–1983* (London: Prince Consort Foundation, 1982)

Cowgill, R., and P. Holman (eds.), *Music in the British Provinces, 1690–1914* (Aldershot: Ashgate, 2007)

Crowest, F., *Phases of Musical England* (London: Remington & Co., 1881)

Darian-Smith, K., P. Grimshaw and S. Macintyre (eds.), *Britishness Abroad: Transnational Movements and Imperial Cultures* (Melbourne: Melbourne University Press, 2007)

Darwin, J., *The Empire Project: The Rise and Fall of the British World-System, 1830–1970* (Cambridge: Cambridge University Press, 2009)

Dibble, J., *C. Hubert H. Parry: His Life and Music* (Oxford: Oxford University Press, 1992)

—— *Charles Villiers Stanford: Man and Musician* (Oxford: Oxford University Press, 2002)

—— 'Stainer, Sir John (1840–1901)', *ODNB*

—— *John Stainer: A Life in Music* (Woodbridge: Boydell Press, 2007)

Dobrée B. (ed.), *The Letters of Philip Dormer Stanhope, 4th Earl of Chesterfield* (London: Eyre & Spottiswoode, 1932)

Doctor, J., *The BBC and Ultra-Modern Music, 1922–1936: Shaping a Nation's Tastes* (Cambridge: Cambridge University Press, 1999)

Doctor, J., N. Kenyon and D. Wright (eds.), *The Proms: A New History* (London: Thames & Hudson, 2007)

Edwards, R. A., *And the Glory: A History in Commemoration of the 150th Anniversary of the Huddersfield Choral Society* (Leeds: W. S. Maney, 1985)

Ehrlich, C., *The Music Profession in Britain since the Eighteenth Century: A Social History* (Oxford: Clarendon Press, 1985)

—— *The Piano: A History*, rev. edn (Oxford: Clarendon Press, 1990)

Federation of British Conservatoires, *Teaching Performance: The Employment of Musical Instrument Teaching Specialists*, HEFCE Good Management Practice Project, 41 (2003)

Finnegan, R., *The Hidden Musicians: Music-Making in an English Town*, 2nd edn (Middletown, CT: Wesleyan University Press, 2007)

Foreman, L., *Music in England 1885–1920 as Recounted in Hazell's Annual* (London: Thames Publishing, 1994)

Galloway, W. J., *Musical England* (London: Christophers, 1910)

Gardiner, J., *Wartime Britain* (London: Headline, 2004)

Gillett, P., *Musical Women in England, 1870–1914: 'Encroaching on all Man's Privileges'* (Houndmills: Macmillan Press, 2000)

Glock, W., *Notes in Advance: An Autobiography in Music* (Oxford: Oxford University Press, 1991)

Grove, G., *A Dictionary of Music and Musicians (AD 1450–1879) by Eminent Writers, English and Foreign* (London: Macmillan, 1879)

Hadley, H., 'Frederic Cliffe', *RCM Magazine* 28/1 (1932), 21–2

Hallam, S., and V. Prince, *Research into Instrumental Music Services* (London: DfEE, 2000)

Hallam, S., L. Rogers and A. Creech, *Survey of Local Authority Music Services, 2005* (London: DES, 2005)

Handford, M., *Sounds Unlikely: Music in Birmingham*, rev. edn (Studley: Brewin Books, 2006)

Hargreaves, D. J., A. C. North and R. M. Hatcher, *Establishing Benchmarks and Reliability of Assessments in the ABRSM Examinations* (University of Leicester Department of Psychology, Music Research Group, 1998)

Harris, A., *Romantic Moderns* (London: Thames & Hudson, 2010)

Haskell, H., *The Early Music Revival: A History* (New York: Dover, 1996)

Haweis, H. R., *Music and Morals* (London: Stathan & Co., 1871)

Herbert, T. (ed.), *The British Brass Band: A Musical and Social History* (Oxford: Oxford University Press, 2000)

Horrall, A., *Popular Culture in London, c. 1890–1918* (Manchester: Manchester University Press, 2001)

Howe, B., *Arbiter of Elegance* (London: Harvill Press, 1967)

Howes, F., *The English Musical Renaissance* (London, Secker & Warburg, 1966)

Hudson, D., and K. Luckhurst, *The Royal Society of Arts, 1784–1954* (London: John Murray, 1954)

Jenkins, P., *Mrs Thatcher's Revolution*, 2nd edn (London: Pan Books, 1989)

Kennedy, M., *The History of the Royal Manchester College of Music, 1893–1972* (Manchester: Manchester University Press, 1971)

—— *Adrian Boult* (London: Papermac, 1989)

Kenyon, N., *The BBC Symphony Orchestra: The First Fifty Years, 1930–1980* (London: British Broadcasting Corporation, 1981)

Kneschke, E., *Das Conservatorium der Musik in Leipzig … Festgabe zum 25jährigen Jubiläum zum 2. April 1868* (Leipzig, [1872])

Kraus, R. C., *Pianos and Politics in China: Middle-Class Ambitions and the Struggle over Western Music* (New York: Oxford University Press, 1989)

Langley, L., *Unlocking Classical Music: Queen's Hall and the Rise of Public Orchestral Culture in London, 1880–1930* (forthcoming)

Lau, F., 'Teacher's Friend', *Music Teacher* 89/12 (December 2010), 42–3

Lawson, C., and R. Stowell (eds.), *The Cambridge History of Musical Performance* (Cambridge: Cambridge University Press, 2012)

LeMahieu, D. L., *A Culture for Democracy: Mass Communication and the Cultivated Mind in Britain between the Wars* (Oxford: Clarendon Press, 1998)

Lowenthal, D., *The Past is a Foreign Country* (Cambridge: Cambridge University Press, 1985)

Lowerson, J., *Amateur Operatics: A Social and Cultural History* (Manchester: Manchester University Press, 2005)

Lowerson, J., and J. Myerscough, *Time to Spare in Victorian England* (Hassocks: Harvester Press, 1977)

Mackenzie, A. C., *A Musician's Narrative* (London: Cassell & Co., 1927)

Mackerness, E. D., *A Social History of English Music* (London: Routledge & Kegan Paul, 1964)

Maine, C. S., 'A Conservatoire of Music for England: Report of Prince
    Christian's Executive Committee since its Foundation by the Prince of Wales',
    Macmillan's Magazine 41/242 (November 1879), 145–53
Martin, P. J., *Sounds and Society: Themes in the Sociology of Music* (Manchester:
    Manchester University Press, 1995)
Maschler, T. (ed.), *Declaration* (London: MacGibbon & Key, 1957)
Mathew, H. C. G., *Gladstone, 1809–1898* (Oxford: Clarendon Press, 1997)
McKinstry, L., *Rosebery: Statesman in Turmoil* (London: John Murray, 2005)
Mitchell, D., and P. Reed (eds.), *Letters from a Life: Selected Letters and Diaries of
    Benjamin Britten, 1913–1976*, vol. 1: *1923–1939* (London: Faber & Faber, 1991)
MORI, *Musical Instrument Tuition in Schools – Survey* (London, 1999)
Munson, J., *The Nonconformists: In Search of a Lost Culture* (London, SPCK, 1991)
Musgrave, M., *The Musical Life of the Crystal Palace* (Cambridge: Cambridge
    University Press, 1995)
Neighbour, O. (ed.), *Music and Bibliography: Essays in Honour of Alec Hyatt King*
    (London: Clive Bingley, 1980)
Nettel, R., *Music in the Five Towns, 1840–1914* (London: Oxford University Press,
    1944)
Nott, J. J., *Music for the People: Popular Music and Dance in Interwar Britain*
    (Oxford: Oxford University Press, 2002)
Pearsall, R., *Edwardian Popular Music* (Rutherford, NJ: Fairleigh Dickinson
    University Press, 1975)
Phillips, L. M., 'The Leipzig Conservatory, 1843–1881' (PhD diss., Indiana
    University, 1979)
Poole, T., 'China's elite music school starts a pop revolution', *Independent on
    Sunday*, 14 March 1993
Porter, R., *Quacks: Fakers and Charlatans in Medicine* (Stroud: Tempus
    Publishing, 1989)
Raban S. (ed.), *Examining the World: A History of the University of Cambridge
    Local Examinations Syndicate* (Cambridge: Cambridge University Press, 2008)
Rainbow, B., 'Hunt, Henry George Bonavia', rev. A. Pimlott Baker, *ODNB*
Rainbow, B., and G. Cox, *Music in Educational Thought and Practice*, 2nd edn
    (Woodbridge: Boydell Press, 2006)
Richards, J., *Imperialism and Music: Britain, 1876–1953* (Manchester: Manchester
    University Press, 2001)
Rodmell, P. (ed.), *Music and Institutions* (Aldershot: Ashgate, 2012)
Rohr, D., *The Careers of British Musicians, 1750–1850: A Profession of Artisans*
    (Cambridge: Cambridge University Press, 2001)
Ross, H. M., 'Dewar, Sir James (1842–1923)', rev. T. I. Williams, *ODNB*
Rowland, D. (ed.), *The Cambridge Companion to the Piano* (Cambridge:
    Cambridge University Press, 1998), 117–34
Rubinstein, W. D., 'The End of Old Corruption in Britain, 1780–1860', *Past and
    Present* 101/1 (November 1982)
Russell, D., *Popular Music in England, 1840–1914*, 2nd edn (Manchester:
    Manchester University Press, 1997)
Sanderson, M., *Education, Economic Change and Society in England, 1780–1870*,
    2nd edn (Cambridge: Cambridge University Press, 1995)

—— *Education and Economic Decline in Britain, 1870 to the 1990s*, 2nd edn (Cambridge: Cambridge University Press, 1999)

Schmitz, O. A. H., *Das Land ohne Musik: Englische Gesellschaftsprobleme*, trans. H. Herzl as *The Land without Music* (London: Jerrolds, [1926])

Scholes, P., *The Mirror of Music, 1844–1944* (London and Oxford: Novello and Oxford University Press, 1947)

Scott, D., *The Singing Bourgeois*, 2nd edn (Aldershot: Ashgate, 2001)

Searle, G. R., *A New England?: Peace and War, 1886–1918* (Oxford: Oxford University Press, 2004)

Sewell, G. F., *A History of the Bradford Festival Choral Society: From its Formation in 1856 to its Jubilee in 1906* (Bradford: G. F. Sewell, 1907)

Shera, F. H., 'Coward, Sir Henry (1849–1944)', rev. J. J. Nott, *ODNB*

Sherman, B. D., *Inside Early Music* (New York: Oxford University Press, 1997)

Shi-guang, C., 'Three Centuries of Cultural Interfacing: A History of Western Music in China', *American Music Teacher*, April/May 1990, 14–17, 51

Smith, A., *The Wealth of Nations* (1776), ed. E. Cannan (New York: Random House, 2000)

Society for the Encouragement of Arts, Manufacturers, and Commerce, *First Report of the Committee ... on the State of Musical Education at Home and Abroad* (London: Bell & Daldy, 1866)

Stanford, C. V., *Pages from an Unwritten Diary* (London: Arnold, 1914)

Stanton, W. K., 'Allen, Sir Hugh Percy (1869–1946)', rev., *ODNB*

Stockwell, S. (ed.), *The British Empire: Themes and Perspectives* (Oxford: Blackwell Publishing, 2008)

Temperley, N. (ed.), *The Athlone History of Music in Britain*, vol. 5: *The Romantic Age, 1800–1914* (London: Athlone Press, 1981)

Thompson, A., *The Empire Strikes Back?: The Impact of Imperialism on Britain from the Mid-Nineteenth Century* (Harlow: Pearson Longman, 2005)

Thompson, F. M. L., *Chartered Surveyors: The Growth of a Profession* (London: Routledge & Kegan Paul, 1968)

—— (ed.), *The Cambridge History of Britain*, vol. 2: *People and Their Environment* (Cambridge: Cambridge University Press, 1990)

Thomson, H. B., *The Choice of a Profession: A Concise Account and Comparative Review of the English Professions* (London: Chapman & Hall, 1857)

Toop, R., 'Four Facets of "The New Complexity"', *Contact* 32 (Spring 1988), 4–50

Training Musicians: A Report to the Calouste Gulbenkian Foundation on the Training of Professional Musicians (London: Calouste Gulbenkian Foundation, 1978)

Trentmann, F., *Free Trade Nation* (Oxford: Oxford University Press, 2008)

Venables, L. C., *Choral and Orchestral Societies: A Book of Hints on their Organisation, and Business and Musical Management*, 3rd edn (London: J. Curwen & Sons, [1900])

Warrack, G., *Royal College of Music: The First Eighty-Five Years, 1883–1968 and Beyond*, 2 vols. (unpublished: Royal College of Music, 1977)

Williams, G., *Valleys of Song: Music and Society in Wales, 1840–1914* (Cardiff: University of Wales Press, 1998)

Wright, D. C. H., 'Grove's Role in the Founding of the RCM', in *George Grove, Music and Victorian Culture*, ed. Michael Musgrave (Basingstoke: Palgrave Macmillan, 2003)

—— 'The London Sinfonietta, 1968–2004: A Perspective', *Twentieth-Century Music* 2/1 (2005), 109–36

—— 'The South Kensington Music Schools and the Development of the British Conservatoire in the Late Nineteenth Century', *Journal of the Royal Musical Association*, 130/2 (2005), 236–82

—— 'Situating Stainer', *The Musical Times* 149/3 (Summer, 2008), 95–103

—— 'Music and Performance: Histories in Disjunction?', in *The Cambridge History of Musical Performance*, ed. C. Lawson and R. Stowell (Cambridge: Cambridge University Press, 2012), 169–206

—— 'The Music Exams of the Society for the Encouragement of Arts, Manufactures and Commerce, 1859–1919', in *Music and Institutions*, ed. P. Rodmell (Aldershot: Ashgate, 2012)

Index

accordion, free bass, 187–8, 189
Aitken, Samuel, 81, 94, 95
Alcock, (Sir) Walter, 82
Alexander, Arthur, 145
Allen, (Sir) Hugh, 84, 90–1, 96, 105, 107–8,
    109, 111, 115, 117, 119, 120, 125, 126, 127,
    132, 135, 137, 141, 176
Alwyn, William, 97
amateur music-making, 19–21, 24–7, 105,
    110, 123
Anderson, Lindsay, 144
apprenticeship, 29
Armstrong, (Sir) Thomas, 145–6, 162
Associated Board of the Royal Schools of
    Music (ABRSM)
    administration and operational aspects,
        89–90, 131–2, 161–6, 183–4, 199–201,
        211, 218–19, 228
    annual general meetings, 73, 110, 131,
    annual lunch, 87, 109, 136, 152
    authority conveyed by royal charters,
        4–5, 37, 47, 68, 105, 135, 139
    brand, 9, 16, 42, 48, 59, 105, 139, 180, 212
    business aspects, 16, 76, 148, 160–3, 173,
        175–6, 179–80, 184–5, 188, 211, 216,
        218, 228, 242, 254
    centenary, 184–5
    Chairmen, 84, 89, 108–10, 164, 166, 171,
        174, 177, 184, 188, 210, 215–16
    character and culture, 1, 13, 16, 76,
        105–9, 110–11, 122–5, 139, 145–7, 183,
        212–14, 241
    charitable status, 177, 185, 209, 215–6,
        238, 244
    Chief Examiner, 194–5, 200, 219
    Chief Executive, 14, 109, 166–7, 171–2,
        174, 181, 184–6, 187, 194, 200, 209,
        210, 213, 217, 218, 219, 254
    composers, 107, 119, 124, 144–7
    constitution, 84, 135–6, 160, 164, 166–7,
        171–80, 188
    contemporary music, attitudes to, 122–5,
        144–7, 190, 250
    Directorate membership (2007), 218–19
    Distribution of Certificates ceremonies,
        59, 72, 87, 121, 129
    donations, charitable, 14, 16, 175–6,
        178–9, 193, 198–9, 210–11, 215, 218

Associated Board of the Royal Schools of
    Music, *continued*
    as emblematic of the RSMs, 5, 105,
        107–8
    examinations, *see* examinations, ABRSM
    examiners, *see* examiners, ABRSM
    executive, 184, 186–9, 193–4, 196, 197–9,
        201, 210, 215–7, 228, 241
    exhibitions, *see* scholarships *below*
    finances, 72–4, 86, 92, 110, 129–34,
        136–40, 160, 161, 163–6, 173, 174–5,
        179, 184, 189–90, 197–8, 218, 251
    foundation, 47–8, 63–75, 180
    Governing Body, 13, 71–2, 83–4, 87, 135,
        142, 146, 164–6, 176, 180, 184, 186–8,
        190, 191–3, 196, 196–9, 201–2, 203,
        210–11, 215–18, 227, 227–8, 242–4,
        251
    Examinations Board, 186, 187–8, 216,
        242
    Finance Committee, 84, 164–6, 177,
        216, 217, 244
    Honorary Local Representatives (HLRs),
        47, 67–8, 72, 73, 75, 109, 111, 131, 189,
        200, 229, 230, 238
    international development, 202–6, 215,
        217; *see also* China, Hong Kong,
        Japan, Malaysia, Singapore, Taiwan,
        USA
    musical ethos, 11, 105, 107–8, 122–5,
        126–8, 144–7, 206–7
    perceptions of, 9–10, 11, 99, 110, 175, 183,
        192, 198, 209, 217, 229–30, 233, 240,
        243
    premises
        Bedford Square, London, WC1, 84, 86,
        129, 198, 219
        Hanover Square, London, W1, 84, 219
        New Bond Street, London, W1, 66
        Portland Place, London, W1, 219
    President, 3, 67, 73, 93, 136, 185, 219
    professional development of teachers,
        9, 14, 122, 172, 186, 191, 195, 212, 214,
        217, 225–6, 235, 242–6, 254; *see also*
        Certificate of Teaching
    public image, 16, 69, 75, 148, 176, 180,
        184, 196, 243
    publishing, *see* publishing, ABRSM

Associated Board of the Royal Schools of
    Music, *continued*
  purpose, 7–8, 108, 139, 160–1, 163, 172,
    174, 176–7, 184–6, 192, 214–5, 228
  Reconstitution (1985), 14, 108, 136, 148,
    159, 161, 163–4, 171–80, 184, 201, 207,
    216, 250
  relations with teachers and candidates,
    3, 7–9, 10, 12, 16, 110–11, 138–40,
    151, 164, 171, 183, 186, 191–2, 197, 198,
    200, 207, 213, 230, 231–3, 235, 254–5
  relationship with the Royal Schools, 1,
    93, 105–9, 135, 160, 161, 163–4, 173–4,
    184, 198–9, 201, 209–11, 214, 216–17,
    254
  repertoire, 2, 11, 79–80, 107–8, 113–4,
    122–3, 126, 146–7
  research (*Making Music*), 172, 191, 219,
    221, 224–6, 229, 244
  scholarships, 6, 78, 92, 136, 176
  Secretary, 109, 130, 141, 162–3, 166, 171,
    181, 194
  technology, 105, 110, 119–22, 126, 157,
    200, 206, 213–14
  title, 66, 67, 110, 135
  website, 10, 14, 213, 217, 242
Aston, Peter, 181, 190
Augener (publisher), 87, 116
aural training or testing, 12, 80, 81–2, 114,
    212, 214, 235, 237, 238, 239, 249
Australia, 6, 48, 49, 90, 92–5, 97, 98, 99,
    100, 101, 130, 203
autodidacticism, 29, 54, 241

Bainton, Edgar, 6
Bairstow, (Sir) Edward, 90
Baker, (Sir) John, 215–16
Bartók, Béla, 146, 158
BBC (British Broadcasting Corporation),
    108, 120, 121, 123–5, 126–8, 134, 144,
    181
BBC Music Advisory Committee, 127–8
Benjamin, Arthur, 6, 83, 100
Bennett, (Sir) William Sterndale, 45
Benson, Helen (Assistant Secretary), 89
Berg, Alban, 124, 125
Beringer, Otto, 67, 83, 87
Besley, Maurice, 97
Bigge, (Sir) William, 83, 84, 89
Birmingham and Midland Institute School
    of Music, 30

Bliss, (Sir) Arthur, 127
Boosey & Hawkes, 150
Boult, (Sir) Adrian, 124, 127
Bradshaw, Susan, 158
brass bands, 20, 24, 25, 28, 148–51, 172
Brendel, Alfred, 253
Bridge, Frank, 125
British Council, 215, 248
British Empire, 6, 76, 92, 96, 97, 110; *see
    also* British World
British Medical Association, 36
British musical culture, 123, 126–8
British World, 76, 92–102
Britten, (Lord) Benjamin, 124–5
Bruce, (Lord) Charles, 65, 81
Buck, (Sir) Percy, 11, 117
Bullock, (Sir) Ernest, 136, 137, 153
Burgh, (Sir) John, 215
Burnham Salary Scale, 158
Bury Music Service, 150
Butler, Lynne, 200

Cambridge Local Examinations Syndicate,
    University of, 40, 41, 248; *see also*
    'Oxbridge' Local Examinations
Canada, 6, 93, 94–6, 98, 101, 202
Centenary Travel Grant scheme, 185–6,
    203
Certificate of Teaching (CT ABRSM), 192,
    235–6, 245
Ceylon (Sri Lanka), 49, 101, 205
chartered associations, 35, 36
Cheung, Lawrence, 185
China, 14, 205, 209, 246–9
  Beijing, 205, 247–9
  Guangdong, 249
  Shanghai, 247–8
  Shenzhen, 249
  Wuhan Conservatory of Music, 246–8
  see also Hong Kong
Chorley, Henry, 30
Classical music
  challenge to cultural status, 9, 16, 213–14,
    255
  social image, 15–6, 206, 213
Cliffe, Frederic, 67, 83, 99–100
Cole, William, 14, 109, 152–3, 162, 194, 199
College of Organists, *see* Royal College of
    Organists
College of Violinists, 57

Cooper, Barry, 115n20, 117, 172, 250, 251–4
Coward, (Sir) Henry, 53–4
Cranmer, Philip, 14, 109, 152–3, 163–4,
    166–7, 183, 194, 199
Craxton, Harold, 117, 119, 130, 136–7, 251
Crowest, Frederick, 31, 33, 42
Crozier, Richard, 218, 245
Cyprus, 205

Dale, Benjamin, 96, 119, 121
Davies, (Sir) (Henry)Walford, 120
degrees in music, external, 39
Department of Culture, Media and Sport
    (DCMS), 219, 241
Department for Education and
    Employment (DfEE), 223
Department of Education and Science
    (DES), 158, 161, 176–8, 189, 192, 221
Dewar, (Sir) James, 65
Dinn, Freda, 152
diplomas (music), 34, 39, 42, 44, 55–9
    ARCM, 38, 42, 55, 57, 108, 191, 235
    LRAM, 38, 46, 55, 58, 108, 142, 191, 235
    LRSM, 108, 186, 190, 191–2, 203–4,
        235–6
    Trinity College London, 41, 49, 58, 236
Dunhill, Thomas, 100, 119, 124, 147
Dyson, (Sir) George, 11, 12, 90, 117, 124, 137,
    138–9, 147

East, Leslie, 218–19, 250–1, 253
Education Reform Act, 1988, 15, 172–4, 192,
    207, 213, 221–2
Ehrlich, Cyril, 31, 44, 51, 60
English Musical Renaissance,
    historiography of, 22–3, 25
Eriksson, Hildur Sanquist, 101
European String Teachers Association
    (ESTA), 242
examination market, 14–15, 26–9, 59
examinations, ABRSM
    1890 exams, 68, 69–73
    accordion, 187–8, 189
    advanced certificate, 190, 192, 235
    appeals process, 196–7, 230–3, 235
    assessment criteria, 79
    candidate base
        character of, 12, 13, 14–15, 119, 148, 225,
            227, 228
        orchestral instruments, 147–52

examinations, ABRSM, *continued*
    candidate base, *continued*
        Theory, 154–6
        woodwind and brass instruments, 14,
            148–51
    candidate numbers, 13, 72, 74, 77, 81,
        86–7, 109, 129–34, 137–40, 151, 165,
        174, 189, 190, 198, 204–6, 217, 224–5,
        227, 241
    character of, 5, 40–1, 52, 55, 59, 186, 190
    choral singing, 228
    colonial exams, 77, 81, 92–102
    diplomas, 172, 191, 210, 235–6
        LRSM, 108, 186, 190, 191–2, 203–4,
            235–6
    fees, 63, 113, 137, 156, 165–6, 177, 189,
        196–8, 210, 217, 227–9
    Grade music exams, 3, 6, 8, 15, 19, 33,
        60, 75,
        as educational consensus, 7, 212, 219
        dramatis personae, 7, 8, 254
        early development, 69, 72, 73–5, 76–9,
            82
        eight-grade pattern, 1, 111
        equivalence between exams, 11, 76–7
        exam system as interaction of
            interests, 9, 233
        fragmentation of grade market, 212
        as musical formation and training, 6,
            8–9, 55, 123–4, 212, 214
        qualifications framework (Quality and
            Curriculum Authority), 230
    guitar, 151–2
    harpsichord, 187, 188
    jazz, 211, 217, 228, 229, 236–7, 238–9,
        250, 253, 254
    Local Centre Examinations (Music), 55,
        59, 68, 72, 73, 74–5, 76–8, 82, 86–7,
        111
    Local School Examinations (Music), 56,
        68, 73–4, 76–8, 82, 86–7, 111
    Music Medals, 16, 211–12, 217, 219, 224,
        228, 229, 236, 238–42, 250, 254
    percussion, 187, 188, 189, 234
    piano, 79, 80
    practical musicianship, 237
    Preliminary (Musical Rudiments) Exam,
        68, 69, 72
    Preliminary (Practical) Exam, 77, 112,
        139, 235

examinations, ABRSM, *continued*
Preparatory Test (Prep Test), 189, 192,
    235, 240
recorder, 152, 189, 198
saxophone, 152, 183, 189, 198, 250
speech and drama, 141
syllabuses, 2, 3, 5, 6, 8, 9, 92–3, 99, 113–5,
    122–3, 150, 151–2, 186–7, 188–9, 190,
    214
Theory, 69–71, 78, 152–7, 189–90, 192,
    205–7, 244–5
Theory as prerequisite to higher grades,
    74, 80–1, 111, 131, 138–9, 152, 155–7,
    190, 206–7, 211–12, 238
violin, 71–2, 77, 79, 113, 235
woodwind and brass, 14, 15, 148–51, 183,
    237, 250
examiners, ABRSM
Chief Examiner, 194–5, 200, 219
complaints against, 82–4, 100, 162, 194,
    196–7, 230–3
drinking, 82, 98
employment, 5, 12, 67, 91, 108, 137, 141,
    158–9, 166, 175
ethos, 10, 105, 107, 122–3, 137, 184
examination criteria, 9–10, 79, 183, 187,
    194
Examinations Board, 186, 187–8, 216, 242
examiner as representative, 7, 10, 93, 122
examiners overseas, 92, 99–102
examiners' panel, nature of, 5, 10, 11–12,
    58, 69, 82, 96, 107, 111, 124, 138,
    194–7, 232, 236
examiners' reports, 10, 78–9, 96, 195
fees, 67, 72, 74, 129–31, 136–7, 159–60,
    196
moderation, 11, 194–7, 230, 234
selection and appointment, 90, 124, 137,
    141, 175, 186, 195–6
smoking, 162–3
specialist examiners, issue of, 12, 111, 164,
    187, 189, 234, 236–7
standards, 9–11, 79–80, 183, 186, 192, 195,
    197, 230–5
training, 10–11, 122, 186, 195, 197, 217–18,
    228, 233–4, 237
wartime conditions and travel, 90,
    129–34
women examiners, 11–12, 124, 130, 132,
    137–8, 139, 140–3

Fanning, Eaton, 83
Falkner, (Sir) Keith, 162
Far East, 14, 156, 202–5, 212, 217, 218, 227,
    246
Federation of Music Services, 221, 226
Ffennell, Raymond, 110–11
fiduciary principle, 35, 197, 232
Fielden, Thomas, 130–1
Foggin, Myers, 144–6
Forbes, Robert, 136
formation: technical and cultural, 2, 8–9,
    55, 123
Forster, Ivor, 147
free trade, 26, 35, 50, 51, 60
Furze, Jessie, 147

Galloway, William Johnson, 26
Gardner, John, 153–4, 156, 189
German, (Sir) Edward, 25, 28
Germany, 204, 205
Gibraltar, 90
Glasgow Atheneum School of Music, 30
Glock, (Sir) William, 144
Graduate of the Royal Schools of Music
    (GRSM), 107–8
Grove (Sir) George, 4, 5, 24, 37, 45, 46, 47,
    48, 63, 66, 67
Guildhall School of Music and Drama, 30,
    44, 127, 228–9
Gwilt, David and Shirley, 249

Hallam, Susan, 223–5
Hamilton (Sir) Edward, 65
Handel, G. F.: *Messiah*, 27
Harding, Miss J. L., 132
Hargreaves, David, 232–5
Harriss, Charles A. E., 95
Harvey, Jean, 194–5, 200, 203–4
Harwood, Pamela, 194n11, 199–200
Haweis (Rev) H. R., 31–2, 33n49
Hickman, Richard, 242
historiographical attitudes, 3, 19–23, 92
Hodgson, Julian, 201, 218, 250
Hogwood, (Sir) Christopher, 157
Holmes, Anne, 246–7n23
Holmes, Henry, 58, 67
Hong Kong, 203–5, 245, 246–7, 249
Hosier, John, 181
Howell, Edward, 67, 72
Howells, Herbert, 119, 124, 146
Howes, Frank, 22–3

Hull, Arthur C., 97
Humphries, Richard, J. R., 165, 200, 218
Hunt, (Rev) Bonavia, 48–50

Illiffe, Dr, 71, 73
Incorporated Society of Musicians (ISM),
    37, 112, 120, 140, 142, 160, 235, 244
India, 47, 49, 109, 121, 199
Indonesia, 245
Inner London Education Authority (ILEA),
    181, 239, 244
Institute of Education, University of
    London, 223–4
International Society of Music Education
    (ISME), 167, 202
Ireland, John, 90, 124, 125, 147
Isaacs, Harry, 101–2
Ives, Joshua, 94, 99

Jamaica, 205
Japan, 203
jazz, 9, 113, 120
Joachim, Joseph, and Andreas Moser:
    Violinschule, 79
Jones, Alan, 201, 214
Jones, Jean (Jenny), 199–200
Jones, Richard, 172, 202, 250
Joseph (Sir) Keith, 175
Joseph Williams (music publisher), 87, 116

Kenya, 205
Kreisler, Fritz, 79

Land ohne Musik, Das, see Schmitz, Oskar
    A. H.
Landon, (Sir) Ronald, 127
Latham, Richard O., 101–2
Leates, Timothy, 218
Lee, (Ernest) Markham, 124, 147
Leicestershire Schools Symphony
    Orchestra, 181
Leipzig Conservatoire, 30
LeMahieu, D. L., 126
Lewis, (Sir) Anthony, 160, 164
Lloyd, Charles H., 67, 100
Lloyd Webber, William, 153
Local Education Authority (LEA) music
    provision, 13, 14–15, 148–51, 164, 167,
    172–3, 181–4, 189, 192–3, 198, 207, 217,
    219, 221–3, 228, 233

Local Examinations
    in general school subjects, 40, 41, 55
    music, *see under* examinations, ABRSM
Lofthouse, Thornton, 130, 159
London Academy of Music (London
    Academy of Music and Dramatic Art),
    30
London College of Music, 38
London Royal Schools of Music, 107, 135,
    137, 139, 148, 160–2, 164–6, 173, 174,
    175, 176–80, 184, 191
London Sinfonietta, 157
London, University of, 41, 49, 50; *see also*
    Institute of Education
London Vocal Academy, 30
Long, Kathleen, 142
Lumsden, (Sir) David, 202

Macfarren, (Sir) George, 46
Mackenzie, (Sir) Alexander, C., 4, 5, 46, 47,
    58, 63, 65, 66, 67, 71, 72, 180
Macklin, Hilary, 109–11, 132, 139–40, 142,
    161–2, 199
Malaysia, 203, 205, 246
Malta, 90, 96, 130, 205
Manchester College of Music, *see* Royal
    Manchester College of Music
Manduell, (Sir) John, 215
Marchant, (Sir) Stanley, 11, 12, 139
Marychurch, (Sir) Peter, 215
Mathews, Ernest, 89
Matthay, Tobias, 121
McEwen, John B., 97, 121, 127
McNaught, William G., 25, 53–4
Mechanics' Institutes, 39, 40, 52, 53
medicine and music, issues of coherent
    professional identity, 35–6
Mendelssohn, Felix, 30, 32, 80, 119
Military School of Music, Kneller Hall, 31
Mitchell, Donald, 145–6
modernist repertoire, 123–4, 126–8
Morpeth, (Sir) Douglas, 175
Morris, Richard, 14, 172, 186, 198, 205,
    209–55
Moule, Henry, 98
Muir, James, 110
Mundey, Philip, 200, 203–4, 218, 236, 248
Munrow, David, 152, 157
music colleges, 30–1, 38–9, 44, 48, 50, 59,
    126–8, 158–9, 161, 173n2

music education, politics of, 172–3, 193, 213–14, 223, 225, 227

Music Education Council, 223

music examinations, 1, 2, 23
culture, 19, 33, 34, 51
see also examinations, ABRSM

music festivals, 20, 23, 25–6

Music for Youth, 221

music publishing, 26–7

music retail, 7, 25, 27, 29, 250–1

music services, 15, 219, 222–4, 226–7, 235, 238, 240, 243; *see also* Federation of Music Services; Local Education Authority (LEA) music provision

Music Standards Fund, 223, 226

music teachers
condition of music teaching, the, 9, 19, 42, 114, 123, 143, 172, 174, 191, 213–14, 225–6, 238–41, 244–6
group teaching, 224, 238–9
peripatetic, 148, 173, 181, 221, 240, 246
piano teachers, 79, 133, 234
professionalization of music teaching, 5, 7, 8, 19, 21, 33, 36, 42, 55, 59, 75, 235, 241, 244
registration of, 37, 38n64,
relationship with exam board, 3, 7–10, 12, 16, 207, 231, 233, 254–5
statistics, 29, 114, 151, 191n8,
status and standing, 19, 21, 33, 42, 114, 244

Music Teachers' Association, 141–2, 145

Musical Standard, 32n48, 37, 38

musical training, 23, 29–30, 33, 42–3, 45, 51, 55n37, 59, 87

Musical Times, 27, 48, 49, 51, 69, 75

Musical World, 37n62, 46–7

Myers, Thalia, 250

Nash, Paul, 128

National College of Music, 30

National Curriculum, 191, 221, 241

National Training School for Music (NTSM), 45, 50

New Zealand, 49, 90, 93, 94, 97, 98–100, 130, 202–3, 205, 246

North, Adrian, 232–5

Northcote–Trevelyan Report (1854), 34

northern Royal Schools, 135–6, 160, 166, 173, 177, 179–80

Novello (publishers), 27, 28, 152–3

'Oxbridge' Local Examinations, 40, 41, 55, 67, 75

Oxford Delegacy of Local Examinations, University of, 40; *see also* 'Oxbridge' Local Examinations

Oxford Music Service, 71

Oxford University Press, 175, 202

Paris Conservatoire, 30, 42, 43

Parratt, (Sir) Walter, 4, 58, 67, 72

Parry, (Sir Charles) Hubert, 4, 23, 41n76, 58, 65, 67, 71, 81, 82, 84, 87, 93, 100, 112

Pauer, Ernest, 28, 58, 67

Paynter, John, 181

Perricone, Guy, 109n9, 254

pianos, 26, 119–20

power relations (in exams), 7–11, 254

Preceptors, College of, 38–9

Prince of Wales (King Edward VII), 3, 45, 67, 73, 93–4, 219

prisoners of war, 131

professions, chartered, growth of, 21, 34–6

publishing, ABRSM
ABRSM (Publishing) Ltd, 172, 178, 185, 187, 201–2, 214, 216, 218, 250–1
Beethoven Sonatas, 115, 117, 119, 133, 136, 172, 250, 251–4
editions, 115, 117, 119, 133, 172, 185, 202, 214, 218, 250
income to selected composers (1925–47), 119
Music Publishing Department (1921–85), 87, 132–3, 172, 178, 201
Spectrum series, 145, 190, 250

Quality and Curriculum Authority, 230

Quine, Hector, 151–2

Randegger, Alberto, 65, 67, 72

Raymar, Aubin, 117

Reeves, Jonathan, 116–17, 132

Registered Teachers', ABRSM scheme, 3, 74

Reith, (Lord) John, 126–7

Robinson, David, 249

rock and pop exams, 237

Royal Academy of Dance, 247

Royal Academy of Music (RAM), 1, 4, 5, 11,
    30, 36, 43, 44, 45, 46, 47, 54, 63, 65, 67,
    76, 81, 84, 90, 97, 105, 107, 108, 110, 121,
    127, 137, 155, 158–9, 160, 161, 162, 176,
    178–80, 187–8, 194, 211
  finances, 86–7, 133–4, 137, 178–9
  Governing Board, 135, 165
  LRAM diploma, 38, 46, 55, 58, 108, 142,
    191, 235
  RAM Foundation, 178–9
  RAM-run music exams, 46–7, 65
  royal charter, 36, 45, 50
royal charters, 35, 36, 37, 38, 50, 57, 68, 135
Royal College of Music (RCM), 1, 4, 5, 11,
    23, 30, 37, 43, 44, 45, 46, 47, 48, 54, 63,
    65, 66, 67, 71, 76, 81, 83, 84, 90, 91, 105,
    107, 108, 120, 125, 126, 129, 141, 142,
    153, 158–9, 160, 161, 162, 180, 188, 211,
    219, 254
  ARCM diploma, 38, 42, 55, 57, 58, 108,
    191, 235
  Centenary Appeal, 176
  Council, 135, 165–6, 175–6
  Finance and Executive Committee, 63
  finances, 86–7, 134, 137–8, 178
  Prince Consort Foundation, 178–9
  Prince Consort Road premises, 4
  Royal Charter, 4, 5, 8, 36, 37, 45, 76, 92,
    139
  student experience, 43, 44
Royal College of Organists (RCO), 29, 55,
    57–8
Royal Institution of Great Britain, 65, 66
Royal Manchester College of Music
    (RMCM) [*later* Royal Northern
    College of Music (RNCM)], 1, 11, 14,
    30–1, 38, 52, 107, 135–6, 137, 160, 165,
    166, 178, 185, 192, 215, 242; *see also*
    northern Royal Schools
Royal Scottish Academy of Music and
    Drama (RSAMD) [*later* Royal
    Conservatoire of Scotland], 1, 11, 14,
    30, 107, 135–6, 137, 160, 165, 166, 178;
    see also northern Royal Schools
Royal Society of Arts, *see* Society of Arts
RSMs (Royal Schools of Music), 1, 3, 4, 5, 6,
    11, 14, 38, 41, 42, 44, 48, 50, 55, 75, 78,
    107, 108, 134, 175, 177, 186–7, 193, 195,
    215–17, 242–3
  employment of professors, 5, 129, 141,
    158–9

Rube, Charles, 84
rubrics, examination, 3

Sadie, Stanley, 251, 253
Salter, Timothy, 153–4, 156, 189
Salvation Army, 150
Samuel, Harold, 90, 117
Schmitz, Oskar A. H.: *Das Land ohne
    Musik* [*The Land Without Music*],
    20, 22
Scholes, Percy, 51, 120
Self, George, 181
Singapore, 156, 202, 205, 245, 246,
Slatford, Rodney, 242
Smith, Ronald, 14, 109n9, 167, 172, 181–207,
    230, 247
Society of Arts, (Royal) [Society for the
    Encouragement of Arts, Manufactures
    and Commerce]
  examination philosophy, 52, 55
  examinations, 40, 42, 52
  music, 53, 54
  Report on the State of Musical
    Education (1866), 30, 33, 44, 45, 50
Society of Corresponding Members
    (ABRSM), 111, 114, 129, 139
Society of Women Musicians, 142
'SoundJunction', 213, 219, 241–2
South Africa, 6, 48, 83, 87, 90, 93, 202, 205
Sowerbutts, J. A., 153
'Speedshifter', 122
Squire, William, 90
Sri Lanka, *see* Ceylon
Stainer, (Sir) John, 27–8, 37–8, 39, 53–4, 65
Stanford, (Sir) Charles Villiers, 4, 23, 39,
    41n76, 43, 58, 67, 83, 84
Staton, Frederick, 94, 131
Stephens, John, 244
Sullivan (Sir) Arthur, 25, 28, 45, 65, 81
Sutherland of Houndwood, Lord, 216
Swinstead, Felix, 90, 101, 119, 124, 147

Taiwan, 203, 205
Taylor, Clara, 219
Taylor, Colin, 90, 100
Taylor, Eric, 156, 190
Taylor, Franklin, 58, 65, 67, 71, 93
Taylor, Kendall, 251, 253
teachers, music, *see* music teachers
Teachers' Registration Council, 37
Thatcher, Reginald, 109, 127n56

Thiman, Eric, 124
Thomas, John, 72
Thorman, Christopher, 199
Threlfall, Thomas, 63, 65, 81
Times, The, 65, 105, 120
Tippett, (Sir) Michael, 181
Tobago, 205
Tonic Sol-fa, 53–4
Tovey, (Sir) Donald, 116–17, 119, 136, 250,
    251, 253
Tower Hamlets, 181, 239
Training Musicians (Gulbenkian
    Foundation, 1978), 157–9
Treasury, H. M., grants-in-aid, 43, 44, 50,
    134, 137, 138
Trinidad, 205
Trinity College London (TCL), 3, 26, 30,
    37, 38, 40, 41, 42, 44, 46, 47, 51, 52, 55,
    59, 60, 67, 69, 94, 95, 114, 158, 228–9,
    244–5
  diplomas, 58, 236
  exam income, 49
  foundation, 48–50
  reaction to founding of ABRSM, 49–50
  scheme of exams, 48–9, 56, 156, 236
Tyson, Alan, 253

Ullswater Commission, 126–8
United States of America, 203–4

university music education, 39, 157–8

Vaughan Williams, Ralph, 125
Victorian society
    attitudes to music, 19–21, 25, 31–3, 172–3
    class culture, 3, 68
    musical life, 20–33, 241

Waddington, Sydney P., 125
Wakefield, Mary, 25
Ward, David, 254
Warrack, Guy, 151
Watson, Angus, 249
Watson, George, 47, 65, 66, 72, 74, 81
Wessely, Hans, 87
Westlake, Frederick, 65, 67, 71
White, (Judge) Meadows, 65
Willcocks, (Sir) David, 160
Williams, C. Lee, 94
Williams, John, 151
Wood, Thomas, 101
World War I, 86–91
World War II, 86, 129–34, 221

Young, (Sir) Brian, 177, 215
Ysaÿe, Eugene, 79

Zimbabwe, 205